D1016192

GERMANY,
AUSTRIA & SWITZERLAND'S
BEST TRIPS
33 AMAZING ROAD TRIPS

WITHDRAWN

This edition written and researched by

Nicola Williams

Kerry Christiani, Marc Di Duca, Catherine Le Nevez, Tom
Masters, Sally O'Brien, Andrea Schulte-Peevers, Ryan
Ver Berkmoes, Benedict Walker

SYMBOLS IN THIS BOOK

✓ Top Tips

📖 History & Culture

📷 Essential Photo

🔗 Link Your Trips

👪 Family

🏃 Walking Tour

💬 Tips from Locals

🍷 Food & Drink

✗ Eating

↱ Trip Detour

🌳 Outdoors

🛏 Sleeping

📞 Telephone Number

@ Internet Access

📖 English-Language Menu

🕐 Opening Hours

🛜 Wi-Fi Access

👪 Family-Friendly

🅿 Parking

🥦 Vegetarian Selection

🐾 Pet-Friendly

⊗ Nonsmoking

🏊 Swimming Pool

❄ Air-Conditioning

MAP LEGEND

Routes
- Trip Route
- Trip Detour
- Linked Trip
- Walk Route
- Tollway
- Freeway
- Primary
- Secondary
- Tertiary
- Lane
- Unsealed Road
- Plaza/Mall
- Steps
-)= = Tunnel
- Pedestrian Overpass
- Walk Track/Path

Boundaries
- International
- State/Province
- Cliff
- Wall

Population
- ✪ Capital (National)
- ◉ Capital (State/Province)
- ● City/Large Town
- ○ Town/Village

Transport
- ✈ Airport
- +Ⓒ+ Cable Car/Funicular
- 🅿 Parking
- +Ⓒ+ Train/Railway
- 🚊 Tram
- Ⓜ Underground Train Station

Trips
- 1 Trip Numbers
- 9 Trip Stop
- 🚶 Walking tour
- ↱ Trip Detour

Route Markers
- E44 E-road network
- M100 National network

Hydrography
- River/Creek
- Intermittent River
- Swamp/Mangrove
- Canal
- Water
- Dry/Salt/Intermittent Lake
- Glacier

Areas
- Beach
- Cemetery (Christian)
- Cemetery (Other)
- Park
- Forest
- Urban Area
- Sportsground

PLAN YOUR TRIP

ON THE ROAD

CONTENTS

Northeastern Germany
p33

Northwestern Germany
p121

Southern Germany
p189

Austria
p273

Switzerland
p335

Contents cont.

ROAD TRIP ESSENTIALS

Classic Trips

Look out for the Classic Trips stamp on our favorite routes in this book.

Stein am Rhein, Switzerland Patrons enjoying the town's Rathausplatz (Trip 29)

NUI7711 / SHUTTERSTOCK ©

WELCOME TO
GERMANY, AUSTRIA & SWITZERLAND

Grandiose cities, storybook villages, vine-stitched valleys and hallucinatory Alpine landscapes that beg you to toot your horn, leap out of the car and jump for joy – road-tripping in this Germanic part of Western Europe is a mesmerising kaleidoscope of brilliant landscapes and experiences.

The 33 trips in this book take you for a spin from Germany's edgy capital to its bracing northern coast and fabled Rhine and Moselle Valley vineyards, from Bavaria to the Black Forest, to the sparkling shores of Lake Constance and beyond into Austria and Switzerland. Motor the castle-strewn banks of Europe's greatest rivers and within a whisker of its mightiest glacial peaks.

Whether you want to navigate hairpins with attitude on high-altitude mountain passes, taste wine, or cool off in romantic cobalt-blue lakes, we have something for you. And if you only have time for one trip, make it one of our eight Classic Trips, which take you to the very best of Germany, Austria and Switzerland. Turn the page for more...

→

GERMANY, AUSTRIA & SWITZERLAND

Classic Trips

24

What is a Classic Trip?

All the trips in this book show you the best of Germany, Austria & Switzerland, but we've chosen eight as our all-time favourites. These are our Classic Trips – the ones that lead you to the best of the iconic sights, the top activities and the unique German, Austrian and Swiss experiences. Turn the page to see the map, and look out for the Classic Trip stamp throughout the book.

8 **German Avenues Route** Wander the streets in Wernigerode, along one of Germany's most picturesque driving routes.

24 **Grossglockner Road** Twist and turn along one of Austria's most spectacular mountain passes.

32 **The Swiss Alps** Enjoy the great outdoors along this route, which includes gorgeous peaks, glaciers and valleys.

32

GERMANY, AUSTRIA & SWITZERLAND

Classic Trips

10 **German Fairy Tale Road**
Learn the fantasies and the horrors in the stories of the Brothers Grimm. **5 DAYS**

12 **Romantic Rhine** Fall under the spell of the castle-lined riverscape along the world-famous Rhine. **5–7 DAYS**

8 **German Avenues Route**
Follow one of Germany's most picturesque, tree-lined driving routes. **5–7 DAYS**

16 **German Castle Road**
Castles, palaces and fortresses galore along this route from Mannheim to Bayreuth. **7 DAYS**

POLAND

DENMARK

NETHERLANDS

17 The Romantic Road A ribbon of historical quaintness running through Bavaria's western reaches. **10 DAYS**

32 The Swiss Alps The greatest of the great outdoors: perfect peaks, gorgeous glaciers, verdant valleys. **7 DAYS**

11

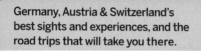

Germany, Austria & Switzerland's best sights and experiences, and the road trips that will take you there.

GERMANY, AUSTRIA & SWITZERLAND
HIGHLIGHTS

Berlin

It can bookend either end of **Trip 6: Berlin & the Jewels of Eastern Brandenburg** – and what a bookend it is! Berlin is a bon vivant feasting on the smorgasbord of urban life. It oozes glamour and grit, and teems with top museums and world-famous landmarks such as the Berlin Wall and Brandenburg Gate that have to be seen. If you love great nightlife, you might dump the car and never leave.

Trip

Berlin Brandenburg Gate and Pariser Platz

Vienna Fiaker (horse-drawn carriage) on Graben (Trip 23)

The Black Forest

Few spots soul-soothe like Germany's Black Forest. Each bend in the road on **Trip 22: Schwarzwaldhochstrasse** unveils a surprise: half-timbered fairy-tale-like villages, thunderous waterfalls, cuckoo clocks the size of houses. Inhale pine-scented air, navigate roller-coaster roads to middle-of-nowhere lakes, frolic in waterfalls and dine in fine restaurants.

Trips

Romantic Rhine

The Rhine has long mesmerised artists, illustrated by the 19th-century paintings in Koblenz on **Trip 12: Romantic Rhine**. From Düsseldorf and Cologne, the majestic river snakes through churning whirlpools, castle-capped cliffs, medieval villages and vineyards. Trails lead to forests and fortresses, or to evenings sipping rieslings under chestnut trees.

Trips

Vienna

There is no finer approach to Austria's elegant capital than through farmland, forest and vineyard-streaked hills on **Trip 23: Along the Danube**. In Vienna, park up and indulge in pedestrian meanderings around imperial Habsburg palaces and castles of unimaginable grandeur. Track down Mozart. Talk, read, dream and indulge like Trotsky and Freud did in a Viennese coffee house.

Trips

Lake Geneva Jet d'Eau fountain (Trip 31)

BEST ROADS FOR DRIVING

Schwarzwaldhochstrasse Altitude trip from Baden-Baden to Freudenstadt past forested peaks and glacial lakes. **Trip** 22

St Gotthard Pass Spectacular drive, partly on cobblestones, over Switzerland's famous mountain pass (2108m). **Trip** 33

Route 28 Wild Alpine scenery in the Swiss National Park. **Trip** 33

Grossglockner Road Heart-in-your-mouth Alpine adventure on a legendary Austrian road. **Trip** 24

Lake Geneva

Europe's largest lake is rarely out of sight on **Trip 30: Lake Geneva & Western Switzerland**. The urban viewpoint is cosmopolitan, French-speaking Geneva, where yellow 'seagulls' ferry locals across the water, overlooked by the icy peak of Mont Blanc. East along the shore, nothing prepares you for the dazzling spectacle of emerald vines marching uphill from the water in the Lavaux wine region.

Trips

The Swiss Alps The great Matterhorn in the distance

The Swiss Alps

You'd think after motoring through 537km of mind-blowing Alpine scenery with **Trip 32: The Swiss Alps** that you'd seen it all. Wrong. After a relentless succession of dramatic green peaks, Alpine lakes, glacial ravines and other hallucinatory natural landscapes, you finally pull into your final destination: Zermatt, a highly desirable Alpine resort built around the iconic, one-of-a-kind Matterhorn. *Nothing* prepares you for that first unforgettable glance.

Trips   32

BEST PICTURESQUE VILLAGES

Soest Medieval village in luminous green stone. **Trip** 11

Annweiler A German mountain gem with waterways and wooden wheels. **Trip** 14

Rothenburg ob der Tauber Bavarian beauty from the Middle Ages. **Trip** 16

Ottenhöfen Black Forest storybook village amid hills and watermills. **Trip** 22

Gruyères Swiss hilltop village with châteaux, dairies and meringues. **Trip** 30

Salzburg Getreidegasse in the Altstadt (old town)

Schloss Neuschwanstein King Ludwig II's fairy-tale castle

Schloss Neuschwan-stein

King Ludwig II's crazy castle rises from Bavaria's mysterious forest like a storybook illustration. Inside, the make-believe continues in a confection that outdoes even the flashiest oligarch's palazzo. Said to have inspired Walt's castle at Disney World, it now inspires tourist masses to make the pilgrimage along **Trip 17: The Romantic Road**, which culminates at its gates.

Trip `17`

Zürich

Ending **Trip 31: Geneva to Zürich** in Zürich is the perfect antidote to wild motoring through dairy pasture, lake and mountain. One of Europe's most liveable cities, this German-speaking Swiss city is a hipster delight (where Google employees shoot down a slide to lunch) with a quaint Old Town, great art and shopping, waterfront bars and dancing till dawn in Züri-West.

Trip `31`

Salzburg

Mozart's birthplace is a fitting finale to **Trip 25: Tyrol & Vorarlberg**, a drive with a 'Wow!' at every turn. Salzburg – baroque masterpiece, classical-music legend, Austria's spiritual heartland – is just as grand. The city stands proud on the banks of the Salzach River, above which rise the Altstadt (old town) and clifftop-fortress Festung Hohensalzburg in their architectural glory.

Trips

19

Dresden

This Saxon city is dubbed 'Florence
on the Elbe' for good reason.
Reconstructed architectural jewels
pair with stunning art collections to
justify Dresden's place in the pantheon
of European cultural capitals. Packaged
with superb museums, baroque
architectural gems and a tiara of villas
and palaces lined up along the river,
Trip 4: Highlights of Saxony is one
handsome road trip.

Trip **4**

Moselle Valley

Germany's oldest city, Trier, with
its Roman ruins and Unesco World
Heritage good looks, opens **Trip 13:
Moselle Valley**. The downstream drive
along the serpentine Moselle River is a
go-slow, curvaceous affair with drop-
dead-gorgeous castles and storybook
half-timbered villages. It's topped by
exhilarating walks through some of the
world's steepest vineyards and tasting
the valley's famed white wine.

Trip **13**

(left) **Moselle Valley** Moselle River, village and vineyards

(below) **Frankfurt** Gerechtigkeitsbrunnen (Fountain of Justice)

Frankfurt

After the natural splendour of **Trip 7: Via Regia**, urbanites need a dose of city life. Frankfurt, Germany's financial capital, brims with cultural, culinary and shopping excitement beneath a corporate demeanour. Discover its soul with an espresso in an old-time cafe, museum-hop along the riverbank, or wash down hearty local fare with tart *Ebbelwei* (apple cider) in an old-world wood-panelled tavern.

Trip 7

BEST FOR WINE LOVERS

Traben-Trarbach Moselle wine town with *Jugendstil* (art-nouveau) architecture and wisteria. **Trip** 13

Bad Dürkheim German spa town with perfumed parks, vineyard trails, the world's largest wine barrel and wine fest. **Trip** 14

St-Saphorin Bewitching village with a tasting cellar among vineyards. **Trip** 30

Rust Nesting storks, reed-filled lake and renowned Austrian wines. **Trip** 26

21

IF YOU LIKE

Tyrolean snack Cheese and smoked sausages (Trip 25)

History

With a history harking back several millennia, the region is littered with reminders of its turbulent past – ancient and uncannily recent.

6 Berlin & the Jewels of Eastern Brandenburg
Explore history's dark side in a concentration camp and the largest WWII battlefield on German soil.

11 Cologne & the Ruhr Valley Romans to 20th-century postindustrialisation in northwest Germany.

13 Moselle Valley
Germany's finest ensemble of Roman remains.

17 The Romantic Road
Ancient walled towns, medieval castles and historic churches pearl Bavaria's romantic east.

Food & Drink

Pepper road trips with sausages and dumplings, black forest gateau, Swiss chocolate and creamy Alpine cheeses. The 'homegrown and seasonal' mantra is picnic perfect.

14 German Wine Route
Eat and drink your way through vine-planted hills in Germany's Palatinate region.

22 Schwarzwaldhoch-strasse Menus sing with earthy, seasonal flavours – from wild game to mushrooms – in this southern Germany foodie region.

33 Graubünden & Ticino
Distinct local flavours and rare Swiss wines create a notable culinary experience.

25 Tyrol & Vorarlberg
Visit cheesemakers along Austria's Bregenz Forest 'cheese road'.

Mountains

Buckle up for Europe's greatest Alpine drives. On sunny days, icy mountain peaks and shimmering white glaciers are spellbinding. Keep your eyes firmly on the hairpin-laced road and go slow.

15 Bergstrasse
Germany's historic 'mountain road', a Roman trade route, shadows the forested Odenwald mountain range.

19 German Alpine Road
This dramatic road trip through the Bavarian Alps showcases Germany's mightiest peaks.

32 The Swiss Alps All the big names are here: Matterhorn, Eiger, Mönch, Jungfrau, Schilthorn and Titlis.

24 Grossglockner Road
A feat of 1930s engineering, this road swings giddily around 36 switchbacks in the Austrian Alps.

Bavaria Berchtesgaden and the Watzmann in the distance (Trip 19)

Castles

Romantic castles and feudal fortresses enhance the region's natural good looks. Teetering on rocky crags, crowning clifftops or lacing a lake shore, their settings are picture perfect.

5 Central Germany's Castles & Palaces Motor between mystical ruins, robust fortresses and exquisite palaces on this scenic trip.

10 German Fairy Tale Road Yes, this trip is straight out of a Brothers Grimm fairy tale: aspiring princesses, let your hair down!

16 German Castle Road Castle-hop in southern Germany along 600km of scenic road and a thousand years of history.

26 Castles of Burgenland Castles abound on this drive through eastern Austria's wine country.

Lakes & Rivers

Stock up on superlatives and ensure cameras are charged. Few parts of Europe have so many of the longest, biggest, deepest...

3 Lakes & Treasures of Mecklenburg–Western Pomerania Take your foot off the pedal along a string of beautiful lakes.

12 Romantic Rhine Powerhouse riverside cities and castle-capped cliffs; this German journey along Europe's longest river is epic.

30 Lake Geneva & Western Switzerland Vineyards, villages, beaches and castles embellish Europe's largest Alpine lake.

23 Along the Danube Abbeys, castles and Austria's resplendent capital unfurl riverside.

Art & Architecture

Romanesque cathedrals, baroque palaces, timber granaries on stilts and chalet farmsteads in the Alps: the region's artistic and architectural legacy will be a memorable part of your trip.

2 Design for Life: Bauhaus to VW Unique Bauhaus and other design-related sights in central Germany.

8 German Avenues Route Renaissance palaces, baroque cathedrals and art-rich 'Florence on the Elbe'.

25 Tyrol & Vorarlberg Ecofriendly contemporary design contrasts with traditional chocolate-box chalets in Austria.

29 Northern Switzerland Human-made wonders are showcased in this art trip, with museum-rich Basel at its helm.

NEED TO KNOW

CURRENCY
Euro (Germany & Austria; €), Swiss Franc (Switzerland; CHF, also Sfr)

LANGUAGE
German region-wide, plus French, Italian, Romansch also in Switzerland.

VISAS
Generally not required for stays of up to 90 days; some nationalities require a Schengen visa.

FUEL
Petrol stations are common on main roads and highways, and in larger towns. Unleaded in Germany/Austria costs around €1.50/1.30 per litre and diesel is €1.25/1.15; pay Sfr1.55 and Sfr1.53 respectively in Switzerland.

RENTAL CARS
Auto Europe (www.autoeurope.com)

Avis (www.avis.com)

Europcar (www.europcar.com)

Hertz (www.hertz.com)

IMPORTANT NUMBERS
Europe-wide emergency covering police, fire and ambulance (𝄞112)

Climate

warm to hot summers, mild winters
warm to hot summers, cold winters
mild summers, cold winters
cold climate

Berlin
GO May, June, Sep & Oct

Frankfurt
GO May–Sep

Munich
GO Apr, May, Sep & Oct

Vienna
GO Late Mar–Oct

Zürich
GO Apr–Aug

When to Go

High Season (Jul & Aug)
» Main holiday season – expect increased traffic on roads and Alpine walking trails.

» Late December to early April is high season in Swiss and Austrian ski resorts.

» Christmas and New Year are busy – warm cockles with *Glühwein* (hot mulled wine) at alfresco Christmas markets.

Shoulder Season (May, Jun & Sep)
» Accommodation rates drop by at least 30% in popular tourist areas.

» September's grape harvest ushers in the year's new wine in vineyards region-wide – it's also the month of Munich's famous Oktoberfest.

Low Season (Oct–Mar)
» Expect heavy discounts on accommodation.

» Snow covers the Alps – Alpine-ski-resort hotels close October to early December.

Your Daily Budget

Budget: Less than €100/Sfr200

》 Double room in a budget hotel: €50-80/Sfr80-170

》 Picnic, dinner out: €15/Sfr25

》 Free admission to some museums first Saturday or Sunday of month

Midrange: €100-200/ Sfr200-300

》 Double room in a midrange hotel: €80-160/Sfr170-350

》 Dish of day or two-course menu: €15-30/Sfr25-50

》 Museum admission: €5-15/ Sfr5-10

Top End: More than €250/Sfr300

》 Luxury double hotel: more than €200/Sfr350

》 Three-course dinner in top restaurant: €50/Sfr100

Eating

Cafes Coffee, drinks, snacks.

Bistros Light meals to full-blown dinners.

Restaurants Simple eateries to Michelin-starred temples.

Vegetarian Few wholly vegetarian places, limited choices on most menus.

The following prices indicate the cost of a two-course set menu:

€	less than €15/Sfr25
€€	€15-30/Sfr25-50
€€€	more than €30/ Sfr50

Sleeping

Hotels From budget to luxury; breakfast included unless indicated.

B&Bs *Chambres d'hôte* in French-speaking Switzerland, *pensiones* elsewhere; rates always include breakfast.

Hostels In cities and large towns; private or HI-affiliated.

Price symbols indicate the cost of a double room with private bathroom in high season:

€	less than €80/ Sfr170
€€	€80-160 (Germany), €80-200 (Austria), Sfr170-350
€€€	more than €160/200 (Germany/Austria), more than Sfr350

Arriving in the Region

Major car-rental agencies offer competitive rates at the airports.

Frankfurt Airport

S-Bahn Commuter rail lines S8 and S9 from Flughafen Regionalbahnhof to Frankfurt centre, 4.30am to 12.30am (€4.55, 15 minutes).

Taxis €25 to €35; 20 minutes to centre.

Vienna Airport

Train & S-Bahn To city centre every 30 minutes, 6am to 11.30pm (€4 to €12, 15 to 30 minutes).

Taxis €35 to €50; 30 minutes to centre.

Zürich Airport

Trains To Zürich centre, 6am to midnight (Sfr7, 14 minutes).

Taxis Sfr50 to Sfr70, 20 minutes to centre.

Mobile Phones

Most European and Australian phones function; turn off roaming to avoid data charges. Buy a local SIM for cheaper rates.

Internet Access

Wi-fi (usually free) is available to guests in most hotels, B&Bs and hostels. Also offered by many cafes, bars, train stations and other public spaces.

Money

ATMs are widespread. Most major credit cards are accepted. Larger cities have money-exchange bureaus.

Tipping

Restaurant and bar prices include a service charge but locals still tip. Taxis expect 10%.

Useful Websites

Lonely Planet (lonely planet.com) Travel tips, accommodation, travellers' forum and more.

Germany: The Travel Destination (www.germany. travel) German tourist board.

Austria (www.austria.info) Austrian tourist board.

My Switzerland (www. myswitzerland.com) Swiss tourist board.

ADAC (www.adac.de) Driving info for Germany and neighbouring countries.

For more, see Road Trip Essentials (p390).

CITY GUIDE

BERLIN

Berlin's glamour-grit combo mesmerises. Allow a couple of days to get your teeth into its vibrant culture, cutting-edge architecture, fabulous food, legendary party scene and tangible history. This is, after all, a city that staged a revolution, was headquartered by Nazis, bombed, divided by a wall and finally reunited – all in the 20th century.

Berlin East Side Gallery

Getting Around

Driving in Berlin is a hassle. The key areas are compact and easily navigated on foot, by bike or public transport. Jump on the U-Bahn (underground) or, for longer distances, the S-Bahn (light rail). A single/day ticket starts at €2.60/6.70.

Parking

Parking is expensive and scarce. Hotel parking (€25 per day) is rare; street parking (€1 to €3 per hour) is limited to three hours; garage parking in commercial areas costs €2.50 per hour. Central Berlin is a low-emission zone – vehicles must display an Umweltplakette (p394) or risk an €80 fine.

Discover the Taste of Berlin

Sample Berlin's *Currywurst* (sausage in tomato sauce with curry powder), *Eisbein* (pork hock with sauerkraut and boiled potatoes) and other classics in historic Mitte. Prenzlauer Berg has a lively cafe scene or enjoy the street-food craze at a weekly market: Markthalle 9 (Thursday), Bite Club (Friday) or Neue Heimat (Sunday).

Live Like a Local

Base yourself in Scheunenviertel's web of narrow lanes in Mitte, packed with trendy boutiques, restaurants and bars, and in walking distance of the sights. Gritty but cool Kreuzberg, with its offbeat flavour, is for party animals and those on a budget.

Useful Websites

Visit Berlin (www.visitberlin.de)
Lonely Planet (www.lonelyplanet.com)

Trip Through Berlin: 6

TOP EXPERIENCES

➡ **Reichstag Panorama**
Ride the free lift up the Reichstag, home to Germany's parliament, for close-ups of the landmark's famous glass dome and dazzling city panorama.

➡ **Berlin Wall**
Trail the legacy of the world's most infamous wall, torn down in 1989, at Checkpoint Charlie, the Gedenkstätte Berliner Mauer and East Side Gallery, with its colourful murals.

➡ **The Holocaust Relived**
Stand in the very room where the Holocaust was planned and feel the presence of uncounted souls at the heart-wrenching Holocaust Memorial and its subterranean exhibit.

➡ **Museum Island**
Explore 6000 years of art and cultural history, from the Stone Age to the 19th century, in the five museums on the Unesco World Heritage site Museumsinsel.

➡ **Berlin Afloat**
Explore the city with a laid-back boat cruise through its historic core or further afield to the lakes.

➡ **High-octane Nightlife**
Party until sunrise or beyond in one of Berlin's legendary electro-techno clubs. Hot addresses include **Berghain** (www.berghain. de), riverside **Watergate** (www. water-gate.de) and **Tresor** (www. tresorberlin.de) in a former power station.

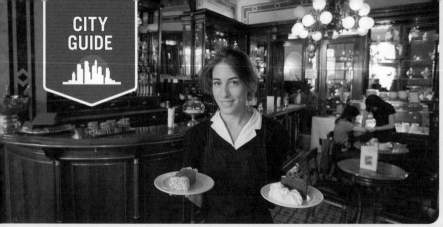

Vienna Fancy cakes at a *Kaffeehäuser* (coffee house)

VIENNA

Austria's capital city is a timeless, oh-so-elegant cocktail of grand imperial history, exciting contemporary museums, lively eating and infectious nightlife. Be it clip-clopping in a horse-drawn open carriage past majestic monuments, waltzing through the Habsburgs' opulent summer palace or taking a spin on the iconic Ferris wheel, Viennese life is uncannily cinematic. Play the part!

Getting Around

Stick with the excellent public transport system, one of Europe's most efficient. Tickets that are good for trams, buses, the underground (U-Bahn) and regional trains (S-Bahn) cost €2 or €6.70 for a 24-hour ticket; validate on board.

Parking

Pay for street parking with prepaid parking tickets (first 15 minutes free, then €2 per hour) sold at tobacconists, petrol stations and U-Bahn stations; street parking is free from 10pm to 9am. Well-signposted car parks cost around €4 per hour.

Few city hotels have their own parking.

Discover the Taste of Vienna

Kaffeehäuser (coffee houses) abound in the historic Innere Stadt. They're as good for a fine meal as they are for a traditional coffee and cake – don't skip the slice of *Sacher Torte* (rich chocolate cake with apricot jam). For goulash and other traditional Austrian dishes hit a *Beisl* (bistro pub). Vienna's historic Naschmarkt, with its food stalls, is a foodie nirvana.

Live Like a Local

The Innere Stadt is ideal for getting around the main sights, eateries and bar-spiked MuseumsQuartier on foot. Money-conscious road trippers will appreciate the good value offered by accommodation around the Ringstrasse (ring road), and its excellent public transport.

Useful Websites

Vienna Tourism (www.vienna. info)

Trips Through Vienna:

Zürich View of downtown

ZÜRICH

Switzerland's largest metropolis is one of Central Europe's hippest destinations, with a post-industrial edge. World-class art in the Kunsthaus and Marc Chagall's stained-glass cathedral windows tick the box for culture vultures, while Zürich's retail strip Bahnhofstrasse is shopping paradise. Few urban experiences climax like Zürich: with a swim 'n' tipple at a trendy lake or river bath-cum-bar.

Getting Around

Dump the car at the hotel or in a car park and navigate one of the world's most liveable cities on foot or public transport – Zürich's public transport system works like a dream. Pay Sfr2.60/8.40 for a single/day ticket.

Parking

Street parking (Sfr1.50 per 30 minutes, free 9pm to 8am) is limited to between 30 minutes and four hours. For all-day parking try a car park run by **Parking Zürich AG** (www. parkingzuerichag.ch); pay around Sfr4.40 per hour or Sfr45 per day.

Discover the Taste of Zürich

The narrow streets of Niederdorf on the River Limmat's east bank are crammed with restaurants cooking up the rich local cuisine, epitomised by Zürich's signature dish, *Zürcher Geschnetzeltes* (sliced veal in a creamy mushroom and white-wine sauce). Swiss chocolate, coffee and cakes at **Café Sprüngli** (www.spruengli. ch), dating to 1836, are obligatory.

Live Like a Local

Accommodation in reborn hip hood Züri-West – epicentre of nightlife, with bags of late-night eateries, bars and dance venues – is as good value as it gets in this expensive city.

Useful Websites

Zürich Tourism (www. zuerich.com)

Trip Through Zürich:

For more, check out our city and country guides. www.lonelyplanet.com

GERMANY, AUSTRIA & SWITZERLAND BY REGION

From zigzagging snail-pace up spectacular Alpine mountain passes to speeding, foot down, along German autobahns, this is a driver's dream. Here's your guide to what each country has to offer, along with suggestions for our top road trips.

Northwestern Germany (p121)

A place for outdoor lovers and wine aficionados: the Rhine and Moselle rivers carve spellbinding paths past chess-piece castles, gingerbread villages and pea-green vineyards. Park and hike, cycle or hit the North Sea beaches for alfresco beauty. Culture vultures can gorge on industrial history in the Ruhr Valley and the Brothers Grimm stuff of fairy tales in lower Saxony.

Taste star rieslings on Trip 13

Switzerland (p335)

The epic natural beauty of this tiny country, with four languages and cosmopolitan cities, is completely disproportionate. Toss your walking boots in the car and rev up for spine-tingling motoring across Alpine mountain passes, around cobalt-blue lakes, and through lush green meadows strewn with timber chalets and wildflowers.

Ogle at the iconic Matterhorn on Trip 32

Northeastern Germany (p33)

Surf's up on the bracing Baltic Sea. Sand beaches and dunes lace a coastline where red-brick Hanseatic jewels Lübeck and Wismar play coastguard. Motoring south, lakes and forests jockey with world-class architectural treasures in Bauhaus meccas Weimar and Dessau, ultimate comeback city Dresden and legendary capital Berlin.

Feast on seafood on Trip

Southern Germany (p189)

Southern Germany keeps its clichéd promise with lofty castles, mountains and dark forests fit for witches. The road ribbons through Bavaria and Baden-Württemberg, from romantic palace to medieval town, glittering glass art to glacial peak, railway to waterway. Every journey ends in a tree-shaded beer garden.

Drink water from Germany's highest lake on Trip

Austria (p273)

Austria meanders along the serpentine banks of Strauss' beautiful 'blue' Danube. It plays off spectacular natural landscapes against elegant urban vignettes such as coffee in a Viennese *Kaffeehaus* or imperial-palace strolls. The cultural might of the Habsburgs is felt everywhere, while rural landscapes are rugged, exhilarating and charged with outdoor adventure.

Explore ice caves on Trip
Ice-dive on Trip

Northeastern Germany Trips

DRIVE INTO THE SPIRITUAL HEART OF GERMANY on these trips, which are found in the regions in and around the compelling capital of Berlin. There's plenty of natural beauty; the shores of the Baltic Sea feature endless beaches and beautiful surf; inland, pristine lakes abound amid ancient beech forests.

But it's the proud and ancient cities that really stand out. Dresden is a baroque wonderland of storied buildings and churches. Beguiling, strollable Lübeck was the capital of the Hanseatic League, which once made this region one of the world's richest and most civilised. And the riches weren't limited to the coasts – wealthy potentates built lavishly from the Harz Mountains all the way to the sea.

On these drives, you'll discover hulking castles, opulent palaces and magnificent gardens, along with excellent German food and drink.

Dresden The Fürstenzug (Procession of the Princes) and the Frauenkirche (Church of Our Lady) in the background (Trip 4).
L. TOSHIO KISHIYAMA / GETTY IMAGES ©

33

1 **Along the Baltic Coast 5 Days**
From Lübeck to Rügen Island, celebrate the bracing, beautiful Baltic. (p37)

2 **Design for Life: Bauhaus to VW 2–4 Days**
Drive through the evocative industrial heart of the old East Germany (GDR). (p47)

3 **Lakes & Treasures of Mecklenburg–Western Pomerania 2–3 Days**
Palaces and jewel-box towns dot land that's also dotted with lakes. (p55)

4 **Highlights of Saxony 5–7 Days**
Follow one of Germany's great rivers past palaces and fortresses to Dresden. (p63)

5 **Central Germany's Castles & Palaces 3–5 Days**
Through Germany's heartland from Leipzig to Kassel, with castles and lavish palaces. (p73)

6 **Berlin & the Jewels of Eastern Brandenburg 4 Days**
A tantalising tour to a watery forest, WWII sites and medieval marvels. (p81)

7 **Via Regia 5–7 Days**
The German portion of the longest historic road link across Europe. (p89)

Classic Trip

8 **German Avenues Route 5–7 Days**
Follow one of Germany's most picturesque, tree-lined driving routes, which includes Dresden and Leipzig. (p101)

Ahrenshoop (Trip 1)

 DON'T MISS

Dresden
Saxony's capital has superb museums, baroque architectural gems and a dynamic alternative scene in its funky Neustadt. Enjoy on Trips **4** **7** **8**

Lübbenau & the Spreewald
Take a punt in the slow lane in this rivulet-laced forest inhabited by exotic locals with a passion for pickles. All on Trip **6**

Berlin
Germany's thriving capital has a past that's operatic in its drama. See how the entire 20th century is writ large here on Trip **6**

Ahrenshoop
Feel the Baltic Sea's surging surf pound the shore, as little beach towns like Ahrenshoop shelter behind dunes. See it on Trip **1**

Schwerin
Regal Schwerin is studded with surprises and delights. Walk the gardens, tour the lakes and make discoveries on Trip **3**

Binz Kurhaus at sunrise

Along the Baltic Coast

1

Head to Germany's north because you love the water. The fabled Baltic historic towns like Lübeck, Wismar and Stralsund mix with long stretches of wave-tossed sand.

TRIP HIGHLIGHTS

199 km

Ahrenshoop
See trees growing sideways and waves pounding golden sand

417 km

Binz
Experience the genteel good life of this classic beach resort

Göhren

FINISH

Kühlungsborn

Greifswald

Rostock

START

Wismar

Lübeck
Revel in the Unesco-listed charms of this old city

0 km

Stralsund
Church steeples built with millions of bricks beckon you from afar

350 km

**5 DAYS
417 KM / 259 MILES**

GREAT FOR...

BEST TIME TO GO
April to October for the best weather.

ESSENTIAL PHOTO
Lübeck's Holstentor, with the city's iconic church steeples rising up behind.

BEST FOR FAMILIES
Riding the Molli steam train along the Baltic coast.

1 Along the Baltic Coast

The Hanseatic cities along the Baltic coast are some of the most beautiful in Germany, perfect for evocative strolling amid huge architectural treasures made from untold millions of bricks. In between, this drive takes you along the wave-tossed coast with its rugged beaches and long sandy vistas. But there are also great places to take a dip, like the fabled promenade at Binz.

TRIP HIGHLIGHT

1 Lübeck

A 12th-century gem boasting more than 1000 historical buildings, Lübeck's picture-book appearance is an enduring reminder of its role as one of the founding cities of the mighty Hanseatic League and its moniker 'Queen of the Hanse'. Behind its landmark 1464 **Holstentor** (Holsten Gate), you'll find streets lined with medieval merchants' homes and spired churches forming Lübeck's 'crown'.

The fine Gothic **Marienkirche** (St Mary's Church; ☎0451-397 700; www.stmarien-luebeck.com; Marienkirchhof 1; adult/child €2/1.50; ⏲10am-6pm Apr-Sep, to 5pm Oct, to 4pm Tue-Sun Nov-Mar) boasts the world's highest brick-vaulted roof and was the model for dozens of churches in northern Germany. A WWII bombing raid brought down the church's bells, which have been left where they fell in 1942 and have become a famous symbol of the city.

Thanks to a lift, even the fitness-phobic get to enjoy panoramic views from the 50m-high platform in the tower of the 13th-century **Petrikirche** (Church of St Peter; ☎0451-397 730; www.st-petri-luebeck.de; Petrikirchhof 1; tower adult/child €3/2; ⏲9am-8pm Apr-Sep, 10am-7pm Oct-Mar).

Opened in 2015, the brilliant **Europäisches Hansemuseum** (European Hanseatic Museum; ☎0451-809 0990; www.hansemuseum.eu; An der Untertrave1; combined ticket adult/child €14.50/8.50; ⏲10am-6pm Mar-Oct, to 5pm Nov-Mar) tells the remarkable story of the Hanseatic League (boxed text; p44), Lübeck and the region. Transfixing exhibits use every modern technology to tell a story as dramatic as anything in *Game of Thrones*.

✕ ▭ p45

The Drive » Take the B75 northeast for 19km to Travemünde.

② Travemünde

Writer Thomas Mann declared that he spent his happiest days in Travemünde, just outside Lübeck (which bought it in 1329 to control the shipping coming into its harbour). Its 4.5km of sandy beaches at the point where the Trave River flows into the Baltic Sea make it easy to see why. Water sports are the main draw, along with a colourful **sailing regatta** (www.travemuender-woche.com) in the last week of July.

The town is all wide streets and has a certain 1960s feel. Vorderreihe on the waterfront is lined with upscale shops and cafes.

The town takes great pride in its historic four-masted sailing-ship-turned-museum, **Passat** (☎0451-122 5202; www.ss-passat.com; Am Priwallhafen 16a; ⏲10am-5pm Apr-Oct), which did the run around South America's Cape

LINK YOUR TRIP

3 **Lakes & Treasures of Mecklenburg–Western Pomerania**

From Greifswald, found on both routes, discover the inland charms and surprises of the region.

6 **Berlin & the Jewels of Eastern Brandenburg**

It's only 180km south (under two hours on the A20) from Greifswald to hit this route's Kloster Chorin, a 13th-century abbey.

Horn from the early to mid-20th century.

The Drive » Take the very short but fun car ferry ride across the Trave River, then take the Siedlung road southeast for 10km to the junction with the B105, which you follow for 39km east to Wismar.

③ Wismar

With its gabled facades and cobbled streets, this small, photogenic city looks essentially Hanseatic. But although it joined the Hanseatic trading league in the 13th century, it spent most of the 16th and 17th centuries as part of Sweden. There are numerous reminders of this era all over town. The entire **Altstadt** (old town) was Unesco-listed in 2002.

The sober red-brick **St-Nikolai-Kirche** (St-Nikolai-Kirchhof; www.kirchen-in-wismar.de; St-Nikolai-Kirkhof; admission €2; ⊙8am-8pm May-Sep, 10am-6pm Apr & Oct, 11am-4pm Nov-Mar) is the largest of its kind in Europe. Its linden-tree-shaded churchyard is next to a small canal and is Wismar's loveliest spot.

Dominating the middle of the **Markt** is the 1602-built Wasserkunst (waterworks), an ornate, 12-sided well that supplied Wismar's drinking water until 1897. Today it remains the town's landmark. The large **Rathaus** (Markt; exhibition adult/child €3/2; ⊙exhibition 9am-5pm

Apr-Sep, 10am-4pm Oct-Mar) at the Markt's northern end was built between 1817 and 1819.

🛏 p45

The Drive » Sand dunes and forests add accents to the placidly flat expanses as you head to the coast. Head north for 42km on the L12 via Neubukow to Kühlungsborn.

④ Kühlungsborn

Get some beach time in Kühlungsborn, one of the most atmospheric beach resorts along this starkly beautiful coast.

Molli (Mecklenburger Bäderbahn Molli; ☎038293-431 331; www.molli-bahn.de; Bad Doberan Bahnhof; return adult/child €13.50/9.50; ⊙year-round; ♿) is a popular tourist train that travels along the coast from Kühlungsborn and Bad Doberan. Alternate taking the train and walking between stops for a gorgeous day out along the often wild Baltic shore before you set out driving again.

The Drive » Enjoy the coastal plains and glimpses of the Baltic as you take the Pfarrweg and L12 16km east to Bad Doberan.

⑤ Bad Doberan

The former summer ducal residence of Bad Doberan was once the site of a powerful Cistercian monastery and is now home to a fantasy in brick. Construction of the magnificent Gothic

Münster Bad Doberan (☎038203-627 16; www.muenster-doberan.de; Klosterstrasse 2; adult/child €3/1; ⊙9am-6pm Mon-Sat, 11am-6pm Sun May-Sep, shorter hours rest of the year) started in 1280 but the scale of the building meant it wasn't consecrated until 1368. Its treasures include an intricate **high altar** and an **ornate pulpit**.

The Drive » Leave town driving north on the L12, which curves around to the east for 16km until it meets the B103. Turn north for 3km to Warnemünde.

Wismar The city's Altstadt

6 Warnemünde

Genteel Warnemünde is all about promenading, eating fish, sipping cocktails and lazing on its long, wide and startlingly white **beach**. Perfect for the last of these activities is the *Strandkörbe*, the iconic German wicker beach chair, complete with its own roof and awning to deflect seaside breezes. Rent one and get cosy on most public beaches.

Walking along **Alter Strom**, the boat-lined main canal, you'll pass a row of quaint cottages housing restaurants.

The Drive » Drive south on the Werftallee for 10km through Rostock's interesting industrial docklands to the centre.

7 Rostock

Rostock was devastated in WWII and later pummelled by socialist architectural 'ideals'. But this large port city still has small but attractive historic enclaves. Perhaps the best feature is the vibrant energy provided by the 11,000 university students.

Central Rostock's pride and joy is the 13th-century **Marienkirche** (📞0381-453 325; www. marienkirche-rostock.de; Am Ziegenmarkt; €1.50 donation requested; ⊘10am-6pm Mon-Sat, 11am-5pm Sun May-Sep, 10am-4pm Mon-Sat, 11am-noon Sun Oct-Apr), the only main Rostock church to have survived WWII unscathed (although restorations are ongoing). Behind the main altar, the church's 12m-high astrological clock was built in 1472 by Hans Düringer.

Red-brick and pastel-coloured buildings on the large **Alter Markt** hark back to the 14th- and 15th-century Hanseatic era.

✕ 🛏 p45

LOCAL KNOWLEDGE: CLASSIC ROADSIDE ATTRACTION: KARLS

Gloriously hokey, **Karls** (📞0382-024 050; www.karls.de; Purkshof 2, off B105; ⏱8am-8pm May-Sep, to 7pm Oct-Apr; 👤) is a roadside attraction in the cheesiest tradition. The schtick here is fruit – strawberries to be exact. In this sprawling hodge-podge of petting zoo, shops, playgrounds, cafes and, yes, strawberry fields, you will find something for anyone in the family. The fresh strawberry ice cream (€1) is really good. Watch them make preserves, then listen to the mechanical bears sing Elvis. Karls is about 12km northeast of Rostock.

The Drive » Leave Rostock, driving for 22km on the B105. Just before the village of Borg, look for the turn north on the L21 and follow this beautiful coastal road 22km north to Ahrenshoop.

- - - - - - - - - -

TRIP HIGHLIGHT

8 Ahrenshoop

Nature lovers and artists will be captivated by the Darss-Zingst Peninsula. This far-flung splinter of land has a seaside that is raw and bracing, with trees growing sideways away from the constant winds. The artists' village of Ahrenshoop is a great place to wander. It has some of the region's most strikingly painted reed-thatched houses.

The Drive » Drive 8km northeast on the L21, then turn due north for 7km to Prerow, right on the coast.

- - - - - - - - - -

9 Prerow

The tiny town of Prerow is renowned for its model-ship-filled seafarers'

church and lighthouse. Look for charming 'captains' houses' – reed-thatched dwellings with colourfully painted doors depicting sunflowers, fish and other regional motifs. Also common are *Zeesenboote* (dragnet fishing boats) with striking brown sails.

The Drive » Take the L21 and L23 44km south via Löbnitz to the A20. Now you get to open up the car while heading east for 31km to exit 25 where you'll take the B109 25km east to Greifswald.

- - - - - - - - - -

10 Greifswald

The skyline of this compact former Hanseatic city is defined by three churches: the 'Langer Nikolas' ('Long Nicholas'), 'Dicke Marie' ('Fat Mary') and 'Kleine Jakob' ('Small Jacob'). Don't miss climbing the tower of the first, 14th-century **Dom St Nikolai** (📞03834-2627; Domstrasse; tower adult/child €3/1.50; ⏱10am-

4pm Mon-Sat, 11am-3pm Sun), for sweeping views.

The richly ornamented buildings ringing the **Markt** hint at Greifswald's stature in the Middle Ages. The **Rathaus**, at the western end, started life as 14th-century shops. Among the red-brick gabled houses on the eastern side, the **Coffee House** (No 11) is gorgeous and a good example of a combined living and storage house owned by Hanseatic merchants.

The Drive » It's an easy 36km northwest on the B105 to Stralsund. Watch for the huge church spires as they appear on the horizon.

- - - - - - - - - -

TRIP HIGHLIGHT

11 Stralsund

Stralsund was once the second-most-important member of the Hanseatic League, after Lübeck, and its square gables interspersed with Gothic turrets, ornate portals and vaulted arches make it one of the leading examples of *Backsteingotik* (classic red-brick Gothic gabled architecture) in northern Germany.

This vibrant city's historic cobbled streets and many attractions make it an unmissable stop. The main square, **Alter Markt** (Old Market), is a hub of its architectural treasures. The soaring 1270 **Nikolai-kirche** (📞03831-299 799; www.nikolai-stralsund.de; Alter

Markt; adult/child €2/free; ⏱9am-7pm Mon-Sat, noon-5pm Sun May-Sep, 10am-6pm Mon-Sat, noon-4pm Sun Oct-Apr) is a masterpiece of medieval architecture. Its interior is colourful and filled with art treasures.

Seven copper turrets and six triangular gables grace the red-brick Gothic facade of the splendid 1370 **Rathaus**.

In an arctic-white wavelike building that leaps out from the surrounding red-brick warehouses, the state-of-the-art **Ozeaneum** (📞03831-265 0610; www.ozeaneum.de; Hafenstrasse 11; adult/child €16/7, combined ticket incl Meeresmuseum €21/10; ⏱9.30am-8pm Jun-Sep, 9.30am-6pm Oct-May) takes you into an underwater world of creatures from the Baltic

and North Seas and the Atlantic Ocean.

Stroll the nearby harbour area for lots of stands selling smoked fish.

✕ 🛏 p45

The Drive ≫ Soar over the water on the bridge to Rügen Island on the B96; once on the island (7km from Stralsund) turn southeast on the L29 and drive through a canopy of trees and pass through villages for 36km to the B196, where another 10km southeast brings you to Göhren.

- - - - - - - - - - - - -

⑫ Göhren

Göhren's stunning 7km-long **beach** – divided into the sleepier Südstrand and the more developed Nordstrand – lives up to its hype as Rügen's best resort beach.

Göhren is the eastern terminus of the **Rügen-**

sche Bäderbahn (RBB; www.ruegensche-baederbahn.de; day pass adult/child €22/11) steam train that chuffs between Putbus and Göhren. En route, it stops in Binz, Jagdschloss Granitz, Sellin and Baabe. Much of the narrow track passes through sun-dappled forest. Its nickname is the ironic 'Rasender Roland' (Rushing Roland).

The Drive ≫ Take the B196 northwest for a mere 12km to the L29, then turn east for the final 3km to the Jagdschloss Granitz parking lot.

- - - - - - - - - - - - -

⑬ Jagdschloss Granitz

A grandiose hunting palace built in 1723 on top of the 107m-high Tempelberg, **Jagdschloss Granitz** (📞038393-667 10; www.jagdschloss-granitz.de; Binz; adult/child €6/1; ⏱9am-6pm daily May-Sep, to 4pm Apr & Oct, 10am-4pm Tue-Sun Nov-Mar) was significantly enlarged and altered by Wilhelm Malte I in 1837. The results will remind you of salt and pepper shakers or a phallic fantasy, depending on your outlook. Malte's flights of fancy also gave Rügen the grandiose Putbus.

The RBB steam train stops at Jagdschloss and Garftitz, which serve the palace. Get off at one, enjoy some lovely hiking and reboard at the other for a trip to either Göhren or Binz where

DETOUR: PEENEMÜNDE

Start: ⑩ Greifswald

Amid the sandy dunes and bleak expanses of Usedom Island, the notorious village of Peenemünde is at the end of a scenic 52km drive via the B109 and B111.

It was here, on the island's western tip, that Wernher von Braun developed the V2 rocket, first launched in October 1942. It flew 90km high and a distance of 200km before plunging into the Baltic – the first time in history that a flying object exited the earth's atmosphere. Displays at the **Historisch-Technisches Museum** (Historical & Technological Museum; 📞038371-5050; www.peenemuende.de; Im Kraftwerk; adult/concession €8/5; ⏱10am-6pm Apr-Sep, 10am-4pm Oct-Mar, closed Mon Nov-Mar) – some in surviving buildings – do a good job of showing how the rockets were developed and the destruction they caused.

THE HANSEATIC LEAGUE

The legacy of the Hanseatic League lives on in many of the towns and cities on this route, including Lübeck, Wismar, Stralsund, Greifswald and more. Its origins go back to various guilds and associations established from about the mid-12th century by out-of-town merchants to protect their interests. After Hamburg and Lübeck signed an agreement in 1241 to protect their ships and trading routes, they were joined in their league by Lüneburg, Kiel and a string of Baltic Sea cities east to Greifswald. By 1356 this had grown into the Hanseatic League, encompassing half a dozen other large alliances of cities, with Lübeck playing the lead role.

At its zenith, the league had about 200 member cities. It earned a say in the choice of Danish kings after fighting two wars against the Danes between 1361 and 1369. The resulting Treaty of Stralsund in 1370 turned it into northern Europe's most powerful economic and political entity. Some 70 inland and coastal cities – mostly German – formed the core of the Hanseatic League, but another 130 beyond the Reich maintained a loose association, making it truly international. During a period of endless feudal squabbles in Germany, it was a bastion of political and social stability.

By the 15th century, however, competition from Dutch and English shipping companies, internal disputes and a shift in the centre of world trade from the North and Baltic Seas to the Atlantic had caused decline. The ruin and chaos of the Thirty Years' War in the 17th century delivered the final blow, although Hamburg, Bremen and Lübeck retained the 'Hanse City' title. Since reunification, however, well over a dozen cities have decided to adopt the title once again.

you might have left your car. The palace parking itself is 2km from the complex.

The Drive » It's only 2km northwest on the L29 to the beachy pleasures of Binz.

⑭ Binz

Rügen's largest and most celebrated seaside resort, 'Ostseebad' (Baltic Sea spa), Binz is an alluring confection of ornate, white Victorian-era villas, white sand and blue water. Its roads are signed in Gothic script and lined with coastal pines and chestnut trees. Even if all the signs of 21st-century capitalism abound, especially along jam-packed Haupt-strasse, you can still feel the pull of history amid the modern-day crowds.

A highlight of Binz is simply strolling its 4km-long north–south **Strandpromenade**, lined with elegant villas. At the southern end of the built-up area, you'll find the palatial **Kurhaus**, a lovely-looking 1908 build-ing containing a luxury hotel. In front of it is the long pier. Strandprom-enade continues further south from here, and becomes markedly less busy. Join the mobs and stop frequently for ice creams.

✕ p45

Eating & Sleeping

Lübeck ❶

🍴 Schiffergesellschaft German €€

(📞0451-767 76; www.schiffergesellschaft.de; Breite Strasse 2; mains €10-25; ⏲ kitchen 11.30am-11pm, bar 10am-1am) In the historic seafarer's guild hall (1535), Lübeck's most atmospheric – if not best – restaurant is a veritable museum. Ships' lanterns, old model ships and revolving Chinese-style silhouette lamps dangle from the beamed ceiling of this wood-lined dining room. White-aproned waitstaff deliver regional specialities to tables here or in the hidden garden out back. Book ahead for dinner.

🛏 Klassik Altstadt Hotel Boutique Hotel €€

(📞0451-702 980; www.klassik-altstadt-hotel.de; Fischergrube 52; s/d from €50/120; 🛜) Each of the 29 rooms at this elegantly furnished boutique hotel is dedicated to a different, mostly German, writer or artist, such as Thomas Mann and Johann Sebastian Bach. Single rooms (some share baths and are great value) feature travelogues by famous authors.

Wismar ❸

🛏 Hotel Reingard Hotel €€

(📞03841-284 972; www.hotel-reingard.de; Weberstrasse 18; s/d from €72/90; 🅿🛜) Wismar's most charming hotel has a dozen artistic rooms, a little garden and wonderfully idiosyncratic touches such as a lightshow to classical music that plays across the facade daily at 8.30pm. The breakfast includes apples from the owners' trees and eggs from their chickens.

Rostock ❼

🍴 Zur Kogge German €€

(📞0381-493 4493; www.zur-kogge.de; Wokrenterstrasse 27; mains €9-20; ⏲11am-9pm Mon-Sat; 🚼) At this Rostock institution, cosy wooden booths are lined with stained-glass Hanseatic coats of arms and monster fish threatening sailing ships, while life preservers hang from the walls, and ships' lanterns are suspended from the ceiling. Local fish dishes dominate the menu.

🛏 Hotel Verdi Hotel €€

(📞0381-252 240; www.hotel-verdi.de; Wollenweberstrasse 28; s/d/apt €70/90/100; 🛜) Opening to an umbrella-shaded, timber-decked terrace is this sparkling little hotel near the Petrikirche and Alter Markt, with a handful of attractively decorated rooms (some with kitchenettes), and two apartments with views.

Stralsund ⓫

🍴 Speicher 8 Modern German €€

(📞03831-288 2898; www.speicher8.de; Hafenstrasse 8; mains €10-20; ⏲10am-10pm) Simply roasted fish is one of the stars of this excellent casual restaurant in an old turreted building right on the waterfront. There are great tables out front; inside it's all glass and exposed wood. Celebrate your love by ordering a meat or fish platter for two. Both are beautifully presented. Sushi and vegie fare are also on offer.

🛏 Hotel Scheelehof Boutique Hotel €€

(📞03831-283 300; www.hotel-stralsund-scheelehof.de; Fährstrasse 23-25; r €105-145; 🛜) One of Stralsund's most appealing places to stay, the Scheelehof's 94 rooms are all individually decorated and scattered about several adjoining historic buildings. Furnishings have a luxurious period feel and there is a small spa. The hotel is noted for its bars and restaurants.

Binz ⓮

🍴 Fischräucherei Kuse Seafood €

(📞038393-322 49; Strandpromenade 3; dishes from €2; ⏲9am-8pm) For some of the most delicious and certainly the cheapest fish on Rügen, follow your nose – literally – to the far southeast end of the Strandpromenade, where fish has been freshly smoked since 1900. Choose from fish sandwiches and meals; dine at its indoor tables, on the terrace or make a picnic.

Dessau-Rosslau *Bauhausgebäude, the former school of Bauhaus art, design and architecture*

BAUHAUS

Design for Life: Bauhaus to VW

2

This pilgrimage for lovers of modern architecture and design takes you from the birthplace of Bauhaus to Volkswagen's global HQ, visiting game-changing sites that helped shape today's world.

TRIP HIGHLIGHTS

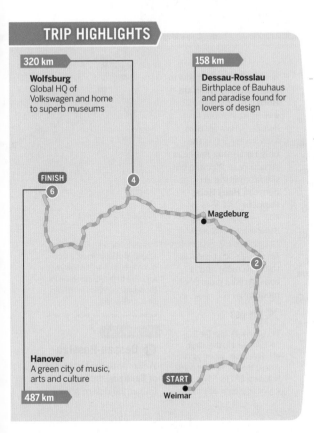

320 km

Wolfsburg
Global HQ of
Volkswagen and home
to superb museums

158 km

Dessau-Rosslau
Birthplace of Bauhaus
and paradise found for
lovers of design

FINISH
6

4

Magdeburg

2

Hanover
A green city of music,
arts and culture

487 km

START

Weimar

2–4 DAYS
487 KM / 304 MILES

GREAT FOR...

BEST TIME TO GO

Long days and clear
skies from May to
September mean
bonus hours.

ESSENTIAL PHOTO

Design-heads'
Holy Grail:
Bauhausgebäude
signage.

BEST FOR FAMILIES

Wolfsburg's fun
museums delight
young and old.

47

Design for Life: Bauhaus to VW

2

Fans of modern architecture, design and technology will find this easy, engaging trip hard to resist. You'll take in the history of the Bauhaus movement in Dessau-Rosslau, where it all took off, get a taste of German art deco and quirky Austrian architect Hundertwasser's off-the-wall ideas in Magdeburg, explore the world's first modern factory in Alfeld, and delve into German automotive genius, firsthand, in Wolfsburg.

9 (130km) **A352** **A7**

Garbsen **FINISH**

6 Hanover

A7

B217 **Hildesheim**

B3

Weser

5 Alfeld

A7

Osterode am Harz

B80

L561 Göttingen

A7

Kassel *Leine*

Werra

A49 **5**

Fulda

---

❶ Weimar

Weimar is best known as the stomping ground for cultural heavyweights Goethe and Schiller, and its post-WWI dalliance with international fame as the place where the constitution of the German Reich (the Weimar Republic) was drafted. Weimar is teeming with historical sights and museums, and is home to the **Bauhaus Museum** (☎ 03643-545 400; www.klassik-stiftung.de; Theaterplatz 1; adult/concession €4/3; ☉10am-6pm Apr-Oct, to 4pm Nov-Mar), which is why you're here. Although the movement did most of its work from Dessau-Rosslau, it was founded here by Walter Gropius in 1919. The tiny **Haus am Horn** (☎ 03643-583 000; www.hausamhorn.de; Am Horn 61; ☉11am-5pm Wed, Sat & Sun Apr-Oct) is the only remaining Bauhaus structure in Weimar, but the fascinating art-nouveau **Haus Hohe Pappeln** (☎ 03643-545 400; www.klassikstiftung.de; Belvederer Allee 58; adult/concession €3/2; ☉11am-4pm Tue-Sun Apr-Oct) predates the movement and is considered a pioneer of modernity.

🗙 🛏 p53

The Drive » Take the B7 for 7.5km east to the village of Umpferstedt, where you'll pick up the B87, heading north. Follow the B87 for 50km as it winds through fields and forests to the pretty Saale River township of Naumburg: a nice place to stop. Take the B180 east for 14km to the A9 autobahn for the remaining 90km north into Dessau-Rosslau.

TRIP HIGHLIGHT

❷ Dessau-Rosslau

Welcome to the birthplace of Bauhaus, the most influential design school of the 20th century, which gave us the mantras 'less is more' and 'form follows function'. There's nowhere else you'll find a greater concentration of structures from the Bauhaus' most creative period, 1925 to 1932. If you're a student of architecture or design, you might not want to leave. Pick up a tour at

LINK YOUR TRIP

5 Central Germany's Castles & Palaces

Fancy some medieval with your modern? From Weimar, take our castles and palaces trip, too.

9 North Sea Coast

If you do like to be beside the seaside, follow the autobahns for 130km northwest from Hanover to Bremen for this nautical jaunt.

the epicentre of activity, the **Bauhausgebäude** (Bauhaus Building; ☎0340-650 8250; www.bauhaus-dessau. de; Gropiusallee 38; exhibition adult/concession €7.50/4.50, tour €5; ⏱10am-6pm, tours 11am & 2pm, also noon & 4pm Sat & Sun), erected in 1925–26 as the school of Bauhaus art, design and architecture. Next, check out the **Meisterhäuser** (Masters' Houses; www. meisterhaeuser.de; Ebertallee 63, 65-67, 69-71; admission to all houses adult/concession €7.50/5.50, tours €11.50/8.50; ⏱11am-6pm Tue-Sun, tours 12.30pm & 3.30pm daily, also 1.30pm Sat & Sun) where the likes of Kandinsky and Gropius once lived. Proceed to the 300-plus homes of the **Törten Estate** (Am Dreieck 1; tours €4; ⏱tours 3pm Tue-Sun) prototype of the first-ever housing estate. To complete the experience, why not spend the night?

✗ 🏠 p53

The Drive » Follow B184 through farms and canola fields for 63km into Magdeburg.

- - - - - - - - - - - - - -

❸ Magdeburg

Few people could deny that Magdeburg is aesthetically challenged, thanks to WWII bombs and socialist city planners in love with sparse boulevards and prefab concrete apartment blocks, the so-called Plattenbauten. Yet this is one of the country's oldest cities, founded some 1200 years

ago, and its imposing **Dom** (www.magdeburgerdom. de; Am Dom 1; tour adult/ concession €3/1.50; ⏱10am-5pm) is the first Gothic cathedral on German soil. The reason you're here, however, is the love-it-or-hate-it, whimsical **Grüne Zitadelle** (Green Citadel; ☎0391-620 8655; www. gruene-zitadelle.de; Breiter Weg 9; tour adult/concession €6/5; ⏱information office 9am-2pm), the last building of eccentric artist-architect Friedensreich Hundertwasser. For a little more architectural contrast, why not stop to admire the ornately detailed dark-green walls of **Die Saison** (☎0391-850 80; www.herrenkrug.de; Herrenkrug Parkhotel an der Elbe, Herrenkrug 3; mains €22-36; ⏱noon-3pm & 5-11pm), or dine alfresco and admire the hotel's handsome art-deco facade and immaculate gardens.

🏠 p53

The Drive » Follow the B71 north for 10km, then pick up the A2 autobahn at exit 69 Magdeburg-Kannenstieg. It's 69km of autobahn action until exit 58 Kreuz Wolfsburg/ Königslutter, before heading north for 15km on the A39 into Wolfsburg.

- - - - - - - - - - - - - -

TRIP HIGHLIGHT

❹ Wolfsburg

Volkswagen is the world's second-largest vehicle manufacturer, and its global headquarters employ about 40% of Wolfsburg's residents: you

can't miss the massive VW emblem on the side of the textbook postwar factory building. Designed by Ferdinand Porsche under Hitler's orders, the Volkswagen Beetle (or 'People's car') influenced the automobile industry in much the same way as the Bauhaus movement influenced architecture. Of Wolfsburg's numerous shiny state-of-the-art museums, loved by adults and kids alike, you'll want to check out Volkswagen's own **AutoMuseum** (automuseum.volkswagen.de/ en; Dieselstrasse 35; adult/ concession/family €6/3/15; ⏱10am-6pm Tue-Sun), or the

Magdeburg The Grüne Zitadelle (Green Citadel)

big draw for rev-heads, **Autostadt** (Car City; ☎05361-400; www.autostadt. de/en; Stadtbrücke; adult/ concession €15/12, car tower discovery tour adult/concession €8/6; ⏰9am-6pm), a celebration of all things automobile spread across 25 hectares. To see where design and science meet, head straight to the informative and engaging **Phaeno** (☎05361-890 1 00; www.phaeno.de; Willy-Brandt-Platz 1; adult/concession €12.50/8; ⏰9am-5pm Tue-Fri, from 10am Sat & Sun), or swap your smarts for the arty side of modern design at the **Kunstmuseum** (Art Museum; ☎05361-266 90;

www.kunstmuseum-wolfsburg. de; Porschestrasse 53; adult/ concession €8/4; ⏰11am-8pm Tue, to 6pm Wed-Sun).

🛏 p53

The Drive ›› Follow the A39 south for 76km to exit 65 Bockenem. Take the B243 north to the tiny village of Nette, then scoot west on the L493 for 6km to another tiny village, Bodenburg. Drive the less than 1km across town to pick up the L490, which winds through picturesque hills and fields for 17km to the township of Alfeld. Your next stop, Fagus Werk, is clearly signposted.

- - - - - - - -

5 Alfeld

Designed and built by Bauhaus founder Walter Gropius in 1911, the **Fagus Werk** (Fagus Factory; ☎05181-7914; www.fagus-werk. com/en; Hannoversche Strasse 58, Alfeld; adult/concession €8/6; ⏰10am-4pm) has been producing shoe lasts – the basic moulds around which shoes are made – for over a century. It's regarded as the first building in the world to conform to the modern architechtural style and is the last Bauhaus stop on your pilgrimage. Given Unesco World Heritage status in 2011,

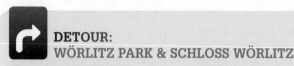

DETOUR:
WÖRLITZ PARK & SCHLOSS WÖRLITZ

Start: ❷ Dessau-Rosslau

The 112-hectare **Wörlitz Park & Schloss Wörlitz** (☎039404-310 09; www.woerlitz-information.de; Förstergasse 26, Wörlitz; palace tours €5; ⏰10am-6pm Apr-Oct, 10am-4pm Mon-Fri Nov-Mar) is the pinnacle of Prince Leopold III's so-named Gartenreich Dessau-Wörlitz (Garden Realm), one of the finest garden ensembles in Germany. A visit, to contemplate Bauhaus in the contrasting context of the culture from which it emerged, is highly recommended. Allow at least a half-day including travel time to appreciate the beauty on display. To get here from Dessau-Rosslau, take the B185 east until the junction with the L133. Follow the L133 for 14.5km until you reach the park.

There are five other parks belonging to the Gartenreich Dessau-Wörlitz, Oranienbaum, Luisium, Georgium, Mosigkau and Grosskühnau: scattered over 142 sq km, each comes with its own palace and other buildings, in styles ranging from neoclassical to neo-Gothic, and reflects the vision of Prince Leopold III Friedrich Franz von Anhalt-Dessau (1740–1817). A highly educated man, he travelled to the Netherlands, Italy, France and Switzerland, gaining inspiration to apply the philosophy of the Enlightenment to the design of a landscape that would create a harmony of nature, architecture and art.

The gardens were added to Unesco's World Heritage list in 2000 and are protected under the Biosphärenreservat Mittelelbe (www.mittelelbe.com). All parks are free and can be roamed during daylight hours, but the palaces charge admission and have their own opening hours.

sections of the building have been turned into a gallery which focuses on Gropius' life, the Bauhaus movement, the history of the Fagus company and footwear in general. Guided factory tours are recommended.

The Drive ≫ The B3 runs north for 45km where it merges with the B6 and proceeds for 5km into the heart of Hanover.

- - - - - - - - - - - - -

TRIP HIGHLIGHT

❻ Hanover

Capital of the state of Lower Saxony, Hanover boasts a wealth of cultural attractions, pretty parks and plenty of top-notch nosh. Few realise that

from 1714, monarchs from the house of Hanover also ruled the entire British Empire, for over a century. In a cruel irony, extensive Allied bombing in 1943 wiped out much of Hanover's rich architectural and cultural heritage. But there are a few highlights to round out your trip.

The **Neues Rathaus** (Trammplatz 2; elevator adult/concession €3/2; ⏰9.30am-6.30pm Mon-Fri, 10am-6.30pm Sat & Sun, elevator closed mid-Nov–Mar; Ⓤ Hannover Kröpcke, Hannover Aegidientorplatz), completed in 1913, features a curved elevator – the only one of its kind in the world – that travels 98m to four observation platforms offering panoramic views.

While for something completely different architecturally, the 1979 **Sprengel Museum** (☎0511-438 75; www.sprengel-museum.com; Kurt-Schwitters-Platz; adult/concession €7/4, Fri free; ⏰10am-6pm Wed-Sun, to 8pm Tue) houses one of Germany's finest art collections. Complete your visit with a stroll through the grandiose, baroque **Herrenhäuser Gärten** (☎0511-1683 4000; www.hannover.de/Herrenhausen; Herrenhäuser Strasse 4; general admission free; ⏰9am-6pm (grotto to 5.30pm) Apr-Oct, to 4.30pm (4pm) Nov-Mar; Ⓤ Hannover Herrenhäuser Gärten), the city's pride and joy.

Eating & Sleeping

Weimar

✖ Hans und Franz German €€

(☎03643-457 3987; www.hanzundfranz.
com; Erfurter Strasse 23; mains €8-14; ☺6-
11pm Mon-Sat, noon-2pm & 6-11pm Sun; ✈)
There's something of a mid-century vibe at
this happy haunt serving up local specialities
such as *Thuringian Klösse* (dumplings) with
red cabbage, and meaty German favourites,
intelligently balanced with a few nice options for
vegetarians and vegans. And, yes, the schnitzel
here is good.

⊫ Design Apartments
Weimar Apartment €€

(☎03643-217 149; www.hier-war-goethe-nie.
de; Fuldaer Strasse 85; apt per person from
€59; ☎) Get in quick to snap up one of these
enormous, self-contained, fully renovated
heritage apartments that could have been
plucked from the pages of a Taschen design
book. Even better is that you'd be hard-pressed
to find friendlier, kinder hosts anywhere. This
is surely the perfect homebase from which to
explore the delights of Weimar and Thuringia.
Exceptional value.

Dessau-Rosslau

✖ Kornhaus Cafe €€

(☎0340-6501 9963; www.kornhaus-dessau.
de; Kornhausstrasse 146; mains €10-21) This
striking Bauhaus riverside beer-and-dance
hall was designed by Carl Flieger, a Gropius
assistant. Apart from being a piece of modern
architectural history, it offers the perfect spot to
sit and enjoy a beer and some refreshingly light,
modern German fare in the sun.

⊫ Bauhaus 'Prellerhaus' Hostel €

(☎0340-650 8318; www.bauhaus-dessau.de;
Gropiusallee 38; s/d from €35/55; ⓟ) This is
one for architecture and design purists who'll

first need to come to terms with the fact that
all rooms share showers and toilets. If you
can swallow that, you'll be able to channel
your modernist dream into something highly
functional by staying in these minimally super-
cool former students' rooms.

Magdeburg ❸

⊫ Herrenkrug Parkhotel
an der Elbe Heritage Hotel €€

(☎0391-850 80; www.herrenkrug.de;
Herrenkrug 3; s/d from €86/122; ⓟ@☎☎☎)
Rise to chirping birds at this riverside mansion,
then start the day with a wake-up stroll through
the lush surrounding park. Rooms are spacious
and stylish, with access to the sauna and steam
bath included in the rate. The hotel's best
feature is its bold, handsome art-deco facade:
one for lovers of the period.

Wolfsburg ❹

⊫ Innside by Melia Hotel €€

(☎6128-015 5294; www.melia.com; Heinrich-
Nordhoff-Strasse 2; s/d from €94/111) Opened in
2014, this spotless, stylish property is in a great
spot a hop, skip and a jump from the station. Its
slick black and sleek steel guest rooms afford
every comfort and convenience, including
ports in all the right places, wi-fi and a killer LED
smart TV.

⊫ Ritz-Carlton Hotel €€€

(☎05361-607 000; www.ritzcarlton.com;
Stadtbrücke; r from €305, ste from €405;
ⓟ✳☎☎) This hotel is a hard act to beat.
The hotel swimming pool is integrated into the
harbour basin of the canal, giving it a lakeside
feel, while the building forms a stunning arc on
one side of Autostadt. The decor is elegant and
breathes natural tones. Expect full five-star
facilities, complemented by a Michelin-starred
restaurant and numerous bars. You can take
high tea overlooking the harbour.

Schwerin *Tulips in the picturesque Schlossgarten*

Lakes & Treasures of Mecklenburg– Western Pomerania

3

Beautiful old towns mix with pastoral landscapes on this drive through the heart of one of Germany's oldest provinces. You can almost see the knights riding in the mists.

TRIP HIGHLIGHTS

127 km

Schwerin
The local dukes left a beautiful palace for this beautiful town

190 km

Güstrow
A tiny town that's big on art and architecture

FINISH Greifswald

4

3

5

● Neubrandenburg

● Neustrelitz

1 **START** Ludwigslust

Lüneburg
Enjoy wandering an old town where the buildings look drunk

0 km

Waren
Get back to nature in the heart of the lakes district

249 km

2–3 DAYS
377 KM / 235 MILES

GREAT FOR...

BEST TIME TO GO
May to October the beautiful forests and lakes are at their best.

ESSENTIAL PHOTO
Schwerin's Schloss at dawn, with the stones glowing rose.

BEST FOR FAMILIES
Exploring Schwerin's lakes and gardens on a family bike ride.

Lakes & Treasures of Mecklenburg– Western Pomerania

3

During the 15th century the dukes of Mecklenburg–Western Pomerania built palaces across the lake-strewn plains of Germany's north so they could luxuriate in their wealth. Get a taste of their coddled lives while you also taste the hearty fare of the north at the many excellent restaurants and cafes. Walk it off in the ancient and fabled beech forests of Müritz National Park.

TRIP HIGHLIGHT

❶ Lüneburg

An off-kilter church steeple, buildings leaning on each other and houses with swollen 'beer-belly' facades: in parts it looks like the charming town of Lüneburg has drunk too much of the pilsner lager it used to brew. Of course, the city's wobbly angles and uneven pavements have a more prosaic cause: shifting ground and subsidence due to salt mining has caused many buildings to tilt sideways.

The medieval **Rathaus** (☎04131-207 6620; Markt; tours adult/child €5/3; ⏱tours 11am & 2pm Tue-Sun Jan-Mar, noon & 3pm Tue-Sat, 11am & 2pm Sun Apr-Dec) on the **Markt** has a spectacular baroque facade, added in 1720 and decorated with coats of arms and three tiers of statues. The top row represents (from left to right) Strength, Trade, Peace (the one with the staff), Justice and Moderation.

The cobbled, slightly wobbly street and square **Am Sande** is full of red-brick buildings with typically Hanseatic stepped gables.

✗ p61

The Drive » Take the B5 north and east 89km to Ludwigslust (at 20km watch for the crossing of the historic Elbe River, which flows towards Hamburg).

- - - - - - - - - - - - -

❷ Ludwigslust

Such was the allure of the grand palace, **Schloss Ludwigslust** (☎03874-571 90; www.schloss-ludwigslust. de; Schloss Strasse; ⏱10am-6pm Tue-Sun mid-Apr–mid-Oct, to 5pm mid-Oct–mid-Apr),

that when the ducal seat moved 36km north to Schwerin in 1837, some family members continued living here until 1945. Now part of the Schwerin State Museum, its high point is the stately, gilt-columned, high-ceilinged Golden Hall. After lavish renovations, the East Wing was set to reopen in 2016.

A planned baroque town, Ludwigslust showcases a neat, orderly layout that is an attraction in itself.

The Drive » Go straight north for 38km on the B106. As you near Schwerin, you'll start to see some of the lakes that make the district famous, like the Ostorfer See, the Fauler See and Schweriner See.

LINK YOUR TRIP

1 Along the Baltic Coast

This trip ends in Greifswald where you can join the coastal trip.

10 German Fairy Tale Road

From Lüneburg it's only 141km on the A39 and A1 to Bremen in the west, where you can plunge into the world of the Brothers Grimm.

TRIP HIGHLIGHT

❸ Schwerin

Picturesquely sited around seven lakes (or possibly more depending on how you tally them), Schwerin is the unofficial capital of the lakes district. The centrepiece of this engaging city is its **Schloss** (☎0385-525 2920; www.schloss-schwerin. de; Burg Island; adult/child €6/free; ⏰10am-6pm Tue-Sun mid-Apr–mid-Oct, to 5pm mid-Oct–mid-Apr), a castle built in the 14th century during the city's six centuries as the former seat of the Grand Duchy of Mecklenburg. It's an appealing mishmash of architectural styles and is crowned by a gleaming golden dome. Nowadays the Schloss earns its keep as the state's parliament building. Crossing the causeway south from the palace-surrounding **Burggarten** brings you to the baroque **Schlossgarten** (Palace Garden), intersected by several canals.

Schwerin has an upbeat, vibrant energy on its restored streets that befits its role as the capital of Mecklenburg–Western Pomerania. Cafes, interesting shops and flashes of its regal past make wandering the **Altstadt** (old town) a delight. The bustling **Markt** is home to the **Rathaus** and the colonnaded neoclassical Neues Gebäude (1780–83).

Schwerin's central lake, the **Pfaffentiech**, was created by a dam in the 12th century. Through the centuries it was surrounded by some of the city's most elegant buildings. At the southwest corner, the vividly orange **Arsenal** dates from 1840. You can cross the waters on a small **ferry** (Pfaffentiech; adult/child €2/1; ⏰10am-6pm Tue-Sun Apr-Sep).

✗ ⨳ p61

The Drive ❯❯ Drive directly east for 63km on the B104. As you go, the land becomes increasingly moist, with rivers and tiny lakes appearing in profusion.

TRIP HIGHLIGHT

❹ Güstrow

This charming town is over 775 years old and is a great place to explore on foot. The fabulous Renaissance 16th-century **Schloss Güstrow** (☎03843-7520; www.schloss-guestrow. de; Franz-Parr-Platz 1; adult/child €5/3.50; ⏰10am-6pm Tue-Sun mid-Apr–mid-Oct, to 5pm mid-Oct–mid-Apr) is home to a historical museum, luxe rooms and formal **gardens**.

Built between 1226 and 1335, the richly ornamented Gothic **Güstrow Dom** (www.dom-guestrow. de; Philipp-Brandin-Strasse 5; ⏰10am-5pm daily mid-May–mid-Oct, reduced hours rest of year) is an old-town highlight.

Famed 20th-century sculptor Ernst Barlach

spent most of his working life in Güstrow. You can view his deeply felt, humanist works in the **Gertrudenkapelle** (☎03843-844 000; Gertrudenplatz 1; adult/child €4/2.50; ⏰10am-5pm Tue-Sun Apr-Oct, 11am-4pm Tue-Sun Nov-Mar) and at the **Atelierhaus** (☎03843-822 99; www.ernst-barlach-stiftung.de; Heidberg 15; adult/child €6/4; ⏰10am-5pm Tue-Sun Apr-Oct, 11am-4pm Tue-Sun Nov-Mar).

✗ p61

The Drive ❯❯ Leave Güstrow by driving due south for 20km on the B103. At Krakow-am-See (and its large lake) turn

Güstrow Schloss Güstrow and its formal gardens

southeast for 14km on the L204, then continue east for another 14km on the Kastanienallee to the B108, which you take southeast to Waren.

TRIP HIGHLIGHT

⑤ Waren

Right on the sparkling blue waters of **Lake Müritz**, Waren is a lovely village and one of the more popular in the lakes region. You can stroll streets lined with half-timbered buildings, poke in and out of churches and, best of all, relax at a waterfront cafe while you watch small sailboats darting past.

Large-scale renovation schemes have restored much of the 16th-century feel to the town. Should the waters beckon, there are several places where you can rent a kayak or small boat to explore the chain of lakes that includes the **Tiefwarensee** and the **Kölpinsee**.

The Drive » Leave Waren on Kargower Weg and plunge right into the heart of the Müritz National Park. Drive for 32km following the signs for Neustrelitz via Kratzeburg. Then turn south for 10km on the B193.

⑥ Neustrelitz

Situated on the Zierker See within the national park, the pretty, planned baroque town of Neustrelitz centres on its circular **Markt**, from which streets radiate like the spokes of a wheel.

The town's Schloss fell victim to WWII damage, but its beautiful **Schlossgarten** retains its 18th-century orangery (with a restaurant open Tuesday to Sunday May to September), and hosts the **Schlossgartenfestspiele** (www.schlossgartenfestspiele. de), a series of classical and other concerts in summer.

MÜRITZ NATIONAL PARK

Müritz is commonly known as the land of a thousand lakes. While that's an exaggeration, there are well over 100 lakes here, as well as countless ponds, streams and rivers in this beautiful area midway between Berlin and Rostock.

The serene **Müritz National Park** (☎039824-2520; www.mueritz-nationalpark.de) consists of bog and wetlands, and is home to a wide range of waterfowl, including ospreys, white-tailed eagles and cranes. Its two main sections sprawl over 300 sq km to the east and (mainly) west of Neustrelitz, where the park's waterway begins on the Zierker See. Boardwalks and other features let you get close to nature.

The country roads between Waren and Neustrelitz cut through the heart of the park and offer plenty of places to stop and admire the Unesco-recognised **beech forests**.

The **national park office** (☎03981-253 106; ⊙9.30am-6pm Mon-Sat May-Sep, 9.30am-4pm Mon-Fri early–mid-Apr & Oct) is a good stop as it has a lot of information on the lakes, forests and park in English. Fish plucked fresh from the lake is the highlight at simple restaurants along the shore, near the centre.

The Drive » For more than half your 31km drive on the B96 to Neubrandenburg, you'll be passing by a beautiful lake, the Tollensesee.

- - - - - - - - - - - -

❼ Neubrandenburg

Neubrandenburg bills itself as 'the city of four gates on the Tollensesee Lake', and you'll see why during this enjoyable stop. A largely intact medieval **wall**, with those gates, encircles the city, which was founded in 1248. Made of stone, the wall is 2.3km in circumference and averages 7.5m in height. To navigate it, consider the wall as the rim of a clock face, with the train station at 12 o'clock.

The **Friedländer Tor** (2 o'clock), begun in 1300 and completed in 1450, was the first gate. **Treptower Tor** (9 o'clock) is the largest and contains an archaeological collection. At the southern end of the city is the gaudy **Stargarder Tor** (6 o'clock). The simple brick **Neues Tor** (3 o'clock) fronts the east side of the **Altstadt**. Southwest of the train station is the city's former dungeon, the **Fangelturm** (11 o'clock). You'll recognise it by its pointy tower.

Wedged into the stone circumference are the 27 sweet half-timbered houses that remain of the original sentry posts. Most of the surviving homes are now craft shops, galleries and cafes.

✖ p61

The Drive » Fertile fields keep the view from your car green as you go 65km straight north on the L35 to Greifswald.

- - - - - - - - - - - -

❽ Greifswald

The old university town of Greifswald, south of Stralsund, was largely unscathed by WWII thanks to a courageous German colonel who surrendered to Soviet troops (a move usually punishable by execution).

This former Hanseatic city is small and easy to explore on foot. Start at the **Markt** and be sure to see its three famous churches: the 'Langer Nikolas' ('Long Nicholas'), 'Dicke Marie' ('Fat Mary') and 'Kleine Jakob' ('Small Jacob').

Trade the fresh water encountered on this drive for the salt variety with a visit to Greifswald's pretty harbour in the charming district of **Wieck**, reached by a Dutch-style wooden drawbridge; its medieval city walls have been turned into a wide, tree-shaded promenade. If forsaking the car, it's easily reached via a 5km foot/bike path. More paths follow the pretty and sinuous waterfront.

✖ ⍭ p61

Eating & Sleeping

Lüneburg ❶

✕ Annàs Café
Cafe €

(📞04131-884 3181; www.annas-cafe.de; Am Stintmarkt 12a; mains €3-9; ⏲8am-9pm;)
Frilly and cute, Anna's has fabulous baked goods, including some alluring cakes. Breakfasts are served with verve while lunch is a mix of fresh salads, sandwiches and specials. Bric-a-brac on the tables jostles for space with kids' books.

Schwerin ❸

✕ Buschérie
Modern European €€€

(📞0385-923 6066; www.buscherie.de; Buschstrasse 9; mains €16-25; ⏲11.30am-late) Although historic and half-timbered, Buschstrasse is very much the modern bistro. Enjoy seasonal foods of the region at an outdoor table with the Dom seeming to loom overhead. From mains to small plates, everything is well priced. Stop in for just a glass of wine from the long list and listen to live jazz some nights.

✕ Rösterei Fuchs
Cafe €

(📞0385-593 8444; www.roesterei-fuchs.de; Am Markt 4; mains €4-8; ⏲9am-8pm Mon-Fri, to 6pm Sat & Sun) The aroma of fresh coffee fills this chic cafe, which roasts its own coffee in-house and also sells beans as well as gourmet chocolates. Drop by for an espresso or other warming drink. Breakfasts are fresh and healthy while sandwiches and beautiful baked goods fill out the day. Outside tables peak at the Rathaus.

⌶ Hotel Niederländischer Hof
Hotel €€

(📞0385-591 100; www.niederlaendischer-hof.de; Karl-Marx-Strasse 12-13; s/d from €100/115; P🛜) Overlooking the Pfaffenteich, this regal 1901-established hotel has 33 elegant rooms with black marble bathrooms, a library warmed by an open fire, and a lauded restaurant. The decor is plushly period with whimsical touches.

⌶ Zur guten Quelle
Hotel €€

(📞0385-565 985; www.zur-guten-quelle.m-vp.de; Schusterstrasse 12; s/d from €60/90;
P🛜) One of Schwerin's prettiest half-timbered houses, bang in the heart of the Altstadt. Zur guten Quelle is known for its cosy traditional restaurant and beer garden, but it also has six simple but comfortable rooms. Many have ancient timbers running right through the rooms.

Güstrow ❹

✕ Cafe Küpper
Cafe €

(📞03843-682 485; Domstrasse 15; cakes from €3; ⏲9am-6pm) The perfect pause for your Güstrow visit. This cafe has been creating cakes in the shadow of the Dom since 1852.

Neubrandenburg ❼

✕ Wiekhaus 45
German €€

(📞0395-566 7762; www.wiekhaus45.de; 4th Ringstrasse 44; mains €9-20; ⏲11am-11.30pm) Easily the most appealing place to eat in Neubrandenburg is this renovated guardhouse set into the wall. Waiters zip up and down the narrow stairwell carrying huge portions of Mecklenburg specialities (start with the tasty onion soup served with fresh bread). There are outside tables in summer.

Greifswald ❽

✕ Fischer-Hütte
Seafood €€

(📞03834-839 654; www.fischer-huette.de; An der Mühle 12, Wieck; mains €10-22; ⏲11.30am-11pm;) An exquisitely presented meal at the 'fisher's house' might start with Wieck-style fish stew and move onto the house speciality – smoked herring. You know everything is fresh as you can see the boats pulling up to the dock right outside.

⌶ Hotel Galerie
Hotel €€

(📞03834-773 7830; www.hotelgalerie.de; Mühlenstrasse 10; s/d from €80/90; P🛎🛜) The 13 rooms in this sparkling modern property are filled with a changing collection of works by contemporary artists. Room design is a cut above the usual hotel standard.

Saxony *View of Saxon Switzerland National Park*

Highlights of Saxony

4

Saxony's romantic mountains and castles compete for your attention on this wonderful and varied drive, from the perfectly preserved city of Görlitz to the cultural giant that is Leipzig.

TRIP HIGHLIGHTS

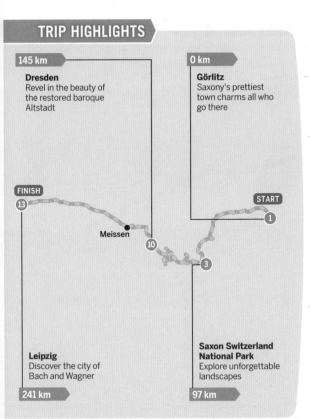

145 km

Dresden
Revel in the beauty of the restored baroque Altstadt

0 km

Görlitz
Saxony's prettiest town charms all who go there

FINISH
13

Meissen
10

START
1

3

Leipzig
Discover the city of Bach and Wagner

241 km

Saxon Switzerland National Park
Explore unforgettable landscapes

97 km

5–7 DAYS
241 KM / 150 MILES

- - -

GREAT FOR...

- - -

BEST TIME TO GO

April to October for warmer hiking weather.

- - -

ESSENTIAL PHOTO

The extraordinary view over the Elbe River from the Bastei lookouts.

- - -

BEST FOR HISTORY

The silhouette of the magnificently rebuilt Altstadt in Dresden.

Highlights of Saxony

On this unforgettable journey through the state of Saxony you'll see castles and fortresses, one of Germany's great rivers, impossibly shaped sandstone mountains, and several magical baroque cities and palaces along the way. These extraordinary landscapes then give way to magnificent Dresden, the erstwhile 'Florence of the North', and then to charming cool kid Leipzig, one-time home to Bach and Wagner but now touted as the 'New Berlin'.

TRIP HIGHLIGHT

1 Görlitz

This border town (half of which, on the other side of the Neisse River, became Polish territory after WWII), is an utter beauty and easily one of Saxony's most charming cities. Having miraculously survived the war intact, Görlitz has been used on numerous occasions as the backdrop to several Hollywood movies, and one look at its skyline of medieval towers and baroque churches

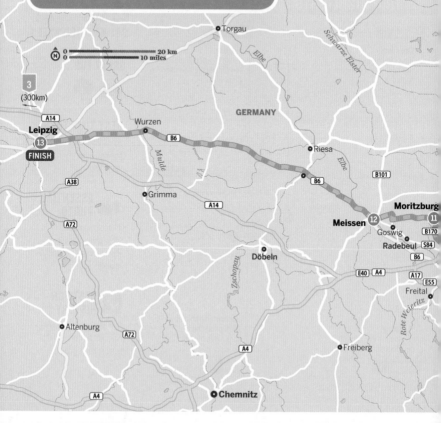

will tell you why. The **Re-ichenbacher Turm** (www.museum-goerlitz.de; Platz des 17 Juni; adult/concession €3/2; ⏰10am-5pm Tue-Sun May-Oct) and the interesting **Barockhaus** (☎03581-671 355; www.museum-goerlitz.de; Neissstrasse 30; adult/concession €5/3.50; ⏰10am-5pm Tue-Sat) are the two most obvious sights, but most visitors simply enjoy strolling around. In recent years Görlitz has grown enormously as a weekend destination and consequently has some excellent restaurants and accommodation options.

LINK YOUR TRIP

3 **Lakes & Treasures of Mecklenburg–Western Pomerania**

From Leipzig take the A14 and then the B71 northwest for 300km to Lüneburg.

6 **Berlin & the Jewels of Eastern Brandenburg**

From Dresden take the A13 north for the 103km drive to Lübbenau to discover this fascinating and multifaceted region.

✕ 🛏 p71

The Drive ≫ It's an easy 50km drive due west out of Görlitz along the A4/E40 directly to Bautzen.

WITOLD SKRYPCZAK / GETTY IMAGES ©

② Bautzen

Quirky Bautzen has an attractive cobblestone old town surrounding a fairy-tale castle and attracts visitors for three main, rather diverse reasons. It's home to the Sorbian people, an ethnic minority within Germany that has its own Slavic language and very distinct cultural identity that can be best explored at the **Sorbisches Museum** (☎03591-270 8700; www.sorbisches-museum.de; Ortenburg 3-5; adult/concession €3.50/2; ☉10am-6pm Tue-Sun). It's also where you'll find Germany's most famous brand of mustard (and on top of numerous mustard shops, there's also an all-mustard restaurant to try!). Finally, Bautzen has two prisons – one of them still works today, while the other, which is now closed but previously hosted political prisoners under the Nazi and communist governments, is the focus of a compelling **Gedenkstätte** (☎03591-404 74; www.gedenkstaette-bautzen.de; Weigangstrasse 8a; ☉10am-4pm Mon-Thu, 10am-8pm Fri, 10am-6pm Sat & Sun), or memorial museum.

The Drive »» Take the picturesque S154 through Neustadt towards the gorgeous scenery of the Saxon Switzerland National Park.

TRIP HIGHLIGHT

③ Saxon Switzerland National Park

Saxony may only have one national park, but Saxon Switzerland is a real stunner. There is an enormous number of hiking and climbing opportunities here, including some 700 peaks to climb and 400 sq km of hiking routes. The entire place is simply stunning, with ethereal sandstone formations that look quite unlike anything else in Europe. It's best to park outside the park itself and then take public transport into it, in particular the solar-powered **Kirnitzschtalbahn** (www.ovps.de; Kirnitzschtalstrasse 8; adult/concession €5/2.50, day pass €8/4; ☉9.30am-7.30pm Apr-Oct), which runs from Bad Schandau to Beutehnfall along the Kirnitzsch River.

The Drive »» From the national park, take the B1725 from Schmilka to Bad Schandau, a gorgeous 8km drive that runs along the banks of the Elbe with mountains visible on both sides.

④ Bad Schandau

The charming 'capital' of Saxon Switzerland, this friendly little town is a good place to bed down for the night after a day of walking in the national park. There's a wonderful early-20th-century lift, the **Personenaufzug**, which takes you to the town's highest point for some breathtaking views. Hikers should not miss the glorious hike to the **Schrammsteinaussicht**, a moderate-to-strenuous trail that leads to a fantastic viewpoint of the rocks, the Elbe Valley and national park beyond. The first 20 minutes up the steep Obrigensteig are tough but then the trail levels out and leads through fabulous rock formations. The final 'ascent' is straight up the rocks via a one-way network of steel stairs and ladders.

Bautzen The old town's cobblestone buildings

The Drive » Leaving Bad Schandau, cross the Elbe at the bridge outside of town and continue along the B1725 to Königstein. This charming small town is a good spot to stop for breakfast or lunch before continuing up to the famous Königstein Fortress high above the town. Park in the car park and walk five minutes to the fortress entrance.

---

❺ Festung Königstein

Festung Königstein
(☎035021-646 07; www. festung-koenigstein.de; adult/ concession Apr-Oct €10/7, Nov-Mar €8/6, audioguide €3; ☺9am-6pm Apr-Oct, to 5pm Nov-Mar; 🅿) is the largest intact fortress in Germany, and so imposing and formidable that no one in history has ever even bothered to attack it, let alone managed to conquer it. Begun in the 13th century, it was repeatedly enlarged and is now a veritable textbook in military architecture, with 30 buildings spread across 9.5 hectares. Inside, the main highlight is the brand new In Lapide Regis, a superb permanent exhibition that tells the dramatic story of the fortress in an engaging and interactive way.

The Drive » Drive back down into the valley along the S168 and in a couple of kilometres you'll come to Rathen. Park in the car park here and take the ferry across the Elbe.

---

❻ Bastei

The resort town of Rathen, in the northwestern corner of the national park, is the access point for the Bastei, the most famous rock formations in the Elbe Valley, and also the most popular spot in the park to visit. It's an easy and gentle hike up to the magnificent **Felsenburg Neurathen** (adult/concession €2/1; ☺9am-6pm), a partly reconstructed medieval castle in the Bastei, from

67

which there are numerous lookouts and viewpoints, including a stunning panorama over the Elbe hundreds of metres below. The much-photographed Basteibrücke, a sandstone bridge built in 1851, leads through the rocks, though this is the busiest part of the park. Try taking the 5km loop back to Rathen to escape the crowds.

The Drive » After returning to Rathen, where there are numerous spots for a meal, cross the Elbe again to get back to your car, and then take the S168 to Pirna. It's a short drive through some lovely countryside.

❼ Pirna

Pirna is a charming town on the Elbe, famous as Canaletto's home during his years in Saxony, and a friendly and easy-going place today. The big attraction in town is the excellent **DDR Museum** (☏03501-774 842; www. ddr-museum-pirna.de; Rottwerndorferstrasse 45; adult/child €7/6; ☺10am-6pm Tue-Sun Apr-Oct, 10am-5pm Tue-Thu, Sat & Sun Nov-Mar), in a former army barracks on the outskirts of the town. You can wander around a fully furnished East German apartment, sit in a classroom with GDR president Walter Ulbricht glowering at you, or find out how much a Junge Pioniere youth organisation uniform cost.

The Drive » It's just 10km along the B172a to Weesenstein, and a lovely drive that wends its way between valleys along the river.

❽ Weesenstein

With its gorgeous setting towering above the valley, **Schloss Weesenstein** (☏035027-6260; www. schloss-weesenstein.de; Am Schlossberg 1, Müglitztal; adult/concession €6/3, audioguide €2; ☺9am-6pm daily Apr-Oct, 10am-5pm Tue-Sun Feb, Mar, Nov & Dec, 10am-5pm Sat & Sun Jan) has an unforgettable setting and looks as fairy-tale perfect as can be. The castle itself is an amazing alchemy of styles, blending medieval roots with Renaissance and baroque embellishments. This resulted in an architectural curiosity where the banquet halls ended up beneath the roof, the horse stables on the 5th floor and the residential quarters in the cellar. There's lots to see inside, with an entire wing of the castle still filled with furniture and an exhibition on life here over the centuries. There's also a wonderful formal garden to explore.

The Drive » Take the B172a and then cross the Elbe at Pirna and follow the signs to Pillnitz. The drive should take around 15 minutes and the views while crossing the river are superb.

❾ Pillnitz

Right on the banks of the Elbe, **Schloss & Park Pillnitz** (☏0351-261 3260; www.schlosspillnitz.de; August-Böckstiegel-Strasse 2; park only adult/concession €2/1, park, museums & greenhouses €8/6; ☺park 9am-6pm, museums 10am-6pm Tue-Sun May-Oct) is a delightful baroque pleasure palace festooned with fanciful Chinese flourishes. This is where the Saxon rulers once lived it up during long, hot Dresden summers. Explore the wonderful formal gardens, then learn about the history of the palace and life at court in the Schlossmuseum inside the palace itself. Two other buildings, the Wasserpalais and the Bergpalais, house the Kunstgewerbemuseum, which is filled with various valuables from the Saxon court, including Augustus the Strong's throne.

The Drive » Take the Pillnitzer Landstrasse from the palace towards Dresden. It's a half-hour, 14km journey that in parts runs along the Elbe's edge. Cross the river at Loschwitz and follow signs for Dresden's Altstadt.

TRIP HIGHLIGHT

❿ Dresden

There are few city silhouettes more striking than Dresden's. The classic view from the Elbe's northern bank takes in spires, towers and domes belonging to palaces, churches and stately buildings, and indeed it's hard to believe that the city was all but wiped off the map by Allied bombings in 1945.

There's an enormous amount to see in the relatively small area that makes up Dresden's **Altstadt** (old town). First on the list should be the **Zwinger** (p118), the incredible pleasure palace of the Saxon electors, which now contains three superb museums. Next up, visit the **Residenzschloss** (p119), the seat of power of the Saxon electors and now the setting for several impressive museums, the most important of which is the **Historisches Grünes Gewölbe** (Historic Green Vault; ☑0351-4914 2000; www.skd.museum; Residenzschloss; admission incl audioguide €14; ☑10am-6pm Wed-Mon), which displays some 3000 precious items on shelves and tables without glass protection in a series of increasingly lavish rooms. Finally, be sure not to miss the famous **Frauenkirche** (p119), which graced the Dresden skyline for two centuries before collapsing after the February 1945 bombings. It was rebuilt from a pile of rubble between 1994 and 2005, and is now Dresden's most enduring symbol.

Also see p118 for a walking tour of Dresden.

DRESDEN & WWII

Between 13 and 15 February 1945, British and US planes unleashed 3900 tonnes of explosives on Dresden in four huge air raids. Bombs and incendiary shells whipped up a mammoth firestorm, and ashes rained down on villages 35km away. Historians still argue over whether or not this constituted a war crime committed by the Allies on an innocent civilian population. Some claim that with the Red Army at the gates of Berlin, the war was effectively won, and the Allies gained little military advantage from the destruction of Dresden. Others have said that as the last urban centre in the east of the country left intact, Dresden could have provided shelter for German troops returning from the east and was a viable target. What's undeniable, though, is that when the blazes had died down and the dust settled, tens of thousands of Dresdners had lost their lives and 20 sq km of this once elegant baroque city lay in smouldering ruins.

✗ 🏠 p71

The Drive » Take the B170 for 16km to reach Moritzburg. It's a picturesque drive through some charming countryside. Park in the car park in the centre of the village and you'll see the castle in the distance ahead of you.

- - - - - - - - - - - -

⑪ Moritzburg

Schloss Moritzburg (☑035207-8730; www.schloss-moritzburg.de; Schlossallee; adult/concession €7/3.50, audioguide €2; ☑10am-5.30pm daily Apr-Oct, 10am-4.30pm Sat-Sun Mar) is the third of the famous palaces surrounding Dresden, but in many ways it's the most impressive, set in the middle of an enormous lake that doubles as a moat, and standing magnificently overlooking a huge park.

It was the preferred hunting palace of the Saxon rulers, and its interiors are dominated by hundreds of framed antlers, which are quite a sight to behold in the sumptuous state rooms. Prized trophies include the antlers of an extinct giant stag and bizarrely misshapen ones in the Hall of Monstrosities. Considerably prettier is the legendary Federzimmer (Feather Room) downstairs, whose centrepiece is a bed made from over a million colourful duck, pheasant and peacock feathers. A walk through the gorgeous formal gardens and then through the wilder, forested park around the ornamental lake will return you to the car park.

The Drive >> It's an easy 16km drive to Meissen along Köhlerstrasse.

⑫ Meissen

Straddling the Elbe around 25km upstream from Dresden, Meissen is the cradle of European porcelain manufacturing and still hitches its tourism appeal to the world-famous china first cooked up in its imposing castle in 1710. But even those left unmoved by August the Strong's 'white gold' will find the impressive position of the town, dominated by its soaring Gothic cathedral, impressive fairy-tale-like castle and wonderful Elbe Valley views, quite compelling. Most visitors will want to head straight up the hillside to glorious **Albrechtsburg** (📞03521-470 70; www. albrechtsburg-meissen.de; Domplatz 1; adult/concession incl audioguide €8/4; ⊙10am-6pm Mar-Oct, 10am-5pm Nov-Feb), Meissen's enormous castle, and the home of European porcelain. After a stroll through the delightful old town, end the day with a visit to the superb **Erlebniswelt Haus Meissen** (📞03521-468 208; www.meissen.com; Talstrasse 9; adult/concession €9/5; ⊙9am-6pm May-Oct, 9am-

5pm Nov-Apr), *the* place to witness the astonishing artistry and craftsmanship that makes Meissen porcelain unique.

The Drive >> Head out of Meissen and take the B6, a pleasant alternative to the motorway, directly to Leipzig. The drive is 88km and takes 1½ hours.

⑬ Leipzig

The final destination on this trip is Leipzig, a fascinating combination of cultural powerhouse and contemporary creative hothouse. Head to the storied **Altstadt** to explore the city's dramatic past, from the choir once led by Bach, which still goes strong at the **Thomaskirche** (📞0341-222 240; www.thomaskirche.org; Thomaskirchhof 18; tower €2; ⊙church 9am-6pm, tower 1pm, 2pm & 4.30pm Sat, 2pm & 3pm Sun Apr-Nov), to the chilling **Stasi Museum** (📞0341-961 2443; www.runde-ecke-leipzig. de; Dittrichring 24; ⊙10am-6pm) and the first-class **Zeitgeschichtliches Forum** (Forum of Contemporary History; 📞0341-222 00; www. hdg.de/leipzig; Grimmaische Strasse 6; ⊙9am-6pm Tue-Fri, 10am-6pm Sat & Sun), which gives a detailed account of the creation and collapse of East Germany.

Another museum not to miss is the excellent **Museum der Bildenden Künste** (📞0341-216 990; www. mdbk.de; Katharinenstrasse 10; adult/concession €5/4; ⊙10am-6pm Tue & Thu-Sun, noon-8pm Wed) or Fine Arts Museum, a first-class art collection in an amazing building. Visit the famous **Oper Leipzig** (📞0341-126 1261; www.oper-leipzig.de; Augustusplatz 12) or see the **Thomanerchor** (📞0341-984 4211; www.thomaskirche. org; Thomaskirchhof 18; tickets €2) perform, before discovering Leipzig's relaxed nightlife and contemporary art and music scenes in the studenty-creative neighbourhoods of the Südvorstadt and Plagwitz. Stroll down Karli, the main street of the Südvorstadt, or Karl-Heine-Strasse, Plagwitz's main thoroughfare, both of which are packed with bars, restaurants, cafes and clubs. Finally, don't miss the amazing **Völkerschlachtdenkmal** (📞0341-241 6870; www. stadtgeschichtliches-museum-leipzig.de; Strasse des 18 Oktober 100; adult/child €8/6; ⊙10am-6pm Apr-Oct, to 4pm Nov-Mar; 🚋2 or 15 to Völkerschlachtdenkmal), the mother of all war monuments.

✕ 🛏 p71

Eating & Sleeping

Görlitz ❶

✖ Vino e Cultura Italian €€

(✆03581-879 6850; www.vinoecultura.de;
Untermarkt 2; mains €10-20; ☺3-11pm Tue-Fri,
noon-11pm Sat & Sun) The vaulted space right on
historic Untermarkt has been glitzily converted
and is now easily Görlitz's most foodie
destination. The menu, courtesy of the clearly
ambitious French chef, is adventurous (try
monkfish with paprika chutney or duck breast
with caramelised apricots), the staff is charming
and the entire place is a great leap forward for
the local eating scene.

▐ Hotel Börse Hotel €€

(✆03581-764 20; www.boerse-goerlitz.de;
Untermarkt 16; s/d from €75/113; P @ 🛜)
Four-poster beds, sparkling glass chandeliers,
marble bathrooms, patterned parquet floors
and elegant antiques are the hallmarks of
this stylish hotel in an 18th-century palais.
With its absolutely perfect location, old-world
atmosphere and surprisingly affordable rates,
this is our best bet for a comfortable and
memorable stay in Görlitz.

Dresden ❿

✖ brennNessel Vegetarian €€

(✆0351-494 3319; www.brennnessel-dresden.
de; Schützengasse 18; mains €9-15; ☺11am-
midnight) This fearfully popular, largely
vegetarian gastropub in a miraculously
surviving 350-year-old building is an oasis in
the otherwise empty and anodyne streets of
the Altstadt. Indeed, reserve for lunch if you'd
like to eat outside in the charming, sun-dappled
courtyard as it's something of a favourite hang-
out for off-duty Semperoper musicians and
nearby office workers.

✖ Raskolnikoff International €€

(✆0351-804 5706; www.raskolnikoff.de;
Böhmische Strasse 34; mains €10-15; ☺11am-
2am Mon-Fri, 9am-2am Sat & Sun) An artist

squat before the Wall came down, Raskolnikoff
now brims with grown-up artsy-bohemian
flair, especially in the sweet little garden at
the back, complete with bizarre water feature.
The seasonally calibrated menu showcases
the fruits of regional terroir in globally inspired
dishes, and the beer is brewed locally. Breakfast
is served until 2pm, with an excellent brunch
(€14.90) on Sundays.

▐ Gewandhaus
Hotel Boutique Hotel €€

(✆0351-4949 3636; www.gewandhaus-hotel.
de; Ringstrasse 1; d from €133; P ✳ @ 🛜 ☒)
Fresh from a total renovation and rebirth as a
boutique hotel, the stunning Gewandhaus, an
18th-century trading house of tailors and fabric
merchants that burned down in 1945, now has
sleek public areas, beautiful and bright rooms,
and a breakfast that sets a high bar for anything
else offered in the city.

Leipzig ⓭

✖ Auerbachs Keller German €€€

(✆0341-216 100; www.auerbachs-keller-leipzig.
de; Mädlerpassage, Grimmaische Strasse
2-4; mains Keller €10-27, Weinstuben €33-35;
☺Keller noon-11pm daily, Weinstuben 6-11pm
Mon-Sat) Founded in 1525, Auerbachs Keller is
one of Germany's best-known restaurants. It's
cosy and touristy but the food's actually quite
good and the setting memorable. There are two
sections: the vaulted Grosser Keller for hearty
Saxonian dishes and the four historic rooms of
the Historische Weinstuben for upscale German
fare. Reservations highly advised.

▐ Quartier M Apartment €€

(✆0341-2133 8800; www.apartment-leipzig.
de; Markgrafenstrasse 10; apt €75-110; P) The
building oozes old-world flair but the roomy
apartments with full kitchens are state-of-the
art and pack plenty of modern design cachet.
Some units come with balcony or terrasse.
Rates drop significantly for stays over seven
days; located above an organic supermarket.

Dornburger Schlösser *Rococo Palace*

Central Germany's Castles & Palaces

5

From the medieval to the romantic, this trip twists through bucolic fields, rustic villages and alongside sparkling rivers, uncovering mystical ruins, robust fortresses and exquisite palaces.

TRIP HIGHLIGHTS

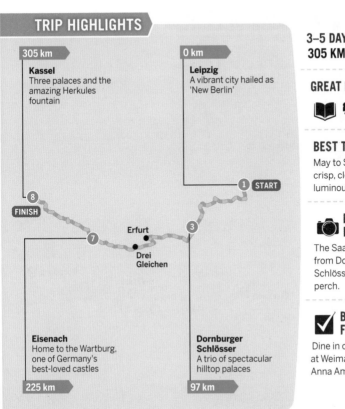

305 km

Kassel
Three palaces and the amazing Herkules fountain

0 km

Leipzig
A vibrant city hailed as 'New Berlin'

1 START

8

FINISH

Erfurt

3

7

Drei Gleichen

Eisenach
Home to the Wartburg, one of Germany's best-loved castles

225 km

Dornburger Schlösser
A trio of spectacular hilltop palaces

97 km

3–5 DAYS
305 KM / 190 MILES

GREAT FOR...

BEST TIME TO GO

May to September has crisp, clear skies and luminous canola fields.

ESSENTIAL PHOTO

The Saale River valley from Dornburger Schlösser's clifftop perch.

BEST FOR FOODIES

Dine in classic style at Weimar's romantic Anna Amalia.

Central Germany's Castles & Palaces

5

Journey into the historical and geographical heartland of Germany, where cultural titans Goethe and Schiller once deliberated. You'll pass through ancient forests and villages, alongside sparkling rivers and working farms to visit spectacular castles and palaces in medieval, Renaissance, baroque and rococo styles. The magnificent Wartburg castle, inspiration for Ludwig II's famous Neuschwanstein, is one of Germany's finest.

TRIP HIGHLIGHT

1 Leipzig

Leipzig could well be Germany's 'it' city, a playground for nomadic young creatives displaced by the fast-gentrifying German capital, but it's also a city of enormous history, set solidly in the sights of music lovers due to an intrinsic connection to the lives and works of Bach, Mendelssohn and Wagner. There's much to see and do here. At the very least, you'll want to check out the enormous art collection of **Museum der Bildenden Künste** (☎0341-216 990; www.mdbk.de; Katharinenstrasse 10; adult/concession €5/4; ⏱10am-6pm Tue & Thu-Sun, noon-8pm Wed) in its modernist glass cube home (for a little architectural contrast), and get an overview of this rapidly changing city in the **Stadtgeschichtliches Museum** (City History Museum; ☎0341-965 130; www.stadtgeschichtliches-museum-leipzig.de; Markt 1; adult/concession €6/4; ⏱10am-6pm Tue-Sun), housed in Leipzig's beautiful Renaissance town hall.

The Drive » Take the B2 south out of Leipzig until you reach the A38 at exit 31 for some 33km of autobahn action, west to exit 26. Head south on the B91 until the junction with the B176 outside Burgwerben. Follow the B176 west for 17km until you reach a roundabout: head straight through then turn left on Merseburger Strasse into Freyburg.

❷ Freyburg

With its cobblestone streets and medieval castle clinging to vine-covered slopes, Freyburg puts the 'r' in rustic. Sparkling wine production has been the town's focus since the mid-19th century. Pop into **Rotkäppchen Sektkellerei** (www.rotkaeppchen.de; Sektkellereistrasse 5; 45min tours €5; ⏱tours 11am & 2pm daily, 12.30pm & 3.30pm Sat &

LINK YOUR TRIP

2 | **Design for Life: Bauhaus to VW**

Have some Bauhaus with your baroque on this exploration of modern German design and architecture, beginning in Weimar.

10 | **German Fairy Tale Road**

Delve into the world of the Brothers Grimm in Kassel, heading north or south along Germany's beloved Fairy Tale Road.

Sun) to toast the start of your trip with a glass of Germany's best-known homegrown bubbles, then head to the imposing medieval **Schloss Neuenburg** (www.schloss-neuenburg.de; Schloss 25; adult/concession €6/3.50, with tour €8/6.50, tower €1.50/1; ⏱10am-6pm daily, tower Tue-Sun), on the hill above town. There's an excellent museum, a rare Romanesque two-storey chapel and a free-standing tower, the Dicker Wilhelm, with splendid views over the Saale River valley. It's possible to spend the night in one of two charming apartments within the castle walls: book ahead if this tickles your fancy.

The Drive » Take the B180 south for 11km to the pretty town of Naumburg. Pick up the B88 for 15km until it meets the Saale River at Camburg. Cross the bridge and follow the scenic L1059 for 9km until you reach a tiny hamlet belonging to Saaleplatte village, where you'll drop south along Wilsdorfer Strasser for 5km to Dornburg.

TRIP HIGHLIGHT

❸ Dornburger Schlösser

There are few places in the world where you can get a snapshot of three distinct historical periods, side by side. The **Dornburger Schlösser** (☎036497-222 91; www.dornburg-schloesser.de; Max-Krehan-Strasse 2, Dornburg; combination ticket (Renaissance & Rococo) €4; ⏱10am-5pm

Köthen

Mulde

Wolfen

Halle

Saale

A14

Leipzig   Wurzen

❶ START

A38   Grimma

Flügraben

A72

Zeitz   Altenburg

Gera   A4

Glauchau

Zwickau

Greiz

Plauen

Thu-Tue Apr-Oct) is one – a hillside trilogy of magnificently restored palaces in medieval, Renaissance and rococo styles, with stunning views and immaculate gardens. The **Altes Schloss**, the oldest, blends Romanesque, late-Gothic and baroque elements but can only be viewed from the outside. You can enter both the 1539 **Renaissance Palace** (where Goethe once stayed) and the gorgeous **Rococo Palace**. It's free to stroll around the magnificent gardens, to enjoy the wonderful views and admire the palaces from the outside.

The Drive » Head south on the B88 for 12km through the picturesque Saale valley. The road hugs the river, even meeting for a brief kiss here and there, until it reaches the outskirts of Jena, where you'll pick up the B7 heading west. Follow it for 21km until you reach Weimar.

- - - - - - - - - -

④ Weimar

A pantheon of intellectual and creative giants lived and worked in Weimar: historical epicentre of the German Enlightenment. Goethe, Schiller, Bach, Nietzsche and Kandinsky are all memorialised throughout town. History buffs may want to linger here a few days. Weimar's **Stadtschloss**

DETOUR:
GEDENKSTÄTTE BUCHENWALD

Start: ④ Weimar

A visit to the sombre **Gedenkstätte Buchenwald** (📞03643-4300; www.buchenwald.de; Gedenkstätte Buchenwald; ◷9am-6pm Apr-Oct, to 4pm Nov-Mar) memorial, in the former concentration camp 10km northwest of Weimar, might be the most memorable of your trip. Drive north out of town along Ettersburger Strasse to Blutstrasse and head west. You'll first pass the striking memorial to your left: be sure to approach the massive hillside monument to fully appreciate it. Publications from the museum store explain the symbolic significance of its many elements. Follow the road for 1km into the camp towards the visitor centre, then wander around the numerous intact structures to deepen your understanding of the horrors that played out here. Between 1937 and 1945, hidden from Weimarers and surrounding villagers, some 56,500, of the 250,000 men, women and children who were incarcerated here, lost their lives.

(Schlossmuseum; 📞03643-545 400; www.klassik-stiftung.de; Burgplatz 4; adult/concession €7.50/6; ◷10am-6pm Tue-Sun), situated in the former residential palace, houses works of art dating from the Middle Ages to the turn of the 20th century. About 4km south of town, baroque **Schloss Belvedere** (📞03643-545 400; www.klassik-stiftung.de; Belvedere Park; adult/concession €6/4.50; ◷10am-6pm Apr-Dec) is set among manicured grounds and has a museum of artefacts from the 17th and 18th centuries. Complete your visit with a comprehensive overview of Weimar's

Weimar Horse-drawn carriage in front of the Goethe-Nationalmuseum

beloved genius at the **Goethe-Nationalmuseum** (☎03643-545 400; www. klassik-stiftung.de; Frauenplan 1; adult/concession €12/8.50; ◷9.30am-6pm Tue-Sun Apr-Oct, to 4pm Nov-Mar).

 p79

The Drive » Take the B7 west through fields of canola and wind turbines for 22km, directly into Erfurt.

- - - - - - - - - - - - - -

❺ Erfurt

Thuringia's capital is a scene-stealing mix of sweeping squares, cobblestone alleyways, perky church towers, idyllic river scenery and

pan-generational architecture. It's a great place to stop for a meal or two and makes a good base if you decide to explore the area over a few days. Perched on the only hill above town, Erfurt's **Zitadelle Petersberg** (☎0361-664 00; tour adult/ concession €8/4; ◷7pm Fri & Sat May-Oct) ranks among Europe's largest and best-preserved baroque fortresses. It sits above a honeycomb of tunnels, which can be explored on guided tours. It's free to roam the external grounds and enjoy the fabulous views.

p79

The Drive » Head south on the L1052 for 9km. Pick up the A4 autobahn at exit 47a Erfurt-Ost, heading west in the direction of Frankfurt. Stay on the A4 until you reach exit 43 Wandersleben, then head south into the pretty village of Mühlburg. You'll be able to see Burg Gleichen to your north.

- - - - - - - - - - - - - -

❻ Drei Gleichen

Allow a few hours to enjoy this fascinating, medieval stop comprising three similar hilltop castles, collectively known as Drei Gleichen, each within eyesight of the other. North of the autobahn, **Burg Gleichen** (📞036202-824 40; Wandersleben; adult/concession €1.50/1; ⊙10am-5pm Apr-Oct) makes a rewarding visit for castle fans, but it's a 30-minute uphill climb from the car park to the ruins. Of the three castles, **Mühlburg** (📞0160-225 0918; www.drei-gleichen. de; adult/concession €2/1.50; ⊙10am-5pm Mar-Oct) is the oldest and closest, dating to around 704. Its moat walls, drawbridge and 22m-high castle tower are intact. **Veste Wachsenburg** (📞03628-742 40; www.wachsenburg.com; Amt Wachsenburg; adult/concession €2/1; ⊙11am-4pm Tue-Sun), 10km south of the A4, is fully preserved, housing a hotel, restaurant and museum; it's possible to drive right up to the castle gate.

The Drive » Take the A4 autobahn west towards Frankfurt for 36km, to exit 40a Eisenach Ost. From here, follow the signs for Eisenach/Wartburg for another 10km.

- - - - - - - - - - - - - -

TRIP HIGHLIGHT

⑦ Eisenach

Hilly Eisenach, on the edge of the Thuringian forest, is best known for its Unesco World Heritage castle **Wartburg** (📞03691-2500; www.wartburg-eisenach. de; Auf der Wartburg 1; tour adult/concession €9/5, museum & Luther study only €5/3; ⊙tours 8.30am-5pm Apr-Oct, 9am-3.30pm Nov-Mar, English tour 1.30pm), where Martin Luther hid while his controversial theses brought

about the Reformation. This huge, medieval fortress is magnificently preserved, offering much by way of its permanent and visiting exhibitions, intact structure and breathtaking views over little Eisenach, the forest and beyond. Allow at least two hours: one for the guided tour, the rest for the museum and the views. If you love classical music, you'll also want to take a look at **Bachhaus** (📞03691-793 40; www. bachhaus.de; Frauenplan 21; adult/concession €8.50/4.50; ⊙10am-6pm) and the **Reuter-Wagner Museum** (📞03691-743 294; Reuterweg 2; adult/concession €4/2; ⊙11am-5pm Tue-Sun), while revheads won't want to miss **Automobile Welt Eisenach** (📞03691-772 12; www.ame.eisenachonline.de; Friedrich-Naumann-Strasse 10; adult/concession €5/3.50; ⊙11am-5pm Tue-Sun).

✗ 🍴 p79

The Drive » Head north on Mühlhäuser Strasse for 2km, then pick up the B19 heading west. Follow the B19 north for 5km until the start of the B7. Follow the B7 northwest as it winds through forests, farmlands and pretty villages for 75km towards Kassel.

- - - - - - - - - - - - - -

TRIP HIGHLIGHT

⑧ Kassel

Although WWII bombing and postwar reconstruction left Kassel looking undeniably utilitarian, you'd hardly know it today. This culture-rich

city on the Fulda River boasts some impressive attractions. The palatial **Schloss Wilhelmshöhe** (📞0561-316 800; www. museum-kassel.de; Schlosspark 1; adult/concession €6/4, Weissenstein wing incl tour €4/3; ⊙10am-5pm Tue & Thu-Sun, to 8pm Wed) contains a premier baroque art collection – time your visit to coincide with the Wednesday and Sunday operation of the spectacular **Herkules** (www.museum-kassel.de; Schlosspark Wilhelmshöhe 26 (Herkules-Terrassen); adult/ concession €3/2; ⊙10am-5pm mid-Mar–mid-Nov) fountain. Both are within **Bergpark Wilhelmshöhe** (www. museum-kassel.de; ⊙9am-sunset), as is the smaller, equally adored **Löwenburg** (📞0561-316 800; www. museum-kassel.de; Bergpark Wilhelmshöhe; adult/student €4/2; ⊙tours hourly 10am-4pm Tue-Sun Mar-Oct, to 3pm Nov-Feb) or 'Lion Castle'. Round out your visit with some fun and fantasy in Kassel's newest attraction, **Grimmwelt** (📞0561-598 610; www.grimmwelt. de; Weinbergstrasse; adult/concession €8/6; ⊙10am-6pm Tue-Sun), paying homage to the Brothers Grimm. Or make a 10km sidetrip to **Schloss Wilhelmsthal** (📞05674-6898; www.museum-kassel.de; Calden; adult/concession €4/3; ⊙10am-4pm Tue-Sun), in Calden; almost due north of Wilhelmshöhe, it's one of Germany's finest rococo palaces.

Eating & Sleeping

Weimar ④

🍴 Anna Amalia   International €€€

(📞03643-8020; www.restaurant-anna-amalia.
com; Markt 19; 3-/5-/7-course menu from
€65/85/110; ⏰6.30-10pm Tue-Sat Mar-Dec)
Inside the Hotel Elephant Weimar, this highly
acclaimed gourmet act is one for those who
appreciate a true fine-dining experience.
Dress to impress, expect the chef to wow your
palate, wait for the staff to make you feel more
important than you know you are, and leave
plenty of room on the credit card.

🛏 Die Kleine Residenz   Pension €

(📞03643-743 270; www.residenz-pension.de;
Grüner Markt 4; d from €70; @) With an enviable
location in the heart of Weimar's Altstadt, this
little inn offers comfortable, light-filled rooms
with high-speed internet and ensuite bathrooms
in a variety of configurations, and a lovely little
terrace restaurant downstairs.

Erfurt ⑤

🍴 Zum Wenigemarkt 13   German €€

(📞0361-642 2379; www.wenigemarkt-13.de;
Wenigemarkt 13; mains €10-18; ⏰11.30am-
11pm) This upbeat restaurant in a delightful
spot serves traditional and updated takes on
Thuringian cuisine, starring regionally hunted
and gathered ingredients where possible.
Tender salt-encrusted pork roast and trout
drizzled with tangy caper-and-white-wine sauce
are both menu stars.

🛏 Hotel Brühlerhöhe   Boutique Hotel €€

(📞0361-241 4990; www.hotel-bruehlerhoehe-
erfurt.de; Rudolfstrasse 48; s/d from €80/95;
P 🛜) This Prussian officers' casino turned

chic city hotel gets high marks for its opulent
breakfast spread (€12.50) and smiling, quick-
on-their-feet staff. Rooms are cosy and modern
with chocolate-brown furniture, thick carpets
and sparkling baths. It's a short tram ride into
the town centre.

Eisenach ⑦

🍴 Trattoria La Grappa   Italian €€

(📞03691-733 860; www.lagrappa-eisenach.
de; Frauenberg 8-10; mains €7-21; ⏰11.30am-
2.30pm & 5.30-11.30pm Tue-Sun) The sunny
terracotta terrace of this local favourite takes
you straight back to the homeland. Pizza,
pasta, fish, soup, salad and meat dishes are well
priced, tasty and generously portioned. *Buon
appetito!* Cash only.

🛏 Pentahotel Eisenach   Hotel €

(📞03691-815 7900; www.pentahotels.com;
Weinbergstrasse 5; d from €63; P ❄ 🛜) Good
for self-drivers, this quirky chain hotel on
the outskirts of town has lovely forest views,
comfortable, modern rooms, free wi-fi and the
kind of bar-restaurant where you can quietly
chill and enjoy a meal or engage your fellow
travellers. A good breakfast buffet and excellent
rates seal the deal.

🛏 Romantik Hotel auf
der Wartburg   Hotel €€€

(📞03691-7970; www.wartburghotel.de; Auf der
Wartburg 2; s/d incl breakfast from €145/240;
P 🛜) Built in 1914, this hotel has subdued
colours and furnishings to match the location
on the historic Wartburg. The gorgeous, cosy
singles with alcove beds are called 'Luther'
rooms, but, for space and luxury, book in the
'Romantik' category. While you're not staying in
the castle, you can't get any closer: the location
is ah-mazing.

Berlin Mauerspringer (wall jumper) memorial sculpture in honour of the Berlin Wall

Berlin & the Jewels of Eastern Brandenburg

6

This tour wraps a lot that's great about Germany into one neat package. A vibrant metropolis, a romantic forest, spirit-lifting gardens and monasteries, and awe-inspiring technology.

TRIP HIGHLIGHTS

366 km

Gedenkstätte & Museum Sachsenhausen
Sobering concentration camp

285 km

Schiffshebewerk Niederfinow
Marvel of technology

FINISH

Kloster Chorin 7

9

START

Gedenkstätte Seelower Höhen

0 km

1

Berlin
Capital of culture and cool

Frankfurt (Oder)

Stift Neuzelle

89 km

2

Lübbenau & the Spreewald
Enchanting watery forest

Schloss Branitz, Cottbus

4 DAYS
366 KM / 228 MILES

GREAT FOR...

BEST TIME TO GO
Any time is possible, but April to October has better weather.

ESSENTIAL PHOTO
Capture a traditional Sorb village in Lehde in the Spreewald.

BEST FOR HISTORY
The heart-wrenching memorial exhibit at Sachsenhausen concentration camp.

Berlin & the Jewels of Eastern Brandenburg

6

This trip gets your head spinning in scintillating Berlin, then slows you back down on a leisurely tour around eastern Brandenburg. You'll meet the Sorbs, a traditional Slavic people at home in the Spreewald, a rivulet-laced fairy-tale forest. You'll visit gardens created by an eccentric prince, soul-stirring monasteries, a technological marvel and socialist model cities. WWII comes hauntingly alive in a concentration camp and on the largest battlefield on German soil.

TRIP HIGHLIGHT

❶ Berlin

Your adventure starts off in the German capital, an intoxicating cocktail of culture, history, off-beat experiences and nightlife. Check off the sightseeing blockbusters on our Stretch Your Legs tour (p116), then devote time to exploring the city's grand museum landscape. A good bet are the five treasure chests on Museum Island that showcase 6000 years worth of art and cultural history, including the ethereal 3300-year-old bust of Egyptian queen Nefertiti at the **Neues Museum** (New Museum; ☎030-266 424 242; www.smb.museum; Bodestrasse 1-3; adult/concession €12/6; ⊙10am-6pm, to 8pm Thu; ◻100, 200, ◻Hackescher Markt), and the radiantly blue Babylonian Ishtar Gate at the **Pergamonmuseum** (☎030-266 424 242; www.smb.museum; Bodestrasse 1-3; adult/concession €12/6; ⊙10am-6pm, to 8pm Thu; ◻100, ◻Hackescher Markt, Friedrichstrasse). To come to grips with Berlin's division during the Cold War, there's no better place than the **Gedenkstätte Berliner Mauer** (Berlin Wall Memorial; ☎030-467

LINK YOUR TRIP

3 **Lakes & Treasures of Mecklenburg–Western Pomerania**

From Berlin head north on the B96 for 120km to pick up this route in Neustrelitz, through the heart of one of Germany's oldest provinces.

4 **Highlights of Saxony**

From Lübbenau head 100km south on the A13 to jewel-like Dresden and on to whimsical sandstone formations.

986 666; www.berliner-mauer-gedenkstaette.de; Bernauer Strasse btwn Schwedter Strasse & Gartenstrasse; ⊙visitor centre 9.30am-7pm Apr-Oct, to 6pm Nov-Mar, open-air exhibit 8am-10pm, documentation centre 10am-6pm Tue-Sun; ◻Nordbahnhof, Bernauer Strasse, Eberswalder Strasse), an indoor-outdoor exhibit along a 1.4km stretch of the former barrier. To see the longest remaining Wall vestige, head to the mural-festooned **East Side Gallery** (www.eastsidegallery-berlin.de; Mühlenstrasse btwn Oberbaumbrücke & Ostbahnhof; ⊙24hr; ⑤Warschauer Strasse, ◻Ostbahnhof, Warschauer Strasse).

✖ ⊨ p87

The Drive » From Berlin, it's a quick one-hour drive to Lübbenau via the A100, the A113 and the A13, where you leave the autobahn at exit 9.

TRIP HIGHLIGHT

❷ Lübbenau & the Spreewald

Lübbenau is the main town in the Spreewald, a unique ice-age-formed landscape of jungle-like forest and marshland criss-crossed by some 300 channels fed by the River Spree – a German Everglades, if you will, minus the alligators. About 100km southeast of Berlin, this is the traditional homeland of the Sorbs, a Slavic tribe whose members still maintain their age-old customs,

costumes and language (all signs are bilingual).

Until the first road was built in 1936, Spreewald villages were accessible only by flat-bottomed punt boats. Today, exploring this Unesco biosphere reserve in a so-called *Kahn* piloted by a ferryman in traditional garb is a Spreewald must-do. Trips last from one hour to all day and depart from various spots, including the **Grosser Hafen** (☎03542-2225; www.grosser-kahnhafen.de; Dammstrasse 77a; boat tours €10-25; ⊙from 10am). A particularly nice one goes out to the Sorb village of Lehde whose **Freilandmuseum** (Open-Air Museum Lehde; ☎03542-2472; www.museum-osl.de; Lehde; adult/concession €5/3.50; ⊙10am-6pm Apr-Sep, to 5pm Oct) gives you a good sense of what rural life in the Spreewald was like a century ago. DIY types can also rent their own canoe or kayak, including from **Bootsverleih Richter** (☎03542-3764; www.bootsverleih-richter.de; Dammstrasse 76a; single kayak per person 2hr/day €7/15-18; ⊙9am-6pm late-Mar–mid-Oct).

✖ p87

The Drive » The A15 takes you from Lübbenau to Cottbus in 30 minutes, but for the scenic drive through Sorb heartland, head south on the L49, turn left on Radduscher Bahnhofstrasse (L51) and follow it via Burg for about 28km to Cottbus.

❸ Schloss Branitz, Cottbus

Cottbus has a handsomely restored historic centre but its star attraction is **Park and Schloss Branitz** (☎0355-751 50; www.pueckler-museum.de; Robinienweg 5; park free, Schloss adult/concession €5.50/4; ⏰10am-6pm daily Apr-Oct, 11am-4pm Tue-Sun Nov-Mar) on the southeastern edge of town. The sprawling park-and-palace ensemble was dreamed up by Prince Hermann von Pückler-Muskau, a kooky 19th-century aristocrat, writer, ladies' man and renowned garden architect. For over 20 years, he feverishly turned his ancestral family estate into an Arcadian English-style landscape park by shaping hills, digging canals and lakes and building earthen pyramids, one of which serves as his tomb. Exhibits in the Schloss (by Gottfried Semper, of Dresden opera house fame) and outer buildings tell the story of the man and his ultimate pet project.

The Drive » The 60km ride to Neuzelle (with a feel-good eating option; p87) takes you northeast on the B168 past the Peitzer Teiche, a huge network of carp-farming ponds, and through the southern reaches of the romantic Schlaube Valley Nature Park, a hikers' and cyclists' paradise. At Schenkendobern turn north onto the B112.

❹ Stift Neuzelle

Gearing up for its 750th anniversary in 2018, the Cistercian **Stift Neuzelle** (Neuzelle Abbey; ☎033652-8140; www.stift-neuzelle.de; Stiftsplatz 7; adult/concession €5/4; ⏰10am-6pm Apr-Oct, to 4pm Nov-Mar) wears the moniker 'Brandenburg's baroque miracle' with pride. Gothic at its core, it got a baroque makeover in the 18th century that included the addition of exuberant gardens with water features, terraced hillsides and an orangery. A new museum presents scenes from the **Passion of Christ** composed of 250-year-old vividly painted, life-sized cut-out figures dramatically arranged in a 'heavenly theatre'. Also make your pilgrimage to the Neuzeller Kloster **brewery** to try their bock, porter, pilsner or 'anti-ageing' beer.

 p87

The Drive » Follow the B112 north for 36km to Frankfurt (Oder), perhaps stopping briefly in Eisenhüttenstadt, a once-thriving East German 'socialist model city'.

❺ Frankfurt (Oder)

Germany's 'other' Frankfurt sits on the Oder River right on the border with Poland. WWII bombs and socialist reconstruction wiped out most vestiges of its one-time grandeur as a medieval trading centre and university town. Still, the scenic river setting

and unique sightseeing gems invite a quick stopover. The Gothic **Marienkirche** (☎0335-224 42; www.st-marien-ffo.de; Oberkirchplatz; ⏰10am-6pm May-Sep, to 4pm Oct-Apr), or Church of St Mary, for instance, boasts stunning medieval stained-glass windows that were squirrelled away by the Soviets as WWII booty and only returned in 2007. For the world's most comprehensive collection of East German art, drop by the **Museum Junge Kunst** (☎0335-552 4150; www.museum-junge-kunst.de; Marktplatz 1 & Carl-Philipp-Emanuel-Bach-Strasse 11; adult/concession €6/4.20;

Cottbus Schloss Branitz

🕐11am-5pm Tue-Sun). And if it's cheap(er) vodka and cigarettes you're after, just walk across the Oder to Słubice, Frankfurt's Polish twin town.

🛏 p87

The Drive » Follow the B112 north for 10km to Lebus, then continue west for 18km on the B167 past hillsides and grassland carpeted in wildflowers from spring to autumn.

- - - - - - - - - - -

⑥ Gedenkstätte Seelower Höhen

This **Seelow Heights Memorial Exhibit** (Seelow Heights Memorial; 📞03346-597; www.gedenkstaette-seelower-hoehen.de; Küstriner Strasse 28a, Seelow; 🕐10am-5pm Tue-Sun Apr-Oct, to 4pm Nov-Mar) documents one of the last major battles of WWII, which took place on this 48m-high plateau above the Oder River valley in April 1945. Some 100,000 German troops fought tooth and nail – but in vain – to stave off a million Soviet soldiers. After three days of fighting, an estimated 50,000 on both sides had fallen. Imagine the horrors of this brutal battle as you climb up to the military cemetery with its striking **memorial**, then pick your way past military vehicles and artillery pieces to the **museum** for the full low-down.

The Drive » Follow the B167 northwest for 55km via Neuhardenberg, with its palace-turned-hotel (p87), and past the Kietzer See birders' paradise. In Niederfinow, turn right on Hebewerkstrasse to arrive at the ships' lift.

- - - - - - - - - - -

TRIP HIGHLIGHT

⑦ Schiffshebewerk Niederfinow

The tiny town of Niederfinow is famous for its spectacular ship lift, the **Schiffshebewerk Niederfinow** (📞033362-215; www.schiffshebewerk-niederfinow.

LOCAL KNOWLEDGE: GHERKIN COUNTRY

The Spreewald is world-renowned for its pickled cucumbers, cherished by connoisseurs for their low acidity, crunchy texture and delicate spicing. The official name 'Spreewälder Gurke' is even an EU-certified Protected Designation of Origin, just like Champagne and Cognac. Flemish cloth-makers introduced the pickle seeds that thrive in the region's watery and humus-rich soil. Only about 20 companies, each using their own 'secret' family recipe, are allowed to produce the vegetable. Discover more pickle secrets on the 260km-long Gurken-Radweg (Gherkin Cycle Path) or at the **Gurkenmuseum** (Gherkin Museum; 📞03542-899 90; www.spreewald-starick.de; An der Dolzke 6; ⏱9am-6pm Apr-Oct & by appointment) in Lehde.

info; Hebewerkstrasse 52; adult/concession €2/1; ⏱9am-6pm mid-Mar–mid-Oct, to 4pm mid-Oct–Dec & mid-Feb–mid-Mar) which links the Oder River and the Oder-Havel Canal. This remarkable feat of engineering was completed in 1934 and measures 60m high, 27m wide and 94m long. Cargo barges sail into a sort of giant bathtub, which is then raised or lowered 36m, water and all. Visitors can enjoy the ride aboard tourist boats operated by **Fahrgastschifffahrt Neumann** (📞03334-244 05; www.schiffshebewerk-niederfinow.info/neumann; adult/child €7/4; ⏱11am, 1pm & 3pm late Mar-Oct). To accommodate larger and multiple barges, an even bigger ship lift is being built adjacent to the historic one. A boat-shaped information

centre has details about this ambitious project.

The Drive » Head north on Hebewerkstrasse as far as Liepe, then turn left on Brodowiner Strasse and continue for 17km through the Schorfheide-Chorin Unesco World Biosphere Reserve (Biosphärenreservat), whose woods, ponds and swamps are a haven for storks, cranes, beavers and other critters.

⑧ Kloster Chorin

A romantically ruined abbey, **Kloster Chorin** (Chorin Monastery; 📞033366-703 77; www.kloster-chorin.org; Amt Chorin 11a; adult/concession €4/2.50; ⏱9am-6pm Apr-Oct, 10am-4pm Nov-Mar) was built by Cistercian monks over six decades starting in 1273, and is widely considered one of the finest red-brick Gothic structures in northern Germany. In summer, the abbey forms an enchanting backdrop for the classical concert

series of **Choriner Musiksommer** (📞03334-818 472; www.musiksommer-chorin.de; ⏱Jun-Aug).

The Drive » Pick up the A11 in Althüttendorf, drive south to exit 14 and follow the B273 in the direction Oranienburg, which takes you through the Nature Park Barnim with its many crystal-clear swimming lakes, including the enchanting Liepnitzsee.

TRIP HIGHLIGHT

⑨ Gedenkstätte & Museum Sachsenhausen

Only 30km north of central Berlin, **Sachsenhausen** (📞03301-200 200; www.stiftung-bg.de; Strasse der Nationen 22; ⏱8.30am-6pm mid-Mar–mid-Oct, to 4.30pm mid-Oct–mid-Mar, museums closed Mon; 🚉S1 to Oranienburg) was built by prisoners and opened in 1936 as a prototype for other concentration camps. Some 200,000 people passed through its sinister gates, most of them political opponents, gypsies, Jews and POWs. By 1945, tens of thousands had died here from hunger, exhaustion, illness, exposure, medical experiments and executions. A tour of the grounds, remaining buildings and exhibits will leave no one untouched. Key stops include the **infirmary barracks**, the **prisoners' kitchen** and the execution area called **Station Z**.

Eating & Sleeping

Berlin ①

✗ La Soupe Populaire   German €€

(☏030-4431 9680; www.lasoupepopulaire.de; Prenzlauer Allee 242; mains €14-21; ☺noon-2.30pm & 5.30-10.10pm Thu-Sat; ⑤Senefelder Platz, 🚇M2) Helmed by local top toque Tim Raue, this industrial-chic gastro destination inside a defunct 19th-century brewery embraces the soulful goodness of German homecooking. The star of the regular menu is Raue's riff on *Königsberger Klopse* (veal meatballs in caper sauce) but there's also a separate one inspired by changing art exhibits in the hall overlooked by the dining room.

⊨ Michelberger Hotel   Hotel €€

(☏030-2977 8590; www.michelbergerhotel.com; Warschauer Strasse 39; d €84-190; ☎; ⑤Warschauer Strasse, 🚇Warschauer Strasse) The ultimate in creative crash pads, Michelberger perfectly encapsulates Berlin's offbeat DIY spirit without being self-consciously cool. Rooms don't hide their factory pedigree, but are comfortable and come in sizes suitable for lovebirds, families or rock bands. Staff are friendly and clued-in, and the restaurant is popular with both guests and locals.

Lübbenau ②

✗ Schlossrestaurant Linari   International €€

(☏03542-8730; www.schloss-luebbenau.de; Schlossbezirk 6; mains €13-22.50; ☺11.30am-10.30pm) This delightful restaurant in the Lübbenau Palace is elegant without being stuffy, and the chef keeps the innovative menu in flux with seasonal and regionally gathered and hunted ingredients. In summer, the terrace with a full-on view of the gardens is the place to sit, while in winter the Sunday roast and goose feasts make reservations de rigueur.

Stift Neuzelle ④

✗ Restaurant Prinz Albrecht   German €€

(☏033652-813 22; www.hotel-prinz-albrecht.de; Frankfurter Strasse 34; mains €10-19; ☺11am-10pm) Attached to a hotel, this country-style restaurant with garden terrace has a feel-good menu that also includes such local dishes as pork marinated in bock beer (from the abbey brewery) or smoked trout from the nearby Schlaube Valley. Portions are generous.

Frankfurt (Oder) ⑤

⊨ Hotel zur Alten Oder   Hotel €

(☏0335-556 220; www.zuraltenoder.de; Fischerstrasse 32; d incl breakfast from €68; P☎) No two of the rooms are alike in this little hotel in a historic building, but all are drenched in bold colours, simply but charmingly furnished and sporting a country-style look. Breakfasts are lavish affairs that should tide you over into the early afternoon.

Neuhardenberg

⊨ Hotel Schloss Neuhardenberg   Hotel €€€

(☏033476-6000; www.schlossneuhardenberg.de; Schinkelplatz, Neuhardenberg; r €162-218; P☎) Spend the night in a palace built in 1786, modified by Prussian starchitect Karl Friedrich Schinkel a few years later, and beautified with a garden designed by Prince Hermann von Pückler-Muskau. Rooms exude understated elegance and come with the gamut of creature comforts. The two on-site restaurants, one serving hearty regional cuisine, the other Mediterranean, are also recommended.

Mainz The beautiful
Romanesque Mainzer Dom

Via Regia

This road trip pays homage to the German section of the Via Regia, or 'Kings Road', the oldest and longest transport route between Western and Eastern Europe.

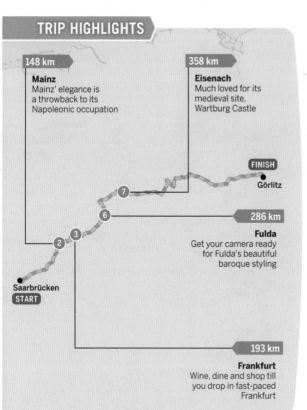

TRIP HIGHLIGHTS

148 km

Mainz
Mainz' elegance is a throwback to its Napoleonic occupation

358 km

Eisenach
Much loved for its medieval site, Wartburg Castle

Görlitz

286 km

Fulda
Get your camera ready for Fulda's beautiful baroque styling

Saarbrücken
START

193 km

Frankfurt
Wine, dine and shop till you drop in fast-paced Frankfurt

5–7 DAYS
771 KM / 481 MILES

GREAT FOR...

BEST TIME TO GO

Fit more in when days are longest from May to July.

ESSENTIAL PHOTO

Fulda's baroque Dom, crowd-less at twilight.

BEST FOR FAMILIES

Frankfurt's myriad attractions entertain young and old.

7 Via Regia

Beginning in Saarbrücken and ending in Görlitz, this spirited west–east romp cuts through the heart of the nation. It juxtaposes Frankfurt's big-city excitement with Fulda's tranquil lanes, gets cultured in Weimar, Dresden and Leipzig, lingers on quiet country highways and roars along autobahns, visiting the key outposts of a road that's no longer in existence, but which was once the way of kings.

❶ Saarbrücken

Vestiges of Saarbrücken's 18th-century heyday survive in the city's beautiful baroque townhouses and churches. The historic centre around **St Johanner Markt** brims with fine restaurants and cafes. Start your trip with a visit to the **Historisches Museum Saar** (www. historisches-museum.org; Schlossplatz 15; adult/student €5/3; ⏰10am-6pm Tue, Wed & Fri-Sun, to 8pm Thu), housed in the basement of the **Saarbrücker Schloss**, where you can descend

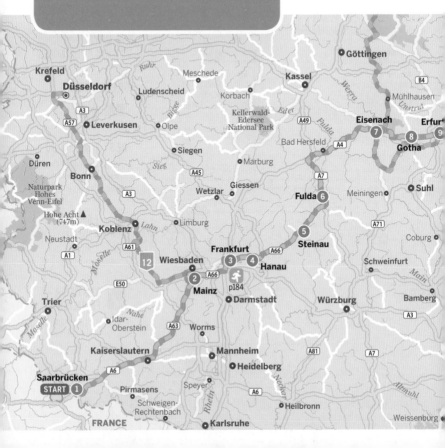

to the castle's massive bastions and casemates. Exhibits look at Saarland from the 1870s, and periods under French and Nazi rule. The Saarland Museum's **Alte Sammlung** (www.kulturbesitz.de; adult/child €5/free, after 3pm Tue free; ⊙10am-6pm Tue & Thu-Sun, to 10pm Wed), or 'old collection', displays a millennium's worth of paintings and artefacts from southwest Germany and France's Alsace-Lorraine. Before you hit the road, why not spend a few minutes' quiet contemplation in the dazzlingly baroque Catholic church, **Basilika**

St Johann (www.basilika-sb.de; Katholisch-Kirch-Strasse 26; ⊙9.30am-7.15pm Mon, Fri & Sat, 8.30am-7.15pm Tue, Thu & Sun, 8.30am-5pm Wed), with its gleaming gold altars, pulpit, organ case and overhead rayburst design?

The Drive » Head south out of town on the A620 for

6km until it becomes the A6 autobahn. Stay on the A6 for 66km until exit 16a Dreieck Kaiserslautern, merging on to the A63 towards Frankfurt. Stay on the A63 for 70km until you reach the outskirts of Mainz, where the road becomes the B40. Keep heading straight for 4km into Mainz.

LINK YOUR TRIP

8 German Avenues Route

Link in with this amazing loop that intersects at Dresden and you have central Germany covered.

12 Romantic Rhine

Hook up with the Rhine while crossing paths in Mainz for some real river romance.

TRIP HIGHLIGHT

2 Mainz

Mainz is located at the confluence of the Rhine and Main Rivers, its elegance a throwback to its Napoleonic occupation. Strolling along the Rhine and sampling local wines in an **Altstadt** (old town) tavern are as essential as viewing the fabulous Romanesque **Mainzer Dom** (☎06131-253 412; www.mainz-dom.de; Markt 10; ☯9am-6.30pm Mon-Fri, to 4pm Sat, 12.45-3pm & 4-6.30pm Sun, shorter hours Nov-Feb), with its octagonal tower, Chagall's ethereal windows in **St-Stephan-Kirche** (www.st-stephan-mainz.de; Kleine Weissgasse 12; ☯10am-5pm Mon-Sat, noon-5pm Sun Mar-Oct, 10am-4.30pm Mon-Sat, noon-4.30pm Sun Nov-Feb), or the first printed Bible in the **Gutenberg-Museum Mainz** (www.gutenberg-museum.de; Liebfrauenplatz 5; adult/child €5/2; ☯9am-5pm Tue-Sat, 11am-5pm Sun), commemorating the native son who perfected movable type. If you're not claustrophobic, head to the dungeon-like **Heiligtum der Isis und Mater Magna** (www.isis-mainz.de; Römer Passage 1; admission by donation; ☯10am-6pm Mon-Sat) archaeological site, with its brilliantly illuminated artefacts uncovered in 1999 during the construction of the Römer Passage shopping mall. If you're desperate to squeeze more in, head to the **Landes-museum Mainz** (www.landesmuseum-mainz.de; Grosse Bleiche 49-51; adult/child €6/3; ☯10am-8pm Tue, 10am-5pm Wed-Sun) for outstanding collections of Renaissance and 20th-century German paintings, baroque porcelain and furniture.

The Drive » Cross the Rhine on the Theodor Heuss Bridge then pick up the B455 at the roundabout and follow it north for 5km until the junction with the A66 autobahn at exit 6 Weisbaden-Erbenheim. Follow the A66 towards Frankfurt for 30km until exit 21 Frankfurt am Main-Miquelallee.

TRIP HIGHLIGHT

3 Frankfurt

Beneath the glinting glass, steel and concrete, you'll discover Frankfurt to be an unexpectedly traditional city, with its medieval **Altstadt**, village-like neighbourhoods, attractive gardens, riverside paths and wealth of museums. The Main River flows from east to west, with the city centre on its northern banks. The **Römerberg** (p185), Frankfurt's ornately gabled old central square, with the **Gerechtigkeitsbrunnen** (Fountain of Justice), marks the centre of the **Altstadt**. To its north, shop till you drop along the **Zeil**, linking **An der Hauptwache** and **Konstablerwache** public squares. Must-sees include the photogenic old town hall **Römer** (p185), comprised of three step-gabled 15th-century

houses, Frankfurt's red-sandstone **Kaiserdom** (p184), dominated by a 95m-high Gothic tower (which you can climb, via 324 steps!), and the world-renowned **Städel Museum** (p185), founded in 1815 and housing an outstanding collection including works by Dürer, Rembrandt, Rubens, Renoir, Picasso and Cézanne.

See p184 for a Stretch Your Legs walking tour of Frankfurt.

🍴 🛏 p99

The Drive » Head south on the B44 for 6.5km to the A3 autobahn at exit 51 Frankfurt Süd. Take the A3 heading east for

Mainz Half-timbered house and a view to Mainzer Dom

19km until exit 54 Hanau, then follow the B45 for 10km north.

- - - - - - - - - - - - - -

❹ Hanau

There are two reasons you've stopped by Hanau: firstly, because Brothers Jacob and Wilhelm Grimm were born here, commemorated by a statue located on the **Markt**; and secondly, for the wonderful **Historisches Museum Schloss Philippsruhe** (☎06181-295 564; www.hanau.de/kultur/museen/hanau; Philippsruher Allee 45; adult/concession €4/3; ⊙11am-6pm Tue-Sun), located within Philippsruhe Palace. Dating

from the early 18th century, this museum has displays on town history and arts and crafts. The parks and gardens are a beautiful place to stroll.

The Drive » Pick up the A66 autobahn at exit 36 Hanau Nord for 48km in the direction of Fulda until exit 47 Steinau an der Strasse.

- - - - - - - - - - - - - -

❺ Steinau

Steinau (an der Strasse) has been firmly planted as a stop on the Via Regia for centuries (*an der Strasse* means 'on the road'). At the entrance to the old town, you'll see two sandstone pillars

commemorating the Via Regia. While you're here, stop by the twinned museums **Brüder Grimm-Haus and Museum Steinau** (☎06663-7605; www.brueder-grimm-haus.de; Brüder Grimm-Strasse 80; adult/concession €6/3.50; ⊙10am-5pm), housed where the Grimm family lived from 1791 to 1796.

The Drive » Return to the A66 at exit 47 Steinau an der Strasse and follow it for 21km until exit 51 Neuhof-Süd. At the roundabout, veer right onto Hanauer Strasse and follow it through the village of Neuhof for 1.6km until the road forks. Take the left fork and follow Alte Heerstrasse for 7km towards Fulda: you're now driving on an

FRANKFURT: THEN & NOW

Around 2000 years ago Frankfurt was a site of Celtic and Germanic settlement and then a Roman garrison town. Mentioned in historical documents as far back as AD 794, Frankfurt was an important centre of power in the Holy Roman Empire. With the election of Frederick I (Barbarossa) in 1152, the city became the customary site of the selection of German kings. In 1372 Frankfurt became a 'Free Imperial City', a status it enjoyed until the Prussian takeover of 1866.

It's hard to believe that about 80% of Frankfurt's medieval city centre was destroyed by WWII Allied bombing raids in March 1944, when over 1000 people lost their lives. The area around Römerberg was reconstructed in its original style and, phoenix-like, the city rose again to prominence as a thriving contemporary centre of commerce. Frankfurt's first international trade fairs began in the 12th century and continue to attract tens of thousands each year, who arrive at its airport, the third-busiest in Europe. Frankfurt's first stock exchange began operating in 1585 and is now in the world's top ten. In the 1760s, the Rothschild banking family began their ascent from Frankfurt, and the city is today home to the gleaming HQ of the European Central Bank.

original Via Regia roadway! Turn left at the junction with the K103 then right onto the L3418 until you reach Frankfurter Strasse: follow it for 3km into Fulda.

TRIP HIGHLIGHT

⑥ Fulda

Founded in 744, photogenic Fulda boasts a treasure trove of sumptuous baroque architecture and a delightfully relaxed atmosphere, with plenty of opportunities for happy snapping and a handful of top spots to pause for a meal or a glass of wine. Fulda's spectacular **Stadtschloss** (☎0661-1020; adult/concession €3.50/2.30; ⏱10am-5pm Tue-Sun) was built from 1706 to 1721 as the prince-abbots' residence. Visitors can enter a selection of ornate historic rooms and the octagonal Schlossturm (April to October) for great views of the magnificent

gardens where locals bronze themselves in summer. Inside the baroque **Dom** (☎0661-874 57; www. bistum-fulda.de; Domplatz 1; ⏱10am-6pm Mon-Fri, to 3pm Sat, 1-6pm Sun), a cathedral built from 1704 to 1712, you'll find gilded furnishings, statues and the tomb of St Boniface, who died a martyr in 754.

The Drive » Take the B27 for 5km north until the interchange with the A7 autobahn at exit 91 Fulda Nord. Follow the A7 north for 35km then merge onto the A4 towards Berlin/Dresden at interchange 86 Kirchheimer Dreieck. Follow the A4 for 60km until exit 39 Eisenach West. Take the B19 south for 6km into Eisenach.

TRIP HIGHLIGHT

⑦ Eisenach

Historically, Eisenach was an important stop on the Via Regia, and its **Wartburg** (☎03691-2500;

www.wartburg-eisenach.de; Auf der Wartburg 1; tour adult/concession €9/5, museum & Luther study only €5/3; ⏱tours 8.30am-5pm Apr-Oct, 9am-3.30pm Nov-Mar, English tour 1.30pm) castle is one of Germany's most significant medieval sites: it held Martin Luther while his actions brought about the Reformation and was the inspiration for better-known Neuschwanstein, whose creator, Ludwig II, saw Wartburg and wanted to build a fortress even more grandiose and impenetrable. Eisenach proudly remembers the birth of Johann Sebastian Bach in the wattle-and-daub home now housing the museum **Bachhaus** (☎03691-793 40; www. bachhaus.de; Frauenplan 21; adult/concession €8.50/4.50; ⏱10am-6pm), and also celebrates its automotive history (the world's first

BMW rolled off the assembly line here in 1929): check out **Automobile Welt Eisenach** (☎03691-772 12; www.ame.eisenachonline. de; Friedrich-Naumann-Strasse 10; adult/concession €5/3.50; ☺11am-5pm Tue-Sun) if four wheels and six cylinders kick-start your heart.

The Drive » Head north on Mühlhäuser Strasse for 2km then turn right on to the L1021 for 6km until the junction with the A4 at exit 40a Eisenach Ost. Head south on the A4 for 9.5km until exit 40b Sättelstädt. Follow the L3007 east for 15km through the small villages of Teutleben and Aspach into Gotha.

- - - - - - - - - - - - - -

 Gotha

Gotha is no longer Thuringia's wealthiest and most beautiful city, as it was once described, but its focal point remains the enormous **Schloss Friedenstein** (☎03621-823 40; www.stiftungfriedenstein. de; Schloss Friedenstein; adult/ concession €10/5, audioguide €2.50; ☺10am-5pm Tue-Sun), built by Duke Ernst I, of House Saxe-Coburg-Gotha, whose descendants reinvented themselves as the House of Windsor after WWI and now occupy the British royal throne. Inside the palace you'll find the exuberantly stucco-ornamented Festival Hall, a neoclassical wing, a curio cabinet jammed with exotica, the Palace Church, and the stunning Ekhof-Theater, one of the oldest baroque theatres in Europe. Gotha's **Hauptmarkt** is dominated by the picturesque **Rathaus** (Hauptmarkt; tower €1; ☺11am-6pm), with its colourful Renaissance facade and 35m-tall tower.

The Drive » Follow Weimarer Strasse, which becomes Eisenacher Strasse, for 21km east, into Erfurt.

- - - - - - - - - - - - - -

❾ Erfurt

Founded as a bishopric on the little Gera River in 742, Erfurt was catapulted to prosperity in the Middle Ages when it began producing a precious blue pigment from the woad plant. In 1392 rich merchants founded

---

LOCAL KNOWLEDGE: FRANKFURT FOR KIDS

Frankfurt is a fun place to linger a little if you have youngsters in your party: they'll jump at the chance to get out of the car. There are plenty of parks to picnic in and several museums have kid-friendly exhibits. Favourites include:

Senckenberg Museum (www.senckenberg.de; Senckenberganlage 25; adult/child €9/4.50, audioguide €3; ☺9am-5pm Mon, Tue, Thu & Fri, to 8pm Wed, to 6pm Sat & Sun; Ⓢ Bockenheimer Warte) Fossils and dinosaurs.

Frankfurt Zoo (Zoologisher Garten; www.zoo-frankfurt.de; Bernhard-Grzimek-Allee 1; adult/child €10/5; ☺9am-7pm late Mar-late Oct, 9am-5pm late Oct-late Mar; Ⓢ Zoo) Animals galore.

Explora (☎069-788 888; www.exploramuseum.de; Glauburgplatz 1; adult/child €16/8; ☺11am-6pm; Ⓢ Glauburgstrasse) Optical illusions.

PalmenGarten (www.palmengarten.de; Siesmayerstrasse 63; adult/child €7/2; ☺9am-6pm Feb-Oct, to 4pm Nov-Jan; Ⓢ Palmengartenstrasse) Parkland and fountains.

Additionally, the **Kinder Museum** (Children's Museum; http://kindermuseum.frankfurt. de; An der Hauptwache 15; adult/child €4/2; ☺10am-6pm Tue-Sun, plus 10am-6pm Mon during school holidays; Ⓢ Hauptwache) and **Halligalli Kinderwelt** (www.halligalli-myzeil.de; Zeil 106, 5th fl; adult/child 2-16yr/1-2yr €4/7.50/4.50, Fri-Sun €1 more; ☺11am-8pm, reduced hours during Christmas; Ⓢ Hauptwache) are both specifically designed for children...and to give wise old elders a break!

Erfurt's university, whose most famous graduate was Martin Luther, harbinger of the Reformation. There's plenty to enjoy here, with the town's history and modernity complementing each other. Head to the **Krämerbrücke** (Merchants' Bridge), a charming 1325 stone bridge flanked by cute half-timbered houses on both sides. Erfurt's is the only one of its kind north of the Alps that's still inhabited. Linger a while in the delightful eateries of nearby **Wenigemarkt**, and consider a visit to the **Augustinerkloster** (☎0361-576 600; www.augustinerkloster. de; Augustinerstrasse 10; tour adult/concession €6/4; ☻tours 9.30am-5pm Mon-Sat, 11am & noon Sun Apr-Oct, 9.30am-3.30pm Mon-Fri, to 2pm Sat & 11am Sun Nov-Mar); this is where Luther lived from 1505 to 1511, was ordained as a monk and read his first Mass. Be sure to stroll about the gorgeous houses on **Fischmarkt** and onwards to the spectacular **Domplatz** and Erfurt's famous **Dom** (Mariendom; ☎0361-6461265; www.dom-erfurt.de; Domplatz; ☻9.30am-6pm Mon-Sat, 1-6pm Sun May-Oct, to 5pm Nov-Apr).

 p99

The Drive » Take the B7 for 22km east, through fields of wind turbines, into Weimar.

- - - - - - - - - - - - - -

⑩ Weimar

Historical epicentre of the German Enlightenment, best known as the town

where intellectual heavyweights Goethe and Schiller did their thing, Weimar appeals to anyone with a passion for German history and culture. In summer, Weimar's many parks and gardens lend themselves to quiet contemplation of the town's cultural onslaught, or to taking a break from it. Must-sees include the museum at **Stadtschloss Weimar** (Schlossmuseum; ☎03643-545 400; www.klassik-stiftung.de; Burgplatz 4; adult/concession €7.50/6; ☻10am-6pm Tue-Sun), the Unesco World Heritage **Herzogin Anna Amalia Bibliothek** (☎03643-545 400; www. anna-amalia-bibliothek.de; Platz der Demokratie 1; adult/concession incl audioguide €7.50/6; ☻9.30am-2.30pm Tue-Sun), and, of course, no visit would be complete without getting up to speed with Germany's literary icon at

the **Goethe-National-museum** (☎03643-545 400; www.klassik-stiftung.de; Frauenplan 1; adult/concession €12/8.50; ☻9.30am-6pm Tue-Sun Apr-Oct, to 4pm Nov-Mar).

The Drive » Follow the B7 for 25km east into Jena.

- - - - - - - - - - - - - -

⑪ Jena

Although signs of East German (GDR) aesthetics remain, Jena enjoys a picturesque setting on the Saale River, flanked by limestone hills and blessed with a climate mild enough for orchids and grapevines. Also an old university town (since 1558), Jena has an entirely different feel to Weimar and Erfurt. Close investigation will unearth fun, fringe, Berlinesque hang-outs and tasty cheap eats. While you're in town, ascend the **JenTower** (📞03641-208 000; www.jentower.de; Leutragraben 1; viewing platform €3; ⏰viewing platforms 10am-11pm) for fabulous views of the surrounding Saale River Valley, learn how Jena's lenses changed the world at the **Optisches Museum** (Optical Museum; 📞03641-443 165; www.optischesmuseum. de; Carl-Zeiss-Platz 12; adult/concession €5/4, combination ticket with Zeiss Planetarium €11/9; ⏰10am-4.30pm Tue-Fri, 11am-5pm Sat), or contemplate the life of a literary giant and his little garden in **Schiller's Gartenhaus** (Schiller's Garden House; 📞03641-931 188; Schillergässchen 2; adult/concession €2.50/1.30; ⏰11am-5pm Tue-Sun).

The Drive >> Follow the B88 north for 34km through forests and fields, as it chases the sparking Saale River into Naumburg.

⑫ Naumburg

At the confluence of the Saale and Unstrut Rivers, Naumburg has a handsome **Altstadt**, striking Renaissance **Rathaus** and **Marientor** double gateway. Its enormous **Dom** (📞03445-230 1133; www.naumburger-dom.de; Domplatz 16-17; adult/concession €6.50/4.50; ⏰9am-6pm Mon-Sat, noon-6pm Sun), the Cathedral of Sts Peter and Paul, is a masterpiece of medieval architecture, featuring elements of

Romanesque and early Gothic design. Medieval stained-glass windows are augmented by ruby-red modern panes by Neo Rauch, one of the premier artists of the New Leipzig School. You may also want to pop into the **Nietzsche Haus** (📞03445-201 638; www. mv-naumburg.de/nietzschehaus; Weingarten 18; adult/concession €3/2; ⏰2-5pm Tue-Fri, 10am-5pm Sat & Sun), where the great philosopher spent most of his childhood.

The Drive >> Head southeast on the B87 for 4km until the intersection with the B180. Continue heading southeast on the B180 for 10km until the junction with autobahn A9 at exit 21a Naumberg. Head north on the A9 for 32km until exit 17 Leipzig West. Head east on the B181 for 13km into Leipzig.

⑬ Leipzig

Leipzig's love affair with music stems from its connection to the lives and work of Bach, Mendelssohn and Wagner. Today, one of the world's top classical orchestras, the Gewandhausorchester, and the 800-year-old Thomanerchor boys' choir continue to delight audiences here. Along this theme, the **Bach-Museum** (📞0341-913 70; www.bachmuseumleipzig. de; Thomaskirchhof 16; adult/concession/under 16yr €8/6/free; ⏰10am-6pm Tue-Sun) lets you treat your ears to any composition Bach wrote, while **Mendelssohn-Haus** (📞0341-127 0294; www. mendelssohn-stiftung.de; Gold-

schmidtstrasse 12; adult/concession incl audioguide €7.50/6; ⏰10am-6pm) teaches you more about Mendelssohn in the Biedermeier-furnished apartment where this remarkable musical prodigy lived until his sudden death, aged 38. At the fabulous **Museum für Musikinstrumente** (📞0341-973 0750; adult/concession €6/3, audioguide €1), housed inside the complex of the **Museen im Grassi** (www.grassimuseum. de; Johannisplatz 5-11; combined ticket adult/concession €15/12; ⏰10am-6pm Tue-Sun), you can discover music from five centuries through an interactive sound laboratory. It's not all music here: linger awhile to find out why Leipzig has been dubbed the 'New Berlin'.

✂ 🍴 p99

The Drive >> Take Torgauer Strasse northeast for 4.5km until the intersection with the A14 autobahn at exit 25 Leipzig Nordost. Head southeast on the A14 for 75km until the A4 interchange 76 Autobahn Dreieck Nossen. Merge here onto the A4 and head east for 20km to exit 78 Dresden Altstadt.

⑭ Dresden

Dresden's cultural heyday came under the 18th-century reign of Augustus the Strong, who produced many of Dresden's iconic buildings, including the **Zwinger** (p118), inspired by the palace at Versailles (and today housing three superb museums within

DETOUR: HALLE

Start: ⑬ Leipzig

Best known as the birthplace of Georg Friedrich Händel – learn all about him in the **Händel-Haus** (☎0345-500 900; www.handel-house.com; Grosse Nikolaistrasse 5; adult/concession €4/2.50; ☺10am-6pm Tue-Sun) – Halle is one of Germany's oldest cities, having celebrated its 1200th birthday in 2006. But the main reason to visit is to check out two impressive museums. The **Landesmuseum für Vorgeschichte** (State Museum of Pre-History; ☎0345-524 7363; www.lda-lsa.de/en/state_museum_of_prehistory; Richard Wagner Strasse 9; adult/concession €5/3; ☺9am-5pm Tue-Fri, 10am-6pm Sat & Sun) houses a phenomenal collection of major archaeological finds, one of the most significant in Europe. Priceless permanent exhibits shed light on the early to late Stone Age and early Bronze Age, and include the oldest known recorded fingerprint, the graves of Eulau and the Nebra Sky Disc. Art lovers will want to make a beeline to **Kunstmuseum Moritzburg** (Moritzburg Art Gallery; ☎0345-212 5911; www.kunstmuseum-moritzburg.de; Friedemann-Bach-Platz 5; adult/concession €8/6; ☺10am-6pm Thu-Tue), where the late-Gothic Moritzburg castle forms a fantastic setting for a superb permanent art collection, from the classics to the modern. When you're done, there are some fine places to wine and dine. Halle is 40km northwest from Leipzig on the A14.

its baroque walls), and the **Frauenkirche** (p119), Dresden's most beloved symbol, rebuilt from a pile of rubble between 1994 and 2005. The original graced the skyline for two centuries until the devastating 1945 Allied firestorm of WWII levelled the church and most of the city. For something completely different, the **Deutsches Hygiene-Museum** (☎0351-484 6400; www.dhmd.de; Lingnerplatz 1; adult/student/under 16yr €7/3/free, valid on 2 consecutive days; ☺10am-6pm Tue-Sun; 🖶) is, in fact, all about human beings. Living and dying, eating and drinking, sex and beauty are all addressed. There's a Children's Museum in the basement. If the kids have made it this far, why not take them to the **Zoo** (☎0351-478 060; www.zoo-dresden.de; Tiergartenstrasse 1; adult/child €12/4; ☺8.30am-6.30pm Apr-Oct, 8.30am-4.30pm Nov-Mar)? They'll love you for it.

See also p118 for a walking tour of Dresden.

📖 p99

The Drive » Pick up the A4 autobahn at exit 78 Dresden Altstadt and follow it east for 102km to the end of your trip at exit 94 Görlitz.

TRIP HIGHLIGHT

⑮ Görlitz

Congratulations, you made it! Görlitz, Germany's most eastern city, is a dreamy coalescence of fabulous architecture, cobbled streets and an intriguing history. Having miraculously escaped destruction during WWII, Görlitz offers the visitor some nearly 4200 heritage buildings in styles from the Renaissance to the 19th century. Be sure to pop in to the **Barockhaus** (☎03581-671 355; www.museum-goerlitz.de; Neissstrasse 30; adult/concession €5/3.50; ☺10am-5pm Tue-Sat), which will fascinate anyone with a taste for the odd with its curiously broad exhibits. For a history of the area, visit the **Schlesisches Museum zu Görlitz** (☎03581-879 10; www.schlesisches-museum.de; Brüderstrasse 8; adult/concession incl audioguide €5/3; ☺10am-5pm Tue-Sun), and drop by **Untermarkt** to see the **Rathaus** and **Peterskirche** (☺10am-6pm Mon-Sat, 11.45am-6pm Sun), with its remarkable Sun Organ.

Eating & Sleeping

Frankfurt ③

✖ Zu den 12 Aposteln   German €€

(☎069-288 668; www.12aposteln-frankfurt.
de; Rosenbergerstrasse 1; mains €9-24;
⊙11am-11pm; Ⓢ Konstablerwache) Glowing
with sepia-toned lamplight, the 12 Apostles
has ground- floor and brick-cellar dining rooms
serving wonderfully traditional German dishes:
Matjes (herring) with sour cream, apple and fried
onion; roast pork knuckle with pickled cabbage;
Frankfurter schnitzel with *Grüne Sosse* (green
sauce); and *Käsespätzle* (handmade cheese
noodles with onions). It brews its own light and
dark beers on the premises.

⌐ Villa Orange   Boutique Hotel €€

(☎069-405 840; www.villa-orange.de;
Hebelstrasse 1; s/d weekday from €128/158,
weekend from €95/119; Ⓟ ✱ 🛜; 🚗12/18
Friedberger Platz) Offering a winning
combination of tranquillity, modern German
design and small-hotel comforts (such as
a quiet corner library), this century-old,
tangerine-coloured villa has 38 spacious rooms,
some with free-standing baths and four-poster
beds. Everything is organic – the sheets, the
soap and the bountiful buffet breakfast.

Erfurt ⑨

✖ Fellini   Italian €€

(☎0361-642 1375; www.fellini-erfurt.de;
Fischmarkt 3; mains €12-22; ⊙10am-11pm)
You can't beat the Fischmarkt location of this
smart Italian affair where local suits and casual
tourists dine side by side. Expect well-prepared
traditional Italian staples, good old-fashioned
service and tourist prices.

⌐ Pullman Erfurt
am Dom   Luxury Hotel €€€

(☎0361-644 50; www.pullmanhotels.com/
Erfurt; Theaterplatz 2; s/d from €102/129;
Ⓟ ✱ 🛜) Situated about 300m west of

Domplatz (off Lauentor), Erfurt's only all-out
luxury address has 160 rooms that exude
effortless sophistication thanks to classy decor
and a soothing natural-hued colour scheme.
Sightseeing fatigue quickly fades in the
impeccable Zen-inspired wellness area. Take
tram 4 from Hauptbahnhof to Theater.

Leipzig ⑬

✖ Reisladen   International €

(Karl-Heine-Strasse 49; mains €3.50-4.50;
⊙11.30am-2.30pm; 🍴) If you're exploring
funky Plagwitz, then this lunch-only joint will
surely be top of your list for a wonderfully good
value, healthy and tasty lunch. Normally with a
line out the door, this local establishment has
daily changing specials of rice dishes that can
be taken away or eaten in; it's a great choice for
vegetarians and vegans.

⌐ Meisterzimmer   Boutique Hotel €

(☎0341-3067 7099; www.meisterzimmer.de;
Spinnereistrasse 7; r from €75) Somewhere
between a hotel and a thoroughly designer
airbnb loft, this selection of minimalist but
supremely style-conscious rooms is inside a
massive converted factory that is now home
to half of Leipzig's creative industries. If you
don't enjoy public areas in hotels, but love a
light-bathed converted factory, this is the place
for you. Booking ahead is essential.

Dresden ⑭

⌐ Gewandhaus
Hotel   Boutique Hotel €€

(☎0351-4949 3636; www.gewandhaus-hotel.
de; Ringstrasse 1; d from €133; Ⓟ ✱ @ 🛜 🏊)
Fresh from a total renovation and rebirth as a
boutique hotel, the stunning Gewandhaus, an
18th-century trading house of tailors and fabric
merchants that burned down in 1945, now has
sleek public areas, beautiful and bright rooms,
and a breakfast that sets a high bar for anything
else offered in the city.

Quedlinburg *Famous for its half-timbered houses and cobblestone streets*

German Avenues Route

8

This quintessential German road trip, along the tree-lined avenues of the Harz Mountains and country highways of central Germany, leaves no stone unturned.

TRIP HIGHLIGHTS

98 km

Quedlinburg
This delightful village has over 1400 half-timbered houses

437 km

Weimar
Goethe was here...and Schiller and a bunch of other cultural titans

Goslar

2

Dessau-
Rosslau

START/
FINISH

Leipzig

13

6

9

Eisenach
Historic Eisenach has a few surprises up its sleeve

311 km

Dresden
Risen again, Dresden is one of Germany's most beautiful cities

694 km

**5–7 DAYS
868 KM / 541 MILES**

GREAT FOR...

BEST TIME TO GO

Visit from May to July for fewer crowds and the best weather.

 ESSENTIAL PHOTO

Dresden by twilight on the banks of the Elbe.

 BEST FOR HISTORY

Few places pack as much punch as Eisenach's Wartburg.

101

Classic Trip

8 German Avenues Route

On this magic loop through the diverse natural beauty of the ancient states of Saxony-Anhalt, Lower Saxony, Thuringia and Saxony, you'll fall in love with the eye-catching villages of Quedlinburg and Goslar, perhaps take a steam train to the top of a mountain, see where Bach was born and Goethe died, keep watch from the Wartburg and ponder the histories written upon the culture-laden cities of Erfurt, Weimar, Dresden and Leipzig.

1 Dessau-Rosslau

The former GDR town of Dessau-Rosslau, 130km south of Berlin, is best known for being the birthplace of the Bauhaus movement, but is also famed for the **Gartenreich Dessau-Wörlitz**, one of the finest garden ensembles in Germany. Begin at the main Bauhaus sites, the **Bauhausgebäude** (Bauhaus Building; 0340-650 8250; www.bauhaus-dessau.de; Gropiusallee 38; exhibition adult/concession €7.50/4.50, tour €5; 10am-6pm, tours 11am & 2pm, also noon & 4pm Sat & Sun), erected in 1925–26 as a school of Bauhaus art, design and architecture, and the three **Meisterhäuser** (Masters' Houses; www.meisterhaeuser.de; Ebertallee 63, 65-67, 69-71; admission to all houses adult/concession €7.50/5.50, tours €11.50/8.50; 11am-6pm Tue-Sun, tours 12.30pm & 3.30pm daily, also 1.30pm Sat & Sun) where the Bauhaus' leading lights lived. Juxtapose these with the 112-hectare **Wörlitz Park & Schloss Wörlitz** (039404-310 09; www.woerlitz-information.de; Förstergasse 26, Wörlitz; palace tours €5; 10am-6pm Apr-Oct, 10am-4pm Mon-Fri Nov-Mar), pinnacle of the Garden Realm, 20km east of town on the L133, before returning to Dessau-Rosslau and heading southwest on the B185 for 11km, for a peek at petite **Schloss & Park Mosigkau** (039404-521 139; www.gartenreich.com; Knobelsdorffallee 3, Dessau-Rosslau; palace admission €7.50; 11am-6pm Wed-Sun May-Sep, 11am-7pm Sat & Sun Apr & Oct), a 'miniature Sanssouci'.

The Drive >> From Schloss & Park Mosigkau, take the B185 for 15km to the pretty village of Köthen, where Bach composed his Brandenburg concertos and *The Well-Tempered Clavier*. Continue on the B185 for 45km until the junction with the B6. Follow the B6 for 20km, to Quedlinburg.

TRIP HIGHLIGHT

2 Quedlinburg

Situated on a fertile plain at the northern cusp of the Harz Mountains, little Quedlinburg, a Unesco World Heritage town, is one of the loveliest in the region. Learn about its centuries-old half-timbered (*Fachwerk*) houses (there are 1400 or so) in the **Fachwerkmuseum im Ständerbau** (03946-3828; Wordgasse 3; adult/concession €3/2; 10am-5pm Fri-Wed), and wander freely around its enchanting cobblestone streets and spectacular medieval marketplace, where you'll find a wonderful mix of original options for wining, dining and resting your

LINK YOUR TRIP

4 Highlights of Saxony

Pick up this scenic jaunt in Dresden to immerse yourself in Saxony's rich history and diverse architecture.

10 German Fairy Tale Road

From Schmalkalden, head southwest for 110km to Steinau to link up with this whimsical journey.

head. Perched high on a 25m plateau above town, Quedlinburg's Renaissance palace houses today's **Schlossmuseum** (☏03946-905 681; Schlossberg 1; adult/concession €4.50/3; ◷10am-5pm), with fascinating Ottonian-period exhibits dating from 919 to 1056. The **Lyonel-Feininger-Galerie** (☏03946-689 5930; www.feininger-galerie.de; Finkenherd

5a; adult/concession €6/3; ◷10am-5pm Wed-Mon) exhibits the work of influential Bauhaus artist Lyonel Feininger (1871–1956), who was born in New York and came to Germany at the age of 16, later fleeing the Nazis and returning to the US in 1937. Timing your visit for a weekday will make all the difference: Quedlinburg is a popular weekend destination.

✕ ⇌ p114

The Drive » Head west on Westerhäuser Strasse (which becomes the B27) through another lovely village – Blankenburg – until the

junction with the B81. Follow the B81 for 4km north: you'll see Blankenburg's handsome castle to your right. Turn left on the L85 and head west for 11.5km into Wernigerode.

---

③ Wernigerode

The winding streets of Wernigerode's attractive **Altstadt** (old town) are flanked by pretty half-timbered houses. This is the northern terminus of the steam-powered narrow-gauge heritage Harzquerbahn railway; the line to the summit of the Brocken also starts here (see boxed text, p105). Dominating Wernigerode's town square, the spectacular towered **Rathaus** (town hall) began life as a theatre around 1277, only to be given its mostly late-Gothic features in the 16th century. Take a stroll along **Breite Strasse**, essentially Wernigerode's main street, for both architectural and gastronomic reasons. A visit to the **Harzmuseum Wernigerode** (☏03943-654 454; Klint 10; adult/concession €2/1.30; ◷10am-5pm Mon-Sat) will top up your knowledge on local geology, history and architecture. Round out a magical day with a castle visit to **Schloss Wernigerode** (☏03943-553 040; www.schloss-wernigerode.de; adult/concession €6/5, tower €1; ◷10am-5pm, closed Mon Nov-Apr), originally built

---

QUEDLINBURG'S HISTORIC BUILDINGS

With so many historic buildings, Quedlinburg is one town in which it's nice just to stroll the streets and soak up the atmosphere. The **Rathaus** (1320) dominates **Markt**, and in front of this is a **Roland** statue from 1426. Just behind the Rathaus is the **Marktkirche St Benedikti** (1233), and nearby is the **Gildehaus zur Rose** (1612) at Breite Strasse 39. Running off Markt is the tiny **Schuhhof**, a shoemakers' courtyard, with shutters and stable-like 'gossip doors'. **Alter Klopstock** (1580), which is found at Stieg 28, has scrolled beams typical of Quedlinburg's 16th-century half-timbered houses.

From Stieg 28 (just north of Schuhhof), it's a short walk north along Pölle to **Zwischen den Städten**, a historic bridge connecting the old town and Neustadt, which developed alongside the town wall around 1200 when peasants fled a feudal power struggle on the land. Behind the Renaissance facade, tower and stone gables of the **Hagensches Freihaus** (1558) is the Wyndham Garden Quedlinburger Stadtschloss. Many houses in this part of town have high archways and courtyards dotted with pigeon towers. A couple of other places of special note are the **Hotel zur Goldenen Sonne** building (1671) at Steinweg 11 and **Zur Börse** (1683) at number 23.

HARZ MOUNTAIN RAILWAYS

Fans of old-time trains will be eager to get out from behind the wheel and into a *wagen* (wagon) on any of the three narrow-gauge railways, a legacy of the GDR, that cross the Harz. This 140km integrated network is the largest in Europe, serving steam and diesel locomotives, and tackling gradients of up to 40% and curves as tight as 60m in radius.

The **Harzquerbahn** runs 60km on a north–south route between Wernigerode and Nordhausen. The serpentine 14km between Wernigerode and Drei Annen Hohne includes 72 bends; you'll get dropped off on the edge of Harz National Park.

From the junction at Drei Annen Hohne, the **Brockenbahn** begins the steep climb to Schierke and the Brocken. Trains to the Brocken (via Drei Annen Hohne) can be picked up from Wernigerode and Nordhausen; single/return tickets cost €24/12 from all stations. Many visitors take the train to Schierke and then follow a trail on foot to the Brocken summit (1142m).

The third service is the **Selketalbahn**, which begins in Quedlinburg and runs to Eisfelder Talmühle or Hasselfelde. At Eisfelder Tal, you can change trains for other lines. The picturesque Selketalbahn crosses the plain to Gernrode and follows Wellbach, a creek with a couple of good swimming holes, through deciduous forest to Mägdesprung, before joining the Selke Valley and climbing past Alexisbad to high plains around Friedrichshöhe, Stiege and beyond.

Check in with the folks at **Harzer Schmalspurbahnen** (☎03943-5580; www.hsb-wr.de; Hauptbahnhof, Wernigerode) for fares and timetables.

in the 12th century but enlarged over the years to reflect late-Gothic and Renaissance tastes. You'll need to leave your car below: it's a 1.5km walk if you fancy it, but the easiest way to get there is by Bimmelbahn wagon from Marktstrasse.

The Drive » Head north on the B244 for 4km to the junction with the B6. Follow the B6 for 32km, over undulating hills, by meadows of golden canola and the odd wind turbine, and through picturesque villages into Goslar.

- - - - - - - - - - - - -

`TRIP HIGHLIGHT`

❹ Goslar

Gorgeous Goslar's beautiful medieval **Altstadt** attracts visitors by the busload. Founded by Heinrich I in 922, the town was important in its early days for silver mining. One of the nicest things to do here is wander through the historic streets around the **Markt**. Opposite the **Rathaus** is the **Glockenspiel**, a chiming clock depicting four scenes of mining in the area. It plays at 9am, noon, 3pm and 6pm. A visit to the **Goslarer Museum** (☎05321-433 94; Königstrasse 1; adult/concession €4/2; ☺10am-5pm Tue-Sun) offers a good overview of local history. The town's pride and joy is its reconstructed 11th-century Romanesque imperial palace, the **Kaiserpfalz** (☎05321-311 9693; Kaiserbleek 6; adult/concession €7.50/4.50; ☺10am-4pm), seat of Saxon kings from 1005 to 1219. After centuries of decay, the building was resurrected in the 19th century and adorned with interior frescos of idealised historical scenes. About 3km south on Rammelsberger Strasse is the **Rammelsberg Museum & Besucherbergwerk** (Rammelsberg Museum & Visitors' Mine; ☎05321-7500; www.rammelsberg.de; Bergtal 19; adult/concession €13/8; ☺9am-6pm, last admission 4.30pm), the shafts and buildings of a 1000-year-old mine that are now a must-see Unesco World Heritage site and museum.

🛏 p114

ANTON_IVANOV / SHUTTERSTOCK ©

URSULA SANDER / GETTY IMAGES ©

WHY THIS IS A CLASSIC TRIP
BENEDICT WALKER, AUTHOR

This trip showcases Germany's evolution from medieval times to the industrialised, environmentally aware nation that's celebrated today. From just over an hour outside Berlin you can pick up this fantastic time warp around one of the longest inhabited regions in the country, along tree-lined avenues, up mountains, down dales, through ancient forests and by sparkling rivers. I promise you won't be bored!

Top: Statues at Erfurter Dom
Left: The charm of the old town in Quedlinburg
Right: Goslar's Altstadt

ANTON_IVANOV / SHUTTERSTOCK ©

The Drive » Allow at least two hours for this scenic Harz Mountains section. Take the B241 as it twists and turns for 31km until the junction of the B243, just through the village of Osterode am Harz. Continue south on the foresty B243 for 30km: you'll cross the border of Lower Saxony into Thuringia, from where it's 49km of country roads, heading south on the L1014 and 1015 to Mühlhausen.

⑤ Mühlhausen

Mühlhausen flaunts medieval charisma. Encircled by nearly intact fortifications, its historic centre is a warren of cobbled alleyways linking proud churches and half-timbered houses. Admire its beauty from the 330m section of the **Town Fortification** (Am Frauentor; adult/concession €3/2; ⏰10am-5pm mid-Apr–Sep), accessible through Inneres Frauentor, and the viewing platform in the **Rabenturm** (Raven's Tower). Originally, the 12th-century fortification ran for 2.8km around the town, of which a remarkable 2km remain. In the early 16th century, the town became a focal point of the Reformation and a launch pad for the Peasants' War of 1525, led by local preacher Thomas Müntzer. With reunification, Mühlhausen became united Germany's most central town, located a mere 5km north of the country's geographical centre in Niederdorla. Mühlhausen's **Rathaus**

(Ratsstrasse 19; ⊙10am-4pm Tue-Sun) is an architecturally intriguing hotchpotch of Gothic, Renaissance and baroque styles. Inside, pay special attention to the Great Hall and the Councillors' Chamber.

The Drive » Follow the L1016 south for 35km to Eisenach.

TRIP HIGHLIGHT

⑥ Eisenach

The modest appearance of hilly Eisenach, a small town on the edge of the Thuringian Forest, belies its association with two German heavyweights: Johann Sebastian Bach and Martin Luther. Luther went to school here and later returned to protective custody in the **Wartburg** (☎03691-2500; www.wartburg-eisenach.de; Auf der Wartburg 1; tour adult/concession €9/5, museum & Luther study only €5/3; ⊙tours 8.30am-5pm Apr-Oct, 9am-3.30pm Nov-Mar, English tour 1.30pm), now itself protected by Unesco World Heritage status. When it comes to medieval castles and their importance in German history, you've hit the mother lode: allow at least two hours for exploration with your camera batteries fully charged. A century after Luther's incarceration, Bach, the

grandest of all baroque musicians, was born in the **Bachhaus** (☎03691-793 40; www.bachhaus.de; Frauenplan 21; adult/concession €8.50/4.50; ⊙10am-6pm), a wattle-and-daub home, now one of Germany's best biographical museums. Admission includes a 20-minute concert played on antique instruments. Music lovers will also appreciate the **Reuter-Wagner Museum** (☎03691-743 294; Reuterweg 2; adult/concession €4/2; ⊙11am-5pm Tue-Sun), honouring composer Richard Wagner in a villa once owned by writer Fritz Reuter. Eisenach also has a century-old automotive tradition – the world's first BMW rolled off the local assembly line in 1929. Since you're on a road trip why not check out **Automobile Welt Eisenach** (☎03691-772 12; www.ame.eisenachonline.de; Friedrich-Naumann-Strasse 10; adult/concession €5/3.50; ⊙11am-5pm Tue-Sun) as well?

🍴 p114

The Drive » Take the B19 south for 37km, admiring the tree-lined avenues, thick forests and lush fields, passing through the occasional sleepy village here and there, then take the L1026 east for 7km into Schmalkalden.

---

⑦ Schmalkalden

As you drive into town, you'll pass the unmissable **Viba Nougat Welt** (☎03683-692 1600; www.viba-sweets.de/worlds-of-

experience; Nougat-Allee 1; ⊙10am-8pm), where you'd be forgiven for being seduced into a sweet-toothed visit, but be sure to press on into Schmalkalden's **Altmarkt** as well, where in 1531 the Protestant princes established the Schmalkaldic League to counter the central powers of Catholic emperor Charles V, so thrusting the little town into the heart of the Reformation. The town's handsome **Rathaus** (1419) once functioned as the meeting place of the Schmalkaldic League. The incongruous towers of the late-Gothic **Stadtkirche St Georg** (1437–1509) overlook the square. You can almost hear the groans and creaks of its half-timbered houses, crowned by the hilltop, late-Renaissance **Schloss Wilhelmsburg** (☎03683-403 186; www.museumwilhelmsburg.de; Schlossberg 9; adult/concession €3.50/2; ⊙10am-6pm Apr-Oct). Conceived by Landgrave Wilhelm IV of Hessen as a hunting lodge and summer residence in the 1580s, it has largely kept its original design, with lavish murals and stucco decorating most rooms.

The Drive » Head north on the L1026, as it skirts the dense Thuringian Forest, with stretches of road fully covered by ancient trees, epitomising the Avenues Route. After 22km you'll come to the village of Friedrichroda, with its pretty castle and mysterious caves, but

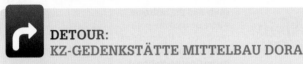

DETOUR:
KZ-GEDENKSTÄTTE MITTELBAU DORA

Start: ➎ Mühlhausen

During the final stages of WWII, when Hitler's grand plan turned to conducting war from underground bunkers, Mittelbau Dora was established as a satellite of the Buchenwald concentration camp, after British bombers destroyed missile plants in Peenemünde. At least 20,000 prisoners were worked to their deaths here. After years of decay under the GDR, the **memorial site** today gives an insight into the horrors that unfolded here, and includes a modern museum that explains the background of the camp and the experiences of the prisoners.

From late 1943, thousands of mostly Russian, French and Polish POWs (many of whom had survived Auschwitz) toiled under horrific conditions. They dug a 20km labyrinth of tunnels in the chalk hills north of Nordhausen, within which were built the V1 and V2 rockets that rained destruction on London, Antwerp and other cities during the final stages of the war. The US Army reached the gates in April 1945, cared for survivors and removed all missile equipment before turning the area over to Russia.

Visitors are free to roam the grounds, crematorium and museum. The tunnels (which are roughly the diameter of an aircraft hangar) are only accessible on free 90-minute guided tours, running at 11am and 2pm Tuesday to Friday and at 11am, 1pm and 3pm on weekends. Within the dank walls you can see partially assembled rockets that have lain untouched for decades.

To get here, head north for 29km on L1015 until you reach the A38 at exit 6 Leinefelde-Worbis, then follow it east for 26km until exit 10 Werther. Follow Kassleler Landstrasse and Strasse der Opfer des Faschismus for 8km until you reach a railway crossing. Turn left and follow the road into the memorial site.

tarry not. A further 8km north brings you to the A4 autobahn at exit 41b Gotha-Boxberg. Head east for 45km of high-octane action to exit 46 Erfurt West. From here, take the L3004 north for 11km into Erfurt.

➑ Erfurt

Thuringia's attractive capital has seen much since being founded by St Boniface in 742 as a bishopric on the Gera River. Known for its churches, steeples and synagogues, today's Erfurt is a vibrant city with an appearance that honours its medieval roots, while adding classy, contemporary flourishes. An overnight stay is recommended. Erfurt has a number of lovely squares to stroll between. Be sure to visit Domplatz and the monumentous **Erfurter Dom** (Mariendom; ☎0361-646 1265; www.dom-erfurt.de; Domplatz; ⊙9.30am-6pm Mon-Sat, 1-6pm Sun May-Oct, to 5pm Nov-Apr); **Anger**, a transport and shopping hub where old meets new; **Wenigemarkt**, the perfect place for a casual meal; and **Fischmarkt**, Erfurt's central square, where you'll find the neo-Gothic **Rathaus** and a collection of spectacular historical buildings. Museums abound, including the worthwhile **Angermuseum** (☎0361-655 1651; www.angermuseum.de; Anger 18; adult/concession €6/4; ⊙1-7pm Tue-Fri, 11am-7pm Sat & Sun), with its strong collection of medieval art, and the fascinating **Alte Synagoge** (☎0361-655 1520; www.juedisches-leben.erfurt.de; Waagegasse 8; adult/concession €8/5; ⊙10am-6pm Tue-Sun), one of Europe's oldest Jewish houses of worship.

✗ ⊫ p114

Classic Trip

The Drive » Take the B7 for 22km east, through fields of canola and wind turbines, into Weimar.

TRIP HIGHLIGHT

9 Weimar

Few German cities of Weimar's size can boast such a wealth of culture and history. Weimar's main claim to fame is that literary and philosophical titans Goethe and Schiller spent the bulk of their days here. If you're interested in these big daddies of German culture, you've come to the right place. You can't get much more authentic than **Goethe Haus** (☏03643-545 401; Frauenplan 1; adult/concession €8.50/7; ☺9am-6pm Tue-Fri & Sun, to 7pm Sat Apr-Sep, 9am-6pm Tue-Sun Oct, to 4pm Tue-Sun Nov-Mar), where for 50 years until his death in 1832 the great man toiled, penning *Faust* and other immortal works. Both his study and the bedroom where he died are both preserved in their original state. Learn all about him in the **Goethe-National-museum** (☏03643-545 400; www.klassik-stiftung.de; Frauenplan 1; adult/concession €12/8.50; ☺9.30am-6pm Tue-Sun Apr-Oct, to 4pm Nov-Mar), then take a peek at the **Nietzsche Archiv** (☏03643-545 400; www.klassik-stiftung.de; Humboldtstrasse 36; adult/concession €3/2; ☺11am-4pm Tue-Sun Apr-Oct), where the philosopher Friedrich Nietzsche spent his final years in illness. Perhaps the most spectacular and thought-provoking site is the Unesco World Heritage **Herzogin Anna Amalia Bibliothek** (☏03643-545 400; www.anna-amalia-bibliothek.de; Platz der Demokratie 1; adult/concession incl audioguide €7.50/6; ☺9.30am-2.30pm Tue-Sun), which has been beautifully reconstructed after a fire in 2004 destroyed much of the building and its priceless contents. Some of the most precious tomes are housed in the

CHRISTIAN HACKER / 500PX ©

magnificent **Rokokosaal** (Rococo Hall).

The Drive » Follow the B7 for 25km east into Jena.

10 Jena

Unlike its neighbours Erfurt and Weimar, Jena owes its beauty more to the Saale River and the surrounding limestone hills than to a wealth

TOP TIP:
WEIMARCARD

Pick up a great-value **WeimarCard** (€27.50 for two days) from the **tourist office** (☏03643-7450; www.weimar.de; Markt 10; ☺9.30am-7pm Mon-Sat, to 3pm Sun Apr-Oct, 9.30am-6pm Mon-Fri, to 2.30pm Sat & Sun Nov-Mar) for free admission to most museums, discounted tours, free iGuides and free travel on local buses if you want to let someone else do the driving for a while.

Jena The city's colourful Marktplatz

of architectural and heritage sites. That said, Jena too has an age-old history as well as a fun, modern vibe courtesy of the 19,000-strong student body that calls Jena home. The birthplace of precision optics – pioneered here by Carl Zeiss, Ernst Abbe and Otto Schott – it is Jena's pedigree as a city of science that sets it apart from other Thuringian towns. Today, several museums attest to this legacy, including the **Stadtmuseum & Kunstsammlung Jena** (City Museum & Art Collection; ☎03641-498 261; www.stadtmuseum.jena.de; Markt 7; Stadtmuseum adult/concession €4/2.40, Kunstsammlung €8/5; ☺10am-5pm Tue, Wed & Fri, 3-10pm Thu, 11am-6pm Sat & Sun), where you can learn how the city evolved into a centre of philosophy and science, and the public **Zeiss Planetarium** (☎03641-885 488; www.planetarium-jena.de; Am Planetarium 5; adult/concession €8.50/7), the world's oldest. Goethe himself planted the ginkgo tree in the wonderful **Botanischer Garten** (☎03641-949 274; www.spezbot.uni-jena.de/botanischer-garten; Fürstengraben 26; adult/concession €4/2; ☺10am-6pm), which boasts more than 12,000 plants from every climatic zone on earth.

 p115

The Drive » Head south for 51km on the delightfully green B88, through thick forests and woodlands into Saalfeld.

11 Saalfeld

Gables, turrets and gates provide a cheerful welcome to Saalfeld, which has been sitting prim and pretty along the Saale River for 1100 years. Aside from the handsome medieval town centre, you might want to check out the **Feengrotten** (Fairy Grottoes; ☎03671-550 40; www.feengrotten. de; Feengrottenweg 2; adult/child €11/6.50, with Grottoneum & Fairy World adult/child €15/8.50; ☺9.30am-5pm) if you're young at heart or travelling with kids. These former alum slate mines (1530–1850) were opened for tours in 1914 and rank among the world's most colourful grottoes, imbued with shades of brown, ochre, sienna, green and blue. Otherwise, take a stroll around the **Markt** then along Brudergasse, uphill to a 13th-century Franciscan monastery, now recycled as the **Stadtmuseum** (City Museum;

☎03671-598 471; Münzplatz 5; adult/concession/family €4/2.50/5; ☺10am-5pm Tue-Sun). Its major allure is the celestial building itself, and the collection of local late-Gothic carved altarpieces.

The Drive » Follow the B281 for 57km until the intersection with the A4 autobahn at exit 56a Hermsdorfer Kreuz. Follow the A7 east for some faster roads for 86km into Chemnitz, at exit 69 Chemnitz Mitte.

12 Chemnitz

Known from 1953 to 1990 as Karl-Marx-Stadt, Chemnitz, like most former East German cities, had to reinvent itself after reunification. It's done so with some measure of success, at least in its revitalised city centre that boasts a pedestrianised glass-and-steel shopping and entertainment district. Although you're here primarily to stretch your legs en route to Dresden, there are some engaging museums that might pique your interest: lovers of modern art should not miss **Museum Gunzenhauser** (☎0371-488 7024; www.kunstsammlungen-chemnitz. de; Falkeplatz; adult/concession €7/4.50; ☺11am-6pm Tue-Sun) and its gallery of 20th-century Expressionist works, housed in a 1930s former bank building, built in the austere New Objectivity style. **DAStietz** (☎0371-488 4397; ww.dastietz.de; Moritzstrasse

20) is a beautifully renovated 1913 former department store and now a one-stop shop for art and culture, housing the city library, **Neue Sächsische Galerie** (☎0371-367 6680; www.neue-saechsische-galerie. de; adult/child €3/free; ☺11am-5pm Thu-Mon, 11am-7pm Tue), which presents contemporary Saxon art, and the **Museum für Naturkunde** (Natural History Museum; ☎0371-488 4551; www.naturkunde-chemnitz. de; adult/concession €4/2.50; ☺10am-5pm Mon, Tue, Thu & Fri, 10am-6pm Sat & Sun), whose most interesting exhibit, the Versteinerter Wald (petrified forest), can be admired for free in the atrium; some of the stony trunks are 290 million years old.

The Drive » To get to Dresden, take the A4 autobahn from exit 69 Chemnitz Mitte for 70km to exit 78 Dresden Altstadt.

TRIP HIGHLIGHT
13 Dresden

Once known fondly as the 'Florence of the North', there are few city silhouettes more striking than Dresden's. The classic view from the Elbe's northern bank takes in spires, towers and domes belonging to palaces, churches and stately buildings, and indeed it's hard to believe that the city was all but wiped off the map by Allied bombings in 1945. Dresden's beloved domed **Frauenkirche** (p118) collapsed after the WWII bombings, and was rebuilt from a pile of rubble between 1994 and 2005. Other must-sees include **Albertinum** (p118), a Renaissance-era former arsenal transformed into the stunning home of the Galerie Neue Meister (New Masters Gallery), and one of Germany's most famous opera houses, the **Semperoper** (p118), which opened in 1841 and hosted premieres of works by Strauss, von Weber and Wagner.

See also p118 for a walking tour of Dresden.

 p115

The Drive » Getting back onto the Avenues Route, take the B6 northwest for 60km to the little town of Oschatz, where there has been a settlement since neolithic times. From here, continue on the B6 through lowlands and fields for another 56km into Leipzig.

- - - - - - - - - - -

14 Leipzig

When it comes to art, the neo-realistic New Leipzig School has stirred up the international art world for over a decade with such protagonists as Neo Rauch and Tilo Baumgär-

LOCAL KNOWLEDGE: NOCH BESSER LEBEN

In Leipzig, this locally beloved **bar** (www. nochbesserleben.com; Merseburger Strasse 25; ⊙7.30pm-4am) at the epicentre of the Plagwitz entertainment district is the perfect spot to meet a cool local crowd drinking an impressive selection of beer. With an upstairs band room, funky downstairs bar and bustling patio, it has a communal, friendly vibe for which only the German word *gemütlich* (approximately translated as cosy) will do.

tel. Such contemporary art in all media is the speciality of the **Galerie für Zeitgenössische Kunst** (☎0341-140 8126; www.gfzk-leipzig.de; Karl-Tauchnitz-Strasse 9-11; adult/concession per space €5/3, both spaces €8/4, Wed free; ⊙2-7pm Tue-Fri, noon-6pm Sat & Sun), presenting exhibits in a minimalist container-like space and a late-19th-century villa. North of Leipzig's **Naschmarkt** is **Sachsenplatz**, a massive square housing the newly built **City History Museum Annexe** (☎0341-965 130; Böttchergässchen 3; adult/child €3/2; ⊙10am-6pm Tue-Sun), hosting temporary exhibitions on a range of Leipzig-related people and themes. The city's beloved **Nikolaikirche** (Church of St Nicholas;

www.nikolaikirche-leipzig.de; Nikolaikirchhof 3; ⊙10am-6pm Mon-Sat, services 9.30am Sun) has Romanesque and Gothic roots but since 1797 has sported a striking neoclassical interior with palm-like pillars and cream-coloured pews. The design is certainly gorgeous but the church is most famous for playing a key role in the nonviolent movement that led to the downfall of the East German government.

 p115

The Drive » Head north on the B2 for 9km until the junction with the A14 autobahn at exit 23 Leipzig Mitte, then follow the A14 west for 14km until it meets the A9 autobahn at exit 15 Schkeuditzer Kreuz. Head north on the A9 for 48km into Dessau-Rosslau.

Eating & Sleeping

NORTHEASTERN GERMANY 8 GERMAN AVENUES ROUTE

Quedlinburg ②

✕ Heilemann's FachwerQ
Italian €

(☎03946-519 8051; www.fachwerq-quedlinburg.
de; Markstrasse 10; bruschetta €6-12; ⊙10am-
8pm Wed-Mon; ☞) This awesome little
bruschetta-ria (yes, there is such a thing)
overlooking the Marktkirche St Benedikti doles
out a clever selection of delicious bruschetta on
freshly baked bread, with local tomatoes and
other goodies. Pasta, wine, coffee and beer are
also served.

🛏 Romantik Hotel
am Brühl
Boutique Hotel €€

(☎03946-961 80; www.hotelambruehl.de;
Billungstrasse 11; s/d/apt from €86/113/176;
P ✳ ☞) Well-appointed, spacious rooms and
suites are individually and classically styled in
this impressive boutique hotel on the outskirts
of the Altstadt. The apartments are delightful
and an excellent option for those travelling
with children or in a small group. A plentiful
breakfast buffet is included.

Goslar ④

🛏 Hotel Alte Münze
Boutique Hotel €€

(☎05321-225 46; www.hotel-muenze.de;
Münzstrasse 10-11; s/d from €69/99; P ☞)
There's very little not to like about this boutique
hotel in the heart of the Altstadt, with a history of
over 500 years on the site. Operating as a mint in
a previous incarnation, the hotel's hotchpotch of
rooms have been beautifully brought up to date
with spotless new bathrooms, flat-screen TVs
and wi-fi to complement the antique-y, creaky,
medieval vibe.

Eisenach ⑥

✕ Weinrestaurant
Turmschänke
German €€€

(☎03691-213 533; www.turmschaenke-eisenach.
de; Karlsplatz 28; mains €15-26, 3-course menu
from €35; ⊙6-11pm Mon-Sat) This hushed
hideaway in Eisenach's only surviving medieval
city gate scores a perfect 10 on the 'romance
meter'. Walls panelled in polished oak, beautiful
table settings and immaculate service are a nice
foil for Ulrich Rösch's flavour-packed concoctions
that teeter between trendy and traditional.

Erfurt ⑧

✕ Glashütte Petersberg
European €€

(☎0361-601 5094; www.glashuette-petersberg.
de; Petersberg 11; mains €9-19; ⊙10am-11pm)
The main reason you'll want to come to this
glass cube perched high atop Erfurt's only
significant hill is for the fabulous views of the
cathedral and city below. The menu offers
a varied selection of modern German and
European fare.

🛏 Mercure Erfurt Altstadt
Hotel €€

(☎0361-594 90; www.accorhotels.com;
Meienbergstrasse 26-27; s/d from €89/109;
P ✳ ☞) The best thing about this above-
average tourist hotel is its prime location a few
blocks from lovely Wenigemarkt and the Anger
transit hub. Rooms tend to be a little pricey for
their styling, but are bright and comfortable.
Wi-fi is free. Online bargains can be found.

Jena 🔟

✖ Landgrafen

Jena   Modern European €€

(☎03641-507 071; www.landgrafen.com;
Landgrafenstieg 25; mains €10-21; ⊙3-11pm
Tue-Thu, 11.30am-11pm Fri & Sat, 11.30am-8pm
Sun) High in the hills, with stunning views over
Jena, this smart, multi-purpose restaurant
is fresh from extensive renovations. There's
a summer beer garden with bratwursts,
beverages and playthings for the kids, but the
real appeal lies within the stylish terrace (for
casual eats) or the dressy, upscale dining room.

🛏 Hotel Rasenmühle   Boutique Hotel €

(☎03641-534 2130; www.hotel-rasenmuehle.
de; Burgauer Weg 1a; s/d incl breakfast €48/55;
🅿🛜) The best thing about this modern, well-
priced, sparsely decorated 11-room private hotel
is its green, leafy location in the midst of Jena's
Paradies park. Most rooms have views over the
Saale River or parklands. Free wi-fi and parking
are a nice bonus, and a communal kitchen is
available to guests.

Dresden 🔢

✖ Raskolnikoff   International €€

(☎0351-804 5706; www.raskolnikoff.de;
Böhmische Strasse 34; mains €10-15; ⊙11am-
2am Mon-Fri, 9am-2am Sat & Sun) An artist
squat before the Wall came down, Raskolnikoff
now brims with grown-up artsy-bohemian flair,
especially in the little garden at the back. The
seasonally calibrated menu showcases the fruits
of regional terroir in globally inspired dishes, and
the beer is brewed locally. Breakfast is served
until 2pm, with an excellent brunch on Sundays.

✖ Restaurant Genuss-
Atelier   German €€

(☎0351-2502 8337; www.genuss-atelier.net;
Bautzner Strasse 149; mains €16-20; ⊙noon-
11pm Wed-Sun; 🚋11 to Waldschlösschen)
Lighting up Dresden's culinary scene is this
fantastic place that's well worth the trip on the
11 tram. The creative menu is streets ahead of
most offerings elsewhere, although the best
way to experience the 'Pleasure-Atelier' is to
book a surprise menu (three/four/five courses

€35/45/55) and let the chefs show off their
craft. Reservations essential.

🛏 Gewandhaus
Hotel   Boutique Hotel €€

(☎0351-4949 3636; www.gewandhaus-hotel.de;
Ringstrasse 1; d from €133; 🅿❄@🛜🏊) Fresh
from a total renovation and rebirth as a boutique
hotel, the stunning Gewandhaus, an 18th-century
trading house of tailors and fabric merchants that
burned down in 1945, now has sleek public areas,
beautiful and bright rooms, and a breakfast that
sets a high bar for anything else offered in the city.

🛏 Hotel Schloss Eckberg   Hotel €€€

(☎0351-809 90; www.schloss-eckberg.de;
Bautzner Strasse 134; d Kavaliershaus/Schloss
from €135/210; 🅿❄@) This romantic
castle set in its own riverside park east of the
Neustadt is a breathtaking place to stay. Rooms
in the Schloss itself are pricier and have oodles
of historic flair, but staying in the modern
Kavaliershaus lets you enjoy almost as many
amenities and the same dreamy setting.

Leipzig 🔢

✖ Auerbachs Keller   German €€€

(☎0341-216 100; www.auerbachs-keller-leipzig.
de; Mädlerpassage, Grimmaische Strasse
2-4; mains Keller €10-27, Weinstuben €33-35;
⊙Keller noon-11pm daily, Weinstuben 6-11pm
Mon-Sat) Founded in 1525, Auerbachs Keller is
one of Germany's best-known restaurants. It's
cosy and touristy but the food's actually quite
good and the setting memorable. There are two
sections: the vaulted Grosser Keller for hearty
Saxonian dishes and the four historic rooms of
the Historische Weinstuben for upscale German
fare. Reservations highly advised.

🛏 Steigenberger Grandhotel
Handelshof   Hotel €€€

(☎0341-350 5810; www.steigenberger.com/
Leipzig; Salzgässchen 6; r from €169; ❄@🛜)
Behind the imposing historic facade of a 1909
municipal trading hall, this exclusive boutique
luxury joint outclasses most of Leipzig's hotels
with its super-central location, charmingly
efficient team, and modern rooms dressed in
crisp white-silver-purple colours and complete
with high ceilings and marble bathrooms. The
stylish bi-level spa is the perfect bliss-out station.

STRETCH YOUR LEGS
BERLIN

Start/Finish: Potsdamer Platz

Distance: 4.5km

Duration: Three hours

An Instagram-worthy cocktail of culture, architecture and history, this easy and entertaining walk checks off many of the famous Berlin landmarks you've seen in newscasts and history books, and even briefly follows the course of the infamous Berlin Wall.

Take this walk on Trip

Potsdamer Platz

The historic Potsdamer Platz quarter underwent a 1990s rebirth and is a showcase of urban renewal masterminded by such international architects as Renzo Piano and Helmut Jahn. Highlights include the glass-tented Sony Center, the **Panoramapunkt** (📞030-2593 7080; www.panoramapunkt.de; Potsdamer Platz 1; adult/concession €6.50/5, without wait €10.50/8; 🕙10am-8pm Apr-Oct, to 6pm Nov-Mar, last entry 30min before closing; 🚌M41, 200, Ⓢ Potsdamer Platz, 🚉 Potsdamer Platz) observation deck and Berlin Wall remnants.

The Walk ≫ There's a large parking garage below Potsdamer Platz; enter via Reichpietschufer, Linkstrasse, Ludwig-Beck-Strasse or Schellingstrasse. After you've seen Potsdamer Platz, follow the course of the Wall by heading north on Ebertstrasse along the eastern edge of the vast Tiergarten park.

Holocaust Memorial

This memorial consists of 2711 sarcophagi-like concrete columns rising in sombre silence from undulating ground. For context visit the subterranean **Ort der Information** (Information Centre; 📞030-7407 2929; www.holocaust-mahnmal.de; Cora-Berliner-Strasse 1; audioguide adult/concession €4/2; 🕙10am-8pm Tue-Sun Apr-Sep, to 7pm Oct-Mar, last admission 45min before closing; 🚉 Brandenburger Tor), whose exhibits will leave no one untouched.

The Walk ≫ Continue north on Ebertstrasse past the US Embassy to the Brandenburg Gate.

Brandenburg Gate & Pariser Platz

A symbol of division during the Cold War, the landmark Brandenburg Gate now epitomises German reunification. Modelled after Athens' Acropolis and completed in 1791, it stands sentinel over Pariser Platz, a harmoniously proportioned square framed by banks and embassies.

The Walk ≫ From Ebertstrasse enter Tiergarten at Simsonweg and walk past the memorial for the Sinti and Roma victims of Nazi Germany to Scheidemannstrasse where the Reichstag will loom in front of you.

Reichstag

It's been burned, bombed, rebuilt, but-
tressed by the Wall, and finally turned
into the modern home of the German
parliament by Norman Foster: the 1894
Reichstag (www.bundestag.de; Platz der Republik
1; ⏱lift ride 8am-midnight, last entry 10pm; 🚌100,
🚇Bundestag, 🚉Hauptbahnhof, Brandenburger
Tor) is one of Berlin's most iconic buildings.
For guaranteed access to its glittering
glass dome, make free reservations online
or try scoring leftover tickets at the Visitors' Service. Bring ID.

The Walk ≫ Backtrack to the Brandenburg Gate,
cross Pariser Platz and walk east on Unter den
Linden, then turn right on Friedrichstrasse and left
on Französische Strasse.

Gendarmenmarkt

Berlin's most graceful square is bookend-
ed by two domed 18th-century French and
German cathedrals and punctuated by a
grandly porticoed concert hall. Climb the
tower of the French Cathedral for views.

The Walk ≫ Consider stopping in one of the
many cafes around the square, then walk west on

Mohrenstrasse to Friedrichstrasse and continue
south to Checkpoint Charlie.

Checkpoint Charlie

The principal gateway for foreigners and
diplomats between the two Berlins from
1961 to 1990, this potent symbol of the
Cold War has largely degenerated into a
tourist trap, but the free open-air exhibit
is one redeeming aspect.

The Walk ≫ Take Zimmerstrasse west to
Niederkirchner Strasse and the Topography of
Terror museum.

Topographie des Terrors

On the site where once stood the Gestapo
headquarters and other feared Nazi insti-
tutions, this compelling **exhibit** (Topography
of Terror; ☎030-2548 0950; www.topographie.
de; Niederkirchner Strasse 8; ⏱10am-8pm; 🚶;
🚇Potsdamer Platz, 🚉Potsdamer Platz) chroni-
cles the stages of terror and persecution,
puts a face on the perpetrators and details
the impact on all of Europe.

The Walk ≫ Follow Niederkirchner Strasse to
Stresemannstrasse, turn right and you'll shortly
be back at Potsdamer Platz.

STRETCH YOUR LEGS
DRESDEN

Start/Finish: Zwinger

Distance: 2km

Duration: Four hours

This walk allows you to discover the sights of Dresden's beautifully restored Altstadt (old town), taking you across and along the Elbe River and past many of the churches, palaces and museums that make Saxony's capital such a beguiling and fascinating place.

Take this walk on Trips

Zwinger

Start by entering the **Zwinger** (☎0351-4914 2000; www.der-dresdner-zwinger.de; Theaterplatz 1; ◷10am-6pm Tue-Sun), a pleasure palace built for Augustus the Strong. It now houses three excellent museums within its baroque walls, though the two most interesting are the **Gemäldegalerie Alte Meister** (www.skd.museum; Zwinger, Theaterplatz 1; adult/student €10/7.50, audioguide €3; ◷10am-6pm Tue-Sun), with its amazing collection of religious art, and the **Porzellansammlung** (www.skd.museum; Zwinger, Theaterplatz 1; adult/student €10/7.50), which has an exquisite collection of European and Asian china.

The Walk >> Park your car on or around Ostra Allee, where there's usually plenty of space (buy a parking ticket from one of the machines on weekdays). After Zwinger, head through the portal on the north side of its courtyard, and you'll emerge onto Theaterplatz.

Semperoper

On Dresden's most famous square, Theaterplatz, you'll see the city's storied opera house, the **Semperoper** (☎0351-320 7360; www.semperoper-erleben.de; Theaterplatz 2; tour adult/concession €10/6; ◷varies) on one side, the Elbe River in the distance and the impressive **Katholische Hofkirche** (Schlossplatz; ◷9am-5pm Mon-Thu, 1-5pm Fri, 10am-5pm Sat, noon-4pm Sun) to your right. This is the heart of Dresden and the history is palpable. It's possible to visit the Semperoper on a tour if you're not going to a performance.

The Walk >> Walk across the square towards the Augustusbrücke and continue over the Elbe. Walk down the steps and continue along the green riverbank, taking in the wonderful views from there before crossing back to the Altstadt along the Carolabrücke.

Albertinum

The gorgeously renovated **Albertinum** (☎0351-4914 2000; www.skd.museum; enter from Brühlsche Terrasse or Georg-Treu-Platz 2; adult/concession/under 17yr €10/7.50/free; ◷10am-6pm Tue-Sun; [P]) holds Dresden's best collection of modern art in a stunning building that's well worth wandering into even if you don't intend to visit the collection. Inside, Claude Monet's landscapes compete with the abstract visions of Marc Chagall. There's also a superb sculpture collection spread over the lower floors.

The Walk » Leaving the Albertinum, follow the walkway along the Brühlsche Terrasse for more epic river views, passing the stunning facade of the Dresden Fine Arts Academy on the way. At the bottom of the stairs, turn left onto Schlossplatz and then head through the archway.

Residenzschloss

The fabulous palace home to the Electors of Saxony, the **Residenzschloss** (☎0351-4914 2000; www.skd.museum; Schlossplatz; adult/concession €12/9; ☺10am-6pm Wed-Mon) has been spectacularly restored and contains a wealth of fascinating museums. A must-see for any visitor is the incredible collection of jewels, diamonds, gold and silver in the **Historisches Grünes Gewölbe** (Historic Green Vault; ☎0351-4914 2000; www.skd.museum; Residenzschloss; admission incl audioguide €14; ☺10am-6pm Wed-Mon) and

the **Neues Grünes Gewölbe** (New Green Vault; ☎0351-4914 2000; www.skd.museum; Residenzschloss; adult/under 17yr incl audioguide €14/free; ☺10am-6pm Wed-Mon). Don't miss the exquisite wall murals found both inside and outside the palace.

The Walk » From the palace walk the short distance to the Neumarkt, the main square of Dresden, which is dominated by the looming presence of the Frauenkirche.

Frauenkirche

Literally rising from the ashes of its WWII destruction, the magnificent **Frauenkirche** (www.frauenkirche-dresden.de; Neumarkt; audioguide €2.50, cupola adult/student €8/5; ☺10am-noon & 1-6pm) is the beloved symbol of Dresden. The original was part of the skyline for 200 years before the wartime bombings, and was rebuilt from a pile of rubble between 1994 and 2005. A spitting image of the original, it's impressive both inside and out.

The Walk » From here, walk down Taschenberg and then up Ostra Allee along the side of the Zwinger to get back to where you started.

Northwestern Germany Trips

LEARN TO LOVE GERMAN WINE AMID GORGEOUS WINERIES on these trips, which take in the fabled vineyards of the Rhine and Moselle Valleys. And you'll find more beauty outdoors as you tour the sheltered towns and pristine beaches of the North Sea.

Inside you'll find plenty to enjoy, from the churches and cultural must-sees of Cologne to the superb museums in the mighty cities of Germany's Ruhr Valley. History as far back as the Romans is found in ancient towns such as Xanten.

History of a much more fanciful sort features in the German Fairy Tale Road. The tales we all loved as children have much more complex pasts, as you'll learn in the string of towns that include the stunning Marburg and Bremen.

Moselle Valley Vineyard-ribboned valley views (Trip 13)
CALLE MONTES / GETTY IMAGES ©

Northwestern Germany Trips

Cologne An overview of the bustling city (Trip 11)

DON'T MISS

Cologne
The star of the region, Cologne makes its statement from the moment you spot the twin spires of the legendary Dom. See it on Trips **11** **12**

Wine Tasting
Learn to love Germany's often excellent white wines. Sip exquisite vintages at the source in cosy wineries amid the vineyards on Trips **12** **13** **14**

Hambacher Schloss
Visit the hilltop castle where the German flag was raised for the first time. It's on Trip **14**

Sylt
Germany's favourite upscale resort island has some of Europe's most beautiful white-sand beaches and some of Germany's most exclusive restaurants and clubs. Enjoy on Trip **9**

Sylt *A candy-striped lighthouse rises above fields and dunes*

North Sea Coast

9

This nautical whimsy whisks you from sleepy sea-shanties and enchanting islands into the heart of high-culture Hanseatic city states and the embrace of Germany's premier seaside resort.

TRIP HIGHLIGHTS

613 km

Sylt
Pamper yourself silly at Germany's favourite seaside resort

FINISH 9

● Husum

383 km

Hamburg
Wealthy Hamburg has an age-old seafaring tradition

● Bremerhaven

7

● Emden
START

263 km

6

Bremen
Cosmopolitan Bremen oozes style and culture

**5–7 DAYS
613 KM / 380 MILES**

GREAT FOR...

BEST TIME TO GO
August to September: long days and thin crowds.

ESSENTIAL PHOTO
Capture the ethereal light of a late-night North Sea sunset.

BEST FOR OUTDOORS
Walk the Wadden Sea to an East Frisian Island.

9 North Sea Coast

From Emden, lightly dusted with the flavours of its Dutch neighbours, travel along the blustery, beautiful Wadden Sea and a take-your-pick selection of enchanting East Frisian Islands, to Bremerhaven, former seat of German emigration, onwards to the high-culture city states of Bremen and Hamburg, before retiring to Sylt, Germany's luxe island resort at the Danish border.

Helgoland
Island

East Frisian
Islands
p130

Norddeich   L5

3   Norden   Wittmund

2 Greetsiel   Jeve
L4   B210   Aurich

1 Emden

Delfzijl   START   A28

NETHERLANDS   Leer

B70

① Emden

You're almost in the Netherlands here: the flat landscape, dikes and windmills outside town and the melodic twang of the local Plattdütsch dialect combine to give this quiet seafaring city a Dutch flavour. Begin your trip with a visit to the **Bunkermuseum** (☎04921-22 25; www.bunkermuseum.de; Holzsägerstrasse; adult/child €2/1; ☺10am-1pm & 3-5pm Tue-Fri, to 1pm Sat & Sun May-Oct), to remind yourself that life wasn't always this peaceful here, and check out the **Ostfriesisches Landesmuseum** (Regional History Museum; ☎0492-872 058; www.landesmuseum-emden.de; Brück-

strasse 1, Rathaus; adult/concession €6/free; ☺10am-6pm Tue-Sun) for an overview of the people whose culture and windblown landscapes you're about to explore. Ferries operated by **AG-Ems** (☎01805-180 182; www.ag-ems.de) depart Emden for Borkum, the largest of the East Frisian Islands, popular with German and Dutch families who rent houses and come for their summer vacations.

The Drive » Follow Auricher Strasse north out of town for 3.5km to Landesstrasse and turn left, through the village of Hinte, then turn right onto the K229 for 8km to the village of Jennelt. Turn right onto the L4 for 750m then follow Greetsieler Strasse for about 5km into the delightful village of Greetsiel.

② Greetsiel

The tiny, photogenic port of Greetsiel was first documented as far back as 1388. There's little to do here but stretch your legs, take a walk around the scenic harbour, check out a windmill or two and admire the handful of handsome buildings

along the harbour wall.
Why not pick up a souv-
enir while you're here?

The Drive » Turning back
the way you came, pass the two
windmills then turn left at the
roundabout towards Norddeich
on the L27: the raised bump the
road follows on your left-hand
side is a dike! Drive 14km across
the moors until you reach the
intersection with the K214 and

LINK YOUR TRIP

1 Along the Baltic Coast

From Hamburg drive
northeast for 65km
to Lübeck to join this
aquatic excursion, and
you'll have Germany's
coasts covered.

2 Design for Life: Bauhaus to VW

It's 130km of autobahn
action from Bremen
southeast to Hanover,
the final stop of our
modern, architectural-
themed jaunt.

turn left, following the road (and the dike) for 5km into Norddeich.

③ Norddeich

There's only one real reason to hang about in the busy port of Norddeich: to take the **Reederei Frisia** (📞04931-9870; www.reederei-frisia. de) ferry to Norderney or Juist, which you might just want to do. If an East Frisian island visit is on your itinerary, consider spending the night here before or after your trip. Watching the late night midsummer sun setting from the dike wall is quite an experience.

🛏 p133

The Drive » Follow Ostermarscher Strasse, which becomes the L5, for 15km to the village of Nessmersiel. This is where you'll alight for walking trips on the Wadden Sea to Baltrum, if you've booked yourself a guide. Otherwise, continue for another 17km to Bensersiel (for ferries to Langeoog), then onwards for 10km to Neuharlingersiel (ferries to Spiekeroog). It's 29km from here to Jever on the B461; follow the signs.

④ Jever

The capital of the Friesland region is also known for 'Fräulein Maria', who peers out from attractions and shop windows in Jever. She was the last of the so-called Häuptlinge (chieftains) to rule the

town in the Middle Ages, and although Russia's Catherine the Great got her hands on Jever for a time in the 18th century, locals always preferred their home-grown queen. Having died unmarried and a virgin, Maria is the German equivalent of England's (in truth more worldly) Elizabeth I. Check out her story in Jever's unique **Schloss** (📞04461-969 350; www. schlossmuseum.de; adult/concession €6/3; ⊗10am-6pm Tue-Sun), then head to the **Friesisches Brauhaus zu Jever** (📞04461-137 11; www.jever.de; Elisabethufer 18; tours adult/concession €8/4; ⊗10am-6pm Mon-Fri, to 2pm Sat) for a brewery tour and a cold pilsner.

The Drive » Head south on Mühlenstrasse then east on Silensteder Strasse until you reach the B210. Follow it south for 6km to the A29. Take the A29 south for 18km to Varel, then head east on the B437 for 38km. Pickup the A27 at exit 11 Stotel, heading north for 17km to exit 7, Bremerhaven Mitte.

⑤ Bremerhaven

Bremerhaven's waterfront Havenwelten area, with its old ships and rusty docks juxtaposed against glistening contemporary architecture, is the product of a recent re-imagining of its harbour as a place to play and learn. It's not only goods that have been shipped out for decades from Bremerhaven, one

of Europe's busiest ports, but people too: almost all German emigrants around the world headed off to their new lives from this very place. Hear their stories in the compelling **Deutsches Auswander-erhaus** (German Emigration Centre; 📞0471-902 200; www. dah-bremerhaven.de; Columbusstrasse 65; adult/concession €12.60/10.60; ⊗10am-6pm Mar-Oct, 10am-5pm Nov-Feb). Continuing on this global theme, the neighbouring **Klimahaus Bremerhaven 8° Ost** (Climate House; 📞0471-902 03 00; www.klimahaus-bremerhaven.de; Am Längengrad 8; adult/concession/family

OLAF JAINZ / GETTY IMAGES ©

NORTHWESTERN GERMANY **9** NORTH SEA COAST

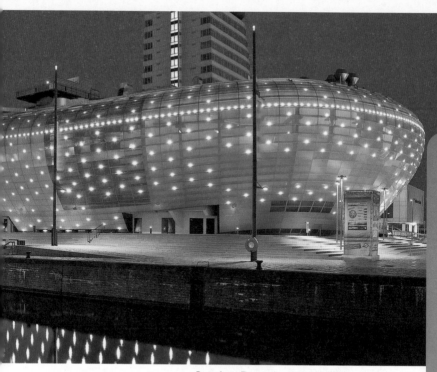

€15/11/45; ⊙10am-6pm, longer hours in summer) takes you on a fascinating journey around the world and its changing climes. If you've an inquisitive mind, both museums are reason enough to come to town.

The Drive ❯❯ Heading back inland, follow the A7 autobahn for a speedy trip south, 60km into Bremen.

- - - - - - - - - -

⑥ Bremen

Bremen, one of Germany's three city states (along with Berlin and Hamburg), has a justi-fied reputation for being among the country's most outward-looking and hospitable places, with a population that strikes a good balance between style, earthiness and good living. Bremen's vibrant districts have a host of fine restaurants, fun bars and a selection of excellent museums. Bremen's must-see **Altstadt** (old town) should be followed by a visit to the **Kunsthalle** (📞0421-329 080; www.kunsthalle-bremen.de; Am Wall 207; adult/concession €8/5; ⊙10am-6pm Wed-Sun, to 9pm Tue) for its collection of paintings and artworks: some are over 600 years old. To mix up the new with the old, take a look at the downtown **Über-see Museum** (Overseas Museum; 📞04214-160 380; www.uebersee-museum.de; Bahnhofplatz 13; adult/concession €6.50/4.50; ⊙9am-6pm Tue-Fri, from 10am Sat & Sun): exhibits on each of the world's continents offer insight into natural evolution with a dazzling collection of exotic artefacts. With over 300 engaging exhibits housed in a unique, shiny silver

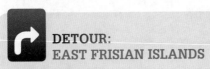

DETOUR: EAST FRISIAN ISLANDS

Start: ❸ Norddeich

Lined up like diamonds in a tiara, from west to east, the seven East Frisian islands are: Borkum, Juist, Norderney, Baltrum, Langeoog, Spiekeroog and Wangerooge. Their long sandy beaches, open spaces and sea air make them a nature-lovers' paradise and peaceful retreat. Like their North Frisian cousins Sylt, Amrum and Föhr, the islands are part of the Unesco World Heritage Wadden Sea (Wattenmeer) National Park.

When the tide recedes on the Wadden Sea, it exposes the mudflats connecting the mainland to the Islands, enabling nature-lovers to waddle their muddy way to Baltrum and its sister 'isles'. *Wattwandern*, as it is known, without an experienced guide is a no-no: tidal changes can quickly cut you off from the mainland. Tourist offices in Emden and Jever can hook you up.

If that's not your thing, a day trip or overnight stay on Norderney, Queen of East Frisia, might do the trick. Founded in 1797 by Friedrich Wilhelm II of Prussia, it fast became one of the most famous bathing destinations in Europe. The island's art-deco **Kurtheater** and the neoclassical **Conversationshaus** (1840), which today houses the tourist office, are worth a visit. But if you need to be pampered, you'll love the sprawling, luxurious **Bade:haus** (www.badehaus-norderney.de; Am Kurplatz 3; pool/sauna per 4hr €18/25; ⏱9.30am-9.30pm, women only from 2pm Wed) aquatic complex, day-spa and sauna housed in the former art-nouveau sea-water baths: reason enough for a day trip.

Tourist season runs from mid-May to September, but opening hours of tourist offices are irregular as are ferry schedules, which are subject to the tides. Same-day return trips are not always possible and advance planning is usually required.

---

building resembling a clamshell, UFO or sperm whale, depending on your interpretation, Bremen's **Universum Science Center** (☎0421-334 60; www.universum-bremen. de; Wiener Strasse 1a; adult/child €16/11; ⏱9am-6pm Mon-Fri, 10am-6pm Sat & Sun; 🚊Universität/NW1) is one of a kind.

 p133

The Drive » Pick up the A1 just outside town for a zippy 105km drive north to Hamburg and its famous port.

---

❼ Hamburg

Germany's second-largest city, and one of the world's busiest ports, has never been shy. A centre of international trade since the 19th century, it amassed great wealth and remains one of the country's richest cities, infused with a maritime spirit and an openness that has given rise to vibrant multicultural neighbourhoods.

Hamburg has more cultural and historical attractions than one can squeeze into a day or three. On **Deichstrasse** (🅄Rödingsmarkt) you can get a feel for the old canal and merchants quarter. For bird's-eye views, take the glass lift up to a 76.3m-high viewing platform in **Mahnmal St-Nikolai** (Memorial St Nicholas; ☎040-371 125; www.mahnmal-st-nikolai.de; Willy-Brandt-Strasse 60; adult/child €5/3; ⏱10am-6pm May-Sep, to 5pm Oct-Apr;

S̲Rödingsmarkt), now a WWII memorial site. Or head to the boisterous **Fischmarkt** (Grosse Elbstrasse 9; ☻5-9.30am Sun Apr-Oct, 7-9.30am Sun Nov-Mar; 🚍112 to Fischmarkt, 🚇Reeperbahn) in St Pauli, running since 1703, where every Sunday in the wee hours some 70,000 locals and visitors converge. **Hamburger Kunsthalle** (☎040-428 131 200; www.hamburger-kunsthalle.de; Glockengiesserwall; adult/child €12/free; ☻10am-6pm Tue, Wed & Fri-Sun, to 9pm Thu; S̲Hauptbahnhof) is one of Germany's most impressive art galleries, while the incredible scale of **Miniatur Wunderland** (☎040-300 6800; www.miniatur-wunderland.de; Kehrwieder 2; adult/child €13/6.50; ☻9.30am-6pm Mon, Wed & Thu, to 7pm Fri, to 9pm Tue, 8am-9pm Sat, 8.30am-8pm Sun; S̲Messberg) delights young and old.

🍴 🛏 p133

The Drive » Follow the A23 north for 105km until it becomes the B3. Continue on, across the moorish landscape for another 70km, to Husum.

----

8 Husum

Warmly toned buildings huddle around Husum's photogenic **Binnenhafen** (inner harbour), colourful gabled houses line its narrow, cobbled lanes, and in late March and early April millions of purple crocuses bloom in Husum's Schlosspark. The **Poppenspäler Museum** (☎632 42; www.pole-poppenspaeler.de; Erichsenweg 23; adult/child/family €2/1/5; ☻2-5pm Sun-Fri Apr-Dec, 2-5pm Mon, Wed & Fri Jan-Mar) has displays of enchanting handmade puppets, and even if you're not familiar with the 19th-century author, the **Theodor-Storm-Haus** (Theodor Storm House; ☎04841-803 8630; www.storm-gesellschaft.de; Wasserreihe 31-35; adult/child €3.50/2.50; ☻10am-5pm Tue-Fri, 11am-5pm Sat & 2-5pm Sun & Mon Apr-Oct, shorter hours Nov-Mar) holds appeal for its intimate depiction of a novelist's life in the rooms where he lived and worked.

The Drive » Follow the B5 north for 80km to the end of the road and about as far north in Germany as you can go. Congratulations, you made it! You can elect to leave your car on the mainland, or take the **car ferry** (☎0180-310 3030; www.syltfaehre.de; one-way/return from €45/76) over to the island.

TRIP HIGHLIGHT

9 Sylt

The star of Germany's North Frisian Islands, glamorous Sylt has

HAMBURG: A CITY SNAPSHOT

Hamburg's commercial character was forged in 1189, when local noble Count Adolf III persuaded Emperor Friedrich I (Barbarossa) to grant the city free trading rights and an exemption from customs duties. This transformed the former missionary settlement and 9th-century moated fortress of Hammaburg into an important port and member of the Hanseatic League.

The city prospered until 1842, when the Great Fire destroyed a third of its buildings. While it managed to recover in time to join the German Reich in 1871, the city was then involved in two devastating world wars. After WWI, most of Hamburg's merchant fleet (almost 1500 ships) was forfeited to the Allies. WWII saw more than half of Hamburg's housing, 80% of its port and 40% of its industry reduced to rubble; tens of thousands of civilians were killed.

In the post-WWII years, Hamburg harnessed its resilience to participate in Germany's economic miracle (Wirtschaftswunder). Its harbour and media industries are now the backbone of its wealth. The majority of Germany's largest publications are produced here, including news magazines *Stern* and *Der Spiegel*.

HELGOLAND

Helgoland's former rulers, the British, really got the better deal in 1891 when they swapped it for then-German-ruled Zanzibar. But Germans today are very fond of this lonesome North Sea outcrop of red-sandstone rock and its fresh air and warm weather, courtesy of the Gulf Stream. The 80m-tall Lange Anna (Long Anna) rock on the island's southwest edge is a compelling sight, standing alone in the ocean. There are also WWII bunkers and ruins to explore, and resurging numbers of Atlantic grey seals. Driving and cycling are not permitted on the tiny 4.2-sq-km island. By an old treaty, Helgoland is not part of the EU's VAT area, so many of the 1130 residents make their living selling duty-free cigarettes, booze and perfume to day-trippers who prowl the main drag, Lung Wai (long way). To swim, many head to neighbouring Düne, a blip in the ocean that is popular with nudists.

Helgoland makes an easy day trip, but if you want to stay, there are more than 1000 hotel beds. Get more information at www.helgoland.de. To get here from Hamburg take the **Helgoline** (📞0180-522 1445; www.helgoline.de; from Hamburg adult/child from €70/35, from Cuxhaven €57/29; ⊙from Hamburg 9am, Cuxhaven 11.30am Apr-Oct) ferry or high-speed catamaran from piers 3/4 at the St Pauli Piers.

designer boutiques housed in quintessential reed-thatched cottages, gleaming luxury automobiles jamming the car parks, luxurious accommodation and some of the country's most acclaimed restaurants. Sylt's candy-striped lighthouses rise above wide expanses of shifting dunes, fields of gleaming canola and expanses of heath. On its west coast, fierce surf and strong winds gnaw at the shoreline. In the east, the retreating low-tidal shallows of the Wadden Sea shore expose vast mudflats. Aside from pampering yourself silly and burning a hole in your wallet, you'll want to visit 5000-year-old **Denghoog** (📞04651-328 05; www.soelring-foriining. de; Am Denghoog; adult/child €4/2; ⊙10am-5pm Mon-Fri & 11am-5pm Sat & Sun Apr-Oct), a Stonehenge-esque archaeological site whose outer walls consist of 12 stones weighing around 40 tonnes, as well as the **Erlebniszentrum Naturgewalten** (Forces of Nature Centre; 📞04651-836 190; www.naturgewalten-sylt. de; Hafenstrasse 37; adult/child €14/8.50; ⊙10am-7pm Jul & Aug, 10am-6pm Sep-Jun), a state-of-the-art ecological museum dedicated to the North Sea.

✖ ⌂ p133

Eating & Sleeping

Norddeich ❸

🛏 Hotel Fährhaus   Hotel €€
(📞04931-988 77; www.hotel-faehrhaus.de; Hafenstrasse 1, Norddeich; d from €105; 🚗)
This delightful hotel by the ferry terminal in Norddeich is a great place to spend the night before or after your visit to the islands. Rooms have been brightly refurbished, there's an excellent restaurant – great for dinner and with one of the best breakfast spreads we've seen – and even a rooftop infinity pool and sauna! Late-night summer sunsets are breathtaking.

Bremen ❻

✕ Bremer Ratskeller   German €€
(📞0421-321 676; www.ratskeller-bremen.de; Am Markt 11; mains €10-20; ⏱11am-11pm)
Ratskellers were traditionally built underneath the Rathaus in every German town, to keep the citizens and civil servants fed. Bremen's is quite the experience, with high vaulted ceilings, an atmosphere that's the real deal on the historical richter scale (in business since 1405!) and good, heavy, no-fuss German food and beer. What's not to like?

🛏 Radisson Blu   Hotel €€
(📞0421-369 60; www.radissonblu.com/hotel-bremen; Böttcherstrasse 2; r from €94; 🅿🚗❄🛜🚗) The 235 guestrooms and suites of this sprawling, full-service international hotel in a premium location by the Markt have been renovated to a high standard. The hotel has annexed what was formerly the Haus Atlantis building, whose striking Himmelssaal room is now an event space. Ask at reception: if it's not in use, you can take a look.

Hamburg ❼

✕ Fischbrötchenbude
Brücke 10   Fish €
(📞040-3339 9339; www.bruecke-10.de; Landungsbrücken, Pier 10; sandwiches €2.50-

7.50; ⏱10am-10pm Apr-Oct, to 8pm Nov-Mar; ⓢLandungsbrücken, ⓡLandungsbrücken)
There are a gazillion fish sandwich vendors in Hamburg, but we're going to stick our neck out and say that this vibrant, clean and contemporary outpost makes the best. Try a classic *Bismarck* (pickled herring) or *Matjes* (brined), or treat yourself to a bulging shrimp sandwich. Lovely tables outside.

🛏 Hotel Atlantic   Luxury Hotel €€€
(📞040-288 80; www.kempinski.com; An der Alster 72-79; s/d from €160/190; ❄🛜🚗; ⓢHauptbahnhof Nord) Imagine yourself aboard a luxury ocean liner in this grand 252-room hotel, which opens onto Holzdamm. Built in 1909 for luxury-liner passengers departing for America, it has ornate stairwells, wide hallways and subtle maritime touches. It has all the services of a five-star hotel; many rooms have lake views.

Sylt ❾

✕ Söl'ring Hof   Modern European €€€
(📞04651-836 200; www.soelring-hof.de; Am Sandwall 1, Rantum; mains from €44; ⏱6.30-9.30pm May-Oct, closed Wed & Sun, shorter hours other times) You'd come here just for the location set among dunes. From the terrace you can hear the crash of the surf, muted by blowing grasses. But Chef Johannes King's kitchen is the draw, with breathtaking takes on local, seasonal produce and seafood.

🛏 Bundersand   Resort €€€
(📞04651-460 70; www.budersand.de; Am Kai 3, Hörnum; s/d from €250/320; 🅿@🛜🚗)
The 21st-century architecture is almost as stunning as the views at Sylt's most luxurious hotel. Many rooms have terraces with their own gardens where you can tickle your toes on grass while looking far out to the North Sea. The spa is legendary, use it to work out kinks generated on the beautiful private golf course.

Marburg The stunning interior of St Elizabeth's Church

Classic Trip

German Fairy Tale Road

10

You might just live happily ever after! You'll certainly end this trip happy, having explored a beautiful swath of Germany and learned the real stories behind Brothers Grimm fairy tales.

TRIP HIGHLIGHTS

642 km

Bremen
See the home (and statue) of the *Town Musicians of Bremen*

Bremerhaven
FINISH

468 km

Hamelin
You don't have to be a rat to be led to this captivating town

Hanover

276 km

Kassel
Brothers Grimm at the unmissable Grimmwelt

Göttingen

160 km

Marburg
Imagine yourself living in a fairy tale in this beautiful old town

Hanau
START

**5 DAYS
705 KM / 440 MILES**

GREAT FOR...

BEST TIME TO GO

Enjoy this trip May to September.

ESSENTIAL PHOTO

Bremen's Town Musicians of Bremen sculpture.

BEST FOR FAMILIES

Grimmwelt, Kassel's new attraction dedicated to all things Brothers Grimm and fairy-tale-worthy.

135

Classic Trip

10 German Fairy Tale Road

Tirelessly roaming the villages and towns of 19th-century Germany, the Brothers Grimm collected 209 folk tales that had been passed down for countless generations. The stories they published often bear little resemblance to the sanitised versions spoon-fed to kids today; rather they are morality tales with blood, gore, sex, the supernatural, magic and much more. See the locations of the stories and learn about these remarkable brothers on this trip, which includes a few non-Grimm fairy-tale sights as well.

❶ Hanau

A mere 20km east of Frankfurt on the Main River, Hanau is the birthplace of the Brothers Grimm (Jacob in 1785 and Wilhelm in 1786) and is a perfect place to begin this trip. Not that their birth is especially commemorated here...

Located within Philippsruhe Palace, dating from the early 18th century, the **Historisches Museum Schloss Philippsruhe** (☑06181-295 564; www.hanau.de/kultur/museen/hanau; Philippsruher Allee 45; adult/concession €4/3; ⏰11am-6pm Tue-Sun) has displays on town history, and arts and crafts. The parks and gardens (free) are a beautiful stroll in snow or in summer.

The Drive » Hop on the A66 for a quick 50km run through the rolling hills to Steinau.

❷ Steinau

Steinau is situated on the historic trade road between Frankfurt and Leipzig. (Note that the full name of the town is

136

'Steinau an der Strasse', an important distinction when using your map app as there's another Steinau way up by the North Sea.)

The twin musuems, **Brüder Grimm-Haus and Museum Steinau** (☎06663-7605; www.brueder-grimm-haus.de; Brüder Grimm-Strasse 80, Steinau; adult/concession €6/3.50; ☺10am-5pm), inside the building where the Grimm family lived from 1791 to 1796, have exhibits on the brothers, their work and the history of Steinau.

The Drive » Exit Steinau to the west on the L3196 for 18km to the B276 where you'll turn north. Weave through the valleys for 64km until the junction with the L3166 and follow the Marburg signs along the L3127, L3089, L3048 and L3125 to your destination. Picnic spots abound along the route.

LINK YOUR TRIP

2 **Design for Life: Bauhaus to VW**

At Hanover, you can join this trip, which covers iconic German centres of design.

5 **Central Germany's Castles & Palaces**

At Kassel, detour through Germany's heartland to castles and lavish palaces all the way to Leipzig.

NORTHWESTERN GERMANY **10** GERMAN FAIRY TALE ROAD

137

TRIP HIGHLIGHT

❸ Marburg

Hilly, historic and delightful, the university town of Marburg is situated 90km north of Frankfurt. It's a delight to wander around the narrow lanes of the town's vibrant **Altstadt** (old town), sandwiched between a palace (above) and the spectacular Gothic church, St Elizabeth's (below). On the south side of the focal **Marktplatz** is the historic **Rathaus** (town hall), dating to 1512. At the base of the **Altstadt's** Reitgasse is the neo-Gothic **Alte Universität** (1891), still a well-used and well-loved part of Philipps-Universität – the world's oldest Protestant university. Founded in 1527, it once counted the Brothers Grimm among its students.

Perched at the highest point in town, a steep walk up from St-Marien-Kirche or the Marktplatz, is the massive **Landgrafenschloss** (☎991 20; www.uni-marburg.de/uni-museum; Schloss 1; adult/concession €4/3; ◷10am-6pm Tue-Sun), built between 1248 and 1300. It offers panoramic views of bucolic hills, jumbled Marburg rooftops and the **Schlosspark**.

DETOUR: FULDA

Start: ❷ Steinau

Although it's not quite on the Fairy Tale Road, photogenic Fulda is well worth a side trip for those interested in sumptuous baroque architecture, historic churches and religious reliquaries. A Benedictine monastery was founded here in 744, and today Fulda has its own bishop.

Inside the baroque **Dom zu Fulda** (☎0661-874 57; www.bistum-fulda.de; Domplatz 1; ◷10am-6pm Mon-Fri, to 3pm Sat, 1-6pm Sun), built from 1704 to 1712, you'll find gilded furnishings, plenty of *putti* (figures of infant boys), some dramatic statues (eg to the left of the altar) and the tomb of St Boniface, who died a martyr in 754.

Fulda's history started in **Michaelskirche** (Michaelsberg 1; ◷10am-5pm). A still-standing reminder of the abbey that made this town, this remarkable church was the monastic burial chapel. Beneath classic witch's-hat towers, a Carolingian rotunda and crypt recall Fulda's flourishing Middle Ages, when the abbey scriptorium churned out top-flight illuminated manuscripts.

Don't miss Fulda's spectacular **Stadtschloss** (☎0661-1020; adult/concession €3.50/2.30; ◷10am-5pm Tue-Sun), built from 1706 to 1721 as the prince-abbots' residence. It now houses the city administration and function rooms. Visitors can enter the ornate **Historiche Räume** (historic rooms), including the grandiose banquet hall, and the octagonal **Schlossturm** (April to October) for great views of the town and magnificent **Schlossgarten** (palace gardens), where locals play *pétanque* (boules) and sunbathe in summer.

The palace's fairy-tale qualities capture the era's extravagance. Don't miss the amazing **Speigelkabinett** (Chamber of Mirrors) and grandiose **Fürstensaal**, a banquet hall decorated with reliefs of tipsy-looking wine queens. Also, there are pretty views from the **Green Room** over the gardens to the Orangerie.

Fulda is a mere 40km northeast of Steinau on the A66.

✕ ⸀ p146

The Drive » Leave Marburg to the north on the B3, after 18km turn north on the L3073. Continue north for 37km through Gemunden and Frankenau to Edertal where you'll find the park. Note how the forest gets thicker and darker as you go.

- - - - - - - - - - -

④ Kellerwald-Edersee National Park

Kellerwald-Edersee National Park (www.national park-kellerwald-edersee.de) encompasses one of the largest extant red-beech forests in Central Europe, the **Kellerwald**, and the **Edersee**, a serpentine artificial reservoir 55km northeast of Marburg and about the same distance southwest of Kassel. In 2011 this national park, along with Hainich National Park in Thuringia and a cluster of other parks and reserves with large beech forests, became a Unesco World Cultural Heritage site.

On a fairy-tale trip, it's fitting to wander into the deep woods, never forgetting that if your name is Grimm, nothing good is bound to happen. If you're lucky, you may see larger land animals including red deer; while overhead you might spot eagles and honey buzzards and, at night, various species of bat. (The brothers would approve of that.)

For information, head to the striking modern **visitors centre** (☏05635-992 781; www.nationalpark zentrum-kellerwald.de; B252, Vöhl-Herzhausen; e-bikes per day €20; ⊙10am-6pm Apr-Oct, to 5pm Nov-Mar) at the western end of the Edersee.

The Drive » Drive east on the L3332, B485 and the B253 for 28km until you reach the A49 autobahn and zip along northeast until you reach Kassel.

- - - - - - - - - - -

TRIP HIGHLIGHT

⑤ Kassel

Visitors to this culture-rich, sprawling hub on the Fulda River discover a pleasant, modern city.

Occupying a prime position atop the Weinberg bunker in the scenic Weinbergpark is the truly most unmissable attraction on this trip: Kassel's newest musuem, **Grimmwelt** (☏0561-598 610; www.grimmwelt.de; Weinbergstrasse; adult/concession €8/6; ⊙10am-6pm Tue-Sun). It could be described as an architect-designed walk-in sculpture housing the most significant collection of Brothers Grimm memorabilia on the planet. Visitors are guided around original exhibits, state-of-the-art installations and fun, hands-on activities, aided by entries from the Grimms' German dictionary: there were more to these famous brothers than just fairy tales, didn't you know?

Billed as 'a meditative space for funerary art', the **Museum für Sepulkralkultur** (Museum of Sepulchral Culture; ☏0561-918 930; www.sepulkralmuseum.de; Weinbergstrasse 25-27; adult/concession €6/4; ⊙10am-5pm Tue & Thu-Sun, to 8pm Wed) aims at burying the taboo of discussing death.

✕ ⸀ p146

The Drive » Your shortest jaunt of the trip takes you 6km west through Kassel's leafy suburbs. Take Wilhelmshöher Allee.

- - - - - - - - - - -

⑥ Wilhelmshöhe

Wilhelmshöhe is the classy end of Kassel. You can spend a full day exploring the spectacular baroque parkland, **Bergpark Wilhelmshöhe** (www.museum-kassel.de; ⊙9am-sunset), which takes its name from **Schloss Wilhelmshöhe** (☏0561-316 800; www.museum-kassel.de; Schlosspark 1; adult/concession €6/4, Weissenstein wing incl tour €4/3; ⊙10am-5pm Tue & Thu-Sun, to 8pm Wed), the late-18th-century palace situated inside the expanse. Walk through the forest, enjoy a romantic picnic and explore the castles, fountains, grottoes, statues and water features: the **Herkules** (www.museum-kassel.de; Schlosspark Wilhelmshöhe 26, Herkules-Terrassen; adult/concession €3/2; ⊙10am-5pm mid-Mar–mid-Nov) statue and Löwenburg castle are also here.

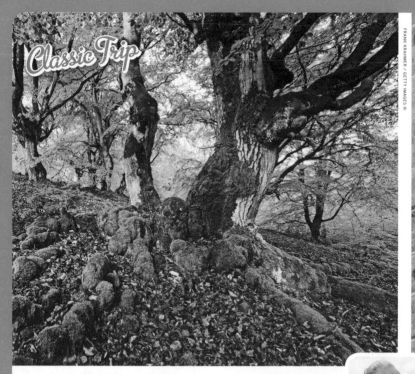

FRANK KRAMER / GETTY IMAGES ©

ONE AND ONLY / SHUTTERSTOCK ©

WHY THIS IS A CLASSIC TRIP
RYAN VER BERKMOES, AUTHOR

Did they give us nightmares or fantasies? Or both? Who can forget hearing the wild stories of the Brothers Grimm as a child? Evil stepmothers, dashing princes, fair maidens, clever animals, mean old wolves and more. With every passing year, these stories become more sanitised. But the real fairy tales are far more compelling, as you'll learn on this trip.

Top: Beech trees in Kellerwald-Edersee National Park
Left: Brothers Grimm sculpture in Hanau
Right: The exterior of an old building in Marburg

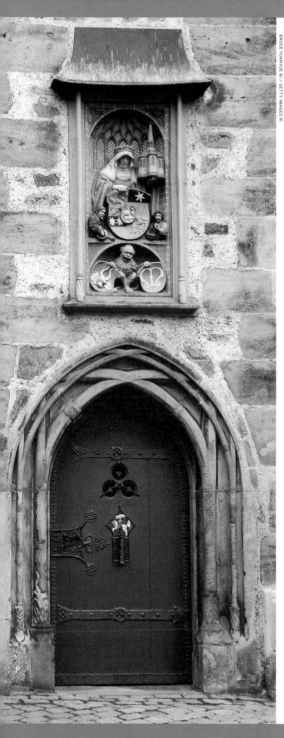

The palace could star in any fairy tale. Home to Elector Wilhelm and later Kaiser Wilhelm II, the opulent complex today houses one of Germany's best collections of Flemish and Dutch baroque paintings, featuring works by Rembrandt, Rubens, Jordaens, Lucas Cranach the Elder, Dürer and many others in the Gemäldegalerie (painting gallery).

✖️ 🛏️ p146

The Drive >> Retrace your 6km drive on Wilhelmshöher Allee into Kassel and take the busy A7 right up to Göttingen.

- - - - - - - - - - -

❼ Göttingen

With over 30,000 students, this historic town nestled in a corner of Lower Saxony near the Hesse border offers a good taste of university-town life in Germany's north. Since 1734, the Georg-August Universität has sent more than 40 Nobel Prize winners into the world. As well as all those award-winning doctors and scientists, it also produced the fairy-tale-writing Brothers Grimm (as German linguistic teachers).

Be sure to stroll around the pleasant **Markt** and nearby Barfüsser-strasse to admire the *Fachwerk* (half-timbered) houses.

The city's symbol, the **Gänseliesel** (little goose girl) statue on Markt is hailed locally as the most kissed woman in the world – not a flattering moniker, you might think, but enough to make her iconic.

 p147

The Drive » Take the L561 22km west to the B80, then head northwest for another 27km to Bad Karlshafen. You'll enjoy the curving panoramas as you follow the Weser River, which links several of the Fairy Tale Road towns and cities.

8 Bad Karlshafen

Bad Karlshafen's orderly streets and whitewashed baroque buildings were built in the 18th century for the local earl Karl by French Huguenot refugees. The town was planned with an impressive harbour and a canal connecting the Weser with the Rhine to attract trade, but the earl died before his designs were completed. The only reminder of his grand plans is a tiny **Hafenbecken** (harbour basin) trafficked by white swans.

Take a stroll around the town centre, on the sinuous Weser River's south bank, with the Hafenbecken and surrounding square, **Hafenplatz**, at its western end.

The interesting **Deutsches Huguenotten Museum** (German Huguenot Museum; 05672-1410; www.huguenot-museum-germany.com; Hafenplatz 9a; adult/concession €4/2; 10am-5pm Tue-Fri, 11am-6pm Sat & Sun mid-Mar–Oct, 10am-noon Mon-Fri Nov–mid-Mar) traces the history of the French Huguenot refugees in Germany, although it fails to mention how many were eaten by big bad wolves in the forest during the journey.

The Drive » Just stay on B83 for the 58km right to Bodenwerder. You'll enjoy Weser vistas for much of the journey – which might lure you to stop for a picnic.

9 Bodenwerder

If Bodenwerder's most famous son were to

GRIMM FAIRY TALES

In the early 19th century the Brothers Grimm travelled extensively through central Germany documenting folklore. Their collection of tales, *Kinder- und Hausmärchen*, was first published in 1812 and quickly gained international recognition. It has 209 tales and includes such fairy-tale staples as:

» *Hansel and Gretel* – A mother tries to ditch her son and daughter, a witch tries to eat them and Gretal outsmarts her. Kids and father reunite and all are happy (the evil mum has died).

» *Cinderella* – The story that gave step-sisters a bad name. Still, when the prince fits the shoe onto our heroine, all is good with the world, although in the Grimm version, the step-sisters are blinded by vengeful doves.

» *Rapunzel* – An adopted girl with very long hair, a prince that goes blind and some evil older women are combined in this morality play that ends on a love note when the prince stumbles upon an outcast Rapunzel and his sight is restored. In the first edition of the Grimm's book, Rapunzel bore children out of wedlock.

For entertaining synopses of all the Grimm fairy tales, see www.shmoop.com/grimms-fairy-tales. One thing you'll note is that the Grimm original versions are much bloodier, more violent and earthier than the ultra-sanitised, Disneyfied versions today.

Although best known for their fairy tales, it should be be noted that the Brothers Grimm were serious academics who also wrote *German Grammar* and *History of the German Language*, enduring works that populate reference shelves to this day.

have described his little hometown, he'd probably have painted it as a huge, thriving metropolis on the Weser River. But then Baron Hieronymous von Münchhausen (1720–97) was one of history's most shameless liars (his whoppers were no mere fairy tales). He inspired the Terry Gilliam cult film, *The Adventures of Baron Munchausen*.

Bodenwerder's principal attraction, the **Münchhausen Museum** (☎05533-409 147; Münchhausenplatz 1; adult/child €2.50/1.50; ⊙10am-5pm Apr-Oct), tackles the difficult task of conveying the chaos and fun associated with the 'liar baron' – a man who liked to regale dinner guests with his Crimean adventures, claiming he had, for example, tied his horse to a church steeple during a snow drift and ridden around a dining table without breaking one teacup. Among other artefacts, it also has paintings and displays of Münchhausen books in many languages.

The Drive » The unofficial spine for some of the Fairy Tale Road route, the B83 again takes you north, for 23km from Bodenwerder to Hamelin.

TRIP HIGHLIGHT

⑩ Hamelin

According to the Brothers Grimm in *The Pied Piper of Hamelin,* in the 13th century the Pied Piper

THE FAIRY TALE ROAD

The 600km **Märchenstrasse** (Fairy Tale Road; www.deutsche-maerchenstrasse.com/en) is one of Germany's most popular tourist routes, with over 60 stops along the way. It's made up of cities, towns and hamlets in four states (Hesse, Lower Saxony, North Rhine-Westphalia and Bremen), which can often be reached by using a choice of roads rather than one single route. The towns are associated in one way or another with the works of Wilhelm and Jacob Grimm. Although most towns can be easily visited using public transport, a car lets you fully explore the route.

(*Der Rattenfänger*) was employed by Hamelin's townsfolk to lure its rodents into the river. When they refused to pay him, he picked up his flute and led their kids away. Today, the rats rule once again – fluffy and cute stuffed rats, wooden rats, and tiny brass rats adorn the sights around town.

Rodents aside, Hamelin (Hameln in German) is a pleasant town with half-timbered houses and opportunities for cycling along the Weser River, on the eastern bank of which lies Hamelin's circular **Altstadt**. The town's heart is its **Markt**.

Many of Hamelin's finest buildings were constructed in the Weser Renaissance style, which has strong Italian influences. Learn more at the town's revamped **Museum Hamelin** (☎05151-202 1215; www.museum-hameln.de; Osterstrasse 8-9; adult/concession €5/4; ⊙11am-6pm Tue-Sun), which has historical displays.

✕ ⊨ p147

The Drive » Leave the pastoral charms of Hamelin as you drive 47km northwest on the B217 to the modern vibe of busy Hanover.

⑪ Hanover

Known for its huge trade shows, Hanover has a past: from 1714, monarchs from the house of Hanover also ruled Great Britain and the entire British Empire for over a century.

Let your hair down at the spectacularly baroque **Herrenhäuser Gärten** (☎0511-1683 4000; www.hannover.de/Herrenhausen; Herrenhäuser Strasse 4; general admission free; ⊙9am-6pm, grotto to 5.30pm Apr-Oct, 9am-4.30pm, grotto to 4pm Nov-Mar; ⓤHannover Herrenhäuser Gärten), the grandiose baroque Royal Gardens of Herrenhausen, which are considered one of the most important historic garden landscapes in Europe. Inspired by the gardens at Versailles, they're a great place to

WESTEND61 / GETTY IMAGES ©

Classic Trip

NORTHWESTERN GERMANY **10** GERMAN FAIRY TALE ROAD

slow down and smell the roses for a couple of hours, especially on a blue-sky day. With its fountains, neat flowerbeds, trimmed hedges and shaped lawns, the 300-year-old **Grosser Garten** (Great Garden) is the centrepiece of the experience.

The Drive » Germany's famed autobahns make quick work of the 127km to Bremen: take the A352 16km to the A7, then shoot northwest on that road and the A27. It will feel like you've arrived before you left, unless you get caught in a *Stau* (traffic jam).

TRIP HIGHLIGHT

⑫ Bremen

Bremen is well known for its fairy-tale character, a unique expressionist quarter and (it must be said, because Bremeners are avid football fans) one of Germany's most exciting football teams.

With high, historic buildings rising up from this very compact square, Bremen's **Markt** is one of the most remarkable in northern Germany. The two towers of the 1200-year-old **Dom St Petri** (St Petri Cathedral; ☎0421-334 7142; www.stpetridom.de; Sandstrasse 10-12; tower adult/concession €1/0.70, museum €3/2; ⏰10am-5pm Mon-Fri, to 2pm

Sat, 2-5pm Sun) dominate the northeastern edge, beside the ornate and imposing **Rathaus**, which was erected in 1410. The Weser Renaissance balcony in the middle, crowned by three gables, was added between 1595 and 1618.

In front of the Rathaus is one of the hallmarks of Bremen, the city's 13m-high Knight Roland statue (1404). As elsewhere, Roland stands for the civic freedoms of a city, especially the freedom to trade independently.

On the western side of the Rathaus you'll find the city's unmissable and famous symbol of the Grimm fairy tale: the **Town Musicians of Bremen** (1951) by the sculptor Gerhard Marcks. The story tells of a donkey, a dog, a cat and a rooster who know their time is up with their cruel masters, so set out for Bremen and the good life. On the way they encounter a forest cottage filled with robbers. They cleverly dispatch the crooks and, yes, live happily ever after. The statue depicts the dog, cat and rooster, one on top of the other, on the shoulders of the donkey. The donkey's nose and front legs are incredibly shiny having been touched by many visitors for good luck.

✕ 🛏 p147

The Drive » Another quick shot up the autobahn, the A27, for 65km will bring you to Bremerhaven and the North Sea.

⑬ Bremerhaven

Anyone who has had the fairy-tale dream of running away to sea will love Bremerhaven's waterfront – part machinery of the trade, part glistening glass buildings pointing to a more recent understanding of its harbour as a recreation spot.

Bremen Knight Roland statue in the Markt

Bremerhaven has long been a conduit that gathered the 'huddled masses' from the verdant but poor countryside and poured them into the world outside. Of the millions who landed in America, a large proportion sailed from here, and an enticing exhibition at the **Deutsches** **Auswandererhaus** (German Emigration Centre; ☎0471-902 200; www.dah-bremerhaven. de; Columbusstrasse 65; adult/concession €12.60/10.60; ☺10am-6pm Mar-Oct, 10am-5pm Nov-Feb), the city's prime attraction, allows you to share their history. The museum stands exactly in the spot where 7.2 million emigrants set sail between 1830 and 1974. Your visit begins at the wharf where passengers gathered before boarding a steamer. You then get to visit passenger cabins from different periods (note the improving comfort levels) before going through the immigration process at Ellis Island.

Classic Trip

Eating & Sleeping

Marburg ❸

✘ Bückingsgarten — German €€
(☎06421-165 7771; www.bueckingsgarten-marburg.de; Landgraf-Philipp-Strasse 6; mains €8-24; ☺noon-10pm) Choose from two separate menus at this historical restaurant with a spectacular hilltop position adjacent to the castle. Dine inside for more upscale ambience and fare, or enjoy a beer and casual meal in the beer garden: both have excellent views.

✘ Café Barfuss — Cafe €
(☎06421-253 49; www.cafebarfuss.de; Barfüsserstrasse 33; meals €4-15; ☺10am-1am; ✎) A local institution, humble Barfuss is a no-fuss, offbeat place with a steady stream of sociable student diners who favour its diverse menu of hearty, healthy plates, including great breakfasts and a variety of vegetarian options.

⊨ Vila Vita Rosenpark — Hotel €€
(☎06421-600 50; www.rosenpark.com; Anneliese Pohl Allee 7-17; s/d from €116/126; P✻@☎☀) Marburg's swankiest and priciest digs are in a lovely spot by the river, a short stroll from the station. If you're going to splurge, superior double rooms and suites offer better value at almost twice the size of classic single rooms. An expansive wellness centre, day spa and two restaurants come with the package.

⊨ Welcome Hotel Marburg — Hotel €€
(☎06421-9180; www.welcome-hotel-marburg.de; Pilgrimstein 29; s/d from €93/122; ✻@☎) Just below the Altstadt, this central hotel has 147 bright, spacious rooms with large windows. Ask for a quieter room at the rear of the building.

Kassel ❺

✘ Lohmann — German €€
(☎0561-701 6875; www.lohmann-kassel.de; Königstor 8; mains €8-18; ☺noon-11pm Sun-Fri, 5-11pm Sat) With roots that go back to 1888, this popular, family-run *Kneipe* (pub) has an old-style birch-and-maple-shaded beer garden with an outdoor grill. Schnitzel (always pork) features heavily on the menu.

⊨ Pentahotel Kassel — Boutique Hotel €
(☎0561-933 9887; www.pentahotels.com; Bertha-von-Suttner Strasse 15; d from €55; P✻☎) This modern, central hotel has compact, stylish rooms with ambient lighting, arty design elements and free high-speed wi-fi. There's a bar and restaurant and free late checkout of 3pm on Sundays (subject to availability).

Wilhelmshöhe ❻

✘ Matterhorn Stübli — Swiss €€
(☎0561-399 33; www.matterhornstuebli.de; Wilhelmshöher Allee 326; mains €14-22; ☺5.30-11pm Tue-Sat, noon-2pm & 5.30-11pm Sun; ✎) If you love cheese, fondue, schnitzel, or all three, you're well advised to hotfoot it to this quaint Swiss restaurant. If you like mushrooms as well, try the *Original Züri Geschnätzläts:* veal escalopes served with mushrooms and crispy rösti.

⊨ Kurpark Hotel Bad Wilhelmshöhe — Boutique Hotel €€
(☎0561-318 90; www.kurparkhotel-kassel.de; Wilhelmshöher Allee 336; s/d from €105/137; P✻☎☀) In an excellent location near the castle and train station, this stylish hotel offers well-appointed rooms and common areas, a restaurant and terrace, and an indoor pool.

Göttingen ➐

✗ Zum Szultenburger   German €€

(📞0551-431 33; Prinzenstrasse 7; mains €8-20;
🕐noon-2.30pm & 5.30-11pm Tue-Sat) This
traditional German pub does things to the
humble schnitzel that will make your mouth
water. It's cosy and cheap, the varied menu is all
kinds of delicious, and the staff seem happy to be
here, which makes all the difference. Cash only.

Hamelin ➓

✗ Klütturm   Modern European €€

(📞05151-962 620; www.kluetturm-restaurant.
de; Klütturm 1; mains €12-22) If you fancy
a splurge, take a drive into the hills above
Hamelin to this classy hotel-restaurant serving
well-executed modern-European dishes. The
setting is wonderful, with an expansive terrace
and magnificent views. If you find yourself in the
mood, you can also stay the night.

✗ Rattenfängerhaus   German €€

(📞05151-3888; www.rattenfaengerhaus.
de; Osterstrasse 28; mains €10-23; 🕐11am-
10pm) One of Hamelin's finest ornamental
Weser Renaissance–style buildings, the
Rattenfängerhaus (from 1602) is also home
to a favourite, unashamedly tourist-centric
restaurant, which has been serving 'rats' tails'
flambéed at your table since 1966; don't fret –
it's all a pork-based ruse. Aside from the novelty
dishes, standard schnitzels, herrings, vegie
dishes, and 'rat killer' herb liquor are also offered.

🛏 Komfort-Hotel Garni
Christinenhof   Boutique Hotel €€

(📞05151-950 80; www.christinenhof-hameln.
de; Alte Marktstrasse 18; s/d incl breakfast
€90/115; 🅿🛜🏊) Historic outside, modern in,
this quaint hotel has some neat touches, such
as a tiny swimming pool in the vaulted cellar, a
sauna, compact but pleasant and uncluttered
rooms, and a generous buffet breakfast.

🛏 Schlosshotel
Münchhausen   Hotel €€€

(📞05154-706 00; www.schlosshotel-
muenchhausen.com; Schwöbber 9, Aerzen bei
Hamelin; s/d tithe barn from €110/140, castle
from €135/180, ste €345-445; 🅿🍴❄🛜)
Palatial Schlosshotel Münchhausen, 15km
outside Hamelin, is a popular spot for weddings
and high-end functions. Stylish, contemporary
rooms in the main wing have historic
touches, while the suites have tasteful period
furnishings. Rooms in the adjacent Tithe barn
are entirely modern. Two restaurants, lavish spa
facilities and two golf courses set in 8 hectares
of parkland round off this luxurious option.

Bremen ⑫

✗ Engel Weincafe   Cafe €

(📞0421-6964 2390; www.engelweincafe-
bremen.de; Ostertorsteinweg 31; dishes €4-13;
🕐8am-1am Mon-Fri, 10am-1am Sat & Sun;
🛜🍴) Exuding the nostalgic vibe of a former
pharmacy, this popular hang-out gets a good
crowd no matter where the hands on the clock.
Come for breakfast, a hot lunch special, crispy
Flammkuchen (regional pizza), carpaccio or
pasta, or just some cheese and a glass of wine.

✗ Ständige Vertretung   German €€

(📞0421-320 995; www.staev.de;
Böttcherstrasse 3-5; mains €9-20; 🕐11.30am-
11pm) An offshoot of Berlin's best-known
restaurant for homesick Rhineland public
servants, this large, bustling place thrives on its
political theme and solid cuisine, washed down
with Rhineland wines and beer.

🛏 Hotel Bölts am Park   Hotel €€

(📞0421-346 110; www.hotel-boelts.de;
Slevogtstrasse 23; s/d €65/85; 🅿🛜) This
cosy family-run hotel in a leafy neighbourhood
has real character, from the wonderfully old-
fashioned breakfast hall to its well-proportioned
doubles.

🛏 Park Hotel Bremen   Hotel €€€

(📞0421-340 80; www.park-hotel-bremen.de;
Im Bürgerpark; s/d from €129/149, ste from
€635; 🅿🍴@🛜🏊) Although it's exterior is
certainly dated, this domed lakeside mansion,
surrounded by parkland, impresses through its
sheer extravagance and could be considered
Bremen's only true five-star, grand hotel. It
offers access to excellent spa, fitness and
beauty facilities, a heated outdoor pool and
views over the lake in a 'spa resort' ambience.

Cologne Houses along the
Rhine riverbank

Cologne & the Ruhr Valley

11

Romans, steel and medieval treasures together forge an unbeatable trip through Germany's former industrial heartland, now the site of myriad and compelling reinventions.

TRIP HIGHLIGHTS

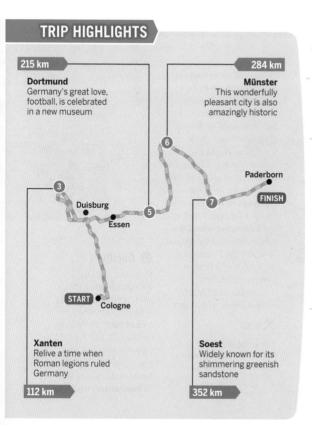

215 km

Dortmund
Germany's great love, football, is celebrated in a new museum

284 km

Münster
This wonderfully pleasant city is also amazingly historic

Paderborn

FINISH

Duisburg

Essen

START **Cologne**

Xanten
Relive a time when Roman legions ruled Germany

112 km

Soest
Widely known for its shimmering greenish sandstone

352 km

4 DAYS
404 KM / 251 MILES

GREAT FOR...

BEST TIME TO GO

Enjoy the food, drink and culture any time, but April to October is more fun for outside.

ESSENTIAL PHOTO

The weirdly green stone of Soest shimmering in the sun.

BEST FOR FAMILIES

Xanten's Römer-Museum brings the past alive for all ages.

11 Cologne & the Ruhr Valley

The Anabaptists were a religious cult that took over the then-pious city of Münster in 1535 – they didn't last but you can learn about their wild ideas at that beautiful city's impressive LWL-Museum für Kunst und Kultur. There are also many other fascinating stories here in one of Germany's most historic regions, which boasts dramatic chapters from Roman times till today.

❶ Cologne

Cologne is like a 3D text-book on history and ar-chitecture. Drifting about town you'll stumble upon an ancient Roman wall, medieval churches such as the magnificent **Dom** (cathedral) and more.

But many don't realise that Germany's fourth-largest city was founded by the Romans in 38 BC and given the lofty name Colonia Claudia Ara Agrippinensium. You can still find evidence of this past around town.

Sculptures and ruins displayed outside the entrance of the **Römisch-Germanisches Museum** (Roman Germanic Museum; ☏0221-2212 4438; www.

museenkoeln.de; Roncalliplatz 4; adult/concession €9/5; �10am-5pm Tue-Sun) are merely the overture to a full symphony of Roman artefacts found along the Rhine. Highlights include the giant Poblicius tomb (AD 30–40) and the magnificent 3rd-century **Dionysus mosaic**. Discover more of Cologne's past at the **Archäologische Zone** (p186), which at its deepest level has the Praetorium, with relics of a Roman governor's palace.

See also p186 for a walking tour of Cologne.

 p155

The Drive » Travel at very un-Roman speeds north on the A3 autobahn 73km to Duisburg.

❷ Duisburg

Duisburg is home to Europe's largest inland port, whose immensity is best appreciated on a **boat tour** (Weisse Flotte Duisburg; ☏0203-713 9667; www.wf-duisburg.de; adult/concession €14/7; �Apr-Nov). Embarkation is at the **Schwanentor**, which is also the gateway to the Innenhafen Duisburg (inner harbour), an urban quarter with a mix of modern and restored buildings.

Now a unique performance space and an all-ages adventure playground, **Landschaftspark Duisburg-Nord** (Landscape Park Duisburg-Nord; 📞0203-429 1942; www.landschaftspark. de; Emscherstrasse 71) is a decommissioned iron works where molten iron used to flow 24/7 from its fiery furnaces.

LINK YOUR TRIP

10 **German Fairy Tale Road**

Join this route at Bad Karlshafen, 66km east from Paderborn on the B64.

12 **Romantic Rhine**

At Cologne, follow the riverscape along the world-famous Rhine.

The Drive » Escape Duisburg on the A40, cross the ship-buzzing Rhine and take exit 10 and the L287 north. At Rheinberg, join the B57, which is helpfully named Xantener Strasse. It's now a straight shot northwest for 19km to Xanten.

TRIP HIGHLIGHT

③ Xanten

Xanten has been the hub of the Lower Rhine ever since it was founded as a Roman military camp in 12 BC. Within a century it grew into a respectable settlement called Colonia Ulpia Traiana.

Revel in all things Roman at the **Archäolo-gischer Park** (Archaeological Park; ☑02801-988 9213; www.apx.lvr.de; Wardter Strasse 2; incl RömerMuseum adult/child €9/free; ☺9am-6pm Mar-Oct, 10am-4pm Nov-Feb; ♿). Its highlight is the **RömerMuseum** (☑02801-988 9213; www.apx.lvr.de; Siegfriedstrasse 39; incl Archäologischer Park adult/child €9/free; ☺9am-6pm Mar-Oct, 10am-4pm Nov-Feb; ♿), which takes you on a journey through 400 years of Roman presence in the Lower Rhine region.

The crown jewel of Xanten's **Altstadt** (old town) is the **Dom St Viktor** (☑02801-713 10; www.stviktor-xanten.de; Kapitel 8; ☺10am-6pm Mon-Sat, 12.30-6pm Sun Apr-Oct, to 5pm Nov-Mar), which has Romanesque roots but is now largely Gothic.

✗ 🛏 p155

The Drive » Leave Xanten driving south for 14km to the well-sign-posted A57. Continue south on this autobahn for 18km to the A40 and go due east 33km to the post-industrial surrounds of Essen and head directly to the centre.

④ Essen

It's taken a few decades, but Germany's seventh-largest city has mastered the transition from industrial powerhouse to city of commerce and culture like few others.

A grande dame among Germany's art repositories, the **Museum Folkwang** (☑0201-884 5314; www.museum-folkwang.de; Goethestrasse 41; ☺10am-6pm Tue-Sun, to 8pm Thu & Fri) has sparkling digs with galleries radiating out from inner courtyards and gardens.

Do not miss a visit to the **Zollverein Coal Mine** (☑0201-830 3636; www.zollverein.de; Gelsenkirchener Strasse 181; ice skating rink €6.50; ☺visitors centre 10am-7pm Apr-Oct, 10am-5pm Nov-Mar), the Unesco-listed vast industrial complex whose star is the **Ruhr Museum** (☑0201-2468 1444; www.ruhrmuseum.de; Fritz-Schupp-Allee 15; adult/child €8/free; ☺10am-6pm). Engaging exhibits span the history of the region. Just as the coal was transported on conveyor belts, a long escalator whisks you up to the foyer from where you descend into the building's dark bowels.

LOCAL KNOWLEDGE: WHAT'S A RUHRGEBIET?

Once known for its belching steelworks and filthy coal mines, the Ruhrgebiet – a sprawling postindustrial region of 53 cities and 5.3 million people – has worked hard in recent years to reinvent itself for the post-industrial future. It includes Dusiburg, Essen and Dortmund, all stops on this route.

Xanten The altar of Dom St Viktor

The Drive >> You are back on the busy A40 for the 38km to Dortmund. Evidence of the once-great industrial might of the Ruhrgebiet are everywhere as you travel.

TRIP HIGHLIGHT

❺ Dortmund

Football (soccer) is a major Dortmund passion. Borussia Dortmund, the city's team in the Bundesliga (Germany's first league), has been national champion eight times, including for the 2011–12 season (they were runners-up in 2013–14).

So it's appropriate that the city is home to

the new **DFB-Museum** (German Football Museum; ☎0231-476 4660; www. fussballmuseum.de; Königswall; adult/concession €17/14; ⏰9am-5pm Tue-Sun). Classic scenes of German football triumphs play across the facade of this vast new shrine to the nation's passion. Right outside the Hauptbahnhof (central train station), the museum has 6900 sq metres of exhibits dedicated to the nation's football passion.

✕ p155

The Drive >> Leave the bustle of Dortmund on the B1 heading east for 13km. At the A1

autobahn, turn north and head up to Münster.

TRIP HIGHLIGHT

❻ Münster

One of the most appealing cities between Cologne and Hamburg, Münster has a beautiful centre with many architectural gems. The **Altstadt** is ringed with beautiful lakes and parks, buzzing with cyclists.

The two massive towers of **Dom St Paul** (☎0251-495 6700; www.paulusdom.de; Domplatz 28; ⏰6.30am-7pm Mon-Sat, to 7.30pm Sun) match the proportions of this 110m-long structure and the vast

153

THE KRUPP DYNASTY

In the Ruhrgebiet, steel and Krupp are virtually synonyms. So are Krupp and Essen, for it's this bustling Ruhrgebiet city that is the ancestral seat of the Krupp family and the headquarters of one of the most powerful corporations in Europe.

It all began rather modestly in 1811 when Friedrich Krupp and two partners founded a company to process 'English cast steel', but, despite minor successes, he left a company mired in debt upon his death in 1826. Enter his son Alfred, then a tender 14, who would go on to become one of the seminal figures of the industrial age.

It was through the production of the world's finest steel that the 'Cannon King' galvanised a company that – by 1887 – employed more than 20,000 workers. In an unbroken pattern of dazzling innovation, coupled with ruthless business practices, Krupp produced steel and machinery that was essential to the world economy.

Krupp will forever be associated, however, with the Third Reich. Not only did the corporation supply the hardware for the German war machine, it also provided much of the financial backing that Hitler needed to build up his political power base. Krupp plants were prime targets for Allied bombers. After the war, the firm slowly lost its way and in 1999 merged with arch-rival company Thyssen.

square it overlooks. It's a three-nave construction built in the 13th century. Nearby, the **Historisches Rathaus** (Historic City Hall; ☏0251-492 2724; Prinzipalmarkt 8-9; Friedenssaal adult/child €2/1.50; ☺Friedenssaal 10am-5pm Tue-Fri, to 4pm Sat & Sun) is a Gothic gem. In the newly expanded **LWL-Museum für Kunst und Kultur** (Museum for Art and Culture; ☏0251-590 701; www.lwl-museum-kunst-kultur.de; Domplatz 10; adult/concession €8/4; ☺10am-6pm Tue-Sat), you can explore a collection spanning the Middle Ages to the latest avant-garde creations.

✕ 🏠 p155

The Drive » The next stretch of driving will get you off the frenetic autobahns and onto quieter country roads that wander past little villages amid verdant farmland. Take the L585 out of Münster and drive southeast over a series roads for 42km to Beckum where you'll

switch to the B475 for the final 26km to Soest.

- - - - - - - - - - - -

TRIP HIGHLIGHT

7 Soest

Soest is a tranquil place with half-timbered houses and a clutch of treasure-filled churches that reflect the wealth it enjoyed during its Hanseatic League days. It's a maze of idyllic, crooked lanes that has been beautifully rebuilt and preserves much of its medieval character.

Soest's one remarkable feature is its stone: a shimmering greenish local sandstone used in building the town wall, churches and other public structures. Among the treasures, check out the late-Gothic **St Maria zur Wiese** (Wiesenkirche; Wiesenstrasse; ☺11am-6pm Mon-Sat, noon-6pm Sun Apr-Sep, to 4pm Oct-Mar) and 10th-century Romanesque **St**

Patrokli (www.sankt-patrokli.de; Propst-Nübel-Strasse 2; ☺10am-5.30pm).

✕ p155

The Drive » Like the arrows of the medieval legions who once roamed these lands – you have a straight shot for 52km from Soest to Paderborn on the B1.

- - - - - - - - - - -

8 Paderborn

From the 8th century AD, Charlemagne used Paderborn as a power base to defeat the Saxons and convert them to Christianity, giving him the momentum needed to rise to greater things. Paderborn remains a pious place to this day – churches abound, and religious sculpture and motifs adorn facades, fountains and parks. Start at the massive **Dom** (☏05251-125 1287; Markt 17; ☺7am-6.30pm), a three-nave Gothic hall church.

✕ p155

154

Eating & Sleeping

Cologne ❶

✖ Café Reichard   Cafe €€
(📞0221-257 8542; www.cafe-reichard.de; Unter
Fettenhennen 11; mains €6-16; ⏰8.30am-8pm)
There are plenty of cafes around the Dom,
but this slightly hidden one is a true luxe gem.
Cologne grannies have been bringing their
granddaughters here for luscious cakes and
treats for generations. Great people-watching
from the terrace tables.

Xanten ❸

✖ Emilie's Le Petit Joli   Cafe €
(📞02801-985 0961; www.lepetitjoli.de; Klever
Strasse 6; mains €4-8; ⏰9am-6pm Thu-
Sun) Emilie has a reason to smile – as do her
many happy customers: the food here, from
breakfasts to afternoon cakes, is sensational.
The menu changes daily, but whatever you
order, whether in the artfully chaotic dining
room or in the lovely garden, will be a delight.

🛏 Neumaier   Hotel €€
(📞02801-715 70; www.hotel-neumaier.de;
Orkstrasse 19-21; s/d from €70/100; P📶)
The 16 rooms are sprightly at this family-run
hotel close to the Markt in the Altstadt. Cute
touches abound, including house plants and
rubber ducks for rooms with bathtubs. There's
a beautiful beer garden in a courtyard that
makes a perfect pause between the town's
museums.

Dortmund ❺

✖ Brauhaus Wenkers   German €€
(📞0231-527 548; www.wenkers.de;
Betenstrasse 1; mains €7-20; ⏰11am-midnight)
A legendary place for quaffing before and after
football matches, long-running Wenkers has
a sea of tables outside on a centrally located
square. It brews its own beer (try the dark one)
and the German classics spill over the plates.

Münster ❻

✖ Holstein's
Bistro   Modern European €€
(📞0251-449 44; www.butterhandlung-holstein.
de; Bogenstrasse 9; mains €8-16; ⏰11.30am-7pm
Tue-Fri, 11am-5pm Sat; �) Münster's slow food
outpost has been raising the bar of innovative
seasonal fare for almost 20 years. The ever-
changing menu reflects what's fresh, but there's
usually a variety of soups, salads and pastas on
offer. Snare one of the tables in the shadow of the
Dom along the alley. An excellent deli adjoins.

🛏 Hotel Feldmann   Boutique Hotel €€
(📞0251-414 490; www.hotel-feldmann.de;
An der Clemenskirche 14; s/d from €76/106;
📶) Four generations of the same family have
run this refined hotel. The 20 rooms have an
understated elegance, some have huge, glassy
walk-in showers. The restaurant is good and
you can relax with a drink after a hard day
enjoying yourself at one of the outdoor tables
on the quiet pedestrian lane overlooking the
Clemenskirche.

Soest ❼

✖ Brauhaus Zwiebel   German
(📞02921-2921 4424; brauhaus-zwiebel.de;
Ulricherstrasse 24; ⏰11am-midnight) A one-
stop shop for myriad forms of pleasure in Soest.
This long-running brewery produces a bevy
of excellent seasonal beers through the year,
which can all be enjoyed in the beer garden. The
food is predictably hearty and tasty (yes, many
dishes come with *Zwiebel* – onion), while various
games keep the mood boisterous and jolly.

Paderborn ❽

✖ Eiscafe Artusa   Ice Cream €
(📞05251-288 7625; artusa.state-art.de;
Westernstrasse 2; treats from €2; ⏰9am-8pm)
Enjoy Paderborn's best ice cream and gelato
at this always-crowded cafe overlooking
Marienplatz.

Bacharach *View over the tiny town*

Classic Trip

Romantic Rhine

12

After traversing powerhouse riverside cities Düsseldorf, Cologne and Bonn, watch epic scenery unfold as Germany's Romantic Rhine valley carves between towering cliffs clad in forest and capped by castles, to delightful Mainz.

TRIP HIGHLIGHTS

START
● Düsseldorf

198 km
Rüdesheim
Escape the crowds by hiking into the picturesque vineyards

● Cologne

Koblenz ●
7

Loreley ●
13 **14** FINISH

Boppard
One of the Romantic Rhine's prettiest towns
155 km

Mainz
Home to rustic wine taverns and a magnificent cathedral
235 km

**5–7 DAYS
235 KM / 146 MILES**

GREAT FOR...

BEST TIME TO GO
April to October offers the best weather, but July and August can be crowded.

ESSENTIAL PHOTO
Boat-shaped toll castle Pfalzgrafstein on a Rhine island.

BEST FOR OUTDOORS
Hike through the vines above Rüdesheim.

Classic Trip

12 Romantic Rhine

Boats gliding down the Rhine give passengers mesmerising views of the medieval villages, craggy hillsides, and castle after castle floating past. But on this trip you'll get up close to its mightiest sights, hike through its loftiest vineyards and discover hidden treasures and romantic hideaways you'd never see from the water. (Though you'll have plenty of opportunities en route to board a cruise, too.)

1 Düsseldorf

Survey the mighty Rhine from Düsseldorf's **Medienhafen**. This old harbour area continues to attract red-hot restaurants, bars, hotels and clubs. Crumbling warehouses have transformed into high-tech office buildings and now rub shoulders with bold new structures designed by celebrated international architects, including Frank Gehry.

Of course, no visit to Düsseldorf is complete without exploring its **Altstadt** (old town), which claims to be the 'longest bar in the world'.

The Drive » It's a 44km drive from Düsseldorf south via the B1 and the A57 to Cologne (fear not: although this section mainly travels through built-up areas and industrial estates, later stages of the drive become much more scenic).

2 Cologne

A walking tour (see p186) is the best way to appreciate this engaging city (Germany's fourth-largest) on the Rhine.

Must-sees include Cologne's world-famous **Kölner Dom** (Cologne Cathedral; ☎0211-1794 0200; www.koelner-dom.de; tower adult/concession €4/2; ⏱6am-9pm May-Oct, to 7.30pm Nov-Apr, tower 9am-6pm May-Sep, to 5pm Mar-Apr & Oct, to 4pm Nov-Feb), whose twin spires dominate the skyline, as well as superb museums such as the **Römisch-Germanisches Museum** (Roman Germanic Museum; ☎0221-2212 4438; www.museenkoeln.de; Roncalliplatz 4; adult/concession €9/5; ⏱10am-5pm Tue-Sun); sculptures and ruins displayed outside its entrance are the overture to its symphony of Roman artefacts found along the Rhine.

The Drive » Drive south along the B51 along the Rhine's western bank before joining the A555 to bring you into Bonn (29km all-up).

LINK YOUR TRIP

11 Cologne & the Ruhr Valley

At Cologne you can also pick up this absorbing route, visiting vibrant Ruhr cities such as Essen and Münster.

13 Moselle Valley

Koblenz sits at the confluence of the Rhine and Moselle Rivers, where you can set out for more vineyard-ribboned valley views and irresistible wines.

CROSSING THE RHINE

No bridges span the Rhine between Koblenz and Mainz; the only way to cross the river along this stretch is by **Autofähre** (car ferry). Prices vary slightly but you can figure on paying about €4.20 per car, including driver; €1.20 per car passenger; €1.30 per pedestrian (€0.80 for a child); and €2.50 for a bicycle, including the rider.

Bingen–Rüdesheimer (www.bingen-ruedesheimer.com; ⏱5.30am-9.45pm Sun-Thu & 5.30am-12.50am Fri & Sat May-Oct, 5.30am-9.45pm Nov-Apr)

Boppard–Filsen (www.faehre-boppard.de; ⏱6.30am-10pm Jun-Aug, 6.30am-9pm Apr, May & Sep, 6.30am-8pm Oct-Mar)

Niederheimbach–Lorch (www.mittelrhein-faehre.de; ⏱6am-7.50pm Apr-Oct, 6am-6.50pm Nov-Mar)

Oberwesel–Kaub (www.faehre-kaub.de; ⏱6am-8pm Mon-Sat & 8am-8pm Sun Apr-Sep, 6am-7pm Mon-Sat & 8am-7pm Sun Oct-Mar)

St Goar–St Goarshausen (www.faehre-loreley.de; ⏱5.30am-midnight Mon-Sat, 6.30am-midnight Sun)

③ Bonn

In a beautiful riverside setting, Ludwig van Beethoven's home town warrants a stop to visit the **Beethoven-Haus Bonn** (📞0228-981 7525; www.beethoven-haus-bonn.de; Bonngasse 24-26; adult/concession €6/4.50; ⏱10am-6pm Apr-Oct, 10am-5pm Mon-Sat, 11am-5pm Sun Nov-Mar), where the great composer was born in 1770. Other landmarks include the soaring **Münster Basilica** (📞0228-985 880; www.bonner-muenster.de; Münsterplatz; ⏱7am-7pm), built on the graves of the two martyred Roman soldiers who later became the city's patron saints.

Bonn's old government quarter dates from its time as West Germany's 'temporary' capital, between 1949 and 1991 (when a reunited German government decided to move to Berlin). For a romp through recent German history from the end of WWII, pop by the **Haus der Geschichte der Bundesrepublik Deutschland** (Museum of History; 📞0228-916 50; www.hdg.de; Willy-Brandt-Allee 14; ⏱9am-7pm Tue-Fri, 10am-6pm Sat & Sun).

The Drive » From Bonn, take the B9 southeast for 24km to Remagen. When you leave the German state of North Rhine-Westphalia and enter Rhineland-Palatinate the road returns to the river's western bank; on your right-hand side, you'll see the hilly wildlife park Wildpark Rolandseck.

④ Remagen

Remagen was founded by the Romans in AD 16 as Rigomagus, but the town would hardly figure in the history books were it not for one fateful day in early March 1945. As the Allies raced across France and Belgium to rid Germany of Nazism, the Wehrmacht tried frantically to stave off defeat by destroying all bridges across the Rhine.

But the Brücke von Remagen (the steel rail bridge at Remagen) lasted long enough for Allied troops to cross the river, contributing significantly to the collapse of Hitler's western front. One of the bridge's surviving basalt towers now houses the **Friedensmuseum** (Peace Museum; 📞218 63; www.bruecke-remagen.de; adult/child €3.50/1; ⏱10am-5pm early Mar-mid-Nov, to 6pm May-Oct), with a well-presented exhibit on Remagen's pivotal role in WWII.

The Drive » Take the B9 southeast for 49km. The Rhine winds back and forth away from the road until you come to the city of Koblenz. Stay on the B9 until you've crossed the Moselle River to the town centre, or risk getting lost in a maze of concentric flyovers.

⑤ Koblenz

Koblenz sits at the confluence of the Rhine and Moselle Rivers – marked by the expansive **Deutsches Eck** (German Corner), adjoining flower-filled parks and promenades – and the convergence of three low mountain ranges (the Hunsrück, the Eifel and the Westerwald). Its roots date back to the Romans, who founded a military stronghold (Confluentes) here because of the site's supreme strategic value.

On the Rhine's right bank, the 118m-high fortress **Festung Ehrenbreitstein** (www.diefestungehrenbreitstein.de; adult/child €6/3, incl cable car €11.80/5.60; ☉10am-6pm Apr-Oct, to 5pm Nov-Mar) proved indestructible to all but Napoleonic troops, who levelled it in 1801. To prove a point, the Prussians rebuilt it as one of Europe's mightiest fortifications. It's accessible by car, on foot and by cable car.

Inside Koblenz' striking new glass **Forum Confluentes**, exhibits at the **Mittelrhein-Museum** (www.mittelrhein-museum.de; Zentralplatz 1; adult/child €10/7; ☉10am-6pm Tue-Sun) span 2000 years of the region's history, including 19th-century landscape paintings of the Romantic Rhine by German and British artists.

🛏 p167

The Drive » Take the B49 across the Rhine to its eastern bank and travel south on the B42; it's 13km to Braubach. At this point of the drive, you leave the cityscapes behind and enter an older world of cobblestones, half-timbered villages, densely forested hillsides and ancient vineyards.

⑥ Braubach

Framed by forest, vineyards and rose gardens, the 1300-year-old town of Braubach centres on its small, half-timbered **Marktplatz**.

High above Braubach are the dramatic towers, turrets and crenellations of the 700-year-old **Marksburg** (www.marksburg.de; adult/child €64; ☉10am-5pm mid-Mar-Oct, 11am-4pm Nov–mid-Mar), which is unique among the Rhine's fastnesses as it was never destroyed. The compulsory tour takes in the citadel, the Gothic hall and a grisly torture chamber. English tours depart

DETOUR: OBERWESEL

Start: ⑧ **St Goar**

It's a quick 7.8km south from St Goar along the B9 to the village of Oberwesel.

Every April, Oberwesel crowns not a *Weinkönigin* (wine queen), as in most Rhine towns, but a *Weinhexe* (wine witch) – a good witch, of course – who is said to protect the vineyards. Photos of all the *Weinhexen* crowned since 1946 are displayed in the cellar of Oberwesel's **Kulturhaus** (www.kulturhaus-oberwesel.de; Rathausstrasse 23; adult/child €3/1; ☉10am-5pm Tue-Fri, 2-5pm Sat & Sun Apr-Oct), along with 19th-century engravings of the Romantic Rhine and models of Rhine riverboats.

Hidden sky-high up a vineyard-striped hillside, the flagstone terrace of **Günderode Haus** (www.guenderodefilmhaus.de; Siebenjungfrauenblick; ☉11am-6pm Sat-Thu, to 8pm Fri Apr-Oct, reduced hours Nov-Mar) is an incredible spot for a glass of wine, beer or brandy, with sweeping views over the Rhine. The adjacent 200-year-old half-timbered house was used as a film set for *Heimat 3* (2004), and now has a cinema room and hosts live music and literary events, as well as wine tastings. From Oberwesel, take the K93 east for 600m, turn right (north) onto the K95; after 1km, the car park's on your right.

Classic Trip

WHY THIS IS A CLASSIC TRIP
CATHERINE LE NEVEZ, AUTHOR

The romance along this stretch of the Rhine is timeless. Poets and painters including Lord Byron and William Turner are among those who have been inspired by this castle-crowned, forest-and-vineyard-cloaked valley. A fabled stop on the original European Grand Tour, the riverscape here is now a designated Unesco World Heritage site. It doesn't get more classic than that.

Top: The Rhine and the town of Boppard on the bend
Left: Natascha Alexandrova's Lorelei Sculpture
Right: Cologne's Kölner Dom illuminated at dusk

ALLAN BAXTER / GETTY IMAGES ©

at 1pm and 4pm from late March to October.

The Drive » Hug the eastern bank of the Rhine for 11km as it curves around to the car-ferry dock at Filsen. It's a five-minute crossing to charming Boppard.

TRIP HIGHLIGHT

⑦ Boppard

Idyllically located on a horseshoe bend in the river, Boppard (pro-nounced 'bo-*part*') is one of the Romantic Rhine's prettiest towns, not least because its riverfront and historic centre are both on the same side of the railway tracks.

Boppard's riverfront promenade, the **Rhein-allee**, has grassy areas for picnicking and a children's playground.

Many of the town's half-timbered buildings house cosy wine taverns, including its oldest, **Weinhaus Heilig Grab** (www.heiliggrab.de; Zelkesgasse 12; ☺3pm-midnight Wed-Mon). In summer you can sip local rieslings under the chestnut trees, where live music plays on weekends.

Fantastic hiking trails fan out into the coun-tryside, including the **Hunsrück Trails**, accessed by Germany's steepest scheduled railway route, the **Hunsrückbahn** (adult/ child one-way €2.90/1.75; ☺hourly 10am-6pm Apr-Oct, to 4pm Nov-Mar). Around the **Vierseenblick** (Four-Lakes-View), a panoramic outlook reached by **Sesselbahn** (chair lift; http://sesselbahn-boppard.de; adult/child return

163

Classic Trip

€7.50/4.50, one-way €4.80/3; ☺10am-5pm Apr-Oct) **creates the illusion that you're looking at four separate lakes rather than a single river.**

The Drive » Take the B9 south from Boppard for 15km, passing Burg Maus across the river on the eastern bank near the village of Wellmich. Shortly afterwards, you'll spot Burg Rheinfels on the western bank above St Goar.

CAT & MOUSE

Two rival castles stand either side of the village of St Goarshausen. Burg Peterseck was built by the archbishop of Trier to counter the toll practices of the powerful Katzenelnbogen family. The latter responded by building a much bigger castle high on the other side of town, Burg Neukatzenelnbogen, which was dubbed **Burg Katz**, meaning 'Cat Castle'. Highlighting the obvious imbalance of power between the Katzenelnbogens and the archbishop, Burg Peterseck was soon nicknamed **Burg Maus** (Mouse Castle). Both are closed to the public.

the L338 as it twists steeply uphill through thick forest for 1.2km and turn right onto the K89 for 2.5km to reach Loreley.

⑧ St Goar

Lording over the village of St Goar are the sprawling ruins of **Burg Rheinfels** (www.st-goar. de; adult/child €5/2.50; ☺9am-6pm mid-Mar–late Oct, 11am-5pm late Oct–mid-Nov), at one time the mightiest fortress on the Rhine. Built in 1245 by Count Dieter von Katzenelnbogen as a base for his toll-collecting operations, its size and labyrinthine layout are astonishing. Kids (and adults) will love exploring the subterranean tunnels and galleries (bring a torch). From St Goar's northern edge, follow the Schlossberg road to the castle.

✕ ⟝ p167

The Drive » At St Goar, take the five-minute car ferry across to the little village of St Goarshausen. From St Goarshausen's Marktplatz, follow

⑨ Loreley

The most storied spot along the Romantic Rhine, Loreley is an enormous, almost vertical slab of slate that owes its fame to a mythical maiden whose siren songs are said to have lured sailors to their death in the river's treacherous currents. Heinrich Heine told the tale in his 1824 poem *Die Lorelei*.

On the edge of the plateau 4km southeast of the village of St Goarshausen, visitor centre **Loreley Besucherzentrum** (☎06771-599 093; www.loreley-besucherzentrum. de; Loreleyring 7; adult/ child €2.50/1.50, parking €2; ☺10am-6pm Apr-Oct, 10am-5pm Mar, 11am-4pm Sat & Sun Nov-Feb) **covers the Loreley myth and local flora, fauna, shipping and winemaking traditions. A 300m gravel path leads**

to a **viewpoint** at the tip of the Loreley outcrop 190m above the river.

The Drive » Return to the B42 at the bottom of the hill; on your left, you'll see Burg Katz. Travel south for 2km to the car park by the breakwater for the next stop, the Lorelei Sculpture.

⑩ Lorelei Sculpture

At the tip of a narrow breakwater jutting into the Rhine, a bronze sculpture of Loreley's famous maiden perches lasciviously atop a rocky platform. From the car park, you can walk the 600m out to the sculpture, from where there are fantastic views of both riverbanks, but be aware that the rough path is made from jagged slate (wear sturdy shoes!) and the gentler sandy lower path is often underwater.

The Drive » Leaving the car park, take the B42 south for 8km to the little village of Kaub, and park next to the ferry dock.

⑪ Kaub

Kaub is the gateway to one of the river's iconic sights. Like something out of a fairy tale, 1326-built, boat-shaped toll castle **Pfalzgrafstein** (www.burg-pfalzgrafenstein.de; adult/child €3/2; ◷10am-6pm Tue-Sun Apr-Oct, 10am-5pm Mar, 10am-5pm Sat & Sun Nov, Jan & Feb, closed Dec), with distinctive white-painted walls, red trim, and slate turrets, perches on a narrow island in the middle of the Rhine. A once-dangerous rapid here (since modified) forced boats to use the right-hand side of the river, where a chain forced ships to stop and pay a toll. The island makes for a fabulous picnic spot.

Alongside Kaub's car ferry dock you can hop on a little **Fährboot** (propelled boat; adult/child €2.50/1; ◷every 30min 10am-6pm Tue-Sun Apr-Oct, 10am-5pm Mar, 10am-5pm Sat & Sun Nov, Jan & Feb, closed Dec) passenger ferry (it only runs from this side of the river).

The Drive » From Kaub, take the car ferry across to the Rhine's western bank and head south on the B9 for 3km to Bacharach.

⑫ Bacharach

Tiny Bacharach conceals its considerable charms behind a 14th-century wall. Enter one of the thick arched gateways under the train tracks and you'll find yourself in a medieval old town filled with half-timbered mansions.

It's possible to walk almost all the way around the centre on top of the walls. The lookout tower on the upper section of the wall affords panoramic views.

Dating from 1421, **Zum Grünen Baum** (www.weingut-bastian-bacharach.de; Oberstrasse 63; ◷noon-midnight Apr-Oct, reduced hours Nov-Mar) serves some of Bacharach's best whites in rustic surrounds. Its nearby **Vinothèque** (www.weingut-bastian-bacharach.de/vinothek; Koblenzer Strasse 1;

CRUISING THE RHINE

If you'd like to let someone else drive for a while and get a different perspective of the Rhine, it's easy to park up and hop on a cruise boat.

From about Easter to October (winter services are very limited), passenger ships run by **KD** (Köln-Düsseldorfer; ☎0221-208 8318; www.k-d.com) link Rhine villages on a set timetable:

» You can travel to the next village or all the way between Mainz and Koblenz (one-way/return €50/55, downstream Mainz to Koblenz/upstream Koblenz to Mainz 5½/eight hours).

» Within the segment you've paid for (for example, Boppard–Rüdesheim, which costs €25.40/26.80 one-way/return), you can get on and off as often as you like, but make sure to ask for a free stopover ticket each time you disembark.

» Children up to the age of four travel free, while those up to age 13 are charged a flat fee of €6 regardless of distance.

» Return tickets usually cost only slightly more than one-way.

» To bring along a bicycle, there's a supplement of €2.80.

Several smaller companies also send passenger boats up and down the river:

Bingen-Rüdesheimer (www.bingen-ruedesheimer.com)

Hebel Linie (www.hebel-linie.de)

Loreley Linie (www.loreley-linie.com)

Rössler Linie (www.roesslerlinie.de)

🕑 3-5pm Mon-Fri & 11am-6pm Sat & Sun Apr-Oct, 3-5pm Mon-Fri Nov-Mar), by contrast, is state of the art. Owner Friedrich Bastian is a renowned opera singer, so music (and culinary) events take place year-round, including on Bastian's private river island with its own vineyard.

🛏 p167

The Drive » Head south on the B9, passing Burg Reichenstein, then Burg Rheinstein, on your right. Then, on your left, in the river itself, you'll pass the Mäuseturm, a fortified tower used as a signal station until 1974. Drive through the busy working town of Bingen to the car-ferry dock at its eastern edge, and cross the river to Rüdesheim.

TRIP HIGHLIGHT

⑬ Rüdesheim

Depending on how you look at it, Rüdesheim's town centre – and especially its most famous feature, the tunnel-like medieval alley **Drosselgasse** – is either a touristy nightmare or a lot of kitschy, colourful fun. But there's also wonderful walking in the greater area, which is part of the Rheingau wine region, famed for its superior rieslings.

For a stunning Rhine panorama, head up the wine-producing slopes west of Rüdesheim to the

Niederwald Monument. Erected between 1877 and 1883, this bombastic monument celebrates the Prussian victory in the Franco-Prussian War and the creation of the German Reich, both in 1871. To save climbing 203 vertical metres, glide above the vineyards aboard the 1400m-long **Seilbahn** (Kabinenbahn; www.seilbahn-ruedesheim.de; Oberstrasse 37; adult/child one-way €5/2.50, return €7/3.50, with Sesselbahn €8/4; 🕑 10am-5.30pm Mon-Fri, to 6pm Sat & Sun May-Sep, 10am-5pm Mon-Fri, to 5.30pm Sat & Sun Apr & Oct) cable car. A network of hiking trails extends from the monument.

🛏 p167

The Drive » From Rüdesheim, head east on the B42 for 23km and turn south on the A643 to cross the bridge over the Rhine. From here it's 13km southeast to the centre of Mainz.

TRIP HIGHLIGHT

⑭ Mainz

The Rhine River meets the Main at lively Mainz, which has a sizeable university, pretty pedestrian precincts and a *savoir vivre* dating from Napoleon's occupation (1797–1814).

Strolling along the Rhine and sampling local wines in an **Altstadt** tavern are as much a part of any Mainz visit as viewing the sights. Try the 1791 **Weinstube Hottum** (Grebenstrasse 3; 🕑 4pm-

midnight), serving wines purely from the Rheingau and Rheinhessen regions, or vine-draped **Weingut Michel** (www.michel-wein.de; Jakobsbergstrasse 8; 🕑 4pm-midnight), Mainz' only *Weingut* (winery) to exclusively serve its own wines.

Highlights you won't want to miss include the fabulous **Mainzer Dom** (📞 06131-253 412; www.mainz-dom.de; Markt 10; 🕑 9am-6.30pm Mon-Fri, to 4pm Sat, 12.45-3pm & 4-6.30pm Sun, shorter hours Nov-Feb), the ethereal windows of Chagall in **St-Stephan-Kirche** (www.st-stephan-mainz.de; Kleine Weissgasse 12; 🕑 10am-5pm Mon-Sat, noon-5pm Sun Mar-Oct, 10am-4.30pm Mon-Sat, noon-4.30pm Sun Nov-Feb), and the first printed Bible in the **Gutenberg-Museum Mainz** (www.gutenberg-museum.de; Liebfrauenplatz 5; adult/child €5/2; 🕑 9am-5pm Tue-Sat, 11am-5pm Sun). This museum commemorates native son Johannes Gutenberg who ushered in the information age here in the 15th century by perfecting movable type.

Also well worth a visit is the dungeon-like, brilliantly illuminated Roman archaeological site **Heiligtum der Isis und Mater Magna** (www.isis-mainz.de; Römer Passage 1; admission by donation; 🕑 10am-6pm Mon-Sat). The easy-to-miss entrance is on the Römer Passage mall's ground floor just inside the western entrance.

 p167

Eating & Sleeping

Koblenz ⑤

🛏 Hotel Stein   Boutique Hotel €€

(☎0261-963 530; www.hotel-stein.de;
Mayener Strasse 126; s/d from €85/110; 🅿🛜)
Decorated in zesty colours such as tangerine
contrasted with dark timbers, Stein's 30
contemporary rooms are all soundproofed for
a peaceful night's sleep. The hotel is situated
across the Moselle River 2km north of Koblenz'
city centre but you won't need to leave to dine:
its superb gourmet restaurant Schiller's utilises
premium ingredients like white asparagus,
scampi, foie gras and truffles.

St Goar ⑧

🍴 Weinhotel Landsknecht   German €€

(☎06741-2001; www.hotel-landsknecht.de;
Aussiedlung Landsknecht 4; mains €14-27.50,
4-course dinner menu €42; ⊘noon-2.30pm &
6-9pm Apr-Oct, noon-2.30pm & 6-9pm Wed-Sun
Nov, Dec & Mar, closed Jan & Feb) The dining
room and terrace at this wonderful spot 1.5km
north of St Goar feel like being aboard a cruise
boat, with close-up, uninterrupted river views.
Sensational home cooking spans pickled
salmon with quince mousse to schnitzel with
mushroom and riesling sauce, and red-wine-
marinated plums with rosemary-and-vanilla ice
cream. Many of its rooms (doubles from €90)
also have Rhine views.

🛏 Romantik Hotel
Schloss Rheinfels   Historic Hotel €€€

(☎06741-8020; www.schloss-rheinfels.de; s/d
weekday from €95/130, weekend €110/140;
🅿@🛜🏊) Part of the Burg Rheinfels (p164)
castle complex is occupied by a romantic hotel
with 64 rooms and suites that range in size
from tiny to palatial. All have antique-style
furnishings; pricier rooms come with a river
view. The hotel has three fine restaurants: one
rustic, one semiformal and one gourmet.

Bacharach ⑫

🛏 Rhein Hotel   Hotel €€

(☎06743-1243; www.rhein-hotel-bacharach.de;
Langstrasse 50; s €39-68, d €78-136; 🅿❄🛜)
Right on the town's medieval ramparts, this
welcoming family-run hotel has 14 well-lit rooms
with original artwork. Rooms facing the river,
and so the train tracks, have double-glazing.
Guests can borrow bikes for free. Its **Stübers
Restaurant** (☎06743-1243; Langstrasse 50;
mains €17-23; ⊘11.30am-2.15pm & 5.30-9.15pm
Wed-Mon; 🍴) is top-notch.

Rüdesheim ⑬

🛏 Rüdesheimer
Schloss   Boutique Hotel €€

(☎06722-905 00; www.ruedesheimer-schloss.
com; Steingasse 10; s €95-115, d €125-155, ste
€155-165; 🅿🛜) Truly good places to sleep
and eat are thin on the ground in Rüdesheim,
but this 18th-century building has 26 stunning
contemporary rooms designed by local and
regional artists. Its restaurant is excellent,
serving dishes such as cheese and riesling soup,
veal liver with truffled mash, and roast duck
stuffed with dates and figs, with a live pianist
and after-dinner dancing.

Mainz ⑭

🍴 Zur Kanzel   German, French €€€

(☎06131-237 137; www.zurkanzel.de;
Grebenstrasse 4; mains €8-23.50; ⊘kitchen
5-11pm Mon-Fri, noon-4pm & 6-11pm Sat) Germany
meets France at this dark-timber-panelled
Weinstube (wine bar) in dishes such as grilled
tuna with riesling and sage sauce, garlic-crusted
rack of lamb with wilted spinach, schnitzel with
Frankfurt-style *Grüne Sosse* (green sauce) and
rump steak with herb butter, as well as garlic
snails. All ingredients are fresh, so the menu
evolves with the seasons; there's a lovely summer
courtyard. Cash only.

Bremm The Moselle River flows between the village and golden vineyards

Moselle Valley

13

Follow the enchanting Moselle River as it flows, between vineyard-wrapped slopes ribboned with walking trails, from historic Trier through fairy-tale landscapes to park-and-flower-filled Koblenz.

TRIP HIGHLIGHTS

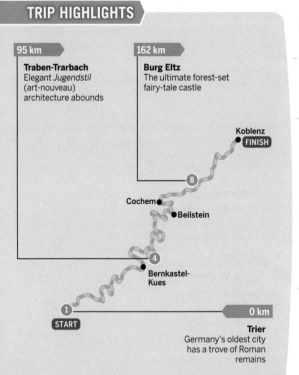

95 km

Traben-Trarbach
Elegant *Jugendstil* (art-nouveau) architecture abounds

162 km

Burg Eltz
The ultimate forest-set fairy-tale castle

Koblenz
FINISH

8

Cochem
Beilstein

4

Bernkastel-Kues

1
START

0 km

Trier
Germany's oldest city has a trove of Roman remains

2–4 DAYS
195 KM / 121 MILES

GREAT FOR...

BEST TIME TO GO

Wine festivals (www.mosel-weinfeste.de) abound between late April and early November.

ESSENTIAL PHOTO

Europe's steepest vineyards – Calmont.

BEST FOR FOODIES

Detour to Liller's Historische Schlossmühle.

169

13 Moselle Valley

As you wind along the river's edge, and criss-cross it over narrow bridges, you'll pass huddled half-timbered villages, precariously perched hilltop castles (or their crumbling remains), and scores of snug, generations-old wineries serving hearty food and exquisite wines. Pack your hiking boots – from every stop along the route you can head up into the vines for sublime views over the valley.

TRIP HIGHLIGHT

1 Trier

Before hitting the road, history buffs especially will want to explore Germany's oldest city, Trier, at the head of the Moselle Valley. A Unesco World Heritage site, this is where you'll find the country's finest ensemble of Roman remains, including the 2nd-century 'black gate' **Porta Nigra** (adult/child €3/2; ⊙9am-6pm Apr-Sep, to 5pm Mar & Oct, to 4pm Nov-Feb); a gladiatorial **Amphitheater**

(Olewiger Strasse; adult/child €3/2; ⏰9am-6pm Apr-Sep, to 5pm Mar & Oct, to 4pm Nov-Feb); thermal baths such as the labyrinthine **Kaiserthermen** (Imperial Baths; Weberbachstrasse 41; adult/child €3/2; ⏰9am-6pm Apr-Sep, to 5pm Mar & Oct, to 4pm Nov-Feb); **Konstantin Basilika** (📞0651-425 70; www.konstantin-basilika.de; Konstantinplatz 10; ⏰10am-6pm Mon-Sat, 1-4pm Sun Apr-Oct, 10am-noon & 2-4pm Mon-Sat, 1-4pm Sun Nov-Mar), constructed around AD 310 as Constantine's throne room (now a Protestant church); as well as Germany's oldest bishop's church, **Trierer Dom** (📞0651-979 0790; www.dominformation.de; Liebfrauenstrasse 12, cnr of Domfreihof; ⏰6.30am-6pm

LINK YOUR TRIP

12 Romantic Rhine

Swap one waterway for another: Koblenz sits at the confluence of the Moselle and Rhine Rivers, where you can also pick up this route.

14 German Wine Route

For more vineyards (and more magnificent wines), drive 129km southeast from Koblenz to the German Wine Route's Bockenheim an der Weinstrasse.

Apr-Oct, to 5.30pm Nov-Mar), which retains Roman sections.

Vineyards climbing the hillsides provide a taste of the road trip to come.

❌ 🏠 p175

The Drive » Cross Germany's oldest bridge, the Römerbrücke (whose 2nd-century stone pilings have held it up since legionnaires crossed on chariots) to the right (western) bank. Turn right onto the B51; after about 1km, the right-hand fork links up to the B53. Following the B53 along the river for 63km brings you to Bernkastel-Kues.

- - - - - - - - - - - -

② Bernkastel-Kues

On the river's right (eastern) bank, higgledy-piggledy half-timbered houses with beautifully decorated gables cluster around Bernkastel's **Marktplatz**, including the Moselle's oldest half-timbered building, dating from 1416. Shaped like a bird's house, with a narrow base topped by a larger, wonkier upper level to allow carriages to pass through the narrow alley, it's now home to **Weinstube Spitzhäuschen** (📞06531-7476; www.spitzhaeuschen.de; Karlstrasse 13; ⏰4pm Mon-Fri, 3pm Sat & Sun Easter-Oct, from 3pm Sat Nov-Dec, other times by appointment) where you can taste the Schmitz family's local wines. Looming above Bernkastel is the ruined 13th-century castle **Burg Landshut**.

Kues, on the left bank, is home to the 1458-founded **St-Nikolaus-Hospital** (www.cusanus.de; Cusanusstrasse 2; guided tour €5; ⏰9am-6pm Sun-Fri, 9am-3pm Sat, guided tour 10.30am Tue & 3pm Fri Apr-Oct), where, for more wine tasting, you'll find the **Mosel Vinothek** (www.moselvinothek.de; ⏰10am-6pm Apr-Oct, 11am-5pm Nov, Dec, Feb & Mar).

🏠 p175

The Drive » From the Bernkastel side of the river, head north, hugging the river as it bends west, for 7km to Zeltingen-Rachtig, then cross to the left (southern) bank: just on your right is one of the trip's biggest surprises.

- - - - - - - - - - - -

③ Kloster Machern

The Moselle might be better known for its wine but a former Cistercian monastery, founded in the 13th century, now houses this extraordinary **brewery** (www.klostermachern.de; An der Zeltinger Brücke, Zeltingen-Rachtig; ⏰bar 11am-2am Easter-Oct, reduced hours Nov-Easter), with a bar made from a copper vat and dry hops hanging from the ceiling. There's a wicker-chair-filled terrace, and excellent local cuisine. Brews, including a *Dunkel* (dark), *Hell* (light) and *Hefe-Weizen* (wheat beer), are also sold at its shop. Also here is a museum exhibiting religious iconography, plus puppets, toys and model railways.

The Drive >> Sticking to the left (eastern) bank, follow the river downstream as it twists, turns and twists again until you arrive at Traben, one of the twin towns making up Traben-Trarbach.

- - - - - - - - - - -

TRIP HIGHLIGHT

❹ Traben-Trarbach

Traben, on the Moselle's left (northern) bank, lost its medieval appearance to three major fires but was compensated with beautiful *Jugendstil* (art-nouveau) villas, many designed by Berlin architect Bruno Möhring.

Across the river in Trarbach, Möhring's works include the 1898-built, medieval-style bridge gate, the **Brückentor**, and a 1906 former winery that's now the unlikely home of 2000-plus wood, bronze and paper Buddha statues

at the **Buddha Museum** (www.buddha-museum. de; Bruno-Möhring-Platz 1, Trarbach; adult/child €15/7.50; ⊙10am-6pm Tue-Sun).

Teetering above Trarbach are the ruins of 14th-century **Grevenburg**. Below the castle is **Weingut Louis Klein** (☎06541-6246; www.klein-wein.de; Enkircher Strasse 20, Trarbach; tastings per 6 wines €10; ⊙10am-6pm Mon-Sat, 10am-noon Sun), which can also arrange vineyard tastings amid the vines.

✗ 🛏 p175

The Drive >> From Trarbach, stay on the river's right (eastern) bank and follow the B53 north for 20km to the wine-producing town of Zell.

- - - - - - - - - - -

❺ Zell

You'll know you've arrived in the charming town of

HANS GEORG EBEN / GETTY IMAGES ©

Zell when you come to its roundabout. In the centre is a gigantic black cat, standing on top of a wine barrel, raising a full glass, backed by vine-planted hills.

So the story goes, in 1863, visiting merchants trying to find the best wine encountered a barrel guarded by a hissing, spitting *Schwarze Katz* (black cat). The merchants snapped up the now-renowned Zeller Schwarze Katz wine; you can taste and buy it at wine shops throughout the town.

The Drive >> After heading 14km north on the left (western) bank, look up (and up!) as you

DETOUR:
LILLER'S HISTORISCHE SCHLOSSMÜHLE

Start: ❹ Traben-Trarbach

From Trarbach, zigzagging uphill for 21km via the L190 brings you to **Liller's Historische Schlossmühle** (☎06543-4041; www.hostorische-schlossmuehle.de; An der Landstrasse 190; mains €18.50-32, 5-/7-course menu €59/79; ⊙kitchen noon-9pm Thu-Tue).

A wonderland of waterwheels, wooden furniture and fairy lights, this ancient mill was moved stone by stone in 1804 to its magical spot in the forest 21km southeast of Traben-Trarbach. Venison carpaccio marinated in plum brandy, trout terrain with dandelion salad and wild garlic-crusted veal with chanterelle ragout encapsulate the flavours of the countryside. Upstairs are enchanting **rooms** (s/d/ste from €91/134/197; Ⓟ🛜).

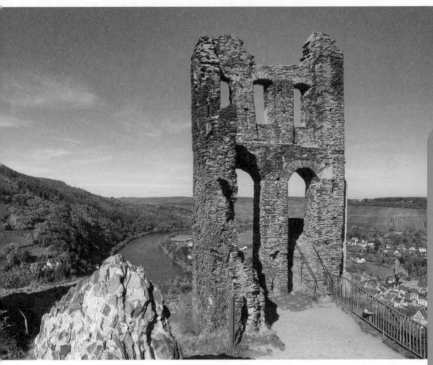

Traben-Trarbach Grevenburg castle ruins

leave the village of Bremm to spot Europe's (and allegedly the world's) steepest vineyards, Calmont, with a 65-degree gradient. Continuing downriver another 15km and crossing to the right (eastern) bank after Nehren takes you into Beilstein.

- - - - - - - - - - -

⑥ Beilstein

Beilstein's storybook-like half-timbered buildings centre on its 14th-century **Marktplatz**. Steep slopes lead to the baroque 17th-century Carmelite monastery church, **Karmeliterkirche St Josef** (www.st-josef-beilstein. de; ⊗8am-6pm). Its spectacular interior has a vaulted ceiling supported by soaring apricot-coloured columns. Also perched above the village is ruined **Burg Metternich** (admission €2.50; ⊗9am-6pm Apr-Nov). Built in 1129, the castle was destroyed by French troops in the Nine Years War in 1689.

The Drive ⟫ Continue along the right (eastern bank) for 11km and cross the bridge to busy Cochem.

- - - - - - - - - - -

⑦ Cochem

Transport hub Cochem is the Moselle at its most touristy. Pastel-coloured, terrace-fronted restaurants line its waterfront. Behind them, Cochem's tangle of narrow, medieval alleyways are crammed with boutiques.

Rising above town is the dazzling **Reichsburg** (☎02671-255; www.burg-cochem.de; Schlossstrasse 36; tours adult/child €6/3; ⊗tours 9am-5pm mid-Mar–Oct, 10am-3pm Nov & Dec, 11am, noon & 1pm Wed, Sat & Sun Jan–mid-Mar). This 11th-century castle fell victim to French troops in 1689, then stood ruined for centuries until it was restored to its current – if not always architecturally faithful – glory. Banquets here include a knighting ceremony.

173

✕ p175

The Drive ≫ Stay on the left (west) river bank and follow the B49 as it winds north, then east, for 17km to the village of Moselkern. At Moselkern, leave the river for 8km to reach Burg Eltz.

TRIP HIGHLIGHT

⑧ Burg Eltz

At the head of the Eltz, a Moselle side valley, **Burg Eltz** (www.burg-eltz.de; Burg-Eltz-Strasse 1, Wierschem; tour adult/child €9/6.50; ⏱9.30am-5.30pm Apr-Oct) is one of the most romantic medieval castles in Germany. Never destroyed, this vision of turrets, towers, oriels, gables and half-timber is still owned by the original family. From the Eltz car park it's a shuttle bus ride or 1.3km walk to the castle.

The Drive ≫ Retrace your route to Moselkern, then follow the B416 along the left (north) bank. After 5.5km you'll pass

tiny Hatzenport (vine-shaded riverfront winery Weinhaus Ibald, in the village centre, makes an idyllic stop). From Hatzenport, it's just another 5km (cross the bridge about halfway along) to Alken.

⑨ Alken

Alken is one of the Moselle's oldest villages, tracing its roots to Celtic and Roman times. Built on Roman foundations from 1197, its hilltop castle, **Burg Thurant** (www.thurant.de; adult/child €3.50/2.50; ⏱10am-6pm May–mid-Nov, to 5pm Mar-Apr, closed mid-Nov–Feb), has an intriguing history. From 1246 to 1248 it was fought over by the archbishops of Cologne and Trier, and divided in two parts (separated by a wall). Fascinating displays include medieval torture devices; the watchtower is accessible by ladder.

The Drive ≫ Along the Moselle's right (east) bank, the B49 squiggles for another 23km to Koblenz.

⑩ Koblenz

Koblenz (p161), with intriguing museums, flower-filled parks and a cable-car-accessed fortress, is a fitting last stop: at the broad **Deutsches Eck** (German Corner), the Moselle ends, emptying into the Rhine.

Specialising in Rhine and Moselle wines by the glass and/or bottle, rustic **Alte Weinstube Zum Hubertus** (www.weinhaus-hubertus.de; Florinsmarkt 6; ⏱3.30pm-midnight Mon-Fri, noon-midnight Sat & Sun) occupies a half-timbered house dating from 1689, with an open fireplace, antique furniture, dark-wood panelling and a summer terrace.

Eating & Sleeping

Trier ❶

✖ Zum Domstein   Roman, German €€

(☎0651-744 90; www.domstein.de; Hauptmarkt 5; mains €9-18.50, Roman menu €17-31; ⊗kitchen 8.30am-11pm, Roman menu 6-9.30pm) Feast like a Roman on dishes based on the recipes of 1st-century local chef Marcus Gavius Apicius: mulled Moselle white wine followed by barley soup, pine-nut-stuffed sausage, artichokes with boiled eggs, ham with figs and almonds, and wine-sautéed pears with custard, honey and green peppercorns. The Roman menu is available of an evening, during the day it serves more conventional German and international fare.

🛏 Becker's Hotel   Design Hotel €€

(☎0651-938 080; www.beckers-trier.de; Olewiger Strasse 206; s €60-75, d €110-170, tr €150-225; P ❋ @ 🛜) In the peaceful wine district of Olewig, across the creek from the old monastery church, 3km southeast of the centre, classy Becker's pairs supremely tasteful rooms – some ultramodern, others rustically traditional – with stellar **dining** (1-course lunch menu incl wine & coffee €18, 3-course lunch menu €28, mains €21-34; ⊗noon-2pm & 6-10pm).

Bernkastel-Kues ❷

🛏 Christiana's Wein & Art Hotel   Boutique Hotel €€

(☎06531-6627; www.wein-arthotel.de; Lindenweg 18, Kues; s/d from €60/89; P 🛜) Each of the 17 rooms at this sleek new hotel is named after a Moselle vineyard and some have dramatic outsized photos of wine glasses or barrels. Bathrooms are state of the art; higher-priced rooms have spas. Its steakhouse restaurant overlooks the vineyards. Lock-up bike storage is available.

Traben-Trarbach ❹

✖ Alte Zunftscheune   German €€

(☎06541-9737; www.zunftscheune.de; Neue Rathausstrasse 15, Traben; mains €11.50-20; ⊗kitchen 5-11pm Tue-Fri, 11.30am-3pm & 5-11pm Sat & Sun Easter-Oct, reduced hours Nov-Easter; 🖋) Dine on delicious Moselle-style dishes such as homemade black pudding and liver sausage, pork medallions with riesling cream sauce, or grilled rump steak with asparagus and fried potatoes in a series of wonderfully atmospheric rooms choc-full of rustic bric-a-brac, with beautiful timber staircases. Its cellar still has its original 1890s lighting. Reservations are recommended. Cash only.

🛏 Hotel Bellevue   Historic Hotel €€€

(☎06541-7030; www.bellevue-hotel.de; An der Mosel 11, Traben; s/d from €95/145; 🛜🏊) Topped by a Champagne-bottle-shaped slate turret, this exquisite *Jugendstil* river-facing hotel was built in 1903 by Bruno Möhring, with an oak staircase in the lobby and beautiful stained-glass windows in its gourmet restaurants Belle Epoque and Michelin-starred Clauss Feist. Individually designed rooms are overwhelmingly romantic; amenities include bike and canoe hire, a pool and a sauna.

Cochem ❼

✖ Alt Thorschenke   German €€

(☎02671-7059; www.thorschenke.de; Brückenstrasse 3; mains €10.50-19; ⊗kitchen 11am-10pm Apr-Oct, reduced hours Nov-Mar) Wedged into the old medieval walls, away from the busy riverfront restaurants, Alt Thorschenke is a diamond find for regional specialities, such as herring with apple and onions, pork neck with mustard-cream sauce, and several different types of schnitzel, washed down with wines from local producers. Upstairs are 27 small but charming **rooms** (d from €99), some with four-poster beds.

German Wine Route

14

Plunge into the heart of the Palatinate (Pfalz) region's vine-planted hills, rambling forests, chess-piece castles, wisteria-draped villages and thermal springs along one of Germany's oldest and loveliest touring routes.

TRIP HIGHLIGHTS

FINISH
● Bockenheim an der Weinstrasse

82 km
Bad Dürkheim
Curative spa waters and pretty parks

6

5

● Neustadt an der Weinstrasse
3

60 km
Hambacher Schloss
Historic hilltop castle with superb dining, too

70 km
Deidesheim
Cobbled streets filled with wineries and galleries

START ● Schweigen-Rechtenbach

● Wissembourg

2–4 DAYS
96 KM / 59 MILES

- - -

GREAT FOR...

- - -

BEST TIME TO GO

Villages here are especially pretty during the spring bloom (March to mid-May).

- - -

 ESSENTIAL PHOTO

Dürkheimer Riesenfass, the world's largest wine barrel.

- - -

 BEST FOR FOODIES

Epicurean treats abound along the entire route.

177

German Wine Route

From the French border, you'll wind north along this venerable route through Germany's largest contiguous wine-growing area, which is blessed with a temperate climate that allows almonds, figs, lemons and kiwi fruit to thrive, and is scattered with half-timbered villages and castles. The route was inaugurated in 1935, and its western edge weaves through the hilly forest of the Pfälzerwald, a Unesco Biosphere Reserve with invigorating hiking and cycling trails.

❶ Schweigen-Rechtenbach

There's no missing the start of the German Wine Route, which is marked by a towering stone gate, the 1936-built **Deutsches Weintor** (German Wine Gate; Weinstrasse 4). Inside is one of Germany's largest wine cooperatives. At this vast **Vinothek** (www.weintor. de; Weinstrasse 4; wine tasting per glass €2-5; ⊙10am-6pm) you can pick up tourist information, stock up on bottles, or sample a variety of wines by the glass.

The Drive 》》 From Schweigen-Rechtenbach, drive north for 16km along the Weinstrasse, which starts as the B38 and becomes the B48 at Bad Bergzabern. Just after pretty

Klingenmünster (look out for its castle, Burg Landeck), the B48 swings west into the forested Pfälzerwald to Annweiler (28km all-up).

❷ Annweiler

At the westernmost edge of the Palatinate wine-growing region, up in the forested Pfälzerwald, Annweiler has a charming core of half-timbered buildings and cobbled squares bisected by a canal-like stream with giant wooden waterwheels.

It's 8.6km via the K2 to **Burg Trifels** (☎06346-8470; adult/child €3/2; ⊙9am-6pm Apr-Sep, to 5pm Oct-Nov & Jan-Mar), looming southeast of the town. Thought to be of Celtic origins, this enormous red-sandstone

hilltop castle was first documented in 1081. Between 1125 and 1298 it was the repository of Imperial treasures including, allegedly, a nail from Jesus' cross and tooth from John the Baptist. Richard the Lionheart (Richard I of England) was imprisoned here from 1193 to 1194 for insulting Leopold V, Duke of Austria – after first having been incarcerated in Austria's Kuenringerburg (see p281) from 1192 to 1193. Today, Burg Trifels' displays include a replica of the Imperial crown jewels. Recent excavations here have uncovered a probable Saxon-era wooden castle.

The Drive 》》 Head east to Albersweiler to rejoin the Weinstrasse (here called L507) and follow it northeast: Hambacher Schloss is west of the hamlet of Hambach along the one-way K9 to the car park at the top of the hill (27.5km in total).

TRIP HIGHLIGHT

❸ Hambacher Schloss

Atop a forested Pfälzerwald hill is the monumental **Hambacher Schloss** (Hambacher Castle; ☎06321-926 290; www.hambacher-schloss.de; Wolfsburg; adult/child €4.50/1.50, incl tour €8/5; ⊙castle 10am-6pm Apr-Oct, 11am-5pm Nov-Mar, tours hourly 11am-4pm Apr-Oct, 11am, noon & 2pm Sat & Sun Nov-Mar). This 'cradle of German democracy' is where idealistic locals, Polish refugees and French citizens held massive protests for a free, democratic and united Germany on 27 May 1832, hoisting the black, red and gold German flag for the first time. An exhibition commemorates the event, known as the Hambacher Fest. Audioguides and tours are available in English.

Inside the castle, opening to a courtyard, **Restaurant 1832** (☏06321-959 7860; www.hambacher schloss.eu; Hambacher Schloss, Wolfsburg; mains €13-21.50; ☻10am-8pm Apr-Oct, to 6pm Nov-Mar) is reason enough to make the trip up, with inspired modern German cuisine: liver dumpling soup; tagliatelle with roasted asparagus in fig sauce; fried calf's liver with glazed grapes and potato and celery cake; and red mullet, shrimp and clams baked in parchment with cuttlefish risotto.

LINK YOUR TRIP

13 Moselle Valley

More wines await in the beautiful Moselle Valley, a 129km drive northwest to Koblenz from Bockenheim an der Weinstrasse.

16 German Castle Road

From Bad Dürkheim, it's a straight 24km shot east to Mannheim to pick up the German Castle Road.

The Drive » Return via the one-way K14 to the Weinstrasse at Hambach and head north for 5.8km into Neustadt an der Weinstrasse. After crossing the railway tracks, turn left for 850m, then right on the B58; after 300m there's a large open-air car park on your left at the edge of the largely pedestrianised Altstadt (old town).

- - - - - - - - - - - - -

❹ Neustadt an der Weinstrasse

Vineyards fan out around Neustadt, a busy wine-producing town at the heart of the German Wine Route.

Neustadt's **Altstadt** (old town) teems with half-timbered houses, especially along Mittelgasse, Hintergasse, Metzgergasse and Kunigundenstrasse. It's anchored by the cobbled **Marktplatz**, which is flanked by the baroque **Rathaus** (town hall), as well as the Gothic **Stiftskirche** (☏06321-841 79; http://stiftskirchenge-meinde-nw.de; Marktplatz 2; church tour adult/child €3/1, tower tour €3/1; ⏱8am-4pm Mon-Thu, 8am-noon Fri, 9am-2pm Sat). Built from red sandstone, this church, dating from the 14th century, has been shared by Protestant and Catholic congregations since 1708. Recent renovations revealed frescos from 1410 that depict a snapshot of life at the time, with bakers, crafts people and market traders. Every Saturday at noon guided tours take you into the tower, reached by 184 steps (book ahead).

DENNIS K. JOHNSON / GETTY IMAGES ©

DETOUR:
WISSEMBOURG, FRANCE

Start: ❶ Schweigen-Rechtenbach

From Schweigen-Rechtenbach, it's an easy 5km detour south over the French border to Wissembourg along the B38 (which becomes the D264 when you enter France).

The chic little town's compact centre is awash with centuries-old architectural treasures along with *boulangeries* (bakeries), *fromageries* (cheese shops) and, yes, *caves viticoles* (wine cellars).

Plaques mark 25 key sights around town that you can follow on a walking circuit. Highlights include the 1448-built **Maison du Sel** (Salt House), first a hospital, then a salt warehouse and later a slaughterhouse; the magnificent **Église Sts-Pierre-et-Paul**, incorporating a square tower from an 11th-century abbey church and dazzling stained-glass windows; and the **Couvent des Augustins**, a 1279-founded convent converted into private residences following the French Revolution.

On Wissembourg's main square, Place de la République, the tourist office sells maps outlining the walking route and has details of local hiking and cycling. Alternatively, visit www.ot-wissembourg.fr for information.

Bad Dürkheim Dürkheimer Wurstmarkt, one of the world's largest wine festivals

✕ 🛏 p183

The Drive » Follow the B38 northeast to the roundabout and continue straight ahead onto the L516, which becomes the Weinstrasse; after 8.2km, you'll arrive in Deidesheim.

- - - - - - - - - -

TRIP HIGHLIGHT

⑤ Deidesheim

Draped in pale purple-flowering wisteria in the springtime, diminutive Deidesheim is centred on its charming **Marktplatz**. This is one of the German Wine Route's most picturesque – and upmarket – villages, with plenty of opportunities for wine tasting, relaxed strolling and sublime dining.

Deidesheim is a 'Cittaslow' town, an extension of the Slow Food movement that aims to rebalance modern life's hectic pace not only through 'ecogastronomy' but also local arts, crafts, nature, cultural traditions and heritage. Galleries and artisans' studios (such as jewellery makers and potters) can be visited along the **Kunst und Kultur** (Art and Culture) Circuit; look for dark-blue-on-yellow 'K' signs.

The town is home to 10 **winemakers** (some closed Sunday) that welcome visitors – look for signs reading *Weingut* (winery), *Verkauf* (sale) and *Weinprobe* (wine tasting) and ring the bell. Many can be found along the small streets west of **Pfarrkirche St Ulrich** (Marktplatz; ⊙8am-5pm).

A Marktplatz landmark with a canopied outdoor staircase, the **Altes Rathaus** (old town hall) dates from the 16th century. Inside is the three-storey **Museum für Weinkultur** (Museum of Wine Culture; Marktplatz 8; ⊙4-6pm Wed-Sun Mar-Dec), featuring displays on winemakers' traditional lifestyle and naive-art portrayals of the German Wine Route.

Shutterbugs will love the **Deutsches Film-und Fototechnik Museum** (www.dftm.de; Weinstrasse 33; admission €2.50; ⊘2-6pm Wed-Sat, 11am-6pm Sun), tucked down an alleyway across from the **Rathaus**, with an impressive collection of historic photographic and movie-making equipment.

Signposted walking and cycling routes lead you through vineyards and the Pfälzerwald.

 p183

The Drive 》 It's a glorious 6.8km drive north from Deidesheim along the Weinstrasse (L516) through gently rolling hills ribboned with vineyards to Bad Dürkheim.

- - - - - - - - - - - -

TRIP HIGHLIGHT

⑥ Bad Dürkheim

Adorned with splashy fountains, the spa town of Bad Dürkheim is famous for its thermal springs, lovely parks such as the azalea-and-wisteria-filled **Kurgarten**

(⊘24hr), and what's claimed to be the world's largest wine festival, the **Dürkheimer Wurst-markt** (www.duerkheimer-wurstmarkt.de; ⊘2nd & 3rd weekends in Sep), as well as the world's largest wine barrel, the enormous **Dürkheimer Riesenfass**. This wine barrel has a diameter of 13.5m and a volume of 1,700,000L, and contains the Restaurant Dürkheimer Fass.

Test the waters at the modern **Kurzentrum** (☎06322-9640; www.kurzentrum-bad-duerkheim.de; Kurbrunnenstrasse 14; treatments from €15; ⊘9am-8pm Mon-Fri, 9am-5pm Sat, 9am-2.30pm Sun) spa. In its lobby, you can taste the salty water (said to be good for your digestion) from a fountain.

Weinwanderwege (vineyard trails) from St Michaelskapelle, a chapel atop a little vine-clad hill, lead to Honigsäckel and the Hochmess vineyards (a 6km circuit).

✗ p183

The Drive 》 At Bad Dürkheim, the Weinstrasse becomes the L271; follow it north via the village of Ungstein for 19km to Bockenheim an der Weinstrasse.

- - - - - - - - - - - -

⑦ Bockenheim an der Weinstrasse

The village of Bocken-heim an der Weinstrasse (not to be confused with the Frankfurt district of Bockenheim), marks the end of the German Wine Route.

Spanning the road at the village's northern edge in Roman castrum style is the modern, brick-and-tile **Haus der Deutschen Weinstrasse** (House of the German Wine Route; http://haus-der-deutschen-weinstrasse.net; Weinstrasse 91b), built in 1995 as a counterpart to the Deutsches Weintor at the route's starting point in Schweigen-Rechtenbach. There's a restaurant inside, but better dining options are elsewhere.

✗ p183

Eating & Sleeping

Neustadt an der Weinstrasse 4

✖ Urgestein   Modern German €€€

(📞06321-489 060; www.restaurant-urgestein.
de; Rathausstrasse 6; 4-course vegetarian
menu €85, 5-/6-course menus €100/120,
paired wines extra €30-50; ⏰6-10pm Tue-Sat;
🍴) For a gastronomic extravaganza, book a
table at Benjamin Peifer's Michelin-starred,
vaulted brick cellar restaurant within a half-
timbered town-centre house. Exquisite dishes
might include pickled trout with sauerkraut
and horseradish, followed by steamed liver
dumplings with riesling foam, hay-roasted
pigeon with foie gras mousse, and nougat
ganache with hazelnut yoghurt. Live jazz plays
in the summer courtyard.

🛏 Gästehaus-Weingut
Helbighof   Guesthouse €€

(📞06321-327 81; www.helbighof.de; Andergasse
40; d €81; 🅿🛜) Beneath the Hambacher
Schloss amid sprawling vineyards, this charming
family-run winery has just five guest rooms,
so book well ahead. The pick is room 3, with
balconies on two sides. Its superb wines are
sold at its honour bar; a sun terrace overlooks
the vines. Turn right after Andergasse 36, then
immediately left to reach the driveway. Cash only.

Deidesheim 5

✖ Gasthaus zur Kanne   German €€€

(📞06326-966 00; www.gasthauszurkanne.de;
Weinstrasse 31; mains €19-23, 4-/5-/6-course
menus €49/59/65; ⏰noon-2pm & 6-10pm Wed-
Sun) The Palatinate's oldest inn, dating from
1160, serves refined, contemporary regional
cuisine in an elegant space with parquet floors.
Its menu changes daily but might include
porcini-stuffed Saumagen (pig's stomach),
venison with riesling jus, or smoked trout with
cream and horseradish. Reservations are
recommended.

🛏 Deidesheimer
Hof   Boutique Hotel €€

(📞06326-968 70; www.deidesheimerhof.de;
Am Marktplatz; s/d from €85/125; 🅿❄@🛜)
In a storybook gabled building, this renowned
hostelry has 28 individually decorated,
ultra-spacious rooms (the smallest are 25 sq
metres), and two fine restaurants: **St Urban**
(mains €17.50-28; ⏰11am-10pm), whose
regional offerings include Saumagen, made
with chestnuts in autumn; and, in the vaulted
basement, the gourmet **Schwarzer Hahn**
(mains €44-59, 4-course menu €95; ⏰6-10pm
Tue-Sat), which specialises in creative French-
and Palatinate-style haute cuisine.

Bad Dürkheim 6

✖ Restaurant Dürkheimer
Fass   German €€

(📞06322-2143; www.duerkheimer-fass.de; St
Michaels-Allee 1; mains €13-23; ⏰11am-10.30pm
Apr-Oct, shorter hours Nov-Mar; 🍴) This convivial
spot occupies the Dürkheimer Riesenfass, a
gargantuan wine barrel that's had a restaurant
inside since a master cooper built it out of 200
pine trees in 1934. Dishes range from suckling
pig and liver dumplings to perch fillet with Grüne
Sosse (green sauce). There's a summer beer
garden, too.

Bockenheim an der
Weinstrasse 7

✖ Bockenheimer Weinstube   German €

(📞06359-409 00; http://bockenheimer
weinstube.de; Weinstrasse 91; mains €7-11;
⏰kitchen 5-10pm Wed-Fri, 11.30am-10pm Sat &
Sun Apr-Oct, reduced hours Nov-Mar) You can just
drop by to try local wines by the glass, but top-
notch local specialities at this rustic Weinstube
(wine tavern) include Saumagen stuffed with
whole chestnuts, bratwurst with sauerkraut, and
Flammkuchen (regional pizza) with toppings such
as ham and garlic or zucchini, tomato and cheese.
When the sun's shining, the sweetest seats are in
the vine-draped, flower-filled summer courtyard.

STRETCH YOUR LEGS
FRANKFURT

Start/Finish: Alte Oper

Distance: 4.4km

Duration: Four hours

Frankfurt's history is chronicled through its architecture on this walk, which takes in its medieval core and magnificent cathedral, its famed museum embankment along the sweeping Main River, and its glittering contemporary skyscrapers.

Take this walk on Trip

7

Alte Oper

Leave your car in the parking station opposite Frankfurt's 'old opera house', the 1880-inaugurated, Italian Renaissance–style **Alte Oper** (Opernplatz 1; ⑤Alte Oper), and check out the statues of Goethe and Mozart gracing its facade.

The Walk ⟫ Head east for 400m on Grosse Bockenheimer Strasse, along the stretch locally known as 'Fressgass' (eat street) for its gourmet shops and restaurants, then north for 50m along Börsenstrasse to Börsenplatz.

Frankfurt Stock Exchange

Built in 1843, Frankfurt's neoclassical **Börse** (☎069-2111 1515; http://deutsche-boerse.com; Börsenplatz; admission free; ☺office 9am-5pm Mon-Fri; ⑤Hauptwache), one of the world's largest stock exchanges, has allegorical statues of the five continents adorning its porch. In the square out front, the **Bulle und Bär** sculpture depicts a showdown between a bull and a bear.

The Walk ⟫ Turn right onto Schillerstrasse for 100m, crossing Fressgass; Café Hauptwache is on your right, opposite mustard-coloured church St-Katharinen-Kirche.

Café Hauptwache

One of the most beautiful buildings in Frankfurt to have escaped WWII's destruction is this 1730-built baroque guardhouse. A **restaurant** (☎069-2199 8627; http://web.cafe-hauptwache.de; An der Hauptwache 15; mains €10-26; ☺kitchen 10am-10pm Mon-Sat, noon-10pm Sun; ⑤Hauptwache) since 1904, it's enveloped by summer terraces that are perfect for a glass of Frankfurt's famous *Apfelwein* (apple wine).

The Walk ⟫ Follow Frankfurt's main pedestrianised shopping street Zeil east for 300m; turn right and follow Hasengasse for 450m to the Kaiserdom.

Kaiserdom

Frankfurt's historic centre was heavily bombed during WWII, but its 13th-century red-sandstone **Kaiserdom** (Imperial/Frankfurt Cathedral; www.dom-frankfurt.de; Domplatz 14; tower adult/concession

€3.50/1.50; ⏱church 8am-8pm Mon-Thu, noon-8pm Fri, 9am-8pm Sat & Sun; S Dom/Römer), topped by a 95m-high Gothic tower, was salvaged and restored.

The Walk » It's just 200m west to Römerberg.

Römerberg

The city's old **central square** (S Dom/Römer), reconstructed after WWII, highlights how beautiful its medieval core once was. Ornately gabled half-timbered buildings include the **Römer** (old town hall). The single-spired Protestant **Alte Nikolaikirche** (www.alte-nikolaikirche.de; ⏱10am-8pm Apr-Sep, 10am-6pm Oct-Mar) was one of the few structures here to survive the war almost intact.

The Walk » Walk 100m south to the river, cross the iron Eiserner Steg bridge and follow Schaumainkai west along the Museumsufer (Museum Embankment) for 750m.

Städel Museum

If you only get to one Frankfurt museum, make it the **Städel** (☎069-605 098; www.staedelmuseum.de; Schaumainkai 63; adult/child

€14/12; ⏱10am-7pm Tue, Wed, Sat & Sun, to 9pm Thu & Fri May-Jun & Sep, 10am-9pm daily Jul & Aug, 10am-6pm Tue, Wed, Sat & Sun, to 9pm Thu & Fri Oct-Apr; 🚌16 Otto-Hahn-Platz). Founded in 1815, this world-renowned art gallery has an outstanding collection of European art from the Middle Ages to today.

The Walk » Cross pedestrian Holbeinsteg back to the north bank and follow the riverfront promenade east for 450m, then north for 560m along Neue Mainzerstrasse to Main Tower.

Main Tower

Survey the ground you've covered by taking a 45-second elevator ride to the observation platform of the 200m-high **Main Tower** (☎069-3650 4878; www.maintower.de; Neue Mainzer Strasse 52-58; elevator adult/child €6.50/4.50; ⏱10am-9pm Sun-Thu, to 11pm Fri & Sat late Mar-late Oct, 10am-7pm Sun-Thu, to 9pm Fri & Sat late Oct-late Mar; S Alte Oper), one of the tallest and most distinctive high-rises in 'Mainhattan'.

The Walk » From Main Tower, walking 400m north along Neue Mainzerstrasse brings you back to the Alte Oper.

STRETCH YOUR LEGS
COLOGNE

Start/Finish: Kölner Dom

Distance: 2km

Duration: Three hours

Cologne's history is everywhere, as you'll see on this walk, which circles through the heart of the bustling city. You can view Roman or medieval ruins, and you'll always be near somewhere to pause for refreshments.

Take this walk on Trips

Kölner Dom

Cologne's geographical and spiritual heart – and its single-biggest tourist draw – is the magnificent **Kölner Dom** (Cologne Cathedral; ☎0211-1794 0200; www. koelner-dom.de; tower adult/concession €4/2; ⏰6am-9pm May-Oct, to 7.30pm Nov-Apr, tower 9am-6pm May-Sep, to 5pm Mar-Apr & Oct, to 4pm Nov-Feb), with its soaring twin spires, art and treasures. Climb the 533 steps up its south tower to the base of the steeple that dwarfed all European buildings until Eiffel built a certain tower in Paris. The underground Domforum visitor centre is a good source of info and tickets.

The Walk ≫ There are large parking facilities around the Dom and the neighbouring Hauptbahnhof (just follow the signs). Then, after Kölner Dom, walk south across the Roncalliplatz to Am Hof, turn east then go south again on Bechergasse to the large, open Rathausplatz.

Altes Rathaus

Dating to the 15th century and much restored, the **old city hall** (Rathausplatz; ⏰8am-4pm Mon, Wed & Thu, to 6pm Tue) has fine bells that ring daily at noon and 5pm. The Gothic tower is festooned with statues of old city notables.

The Walk ≫ Walk to the west side of the Rathaus.

Archäologische Zone

Cologne used the construction of the U-Bahn line to also build this grand **Future Jüdisches Museum** (Archaeological Zone/ Jewish Museum; ☎0221-2213 3422; Kleine Buden-gasse 2; adult/concession €3.50/3; ⏰10am-5pm Tue-Sun) under the Rathausplatz. At the deepest level is the Praetorium, with relics of a Roman governor's palace. One level up are relics from the Middle Ages Jewish community.

The Walk ≫ Cross the Marsplatz on the south side of the square to the museum.

Wallraf-Richartz-Museum

A famous collection of European paint-ings from the 13th to the 19th centuries, the **Wallraf-Richartz-Museum** (☎0221-2212 1119; www.wallraf.museum; Obenmarspforten; adult/concession €8/4.50; ⏰10am-6pm Tue, Wed & Fri-Sun, to 9pm Thu) occupies a postmodern cube designed by OM Ungers. Works are presented chronologically, with the oldest on the 1st floor where stand-outs include examples from the Cologne School, known for its distinctive use of colour.

The Walk » Go west past the shops on Obenmarspforten for four streets, then turn north on Kolumbastrasse.

Kolumba

Art, history, architecture and spirituality form a harmonious tapestry in this spectacular collection of religious treasures of the Archdiocese of Cologne. Called **Kolumba** (☏0221-933 1930; www.kolumba.de; Kolumbastrasse 4; adult/child €5/free; ☉noon-5pm Wed-Mon), the building encases the ruins of the late-Gothic church of St Kolumba and layers of foundations going back to Roman times. Don't miss the 12th-century carved ivory crucifix.

The Walk » Walk west on commercial Breite Strasse, then turn north on Dumont-Strasse.

NS Dokumentationszentrum

Cologne's Third Reich history is poignantly documented in the **NS Documentation**

Centre (☏0221-2212 6332; www.museenkoeln.de; Appellhofplatz 23-25; adult/concession €4.50/2; ☉10am-6pm Tue-Fri, 11am-6pm Sat & Sun). In the basement of this otherwise mundane-looking building was the local Gestapo prison where scores of people were interrogated, tortured and killed.

The Walk » It's just a short jaunt north again along low-key Dumont-Strasse.

Kölnisches Stadtmuseum

The **Kölnisches Stadtmuseum** (Cologne City Museum; ☏0221-2212 2398; www.museenkoeln.de; Zeughausstrasse 1-3; adult/concession €5/3; ☉10am-8pm Tue, to 5pm Wed-Sun), in the former medieval armoury, explores all facets of Cologne history. There are exhibits on Carnival, *Kölsch* (the local beer), eau de cologne and other things that make the city unique. A **model** recreates the city of 1571; it's huge yet minutely detailed.

The Walk » Return to the Dom along Komödienstrasse, with the cathedral towers looming ever closer. Stop off for a much-deserved refreshment at Café Reichard, facing the Dom.

Southern Germany Trips

DREAMY CASTLES AND ROMANTIC ALPINE MEADOWS, glass art and glassy mountain lakes, dark tourism and enigmatic border forests – southern Germany has the lot and tonnes more besides.

Variety is the watchword in Bavaria and Baden-Württemberg (the two states that make up Germany's south); driving this chapter's routes could have you taking a Zeppelin ride above Lake Constance, ascending Germany's highest mountain by train and passing through thickly wooded landscapes of the Bavarian Forest, all in a matter of days.

But all the routes have something in common – the affluent south is infused with that feeling of *Gemütlichkeit,* a state of cosiness and good cheer you'll discover in every traditional tavern and inn from Franconia to the Alps.

Garmisch-Partenkirchen A beautiful area that is popular with outdoorsy types (Trip 19)
DENNIS FISCHER PHOTOGRAPHY / GETTY IMAGES ©

Southern Germany Trips

DON'T MISS

Königssee

Take an eco-friendly electric-boat tour across the tranquil expanse of Germany's most picturesque lake. This day out can be enjoyed on Trip 19

Würzburg Residenz

Ogle the world's largest fresco at Würzburg's magnificent Unesco-listed palace. Get your ticket as part of Trip 17

Rothenburg ob der Tauber

Go full circle around this town's medieval walls before celebrating Christmas in July with a tasty snowball! You'll find it on Trips 16 10 23 13 17

Neuschwanstein Castle

The world's most famous castle inspired Walt Disney's citadel and strikes a fairy-tale pose against Alpine forests. Book your tour on Trip 17

21 Fantastic Road 4–6 Days
Fascinating ring through Baden-Württemberg running through a chunk of the Black Forest. (p255)

22 Schwarzwaldhochstrasse 2–4 Days
High-altitude motoring through the magnificent landscapes of the Black Forest. (p263)

Darmstadt Mathildenhöhe is the best place to see art-nouveau architecture

Bergstrasse

As you drive Germany's beautiful Bergstrasse ('mountain road'), you'll realise it could just as easily be called Burgstrasse ('castle road') for the lofty castles lining this short but attraction-packed route.

TRIP HIGHLIGHTS

START
Darmstadt

13 km
Grube Messel
Archaeological discoveries here date back 49 million years

33 km
Burg Frankenstein
The castle that inspired author Mary Shelley

Lorsch Abbey

91 km
Heidelberg
Renowned for its red-sandstone castle

HockenheimRing

Wiesloch
FINISH

2–4 DAYS
125 KM / 77 MILES

GREAT FOR...

BEST TIME TO GO

Any time of year works but you'll enjoy the best weather between April and October.

ESSENTIAL PHOTO

Wiesloch's statue of Bertha Benz, the world's first road-tripper.

BEST FOR DRIVERS

The HockenheimRing Formula One Grand Prix track.

15 | Bergstrasse

This old Roman trade route along the edge of the Odenwald mountain range, above the Rhine marshland, might be just 125km long, but the diversity you'll encounter is astonishing: stunning *Jugendstil* (art-nouveau) architecture, extraordinary archaeological discoveries, the castle that inspired Mary Shelley's *Frankenstein,* a monumental medieval abbey, romantic Heidelberg, Wiesloch, where trailblazer Bertha Benz made motoring history, and Germany's most famous racetrack.

❶ Darmstadt

Famed for its technical university and the creation of super-heavy element Darmstadtium (Ds; atomic number: 110), Darmstadt is a designated *Wissenschaftsstadt* (City of Science).

Part of the university is housed in Darmstadt's spectacular Schloss, along with a **museum** (☎06151-240 35; www.schlossmuseum-darmstadt.de; Marktplatz 15; adult/child €4/2; ☺tours 10am, 11.30am, 1pm, 2.30pm & 4pm Fri-Sun).

The best place to see the city's renowned *Jugendstil* (art-nouveau) architecture is Mathildenhöhe, the former *Künstlerkolonie* (artists' colony),

established in 1899 by Grand Duke Ernst Ludwig. Surrounded by a fountain-filled hilltop park, its **Museum Künstlerkolonie** (Olbrichweg 13; adult/child €5/3; ☺11am-6pm Tue-Sun Apr-Sep, 11am-5pm Tue-Sun Oct-Mar) showcases *Jugendstil* furniture, tableware, textiles, ceramics and jewellery.

Or simply splash about at the exquisite 1909 indoor/outdoor *Jugendstil* pool and spa complex **Jugendstilbad** (www.jugendstilbad.de; Mercksplatz 1; swimming pools 2hr/4hr/all day €6/8.20/10.40, incl spa €9.30/12.10/14.30, incl spa & saunas €13.60/16.40/19.70; ☺10am-10pm, to midnight 2nd Fri of month, to 2am last Sat of month).

🍴 🛏 p199

The Drive » From Darmstadt's Schloss, head east on Alexanderstrasse, which becomes the L3094. Follow it for 10km through beautiful forest; Grube Messel is signposted 300m off on your left.

TRIP HIGHLIGHT

❷ Grube Messel

A Unesco World Heritage site, this one-time coal-and-oil-shale quarry 10km northeast of Darmstadt, known as **Grube Messel** (Messel Pit; ☎0615-971 7590; www.grube-messel.de; Rossdörfer Strasse 108; visitor centre adult/child €10/8, guided pit tour €7; ☺10am-5pm, tour by reservation), is an archaeological wonder, with superbly preserved animal and plant remains from the Eocene era (around 49 million years ago). Fossils of ancient horses found here illustrate the evolutionary path towards the modern beast.

A pretty half-timbered house 3km south of the visitor centre is a fossil-filled **museum** (www.messelmuseum.de; Langgasse 2; admission free; ☺11am-5pm Apr-Oct, 11am-5pm Sat & Sun Nov-Mar). Better yet, you can visit the pit itself with a German-speaking guide or pre-arrange an English-speaking tour (extra €20 per group).

Other intriguing finds from the site are displayed at the Hessisches Landesmuseum in Darmstadt and the

Senckenberg Museum in Frankfurt.

The Drive » Rejoin the L3094 and travel east towards Dieburg; on its outskirts, turn right (south) on Burgweg. After 1.7km, turn right at the roundabout onto the K128 and follow it for 14km before turning right onto the B426 for 6.7km. Turn left and climb the twisting, precipitous road through shadowed forest to Burg Frankenstein.

TRIP HIGHLIGHT

❸ Burg Frankenstein

Built by Lord Konrad II Reiz von Breuberg around 1250 (who thereafter added *'von und zu* Frankenstein' to his name), hulking, partly ruined hilltop castle **Burg Frankenstein** (www.frankenstein-restaurant.de; Mühltal; admission by donation; ◷ castle 9am-sunset except during events) was visited by Mary Shelley on her

---

🔗 LINK YOUR TRIP

16 German Castle Road

For yet more castles, drive 20km northwest from Heidelberg via the A656 to Mannheim to set out on the German Castle Road.

21 Fantastic Road

The ancient university city of Heidelberg is the starting point for an unforgettable loop through forest-filled Baden-Württemberg.

German travels in 1814, inspiring the title of her Gothic novel and its protagonist. Tours of the castle are in German; you're free to walk around the castle and grounds, or to just stop in for a drink on its restaurant's panoramic terrace.

If you time it right, you can also catch atmospheric events here, including one of Europe's largest – and spookiest – Halloween parties, as well as medieval banquets, costumed adventure castle days, live music including jazz, and theatre nights.

The Drive » Twist back downhill and take the B426 west for 1.4km before turning left (south) onto the B3. After Zwingenberg you'll see Schloss Auerbach looming on your left above the town of Auerbach. Turn west on the B47 for 2.7km then right onto Bensheimer Strasse in the charming village of Lorsch and follow the signs to Lorsch Abbey (29km all up).

- - - - - - - - -

4 Lorsch Abbey

Founded around AD 760 and Unesco-listed in 1991, **Lorsch Abbey** (Kloster Lorsch; www.kloster-lorsch.de; Nibelungenstrasse 35, Lorsch; adult/child €5/3; ⊙10am-5pm Tue-Sun, English tours 11am & 4pm Mar-Oct, 11am & 4pm Sat & Sun Nov-Feb) was a significant religious site in its Carolingian heyday (8th to 10th centuries). Preserved medieval

buildings include the rare, Carolingian-era Königshalle and the Altenmünster; museum exhibits cover the history of the abbey, life in Hesse and tobacco, which was cultivated in Lorsch in the late 17th century.

The Drive » Return to the B3 and take it south for 32km to Heidelberg. En route, look out for castles, including Starkenburg (housing a hostel) on your left above Heppenheim village, and Wachenburg (home to a restaurant) on your left above the town of Weinheim.

- - - - - - - - -

TRIP HIGHLIGHT

5 Heidelberg

In a spellbinding riverside setting surrounded by forest, Germany's oldest university town is renowned for its baroque, red-roofed **Altstadt** (old town), which emerged from WWII almost unscathed, and for its evocative half-ruined **Schloss Heidelberg** (✆06221-658 880; www.schloss-heidelberg.de; adult/child incl Bergbahn €6/4, tours €4/2, audioguide €4; ⊙grounds 24hr, castle 8am-6pm, English tours hourly 11.15am-4.15pm Mon-Fri, 10.15am-4.15pm Sat & Sun Apr-Oct, reduced tours Nov-Mar). You can reach the hilltop castle either via a steep, cobbled trail in about 10 minutes or by Bergbahn (cogwheel train) from Kornmarkt station. Castle highlights include the

world's largest wine cask and fabulous views.

For the best views *of* the Schloss, cross the **Alte Brücke**, Heidelberg's 200m-long, 1786-built 'old bridge', to the right bank of the Neckar River and the **Schlangenweg** (Snake Path), whose switchbacks lead to the **Philosophenweg** (Philosophers' Walk). Don't drive up here, as the road is narrow and there's nowhere to turn around at the top.

Heidelberg's charms draw 11.8 million visitors a year. They follow

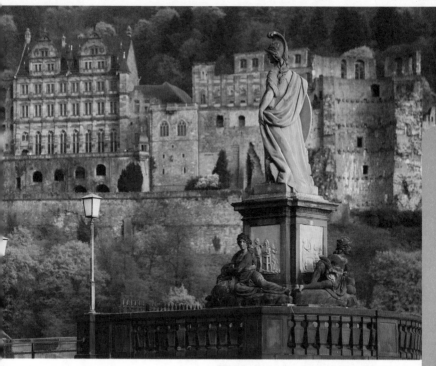

Heidelberg Alte Brücke and Schloss Heidelberg in the distance

in the footsteps of the late-18th- and early-19th-century Romantics, most notably the poet Goethe. Heidelberg also inspired Britain's William Turner to paint some of his greatest landscapes. In 1878, Mark Twain began his European travels in Heidelberg, recounting his observations in *A Tramp Abroad* (1880). Heidelberg's rich literary history, along with its thriving contemporary scene, saw it named a Unesco City of Literature in 2014.

The longer you spend here, the more heart-stopping panoramas and hidden treasures you'll discover.

✕ 🛏 p199

The Drive » It's just 14km south from Heidelberg along the B3 to Wiesloch, at the foot of the Kraichgau hills.

- - - - - - - - - - - - - - -

⑥ Wiesloch

Cute little Wiesloch was pivotal in the evolution of road trips: this is where Bertha Benz – business partner and wife of automobile inventor Karl Benz – refuelled on the first-ever long-distance drive in 1888. Bertha stopped at Wiesloch's pharmacy, the **Stadt-Apotheke** (☎06222-588 120; http://stadtapotheke-wiesloch.de; Hauptstrasse 96; ⊗8.30am-1pm & 2-7pm Mon-Fri, 9am-2pm Sat), still a pharmacy today, which provided her with Ligroin (petroleum ether), making it the world's first filling station. Its small **history museum** only opens a handful of days a year.

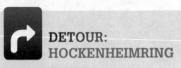

DETOUR:
HOCKENHEIMRING

Start: ❺ Heidelberg

One detour no dedicated road-tripper will want to miss is to the hallowed **HockenheimRing** (☏06205-950 222, track reservations 06205-950 6005; www.hockenheimring.de; Hockenheim).

Signposted 22km southwest of Heidelberg just east of the A6, it has three circuits and stands that accommodate up to 120,000 fans, and hosts some of Germany's most famous car races, including the Formula One German Grand Prix (in even-numbered years).

Start by taking a look behind the scenes on an **Insider Tour** (adult/child incl museum €12/6.50; ⊙11am except during races, advance bookings required Dec-Mar), available in English and German. Tickets are sold at the **Motor Sport Museum** (adult/child €6/3; ⊙10am-5pm Apr-Oct, 10am-5pm Fri-Sun Nov-Mar, longer hours on race days).

While you're here, make time to check out the museum's fantastic collection of historic motorcycles, some a century old, and its ensemble of historic race cars. Upstairs, look out for the reconstruction of the world's first motorcycle, built from wood by Maybach and Daimler in 1885.

If roaring along on a speed-limit-less autobahn doesn't get your adrenaline pumping any more, you can take to the Hockenheim track yourself when it isn't being used for a race:

Action Track Days (per person €399) Three laps on the Grand Prix course with a professional driver in a superfast racing car, such as a Porsche GT3, a Mercedes SLK 350 or an Audi R8 V10.

Drifttaxi (€229) Lets you experience high-speed skids with a professional driver.

Race'n'Roll (€399) Drive a race car yourself.

Touristenfahrten (€15 per 15 minutes) Drive your own car around the track.

Outside on the cobbled square there's a bronze-and-steel **statue** of Bertha driving her three-wheeled contraption.

Bertha set out with her two teenage sons, without her husband's knowledge, to highlight the possibilities of the machine no one had wanted to buy. Repairs en route included clearing a clogged fuel line with her hat pin, and fixing a broken ignition with her garter. Her circuit – from Mannheim to Pforzheim and back, which she took at an average speed of 16km/h – is now the 194km Bertha **Benz Memorial Route** (www.bertha-benz.de).

Eating & Sleeping

Darmstadt ①

🍴 Elisabeth   Cafe €

(www.suppkult.de; Schulstrasse 14; dishes
€3.80-5.80; ⊙11am-4.30pm Mon-Fri, to 4pm
Sat; 🖊️🚼) Hidden down a passageway in a
picnic-table-filled courtyard, this wonderful
spot specialises in homemade soups (which
change daily): pork meatballs and split green
peas; curried apple and potato; lentil, carrot
and leek; and roast tomato with sheep's cheese,
all served with home-baked sourdough or rye
bread. Salads are also available as meals. Finish
off with fabulous cakes.

🛏️ Hotel Jagdschloss
Kranichstein   Historic Hotel €€

(📞06151-130 670; www.hotel-jagdschloss-
kranichstein.de; Kranichstein Strasse 261; d from
€95; 🅿️@🛜) Set on 4.2 hectares of forest
and parkland 5km northeast of Darmstadt, this
1580-built hunting lodge is now a magnificent
hotel, with contemporary countrified rooms
throughout the estate's buildings. Breakfast
starts from €17; epicurean options include a
game-specialist restaurant, bar/bistro, and
Bierstube (beer room) in the armoury, opening
to a beer garden, plus gourmet hampers for
summer picnicking in the grounds.

Heidelberg ⑤

🍴 'S' Kastanie   German €€

(📞06221-728 0343; www.restaurant-s-kastanie.
de; Elisabethenweg 1; 2-course lunch menu €9,
mains €12-28; ⊙11.30am-2.30pm & 6-10pm
Wed-Fri, 5-10pm Sat, 11.30am-8pm Sun) A
panoramic terrace provides sweeping views
of the river at this gorgeous 1904-built former
hunting lodge, with stained glass and timber

panelling, set in the forest near the castle. Chef
Sven Schönig's stunning creations include a
sweet potato and goat's cheese tower with
papaya, and goose-stuffed ravioli.

🍴 Schnitzelbank   German €€

(📞06221-211 89; www.schnitzelbank-heidelberg.
de; Baumamtsgasse 7; mains €15-22; ⊙5pm-
1am Mon-Thu, 11.30am-1am Fri & Sun) Small
and often jam-packed, this cosy wine tavern
has you sampling the local tipples (all wines are
regional) and cuisine while crouched on wooden
workbenches from the time when this was still
a cooperage. It's these benches that give the
place its name, incidentally, not the veal and
pork schnitzel on the menu. Other specialities
include *Schäufele* (stuffed pig's stomach).

🛏️ Hotel Villa
Marstall   Historic Hotel €€

(📞06221-655 570; www.villamarstall.de;
Lauerstrasse 1; s €95-165, d €115-185; ⊙reception
7am-10pm Mon-Sat, 8am-6pm Sun; ❄️🛜) A
19th-century neoclassical mansion directly
overlooking the Neckar River, Villa Marstall is
a jewel with cherrywood floors, solid-timber
furniture and amenities including a lift/elevator.
Exquisite rooms are decorated in whites, creams
and bronzes, and come with in-room fridges
(perfect for chilling a bottle of regional wine). A
sumptuous breakfast buffet (€10) is served in the
red-sandstone vaulted cellar.

🛏️ Kulturbrauerei Hotel   Hotel €€

(📞06221-502 980; www.heidelberger-
kulturbrauerei.de; Leyergasse 6; d €120-180; 🛜)
This stylish Altstadt hotel above the eponymous
microbrewery (⊙7am-midnight) has
romantic cream-coloured rooms with polished
parquet floors, classical furniture and large
windows. Breakfast is €12 for hotel guests (€15
for nonguests).

Bayreuth An ornate fountain stands in front of Neues Schloss

Classic Trip

German Castle Road

16

On this trip you'll follow a ribbon of fairy-tale castles that winds its way across Germany's south, along with the wonderful historic towns that host them.

TRIP HIGHLIGHTS

29 km

Heidelberg
Romantic castle ruins lording over Heidelberg's old town

319 km

Nuremberg
Bavaria's second city is packed with history

FINISH
Bayreuth

Mannheim ②
START

⑤ ⑥

Schwäbisch Hall

Rothenburg ob der Tauber
A romantically walled, perfectly preserved medieval town

208 km

7 DAYS
507 KM / 316 MILES

GREAT FOR...

BEST TIME TO GO

To get the best out of this trip, travel between Easter and October.

ESSENTIAL PHOTO

The view from Nuremberg's Sinwell Tower.

BEST FOR HISTORY

Nuremberg is a treasure trove of European history.

Classic Trip

16 German Castle Road

This romantic trip will take you castle-hopping across 600km of southern Germany and through a thousand years of the country's history. From Germany's biggest baroque pile in Mannheim to Bayreuth's Altes Schloss, it's castle-a-day time on this route, and when palace fatigue sets in, there's nothing easier than escaping to a contemporary art gallery, fascinating museum, or a traditional tavern to sample the local sausages and unsurpassed beer.

1 Mannheim

The Castle Road kicks off in style at the gates of **Barockschloss Mannheim** (www.schloss-mannheim.de; cnr Bismarckstrasse & Breite Strasse). The city's most famous sight is Germany's largest baroque palace. Now occupied by the University of Mannheim, the 450m-long structure was built over the course of 40 years in the mid-1700s but was almost completely destroyed during WWII. Off the main courtyard are the **Schloss Museum** (Ehren-hof; adult/child incl audioguide €6/3, incl guided tour in English €8/4; ⊙10am-5pm Tue-Sun), where you can see the impressively rococo Kabinettsbibliothek, saved from wartime destruction having been stored off-site, and several baroque halls – each a feast of stucco, marble, porcelain and chandeliers – rebuilt after the war.

The **Schlosskirche** (⊙10am-5pm) was constructed between 1720 and 1731, and rebuilt post-WWII. Mozart performed here in 1777. It belongs to the Alt-Katholiken (Old Catholics), a movement that split with Rome over papal infallibility in the 1870s and is now part of the Anglican Communion.

✕ ⊨ p210

The Drive » To reach Heidelberg from Mannheim, take the B36 then the A656 heading southeast. Traffic can be heavy on these roads. Heidelberg is just 19km from Mannheim, meaning it can also be tackled as a day trip by public transport from there; Mannheim's S-Bahn and regional trains make the run every few minutes.

2 Heidelberg

Towering over the **Altstadt** (old town), the ruins of Renaissance **Schloss Heidelberg** (☎06221-658 880; www.schloss-heidelberg.de; adult/child incl Bergbahn €6/4, tours €4/2, audioguide €4; ⊙grounds 24hr, castle 8am-6pm, English tours hourly 11.15am-4.15pm Mon-Fri, 10.15am-4.15pm Sat & Sun Apr-Oct, reduced tours Nov-Mar) cut a romantic figure, especially across the Neckar River when illuminated at night. It's a steep climb, but once you arrive up top, you'll be struck by the far-reaching views over the Neckar River and the Altstadt rooftops. The only way to see the interior is by tour, which can be safely skipped. After 6pm you can stroll the grounds for free.

Another sight in town tourists gravitate to is the **Marktplatz**, the focal point of Altstadt street life. The trickling **Hercules fountain** – that's him

LINK YOUR TRIP

17 The Romantic Road
The Castle Road and the Romantic Road meet up in Rothenburg ob der Tauber.

18 Glass Route
Bayreuth is 60km northwest of Weiden, which is at the northern end of the Glass Route.

up on top of the pillar – in the middle is where petty criminals were chained and left to face the mob in the Middle Ages.

The Drive » To reach the next stop at Burg Guttenberg, the quickest route is to take the A6 autobahn, a journey of 62km which you should cover in a snappy 45 minutes. However, a much more picturesque but considerably slower way to go is to follow country roads along the Neckar Valley where several dramatic castle ruins wait to be discovered.

❸ Burg Guttenberg

Rising high above the Neckar Valley, lonely **Burg Guttenberg** (www.burg-guttenberg.de; Burg-strasse, Hassmersheim-Neckarmü; adult/concession €5/3; ⏱10am-6pm) is one of the most dramatic castles on this part of the route and a fine example of an intact 14th-century castle. In addition to the gobsmacking views of the surrounding vineyards and forests, the award-winning exhibition inside acquaints visitors with the life of medieval knights. The castle has a tavern with great views.

The Drive » From Burg Guttenberg continue south along the attractive Neckar Valley until you reach the town of Neckarsulm. From there take

CONTINUING INTO THE CZECH REPUBLIC

In 1994 the Castle Road was extended into the Czech Republic, a country as rich in castle architecture as southern Germany. The route crosses the border between Bavaria and the Czech Republic at Cheb. Be aware that cars hired in Germany cannot normally be taken over the border into the Czech Republic.

Castle highlights of the Czech section of the route include idyllic Loket, with its perfectly preserved medieval town; Bečov nad Teplou, with its famous reliquary; Křivoklát Castle, set dramatically against the forests of Central Bohemia; 14th-century Karlštejn Castle, built to house the imperial crown jewels of the Holy Roman Empire; and of course Prague Castle, the daddy of all Central European royal residences, where a millennium of history is presented in fascinating exhibitions.

the A6 autobahn as far as exit 43 for Schwäbisch Hall. The whole journey is 72km and should take little more than an hour.

❹ Schwäbisch Hall

Out on its rural lonesome near the Bavarian border, Schwäbisch Hall is an unsung gem. It's a medieval time capsule of higgledy-piggledy lanes, soaring half-timbered houses built high on the riches of salt, and covered bridges that criss-cross the Kocher River – storybook stuff.

Buzzy cafes and first-rate museums add to the appeal of this town, known for its rare black-spotted pigs, which can be seen at the **Hohenloher Freilandmuseum** (Wackershofen; adult/concession €7/5; ⏱9am-6pm May-Sep, 10am-5pm Tue-Sun rest of year; 🚐), an open-air farming museum that will be a sure-fire hit with the kids. It's 6km northwest of Schwäbisch Hall and served by bus 7. However, Schwäbisch Hall's top attraction is the **Kunsthalle Würth** (www.kunst.wuerth.com; Lange Strasse 35; ⏱10am-6pm daily, guided tours 11.30am & 2pm Sun), a contemporary gallery housed in a striking limestone building that preserves part of a century-old brewery. Stellar temporary exhibitions have recently spotlighted the precious silver of London's Victoria & Albert Museum and Op Art kinetics. Guided tours are in German only but audioguides in English are available.

p210

The Drive » The best way to reach the next halt at Rothenburg ob der Tauber 55km away to the northeast is to take the L2218 country road back to the A6 motorway. After a short stretch of superfast autobahn driving, take exit 45 and the L1040 that will take you all the way to your destination. You are now in Bavaria.

TRIP HIGHLIGHT

⑤ Rothenburg ob der Tauber

A medieval gem, Rothenburg ob der Tauber is also a top stop along the Romantic Road (Trip 17; see p216). With its web of cobbled lanes, crooked medieval houses and towered walls, the town is a fairy tale in bricks and plaster.

A striking feature here is the **Stadtmauer** (Town Walls), which forms a 2.5km uninterrupted ring around the historical core.

At the **Käthe Wohlfahrt Weihnachts-dorf** (www.wohlfahrt.com; Herrngasse 1; ◷9am-6pm) you can buy a mind-boggling assortment of high-quality Yuletide

---

NUREMBERG FOR KIDS

No city in Germany's south has more for kids to see and do than Nuremberg. In fact, keeping the little 'uns entertained in the Franconian capital is child's play.

Museums

Children & Young People's Museum (☏0911-600 040; www.kindermuseum-nuernberg. de; Michael-Ende-Strasse 17; adult/family €7/19; ◷2-5.30pm Sat, 10am-5.30pm Sun Sep-Jun) Educational exhibitions and lots of hands-on fun – just a pity it's not open more often.

School Museum (☏0911-530 2574; Äussere Sulzbacher Strasse 62; adult/child €5/3; ◷9am-5pm Tue-Fri, 10am-6pm Sat & Sun) Recreated classroom plus school-related exhibits from the 17th century to the Third Reich.

Deutsche Bahn Museum (☏0800-3268 7386; www.db-museum.de; Lessingstrasse 6; adult/child €5/2.50; ◷9am-5pm Tue-Fri, 10am-6pm Sat & Sun) Feeds the kids' obsession for choo-choo trains.

Play

Playground of the Senses (www.erfahrungsfeld.nuernberg.de; Untere Talgasse 8; adult/child €8/6.50; ◷9am-6pm Mon-Fri, 1-6pm Sat, 10am-6pm Sun May–mid-Sep) Some 80 hands-on 'stations' designed to educate children in the laws of nature, physics and the human body. Take the U2 or U3 to Wöhrder Wiese.

Toys

Playmobil (☏0911-9666 1700; www.playmobil-funpark.de; Brandstätterstrasse 2-10; admission €11; ◷9am-7pm May-Sep, 9am-6pm Oct) This theme park has life-size versions of the popular toys. It's located 9km west of the city centre in Zirndorf; take the S4 to Anwanden, then change to bus 151. Free admission if it's your birthday. Special 'Kleine Dürer' (Little Dürer; €2.99) figures are on sale here and at the tourist office.

Käthe Wohlfahrt Christmas shop (www.wohlfahrt.com; Königstrasse 8) The Nuremberg branch of this year-round Christmas shop.

Spielzeugmuseum (Toy Museum; Karlstrasse 13-15; adult/child €5/3; ◷10am-5pm Tue-Fri, to 6pm Sat & Sun) Some 1400 sq metres of Matchbox, Barbie, Playmobil and Lego, plus a great play area.

Classic Trip

CALLE MONTES / GETTY IMAGES ©

WALTER SCHIESSWOHL / GETTY IMAGES ©

WHY THIS IS A CLASSIC TRIP
MARC DI DUCA, AUTHOR

Think of Central Europe and castles – medieval, Renaissance and in all manner of 'neo' styles – probably come to mind. This route satisfies the longing many history fans have to take a peek into the way dukes, royals, prince-bishops and assorted other gentry once lived, a world away from the crooked medieval streets of the towns that surround them.

Top: Cobbled lanes and medieval houses in Rothenburg ob der Tauber
Left: Barbecued Coburg sausages
Right: Bamberg's beautifully painted Rathaus

decorations, so you can celebrate Christmas every day of the year if you want. Next door is the **Deutsches Weihnachts-museum** (Christmas Museum; ☎09861-409 365; www.weihnachtsmuseum.de; Herrngasse 1; adult/child/family €4/2.50/7; ⊙10am-5pm daily Easter-Christmas, shorter hours Jan-Easter) – also an odd experience in July.

Rothenburg's most popular museum is the **Mittelalterliches Kriminalmuseum** (Medieval Crime & Punishment Museum; www.kriminalmuseum.eu; Burggasse 3; adult/concession €5/3.50; ⊙10am-6pm May-Oct, shorter hours Nov-Apr), where you can view medieval implements of torture and punishment.

The Drive » There are several ways of getting to your next stop, the city of Nuremberg. The simplest is to head south to the autobahn, which will see you get through the 111km in around 1½ hours. Slower routes go via Ansbach, which also has a magnificent Residenz (palace).

TRIP HIGHLIGHT

⑥ Nuremberg

Bavaria's second city is a lively, energetic and moodily historic place. For centuries, it was the undeclared capital of the Holy Roman Empire and the preferred residence of most German kings, who kept their crown jewels at the **Kaiserburg** (Imperial Castle; ☎0911-244 6590; www.kaiserburg-nuernberg.de;

Classic Trip

TOP TIP:
NÜRNBERG CARD

Costing just €25, the Nürnberg Card allows admission to all the city's museums (there are 40 to choose from) and access to the excellent public transport system. It's available from tourist offices in Nuremberg or via www.tourismus.nuernberg.de.

Auf der Burg; adult/concession incl Sinwell Tower €7/6, Palas & Museum €5.50/4.50; ⊙9am-6pm Apr-Sep, 10am-4pm Oct-Mar). This enormous castle complex above the **Altstadt** poignantly reflects Nuremberg's medieval might. The main attraction is a tour of the newly renovated residential wing to see the lavish Knights' and Imperial Hall, a Romanesque double chapel and an exhibit on the Holy Roman Empire. This segues to the Kaiserburg Museum, which focuses on the castle's military and building history. Elsewhere, enjoy panoramic views from the Sinwell Tower or peer 48m down into the Deep Well.

Nuremberg's other stellar sight is the **Germanisches National-museum** (German National Museum; ☎0911-133 10; www.gnm.de; Kartäusergasse 1; adult/concession €8/5; ⊙10am-6pm Tue & Thu-Sun, to 9pm Wed), the German-speaking world's biggest and most important museum of Teutonic culture.

✗ ⊨ p210

The Drive ≫ From busy Nuremberg head north along the A73 via Forchheim, a trip of about 61km. To the east of the road extends the so-called Fränkische Schweiz (Franconian

Switzerland), a soothing area of wooded hills, lazy rivers and village breweries producing Franconia's countless types of tasty *Landbier* (regional beer).

- - - - - - - - - - - - - -

❼ Bamberg
A disarmingly beautiful architectural masterpiece with an almost complete absence of modern eyesores, Bamberg's entire **Altstadt** is a Unesco World Heritage site and one of Bavaria's unmissables. Generally regarded as one of Germany's most attractive settlements, the town is bisected by rivers and canals and was built on seven hills, earning it the inevitable nickname of 'Franconian Rome'. Make your way across its bridges and along the narrow medieval streets to the gaggle of hilltop sights, beginning with the **Neue Residenz** (New Residence; ☎0951-519 390; Domplatz 8; adult/concession €4.50/3.50; ⊙9am-6pm Apr-Sep, 10am-4pm Oct-Mar). This splendid episcopal palace gives you an eyeful of the lavish lifestyle of Bamberg's prince-

bishops who, between 1703 and 1802, occupied its 40-odd rooms. Nearby rises the **Bamberger Dom** (www.erzbistum-bamberg.de; Domplatz; ⊙8am-6pm Apr-Oct, to 5pm Nov-Mar), a cathedral packed with artistic treasures, most famously the life-size equestrian statue of the **Bamberger Reiter** (Bamberg Horseman), whose true identity remains a mystery.

The Drive ≫ The B73 is your road today as you head 53km north to Coburg. Along the way you pass through Lichtenfels, a small town renowned for its basket-weaving traditions and its commanding baroque basilica visible for miles around.

- - - - - - - - - - - - - -

❽ Coburg
Coburg is most famous for its associations with the British royal family – Prince Albert of Saxe-Coburg-Gotha famously married his cousin Queen Victoria in 1857. Albert spent his childhood at **Schloss Ehrenburg** (☎09561-808 832; www.sgvcoburg.de; Schlossplatz; adult/concession €4.50/3.50; ⊙tours

hourly 9am-5pm Tue-Sun Apr-Sep, 10am-4pm Tue-Sun Oct-Mar), a lavish palace and erstwhile residence of the Coburg dukes. Queen Victoria stayed here in a room with Germany's first flushing toilet (1860). The splendid **Riesensaal** (Hall of Giants) has a baroque ceiling supported by 28 statues of Atlas. Prince Albert's statue can be found on Coburg's **Marktplatz**.

However, Coburg's blockbuster attraction is **Veste Coburg** (www.kunstsammlungen-coburg.de; adult/concession €6/3; ⏲9.30am-5pm daily Apr-Oct, 1-4pm Tue-Sun Nov-Mar), a storybook medieval fortress towering over the old centre. With its triple ring of fortified walls, it's one of the most impressive fortresses in Germany. It houses the vast collection of the Kunstsammlungen, with works by star painters such as Rembrandt, Dürer and Cranach the Elder. The elaborate Jagdintarsien-Zimmer (Hunting Marquetry Room) is a superlative example of carved woodwork.

✗ ⊨ p211

The Drive » The most attractive way to cover the 74km between Coburg and Bayreuth is to take the B303 and then the B85 via Kulmbach, where the hilltop Plassenburg is worth making a stop at to explore.

COBURG'S SAUSAGES

Almost every town in this neck of the Wald has its own traditional links, but the sausages of Coburg are special. Around 30cm long, they are grilled over the embers of pine cones, giving them a sappy, smoky flavour. The tasty result is then served in a tiny bread bun with a dollop of mustard. The best places to try them are the unpresuming kiosks on Marktplatz.

⑨ Bayreuth

Bayreuth is best known for its Wagner connections, but its glory days began in 1735 when Wilhelmine, sister of King Frederick the Great of Prussia, was forced to marry stuffy Margrave Friedrich. Bored with the local scene, the cultured Anglo-oriented Wilhelmine invited the finest artists, poets, composers and architects in Europe to court. The period bequeathed some eye-catching buildings, still on display for all to see. The **Altes Schloss** (☎0921-759 6937; adult/concession €4.50/3.50; ⏲9am-6pm Apr-Sep) was Wilhelmine's summer residence. Visits to the palace are by guided tour only and take in the Chinese Mirror room where Countess Wilhelmine penned her memoirs. The **Neues Schloss** (☎0921-759 690; Ludwigstrasse 21; adult/concession €5.50/4.50; ⏲9am-6pm daily Apr-Sep, 10am-4pm Tue-Sun Oct-Mar) lies a short distance south of the main shopping street, Maxmilianstrasse. A riot of rococo style, the margrave's residence post-1753 features a vast collection of 18th-century Bayreuth porcelain. The **Spiegelscherbenkabinett** (Broken Mirror Cabinet), which is lined with irregular shards of broken mirror, is supposedly Margravine Wilhelmine's response to the vanity of her era.

✗ ⊨ p211

Eating & Sleeping

Mannheim ❶

✖ Café Prag
Cafe €

(dishes €1.50-3.50; ⊙10am-7pm Mon-Sat, 1-6pm Sun) A former tailor's shop and cigar store, built in 1902, is now an arty cafe with *Jugendstil* (art-nouveau) woodwork, cranberry-red walls and a pre-war Central European feel. Smooth jazz on the stereo makes a perfect backdrop for enjoying an espresso and light refreshments like croissants or rhubarb cake.

⌂ Maritim Parkhotel
Luxury Hotel €€

(📞0621-158 80; www.maritim.de; Friedrichsplatz 2; d from €118; 🅿 ❄ @ 🛜 ⚟) Built in 1901 in the sumptuous style of the Renaissance, this supremely elegant 173-room hotel overlooks Friedrichsplatz. Amenities include a swimming pool, sauna and steam bath, two top-notch restaurants, and, often, live lobby music in the evenings. Many rooms have balconies or terraces. Breakfast costs €20.

Schwäbisch Hall ❹

✖ Rebers Pflug
International €€€

(📞0791-931 230; www.rebers-pflug.de; Weckriedener Strasse 2; mains €18.50-39, 4-course menu €59-78; ⊙6.30-9pm Mon & Tue, noon-2pm & 6-9pm Wed-Sat, 11.30am-2pm Sun) Hans-Harald Reber mans the stove at this 19th-century country house, one of Schwäbisch Hall's two Michelin-starred haunts. He puts his own imaginative spin on seasonal numbers such as local venison in a pumpernickel crust with sweet potato purée, asparagus and hazelnut *Spätzle* (a kind of soft egg noodle or dumpling). Vegetarians are also well catered for. Dine in the chestnut-shaded garden in summer.

⌂ Hotel Scholl
Hotel €€

(📞0791-975 50; www.hotel-scholl.de; Klosterstrasse 2-4; s €79-109, d €124-169; 🛜) A charming pick behind Am Markt, this family-run hotel has rustic-chic rooms with parquet floors, flat-screen TVs and granite or marble bathrooms. Most striking of all is the attic penthouse with its beams, free-standing shower and far-reaching views over town. Breakfast is a fine spread of cold cuts, fruit and cereals.

Nuremberg ❻

✖ Albrecht Dürer Stube
Franconian €€

(📞0911-227 209; www.albrecht-duerer-stube. de; cnr Albrecht-Dürer-Strasse & Agnesgasse; mains €7-15; ⊙6pm-midnight Mon-Sat, 11.30am-2.30pm Fri & Sun) This unpretentious and intimate restaurant has a Dürer-inspired dining room, prettily laid tables, a ceramic stove keeping things toasty when they're not outside and a menu of Nuremberg sausages, steaks, sea fish, seasonal specials, Franconian wine and *Landbier* (regional beer). There aren't many tables so booking ahead at weekends is recommended.

✖ Goldenes Posthorn
Franconian €€

(📞0911-225 153; Glöckleinsgasse 2, cnr Sebalder Platz; mains €9-19; ⊙11am-11pm; ✐) Push open the heavy copper door to find a real culinary treat that has hosted royals, artists and professors (including Albrecht Dürer) since 1498. You can't go wrong sticking with the miniature local sausages, but the pork shoulder and also the house speciality – vinegar-marinated ox cheeks – are highly recommended as well.

🛏 Agneshof   Hotel €€

(📞0911-214 440; www.agneshof-nuernberg.de; Agnesgasse 10; s/d from €82/96; P 🛜) Tranquilly located in the antiques quarter near the St Sebalduskirche, the Agneshof's public areas have a sophisticated, artsy touch. The 74 box-ticking rooms have whitewashed walls and '90s furniture; some at the top have views of the Kaiserburg. There's a state-of-the-art wellness centre, and a pretty summer courtyard garden strewn with deckchairs. Breakfast is a cheeky extra €7.

🛏 Hotel Deutscher Kaiser   Hotel €€

(📞0911-242 660; www.deutscher-kaiser-hotel.de; Königstrasse 55; s/d from €92/109; @🛜) Epicentral in its location, aristocratic in its design and service, this treat of a historic hotel has been in the same family since the turn of the 20th century. Climb the castle-like granite stairs to find rooms of understated simplicity, flaunting oversize beds, Italian porcelain, silk lampshades and real period furniture (Biedermeier and *Jugendstil*).

Coburg   ⑧

🍴 Ratskeller   Franconian €

(Markt 1; mains €6-16.50; ⊙10am-midnight) Munch on regional dishes from Thuringia and Franconia while kicking back on well-padded leather benches under the heftily vaulted ceiling of Coburg's spectacular town hall.

🛏 Hotelpension Bärenturm   Guesthouse €€

(📞09561-318 401; www.baerenturm-hotelpension.de; Untere Anlage 2; s €85,

d €110-130; P 🛜) For those who prefer their complimentary pillow pack of gummy bears served with a touch of history, Coburg's most characterful digs started life as a defensive tower that was expanded in the early 19th century to house Prince Albert's private tutor. Each of the 15 rooms is a gem boasting squeaky parquet floors, antique-style furniture and regally high ceilings.

Bayreuth   ⑨

🍴 Oskar   Franconian, Bavarian €€

(Maximilianstrasse 33; mains €7-15; ⊙8am-1am Mon-Sat, from 9am Sun) At the heart of the pedestrianised shopping boulevard, this multitasking, open-all-hours bar-cafe-restaurant is Bayreuth's busiest eatery. It's good for a busting Bavarian breakfast, a light lunch in the covered garden cafe, a full-on dinner feast in the dark-wood restaurant, or a *Landbier* and a couple of tasty Bayreuth bratwursts anytime you feel.

🛏 Hotel Goldener Anker   Hotel €€€

(📞0921-787 7740; www.anker-bayreuth.de; Opernstrasse 6; s €98-138, d €168-235; P 🛜) Bayreuth's top address just a few metres from the opera house oozes refined elegance; many of the rooms are decorated in heavy traditional style with swag curtains, dark woods and antique touches. There's a swanky restaurant at ground level, the service is impeccable and there is fresh fruit waiting for you on arrival.

Dinkelsbühl Wander among the coloured houses that line the crooked lanes

Classic Trip

The Romantic Road

17

On this trip you'll experience the Germany of the bedtime story-book – medieval walled towns, gabled townhouses, cobbled squares and crooked streets, all preserved as if time has come to a standstill.

TRIP HIGHLIGHTS

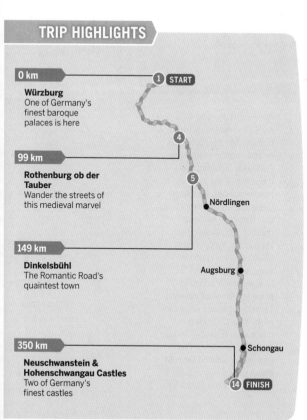

0 km

Würzburg
One of Germany's finest baroque palaces is here

99 km

Rothenburg ob der Tauber
Wander the streets of this medieval marvel

149 km

Dinkelsbühl
The Romantic Road's quaintest town

350 km

Neuschwanstein & Hohenschwangau Castles
Two of Germany's finest castles

Nördlingen

Augsburg

 Schongau

10 DAYS
350 KM / 218 MILES

GREAT FOR...

BEST TIME TO GO
Any time of year.

ESSENTIAL PHOTO

The half-timbered buildings of Rothenburg ob der Tauber's Plönlein.

BEST TWO DAYS

The stretch between stops 4 and 6 takes in the most romantic towns of the Romantic Road.

213

Classic Trip

17 The Romantic Road

From the vineyards of Würzburg to the foot of the Alps, the Romantic Road (Romantische Strasse) is by far the most popular of Germany's touring routes. This well-trodden trail cuts through a cultural and historical cross-section of southern Germany, coming to a climax at the gates of King Ludwig II's crazy castles. The route links some of Germany's most picturesque towns, many appearing untouched since medieval times.

TRIP HIGHLIGHT

1 Würzburg

This scenic town in Bavaria's northeast corner straddles the Main River and is renowned for its art, architecture and delicate wines. A large student population keeps things lively and plenty of hip nightlife pulsates through its cobbled streets.

Top billing here goes to the **Würzburg Residenz** (www.residenz-wuerzburg.de; Balthasar-Neumann-Promenade; adult/concession/under 18yrs €7.50/6.50/free; ⊗9am-6pm Apr-Oct, 10am-4.30pm Nov-Mar, 45 min English tours 11am & 3pm, also 4.30pm Apr-Oct), a vast Unesco-listed palace, built by 18th-century architect Balthasar Neumann as the home of the local prince-bishops. It's one of Germany's most important and beautiful baroque palaces. The wonderful zigzagging Treppenhaus (Staircase) is capped by what is still the world's largest fresco, a masterpiece by Giovanni Battista Tiepolo depicting allegories of the four then-known continents (Europe, Africa, America and Asia). The recently renovated **Dom St Kilian** (www.dom-wuerzburg. de; Domstrasse 40; ⊗8am-7pm

Mon-Sat, 8am-8pm Sun) is a highly unusual cathedral with a Romanesque core and the baroque Schönbornkapelle by Balthasar Neumann.

✗ ⊨ p224

The Drive » The 37km between Würzburg and the next stop, Tauberbischofsheim, is best tackled in the following way: from the centre of Würzburg take the B19 south until it joins the A3 motorway; follow this until the junction with the B81, which goes all the way to Tauberbischofsheim.

② Tauberbischofsheim

The main town of the pretty Tauber Valley, this small settlement has a picturesque marketplace dominated by a neo-Gothic town hall and lined with typical half-timbered houses. Follow the remains of the medieval town walls

🔗 LINK YOUR TRIP

16 German Castle Road

The Romantic Road and the German Castle Road intersect in Rothenburg ob der Tauber.

19 German Alpine Road

The German Alpine Road and the Romantic Road meet up in the Alpine town of Füssen.

215

to the Kurmainzisches Schloss, which now houses the **Tauberfränkisches Landschaftsmuseum** (Schlossplatz; admission €2; ⊙2-4.30pm Tue-Sat, 10am-noon & 2-4.30pm Sun Easter-Oct), where you can learn more about Tauberbischofsheim's past.

The Drive » The 34km dash from Tauberbischofsheim to Weikersheim passes through Lauda-Königshofen, a pretty stop in the Tauber Valley.

❸ Weikersheim

Top billing in under-visited Weikersheim is **Schloss Weikersheim** (www.schloss-weikersheim.de; Marktplatz 11; adult/concession €6.50/3.30; ⊙9am-6pm Apr-Oct, 10am-noon & 1-5pm Nov-Mar), the finest palace on the entire Romantic Road. Renaissance to the core, it's surrounded by beautiful formal gardens inspired by Versailles. Highlights include the enormous Knights Hall dating from around 1600 and over 40m long. The rich decor here includes a huge painted ceiling, each panel depicting a hunting scene, and the amazingly ornate fireplace. The unforgettable rococo mirror cabinet, with its gilt-and-red decor, is also part of the guided tour, after which you can wan-

MUSEUM OF THE BAVARIAN KINGS

Palace-fatigued visitors often head straight for the bus stop, coach park or nearest beer after a tour of the castles, most overlooking the area's third attraction, the worthwhile **Museum der Bayerischen Könige** (Museum of the Bavarian Kings; www.museumderbayerischenkoenige.de; Alpseestrasse 27; adult/concession €9.50/8; ⊙10am-6pm), installed in a former lakeside hotel 400m from the castle ticket office (heading towards Alpsee Lake). The big-window views across the beautiful lake (a great picnic spot) to the Alps are almost as amazing as the Wittelsbach bling on show, including Ludwig II's famous blue-and-gold robe. The architecturally stunning museum is packed with historical background on Bavaria's first family and is well worth the extra legwork. A detailed audioguide is included in the ticket price.

der the elegantly laid-out gardens.

The Drive » The short 28km journey between Weikersheim and Rothenburg ob der Tauber follows minor country roads all the way, with the route passing through a rolling patchwork of fields. You could also detour via Creglingen, a minor stop on the Romantic Road.

TRIP HIGHLIGHT

❹ Rothenburg ob der Tauber

A well-preserved historical town, Rothenburg ob der Tauber is the most popular stop on the Romantic Road. But when you're finished with the main sights, there are a couple of less obvious attractions here.

You'll often see the **Plönlein** on the covers of brochures and tourist bumf, a gathering of

forks in the cobbled road (Obere Schmiedgasse) occupied by possibly the quaintest, most crooked half-timbered house you are ever likely to see.

Hidden down a little alley is the **Alt-Rothenburger Handwerkerhaus** (Alter Stadtgraben 26; adult/concession €3/2.50; ⊙11am-5pm Mon-Fri, from 10am Sat & Sun Easter-Oct, 2-4pm daily Dec), where numerous artisans – including coopers, weavers, cobblers and potters – have their workshops today, and mostly have had for the house's 700-plus-years existence. It's half museum, half active workplace and you can easily spend an hour or so watching the craftsmen at work.

✗ p224

The Drive » The quickest and simplest way between Rothenburg ob der Tauber and

Dinkelsbühl is along the A7 motorway (50km). For a gentler, but slower and longer experience, follow the official Romantic Road route, which tacks along country roads via Schillingsfürst, another quaint halt.

- - - - - - - - - - - -

TRIP HIGHLIGHT

❺ Dinkelsbühl

Immaculately preserved Dinkelsbühl is arguably the Romantic Road's quaintest and most authentically medieval halt. Just like Rothenburg it is ringed by medieval walls, which boast 18 towers and four gates. The joy of Dinkelsbühl is aimless wandering through the crooked lanes, but for a lowdown on the town's history visit the **Haus der Geschichte** (Altrathausplatz 14; adult/child €4/2; ☺9am-6pm Mon-Fri, 10am-5pm Sat & Sun May-Oct, 10am-5pm daily Nov-Apr), in the same building as the tourist office.

✖ 🛏 p224

The Drive ≫ Just 32km separate Dinkelsbühl from Nördlingen along the B25; drivers are accompanied by the Wörnitz River for the first part of the journey. Just a few kilometres short of Nördlingen is Wallerstein, a small market town with the beautiful parish church of St Alban, also a Romantic Road stop.

- - - - - - - - - - - -

❻ Nördlingen

Charmingly medieval, Nördlingen lies within the Ries Basin, a massive impact crater gouged out by a meteorite more than

ROTHENBURG'S SNOWBALLS

Where is it possible to get your hands on a snowball in July? Why, in Rothenburg ob der Tauber, of course! The town's speciality are *Schneeballen* (snowballs), ribbons of dough loosely shaped into balls, deep-fried then coated in icing sugar, chocolate and other dentist's foes. Some 24 types are produced at **Diller's Schneeballen** (Hofbronnengasse 16; ☺10am-6pm); a more limited range can be enjoyed all over town.

15 million years ago. The crater – some 25km in diameter – is one of the best preserved on earth, and has been declared a special 'geopark'. Nördlingen's 14th-century walls, all original, mimic the crater's rim and are almost perfectly circular. The **Rieskrater Museum** (Eugene-Shoemaker-Platz 1; adult/concession €4.50/2.50, ticket also valid for Stadtmuseum; ☺10am-4.30pm Tue-Sun, closed noon-1.30pm Nov-Apr) tells the story. Next door is the **Stadtmuseum** (Vordere Gerbergasse 1; adult/concession €4.50/2.50, ticket also valid for Rieskrater Museum; ☺1.30-4.30pm Tue-Sun Mar-early Nov), which gives an interesting rundown of Nördlingen's story so far.

On a completely different note, the **Bayerisches Eisenbahnmuseum** (www.bayerisches-eisenbahnmuseum.de; Am Hohen Weg 6a;

adult/child €6/3; ☺noon-4pm Tue-Sat, 10am-5pm Sun May-Sep, noon-4pm Sat, 10am-5pm Sun Oct-Mar) near the railway station is a retirement home for locos that have puffed their last. The museum runs steam trains up to Dinkelsbühl, Feuchtwangen and Gunzenhausen several times a year; see the website for details.

✖ 🛏 p225

The Drive ≫ The 19km drive from Nördlingen to Harburg is a simple affair along the arrow-straight B25 all the way. The road crosses the flatlands created by the Ries meteorite, now fertile agricultural land.

- - - - - - - - - - - -

❼ Harburg

Looming over the Wörnitz River, the medieval covered parapets, towers, turrets, keep and red-tiled roofs of the 12th-century

WILLY WONKA'S NÖRDLINGEN

If you've seen the 1970s movie *Willy Wonka & the Chocolate Factory*, you've already looked down upon Nördlingen, from a glass elevator – aerial shots of the town were used in the final sequences of the film.

WHY THIS IS A CLASSIC TRIP
MARC DI DUCA, AUTHOR

This 350km-long ribbon of historical quaintness is the Germany you came to see, but things can get crowded in the summer months, taking away a bit of the romance. Do the trip in winter when Bavaria's chocolate-box towns look even prettier under a layer of snow.

Top: The Main River in Würzburg with a fortress on the hilltop
Left: *Schneeballen* (snowballs), a traditional cake in Rothenburg ob der Tauber
Right: Franconia Fountain in front of Würzburg, Residenz

Schloss Harburg (www.
burg-harburg.de; adult/child
€5/3; ⏰10am-5pm Tue-Sun
mid-Mar–Oct) are so perfectly
preserved they almost
seem like part of a film set.
Tours tell the Schloss' long
tale and evoke the ghosts
that are said to use the
castle as a hang-out.

From the castle, the
walk to Harburg's cute,
half-timbered **Altstadt**
(old town) takes around
10 minutes, slightly
more the other way as
you're heading uphill. A
fabulous panorama of the
village and castle can be
admired from the 1702
stone bridge spanning
the Wörnitz.

The Drive » A mere 12km
separate tiny Harburg with its
bigger neighbour Donauwörth.
The route follows the B25 all the
way across undulating farmland.

- - - - - - - - - - -

⑧ Donauwörth

Sitting pretty at the
confluence of the Danube
and Wörnitz Rivers, the
small town of Donau-
wörth had its heyday
as a Free Imperial City
in the 14th century.
WWII destroyed 75% of
the medieval old town
but three gates and five
town-wall towers still
guard it today. The main
street is Reichsstrasse,
which is where you'll
discover the **Lieb-
fraukirche** (Reichsstrasse),
a 15th-century Gothic
church with original
frescos and a curiously
sloping floor that drops

120cm. Swabia's largest church bell (6550kg) swings in the belfry. The other major attraction in town is the **Käthe-Kruse-Puppenmuseum** (www.kaethe-kruse.de; Pflegstrasse 21a; adult/child €2.50/1.50; ⏰11am-6pm Tue-Sun May-Sep, 2-5pm Thu-Sun Oct-Apr). In a former monastery, it's a nostalgia-inducing place full of old dolls and dollhouses from world-renowned designer Käthe Kruse (1883–1968).

The Drive » The quickest way between Donauwörth and the next stop in Augsburg 47km away is via the B2 and the A8 motorway. The scenic route via backroads east of the A8 passes close to the pretty town of Rain, another minor halt on the Romantic Road.

❾ Augsburg

Augsburg is the Romantic Road's largest city and one of Germany's oldest, founded by the stepchildren of Roman emperor Augustus over 2000 years ago. This attractive city of spires and cobbles is an engaging stop, though one with a less quaint atmosphere than others along the route.

Augsburg's top sight is the **Fuggerei** (www.fugger.de; Jakober Strasse; adult/concession €4/3; ⏰8am-8pm Apr-Sep, 9am-6pm Oct-Mar), Europe's oldest Catholic welfare settlement, founded by banker and merchant Jakob Fugger in 1521. Around 200 people inhabit the complex today; see how the residents of yesterday lived by visiting the **Fuggereimuseum** (Mittlere Gasse 14; admission incl with entry to the Fuggerei;

⏰9am-8pm Mar-Oct, 9am-6pm Nov-Apr).

Two famous Germans have close associations with Augsburg. The Protestant Reformation leader Martin Luther stayed here in 1518 – his story is told at the **St Anna Kirche** (Im Annahof 2, off Annastrasse; ⏰noon-5pm Mon, 10am-12.30pm & 3-5pm Tue-Sat, 10am-12.30pm & 3-4pm Sun). The birthplace of the poet and playwright Bertolt Brecht is now a museum called the **Bertolt-Brecht-Haus** (📞0821-324 2779; Auf dem Rain 7; adult/concession €2.50/2; ⏰10am-5pm Tue-Sun).

✕ 🛏 p225

The Drive » The 41km drive from Augsburg to Landsberg am Lech is a simple affair along the B17. The route mostly follows the valley of the Lech River, which links the two towns. Look out for signs to the amusingly named town of Kissing!

DETOUR: EICHSTÄTT & THE ALTMÜHLTAL NATURE PARK

Start: ❽ Donauwörth

A short 55km off the Romantic Road from Donauwörth lies the town of Eichstätt, the main jumping-off point for the serenely picturesque 2900-sq-km Altmühltal Nature Park, which follows the wooded valley of the Altmühl River. Canoeing the river is a top activity here, as is cycling the same route and camping. The park is an ideal break from the road and a relaxing place to spend a few days in unspoilt natural surroundings. Eichstätt itself has a wealth of architecture, including the richly adorned medieval **Dom** (www.bistum-eichstaett.de/dom; Domplatz; ⏰7.15am-7.30pm), with its museum, the baroque **Fürstbischöfliche Residenz** (Residenzplatz; admission €1; ⏰7.30am-noon Mon-Fri, 2-4pm Mon-Wed, 2-5.30pm Thu), where the local prince-bishops once lived it up, and the **Willibaldsburg** (📞08421-4730; Burgstrasse 19; adult/concession €4.50/3.50; ⏰9am-6pm Tue-Sun Apr-Oct, 10am-4pm Tue-Sun Nov-Mar), a 14th-century castle that now houses a couple of museums.

TOP TIP: GUEST CARDS

Overnight anywhere in the Alps and your hotel should issue you with a free *Gästekarte,* which gives free bus travel as well as many other discounts on admission and activities.

⑩ Landsberg am Lech

A walled town on the River Lech, lovely Landsberg has a less commercial ambience than others on the route. Just like the Wieskirche further south, the small baroque **Johanniskirche** (Vorderer Anger) is a creation by the baroque architect Dominikus Zimmermann, who lived in Landsberg and even served as its mayor. The town's **Neues Stadtmuseum** (www.museum-landsberg. de; Von-Helfenstain-Gasse 426; adult/concession €3.50/2; ⊙2-5pm Tue-Fri, from 11am Sat & Sun May-Jan, closed Feb-Apr) tells Landsberg's tale from prehistory to the 20th century.

The Drive » Still tracing the valley of the River Lech, the 28km drive along the B17 between Landsberg am Lech and Schongau shouldn't take more than 30 minutes. En route you pass through Hohenfurch, a pretty little town regarded as the gateway to the Pfaffenwinkel, a foothill region of the Alps.

⑪ Schongau

One of the lesser-visited stops on the Romantic Road, the attractive town of Schongau is known for its largely intact medieval defences. The Gothic **Ballenhaus** (Marienplatz 2) served as the town hall until 1902 and has a distinctive stepped gable. It now houses a cafe. Other attractions include the **Church of Maria Himmelfahrt** (Kirchenstrasse 23), which sports a choir by Dominikus Zimmermann.

The Drive » To reach the next Romantic Road stop, the Wieskirche (21km away), take the B17 south until you reach Steingaden. From there country roads lead east and then south to Wies. This is where Bavaria starts to take on the look of the Alps, with flower-filled meadows in summer and views of the high peaks when the weather is clear.

⑫ Wieskirche

Located in the village of Wies, the **Wieskirche** (☎08862-932 930; www. wieskirche.de; ⊙8am-8pm Apr-Oct, to 5pm Nov-Mar) is one of Bavaria's best-known baroque churches and a Unesco-listed site, the monumental work of the legendary artist-brothers, Dominikus and Johann Baptist Zimmermann.

In 1730 a farmer in Steingaden claimed he'd witnessed the miracle of his Christ statue shedding tears. Pilgrims poured into the town in such numbers over the next decade that the local abbot commissioned a new church to house the weepy work. Inside the almost-circular structure, eight snow-white pillars are topped by gold capital stones and swirling decorations. The unsupported dome must have seemed like God's work in the mid-17th century, its surface adorned with a pastel ceiling fresco

LANDSBERG'S DARK LITERARY CONNECTIONS

Landsberg am Lech can claim to be the town where one of the German language's best-selling books was written. Was it a work by Goethe, Remarque, Brecht? No, unfortunately, it was Adolf Hitler. It was during his 264 days of incarceration in a Landsberg jail, following the 1923 beer-hall putsch, that Hitler penned his hate-filled *Mein Kampf,* a book that sold an estimated seven million copies when published. The jail later held Nazi war criminals and is still in use.

Classic Trip

celebrating Christ's resurrection.

The Drive » From the Wieskirche, the best way to reach the next stop at Füssen is to backtrack to Steingaden and rejoin the B17 there. The entire journey is 27km through the increasingly undulating foothills of the Alps, with some gorgeous views of the ever-nearing peaks along the way.

⑬ Füssen

Nestled at the foot of the Alps, tourist-busy Füssen is all about the nearby castles of Neuschwan stein and Hohenschwan-gau, but there are other reasons to linger longer in the area. The town's historical centre is worth half a day's exploration and, from here, you can easily escape from the crowds into a landscape of gentle hiking trails and Alpine vistas. When you've had your fill of these, take an hour or two to drop by Füssen's very own castle, the

Hohes Schloss (Magnus-platz 10; adult/concession €6/4; ☺galleries 11am-5pm Tue-Sun Apr-Oct, 1-4pm Fri-Sun Nov-Mar), today home to an art gallery.

✗ ⊨ p225

The Drive » To drive to King Ludwig II's castles, take the B17 across the river until you see the signs for Hohenschwangau. Parking is at a premium in summer. However, as the castles are a mere 4km from the centre of Füssen it's probably not worth driving at all. RVO buses 78 and 73 (www.rvo-bus.de) run there from Füssen Bahnhof (€4.40 return, eight minutes, at least hourly, buy tickets from the driver).

TRIP HIGHLIGHT

⑭ Neuschwanstein & Hohenschwangau Castles

The undisputed high-lights of any trip to Bavaria, these two castles make a fitting climax to the Romantic Road.

Schloss Neuschwan-stein (☎tickets 08362-930 830; www.neuschwanstein.de; Neuschwansteinstrasse 20; adult/concession €12/11, incl Hohenschwangau €23/21; ☺9am-6pm Apr–mid-Oct,

10am-4pm mid-Oct–Mar) was the model for Disney's *Sleeping Beauty* castle.

✓ TOP TIP:
VISITING NEUSCHWANSTEIN & HOHENSCHWANGAU CASTLES

The castles can only be visited on guided tours (35 minutes). Buy timed tickets from the **Ticket Centre** (☎08362-930 830; www.hohenschwangau.de; Alpenseestrasse 12; ☺8am-5.30pm Apr–mid-Oct, 9am-3.30pm mid-Oct–Mar) at the foot of the castles. In summer, arrive as early as 8am to ensure you get in that day.

Bavaria Schloss Neuschwanstein

King Ludwig II planned this fairy-tale pile himself, with the help of a stage designer rather than an architect. He envisioned it as a giant stage on which to recreate the world of Germanic mythology, inspired by the operatic works of his friend Richard Wagner.

It was at nearby **Schloss Hohenschwangau** (☏08362-930 830; www.hohenschwangau.de; Alpseestrasse 30; adult/concession €12/11, incl Neuschwanstein €23/21; ⊙8am-5.30pm Apr–mid-Oct, 9am-3.30pm mid-Oct–Mar) that King Ludwig II grew up and later enjoyed summers until his death in

1886. His father, Maximilian II, built this palace in a neo-Gothic style atop 12th-century ruins. Less showy than Neuschwanstein, Hohenschwangau has a distinctly lived-in feel, where every piece of furniture is a used original. It was at Hohenschwangau where Ludwig first met Wagner.

Eating & Sleeping

Würzburg ❶

✖ Bürgerspital
Weinstube   Wine Restaurant €€

(☎0931-352 880; Theaterstrasse 19; mains €13-24; ⏱10am-11pm) If you are going to eat out just once in Würzburg, the aromatic and cosy nooks of this labyrinthine medieval place probably provide the top local experience. Choose from a broad selection of Franconian wines (some of Germany's best) and wonderful regional dishes and snacks, including *Mostsuppe* (a tasty wine soup).

🛏 Hotel Rebstock   Hotel €€

(☎0931-309 30; www.rebstock.com; Neubaustrasse 7; s/d from €92/113; ❊@🛜) Würzburg's top digs, in a squarely renovated rococo townhouse, has 70 unique, stylishly finished rooms with the gamut of amenities, impeccable service and an Altstadt location. A pillow selection and supercomfy 'gel' beds should ease you into slumberland, perhaps after a fine meal in the dramatic bistro or the slick Michelin-star restaurant.

Rothenburg ob der Tauber ❹

✖ Mittermeier   Bavarian €€

(☎09861-945 430; www.villamittermeier. de; Vorm Würzburger Tor 7; mains €12-19; ⏱6-10.30pm Tue-Sat; 🅿🛜) Supporters of the slow food movement and deserved holders of a Michelin Bib Gourmand, this hotel restaurant pairs punctilious craftsmanship with top-notch ingredients, sourced regionally whenever possible. There are five different dining areas including a black-and-white tiled 'temple', and alfresco terrace and a barrel-shaped wine cellar. The wine list is one of the best in Franconia.

✖ Zur Höll   Franconian €€

(☎09861-4229; www.hoell.rothenburg.de; Burggasse 8; mains €6.80-20; ⏱5-11pm) This medieval wine tavern is in the town's oldest original building, with sections dating back to the year 900. The menu of regional specialities is limited but refined, though it's the superb selection of Franconian wines that people really come for.

Dinkelsbühl ❺

✖ Haus
Appelberg   Franconian, International €€

(☎09851-582 838; www.haus-appelberg.de; Nördlinger Strasse 40; dishes €6-11; ⏱6pm-midnight Mon-Sat) At this 40-cover wine restaurant, the owners double up as cooks to keep tables supplied with traditional dishes such as local fish, Franconian sausages and *Maultaschen* (pork and spinach ravioli). On warm days swap the rustic interior for the secluded terrace, a fine spot for some evening idling over a Franconian white.

🛏 Dinkelsbühler
Kunst-Stuben   Guesthouse €€

(☎09851-6750; www.kunst-stuben.de; Segringer Strasse 52; s €60, d €80-85, ste €90; 🚭@🛜) Personal attention and charm by the bucketload make this guesthouse, situated near the westernmost gate (Segringer Tor), one of the best on the entire Romantic Road. Furniture (including the four-posters) is all handmade by Voglauer, the cosy library is perfect for curling up in with a good read, and the suite is a matchless deal for travelling families. The artist owner will show his Asia travel films if enough guests are interested.

Nördlingen ⑥

✖ La Fontana   Italian €

(Bei den Kornschrannen 2; mains around €8;
🕙11am-11pm) Nördlingen's most popular
restaurant is this large Italian pizza-pasta place
occupying the terracotta Kornschrannen as well
as tumbling tables out onto Schrannenstrasse.
The menu is long, the service swift and when
the sun is shining there's no lovelier spot to fill
the hole.

🛏 Kaiserhof Hotel Sonne   Hotel €€

(☎09081-5067; www.kaiserhof-hotel-sonne.de;
Marktplatz 3; s €55-75, d €80-120; 🅿🛜) Right
on the main square, Nördlingen's top digs once
hosted crowned heads and their entourages,
but have quietly gone to seed in recent years.
However, rooms are still packed with character,
mixing modern comforts with traditional charm,
and the atmospheric regional restaurant
downstairs is still worth a shot.

Augsburg ⑨

✖ August   International €€€

(☎0821-352 79; Frauentorstrasse 27; dinner
€130; 🕙from 7pm Wed-Sat) Most Augsburgers
have little inkling their city possesses two
Michelin stars, both of which belong to chef
Christian Grünwald. Treat yourself to some
of Bavaria's most innovative cooking in the
minimalist dining room, though with just 16
covers, reservations are essential.

✖ Bauerntanz   German €€

(Bauerntanzgässchen 1; mains €7-17; 🕙11am-
11.30pm) Belly-satisfying helpings of creative
Swabian and Bavarian food – Spätzle (a kind of
soft egg noodle or dumpling) and more Spätzle –
are plated up by friendly staff at this prim Alpine
tavern with lace curtains, hefty timber interior
and chequered fabrics. When the sun makes
an appearance, everyone bails for the outdoor
seating.

🛏 Dom Hotel   Hotel €€

(☎0821-343 930; www.domhotel-augsburg.
de; Frauentorstrasse 8; s €70-150, d €95-190;

🅿😊@🛜🏊) Augsburg's top choice packs
a 500-year-old former bishop's guesthouse
(Martin Luther and Kaiser Maxmilian I stayed
here) with 57 rooms, all different but sharing a
stylishly understated air and pristine upkeep;
some have cathedral views. However, the big
pluses here are the large swimming pool, fitness
centre and solarium. Parking is an extra €6.

Füssen ⑬

✖ Zum Franziskaner   Bavarian €€

(Kemptener Strasse 1; mains €6-19.50; 🕙noon-
11pm) This revamped restaurant specialises
in Schweinshaxe (pork knuckle) and schnitzel,
prepared in more varieties than you can shake
a haunch at. There's some choice for non-
carnivores such as Käsespätzle (rolled cheese
noodles) and salads, and when the sun shines
the outdoor seating shares the pavement with
the 'foot-washing' statue.

✖ Zum Hechten   Bavarian €€

(Ritterstrasse 6; mains €8-19; 🕙10am-10pm)
Füssen's best hotel restaurant keeps things
regional with a menu of Allgäu staples like
schnitzel and noodles, Bavarian pork-themed
favourites, and local specialities such as
venison goulash from the Ammertal. Post-
meal, relax in the wood-panelled dining room
caressing a König Ludwig Dunkel, one of
Germany's best dark beers brewed by the
current head of the Wittelsbach family.

🛏 Hotel Sonne   Design Hotel €€

(☎08362-9080; www.hotel-sonne.de;
Prinzregentenplatz 1; s/d from €89/109; 🅿🛜)
Although traditional looking from outside,
this Altstadt favourite offers an unexpected
design-hotel experience within. Themed rooms
feature everything from swooping bed canopies
to big-print wallpaper, huge pieces of wall art
to sumptious fabrics. The public spaces are
littered with pieces of art, period costumes and
design features – the overall effect is impressive
and unusual for this part of Germany.

Passau *Priceless glassware at the Passauer Glasmuseum*

Glass Route

18

Strung along Bavaria's eastern flank like a necklace of gleaming beads, this glass-themed route takes in museums, workshops and theme parks, all set in some wonderfully forested landscapes.

TRIP HIGHLIGHTS

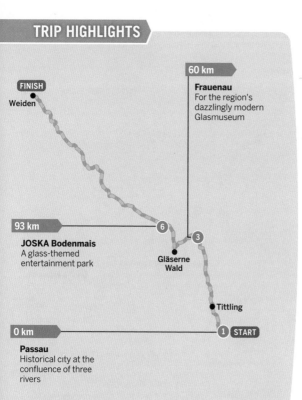

FINISH
Weiden

60 km

Frauenau
For the region's dazzlingly modern Glasmuseum

93 km

JOSKA Bodenmais
A glass-themed entertainment park

6

3

Gläserne Wald

Tittling

0 km

1 **START**

Passau
Historical city at the confluence of three rivers

---

7 DAYS
209 KM / 130 MILES

GREAT FOR...

BEST TIME TO GO
Easter to October when all sights are open.

ESSENTIAL PHOTO
The confluence of three rivers in Passau.

BEST FOR SHOPPING
JOSKA Bodenmais for authentic local glassware.

18 | Glass Route

Think Bavaria, think Alpine meadows, tankards of beer and fast cars – but few may know that the eastern part of the region along the border with the Czech Republic has a long tradition of making glass. However, viewing the region's glazed and glittering creations is just one of the delights of this low-key route – you'll also be passing through the semi-wilderness of the mysterious and undervisited Bavarian Forest National Park.

TRIP HIGHLIGHT

❶ Passau

Passau is a delightful town; its **Altstadt** (old town) is stacked atop a narrow peninsula that jabs its sharp end into the confluence of three rivers: the Danube, the Inn and the Ilz. The glass highlight here is the **Passauer Glasmuseum** (☎0851-350 71; www. glasmuseum.de; Hotel Wilder Mann, Am Rathausplatz; adult/ concession €7/5; ◷10am–5pm) within the Hotel Wilder Mann.

This warren-like glass museum is filled with some 30,000 priceless pieces of glass and crystal from the baroque, classical, art-nouveau and art-deco periods. Much of what you see hails from the glassworks of Bohemia, but there are also works by Tiffany and famous Viennese producers.

Passau's other unmissable sight is the **Dom St Stephan** (www.bistum-passau.de; Domplatz; ⏲6.30am-7pm), a late 17th-century confection by a team of Italians, notably the architect Carlo Lurago and the stucco master Giovanni Battista Carlone. The interior is a top-heavy baroque affair with a mob of saints and cherubs gazing down at the congregation from countless cornices and capitals.

 p233

The Drive ≫ A mere 22km on the B85 divide Passau with Tittling, an easy drive across rolling farmland.

---

❷ Tittling

Tiny Tittling on the southern edge of the Bavarian Forest is home to a big attraction – the **Museumsdorf Bayerischer Wald** (✆08504-8482; www.museumsdorf.com; Am Dreiburgensee; adult/concession €6/4; ⏲9am-5pm Apr-Oct), the largest open-air museum in Europe. This 20-hectare site hosts 150 typical Bavarian Forest timber cottages and farmsteads, as well as mills, schools and stables, all from the 17th to 19th centuries. There are exhibitions here ranging from clothing and furniture to pottery and farming implements. You certainly get a lot for the admission price – you could spend hours ducking in and out of the various buildings. If you are feeling peckish at the end of your tour, drop into the **Gasthaus Mühlhiasl** (mains €7-18; ⏲10am-6pm Apr–mid-Jun & mid-Sep–Oct, 10am-9pm mid-Jun–mid-Sep) for some belly-filling east Bavarian fare.

🛏 p233

The Drive ≫ This section of the route takes you deep into the dark hills of the Bavarian Forest as you head north for 38km on minor road 2132 then the B85. Along the way you'll pass by Grafenau, which has one of the best places to stay (p233) in the Bavarian Forest.

---

❸ Frauenau

For as long as the region has been producing glass, Frauenau has been a key location and still boasts three glass factories. So when it came to deciding where to put the region's dazzlingly modern **Glasmuseum** (✆09926-941 020; www.glasmuseum-frauenau.de; Am Museumspark 1, Frauenau; adult/concession €5/4.50; ⏲9am-5pm Tue-Sun), Frauenau won the day. The superb exhibition covers four millennia of glass-making history, starting with the ancient Egyptians and ending with modern glass art from around the world. Demonstrations and workshops for kids are regular features, as are superb temporary exhibitions. It goes without saying that the museum is an essential stop on any trip along the *Glasstrasse*.

The Drive ≫ From Frauenau it's a short 8km jaunt to your next stop in Zwiesel. Most base themselves in Zwiesel and make day trips out to Frauenau. The two towns, and others, are linked by the Waldbahn, a private railway line serving the communities of the Bavarian Forest.

LINK YOUR TRIP

16 German Castle Road

Weiden, the northern terminus of this route, is just 60km southeast from Bayreuth where it links up with the castle route.

19 German Alpine Road

Passau, at the southern end of the Glass Route, is a 145km drive north from Berchtesgaden on the Alpine Road (the route passes through Austria so you'll need an Austrian motorway vignette).

❹ Zwiesel

Zwiesel is the main settlement in the Bavarian Forest National Park and the traditional centre of glass production in the region. The **Zwieseler Glasfachschule** (Zwiesel Glassmaker's School; www.glasfachschule-zwiesel.com; Fachschulstrasse 15-19) is where many of the craftsmen of eastern Bavaria learn their trade. The town's main place of interest is the **Waldmuseum** (📞09922-503 706; www.waldmuseum.zwiesel.de; Kirchplatz 3; adult/concession €6/4; ⏰10am-5pm Wed-Mon), housed in a former brewery. This 'Forest Museum' has exhibitions on local customs, flora and fauna, life in the forest and, of course, glass-making.

🛏 p233

The Drive » This 16km drive takes you through more wooded hills on country roads to the next stop at the castle of Weissenstein (for the Gläserne Wald), 5km south of the town of Regen.

DETOUR:
REGENSBURG

Start: ❻ JOSKA Bodenmais

It would be a pity to pass through eastern Bavaria without calling in at one of the state's most engaging cities, Regensburg. A Roman settlement completed under Emperor Marcus Aurelius, the city was the first capital of Bavaria, the residence of dukes, kings and bishops, and for 600 years a Free Imperial City. Two millennia of history bequeathed the city some of the region's finest architectural vestiges, a fact recognised by Unesco in 2006.

One of Regensburg's top attractions is the **Schloss Thurn und Taxis** (www.thurnundtaxis.de; Emmeramsplatz 5; tours adult/concession €13.50/11; ⏰tours hourly 10.30am-4.30pm late Mar–early Nov, to 3.30pm Sat & Sun Nov–Mar). In the 15th century, Franz von Taxis (1459–1517) set up the first European postal system, which remained a monopoly until the 19th century. In recognition of his services, the family was given the former Benedictine monastery St Emmeram, henceforth known as Schloss Thurn und Taxis. It soon became one of the most modern palaces in Europe, and featured such luxuries as flushing toilets, central heating and electricity. Tours include the Basilika St Emmeram.

A chunk of Regensburg's Roman heritage has survived in the shape of the Roman Wall in a street called Unter den Schwibbögen. Dating from AD 179 the rough-hewn Porta Praetoria arch is the tallest Roman structure in Bavaria and formed part of the city's defences for centuries. A short walk away is the **Steinerne Brücke** (Stone Bridge), a 900-year-old bridge that was at one time the only fortified crossing of the Danube. Neglected and damaged (especially by the buses that once used it) for centuries, the entire expanse was under renovation at the time of research. At the old town end of the bridge, the **World Heritage Visitors Centre** (📞0941-507 4410; www.regensburg-welterbe.de; Weisse-Lamm-Gasse 1; ⏰10am-7pm daily) focuses on the city's Unesco World Heritage sites using interesting interactive multimedia exhibits.

Frauenau Gläsern Gärten near the Glasmuseum

BAVARIAN FOREST NATIONAL PARK

A paradise for outdoor fiends, the Bavarian Forest National Park extends for around 243 sq km along the Czech border, from Bayerisch Eisenstein in the north to Finsterau in the south. Its thick forest, most of it mountain spruce, is criss-crossed by hundreds of kilometres of marked hiking, cycling and cross-country skiing trails, some of which now link up with a similar network across the border. The region is home to deer, wild boar, fox, otter and countless bird species.

Around 1km northeast of the village of Neuschönau (a short detour north of your route from the village of Grafenau) stands the **Hans-Eisenmann-Haus** (☏08558-961 50; www.nationalpark-bayerischer-wald.de; Böhmstrasse 35; ⏰9am-6pm daily Apr-Oct, 9.30am-5pm daily Nov-Mar), the national park's main visitor centre. The free (but slightly dated) exhibition has hands-on displays designed to shed light on topics such as pollution and tree growth. There's also a children's discovery room, a shop and a library.

⑤ Gläserne Wald

One of the more unusual sights along the Glass Route is the **Gläserne Wald** (Glass Forest; www.glaeserner-wald.de; Weissenstein, Regen) near the town of Regen. Here glass artist Rudolf Schmid has created a forest of glass trees, some as much as 8m tall. The trees, in a number of transparent shades, are set in a flowery meadow next to Weissenstein Castle and are an intriguing sight; many more are set to be added in coming years.

The Drive ≫ Some 16km divide the Glass Forest from the next halt in Bodenmais, following roads 2135 and 2132 through the thickly forested landscape.

TRIP HIGHLIGHT

⑥ JOSKA Bodenmais

The glass highlight of the small town of Bodenmais is **JOSKA Bodenmais** (www.joska.com; Am Moosbach 1; ⏰9.30am-6pm Mon-Fri, to 5pm Sat year-round, 10am-5pm Sun May-Oct), a crystal theme park complete with crystal shops, public artworks, a beer garden, a year-round Christmas market, a crystal gallery and a workshop where visitors can try their hand at glass-blowing.

The Drive ≫ The biggest distance of the route; it's around 117km to Weiden, sticking to the 2132 and B22. You quickly leave the Bohemian forest and enter a hilly landscape of huge agricultural fields, passing through the towns of Cham and Rötz on the way.

⑦ Weiden

Boasting several sheet-glass factories, the large town of Weiden often hosts glass-art exhibitions (ask the tourist office for details), many of them in cooperation with partners across the border in the Czech Republic, which itself has a huge glass- and crystal-producing tradition. Otherwise, the town is a pleasantly low-key place to end your exploration of Bavaria's glassy traditions.

✗ 🛏 p233

Eating & Sleeping

Passau ❶

✕ Heilig-Geist-Stifts-Schenke
Bavarian €€

(☎0851-2607; www.stiftskeller-passau.de; Heilig-Geist-Gasse 4; mains €10-20; ⊙11am-11pm, closed Wed; ☎) Not only does this historical inn have a succession of walnut-panelled ceramic-stove-heated rooms, a candlelit cellar (from 6pm) and a vine-draped garden, but the food is equally inspired. Amid the river fish, steaks and seasonal dishes there are quite gourmet affairs such as beef fillet in flambéed cognac sauce. Help it all along with one of the many Austrian and German wines in stock.

⌂ Hotel Schloss Ort
Boutique Hotel €€

(☎0851-340 72; www.hotel-schloss-ort.de; Im Ort 11; s €68-121, d €97-184; P☎) This 800-year-old medieval palace by the Inn River conceals a tranquil boutique hotel, stylishly done out with polished timber floors, crisp white cotton sheets and wrought-iron bedsteads. Many of the 18 rooms enjoy river views and breakfast is served in the vaulted restaurant. Parking is an extra €4.

⌂ Hotel Wilder Mann
Hotel €€

(☎0851-350 71; www.wilder-mann.com; Höllgasse 1; s €55-77, d €88-200; P☎) Sharing space with the Glasmuseum (p228), this historic hotel boasts former guests ranging from Empress Elisabeth (Sisi) of Austria to Yoko Ono. In the rooms, folksy painted furniture sits incongruously with 20th-century telephones and 21st-century TVs. The building is a warren of staircases, passageways and linking doors, so make sure you remember where your room is. Guests receive a miserly discount to the museum.

Tittling ❷

⌂ Das Reiners
Hotel €€

(☎08552-964 90; www.dasreiners.de; Grüb 20, Grafenau; s €66-75, d €112-190; P☎⌀) Recently revamped and rebranded, this snazzily elegant hotel in Grafenau offers good value for the weary traveller. The stylish rooms are spacious and most have balconies. Guests are treated to a pool and sauna, and scrumptious buffet meals. Prices are for half-board.

Zwiesel ❹

⌂ Hotel Zur Waldbahn
Hotel €€

(☎09922-8570; www.zurwaldbahn.de; Bahnhofplatz 2; s €60-66, d €80-100; P☎) Opposite Zwiesel train station, many of the rooms at this characteristic inn, run by three generations of the same family, open to balconies with views over the town. The breakfast buffet is an especially generous spread and even includes homemade jams. The restaurant, serving traditional local fare, is the best in town.

Weiden ❼

✕ Die Villa
International €€

(www.villa-weiden.com; Hinterm Zwinger 14; mains €8-14; ⊙9am-3pm Tue-Fri, 6-11.30pm Sat; ☎) This new cafe-restaurant on the southern edge of the old town serves up an eclectic menu of vegetarian curries, Greek veal steaks, saltimbocca and tofu-based dishes in an elegant villa setting.

⌂ Altstadthotel Brauwirt
Hotel €€

(☎0961-388 1800; www.altstadthotel-braeuwirt.de; Türlgasse 10-14; s/d €74/109; ☎) A bull's-eye location in the centre, one of the town's best restaurants, a house brewery, 25 very well-appointed, spacious business-class rooms and a sauna with fitness facilities all make this the inn of choice in Weiden. Breakfast is an extra €10 per person.

Bavaria *Small but sumptuous*
Schloss Linderhof

Classic Trip

German Alpine Road

19

This exciting drive winds through the foothills of the Bavarian Alps, taking in romantic castles, lakes of drinkable pure water and high peaks whose mantle of snow remains year-round.

TRIP HIGHLIGHTS

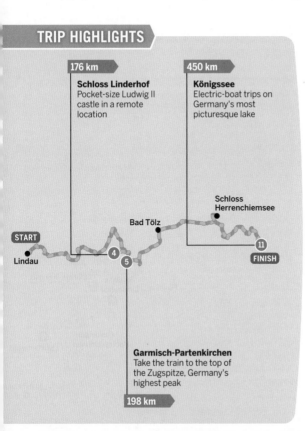

176 km
Schloss Linderhof
Pocket-size Ludwig II castle in a remote location

450 km
Königsee
Electric-boat trips on Germany's most picturesque lake

Schloss Herrenchiemsee

Bad Tölz

START
Lindau

4
5

11
FINISH

Garmisch-Partenkirchen
Take the train to the top of the Zugspitze, Germany's highest peak

198 km

---

7 DAYS
450 KM / 280 MILES

GREAT FOR...

BEST TIME TO GO

From Easter to October you'll encounter warmer weather and better road conditions.

 ESSENTIAL PHOTO

Pretty Schloss Linderhof makes for a beautiful shot.

 BEST FOR OUTDOORS

Vista-rich hiking trails ring the Königssee.

235

Classic Trip

19 German Alpine Road

The Alpenstrasse, as it's known in German, was the country's first touring road, dating from 1858. Since then generations of horse riders, motorbikers, cyclists and campervanners have been discovering the magnificence of the Bavarian Alps. A bonus of this route is its variety – one day you can be exploring one of King Ludwig II's castles, the next picnicking on an Alpine meadow, and the day after that taking a boat trip across a glassy Alpine lake.

❶ Lindau

Brochures rhapsodise about Lindau being Germany's 'Garden of Eden' and the 'Bavarian Riviera'. Paradise and southern France it ain't but it is, well, pretty special. Cradled in the southern crook of Lake Constance and almost dipping its toes into Austria, this is a good-looking, outgoing little town, with a candy-coloured postcard of an **Altstadt** (old town), Alpine views (on clear days) and lakefront cafes that use every sunray to

the max. And it's the lake that really is the main draw here, and the harbourside **Seepromenade**, with its palms, bobbing boats and folk sunning themselves in pavement cafes, is an unmissable part of the experience. Out at the harbour gates,

looking across the Alps, is Lindau's signature 33m-high **Neuer Leucht-turm** (New Lighthouse; adult/concession €1.80/0.70; ⏱10am-7.30pm), which can be climbed for cracking views out over Lindau and the lake.

LINK YOUR TRIP

17 The Romantic Road

The Romantic Road and German Alpine Road routes come together in Füssen.

20 Lake Constance

Lindau is the starting point for both the Lake Constance and German Alpine Road trips.

Map locations: Munich, Bad Aibling, Rosenheim, Bad Tölz, Chiemsee ❽, Schloss Herrenchiemsee ❾, Traunstein, Bad Reichenhall, Salzburg, St Gilgen, Hallein, Berchtesgaden ❿, FINISH ⓫ Königssee, Berchtesgaden NP, Kufstein, St Johann, Saalfelden, Wörgl, Kitzbühel, Jenbach, Aschau, Bramberg, Bruck, Mayrhofen, Hohe Tauern National Park, Bad Hofgastein, Böckstein, Braunau am Inn, Ried im Innkreis, Burghausen, AUSTRIA, Strasswalchen, Mondsee. Rivers/lakes: Inn, Waginger See, Chiemsee, Tegernsee, Achensee. Roads: A94, B472, B13, B305, A10.

Lindau's biggest architectural stunner is the 15th-century step-gabled **Altes Rathaus** (Old Town Hall; Bismarckplatz), a frescoed frenzy of cherubs, merry minstrels and galleons.

✗ ⨝ p245

The Drive ≫ The most scenic way to go from Lindau to Füssen is to follow the B308 then the B310 via Immenstadt and Pfonten. This 104km route takes in many minor stops along the Deutsche Alpenstrasse.

- - - - - - - - - - - - - -

❷ Füssen

Bustling with tourist traffic year-round, Füssen is one of the liveliest towns in the Alps. Most stay over here to access King Ludwig II's castles at nearby Hohenschwangau; see The Romantic Road (Trip 17; p222) for details. But there are other attractions around here. For fabulous views of the Alps and the Forggensee, take the **Tegelbergbahn** (www.tegelbergbahn.de; one-way/return €12.40/19.40; ⊙9am-5pm) to the top of the Tegelberg (1730m), a prime launch point for hang-gliders and parasailers. From here it's a wonderful hike down to the castles (two to three

hours; follow the signs to Königsschlösser).

The river that flows through Füssen is the Lech – walk a kilometre south from the bridge across the river to the Lechfall where the chilly water squeezes through a tight gorge. There are forest trails to the castles from here, too.

✗ ⨝ p245

The Drive ≫ A hefty chunk of the Alps stands between Füssen and your next stop in Oberammergau, making for a photogenic if roundabout route. Take the B17 as far as Steingaden, then the minor St2058 until the Ammer River, where you head south along the B23.

- - - - - - - - - - - - - -

❸ Oberammergau

Quietly quaint Oberammergau occupies a wide valley surrounded by the dark forests and snow-dusted peaks of the Ammergauer Alps. The centre is packed with traditional painted houses, woodcarving shops and awestruck tourists who come here to learn about the town's world-famous Passion Play.

The top attraction here is the **Passionstheater** (☎08822-945 8833; www.passionstheater.de; Othmar-Weis-Strasse 1; combined tour & Oberammergau Museum entry adult/concession €8/7; ⊙tours 10am & 2pm in German, 11pm in English Apr-Oct & Dec), where the Passion Play is performed every

decade (the next one is in 2020). The building can be visited as part of a guided tour, which provides ample background on the play's history and lets you peek at the costumes and sets. Also unmissable is the **Oberammergau Museum** (☎08822-941 36; www.oberammergaumuseum. de; Dorfstrasse 8; combined museum entry & Passiontheater tour adult/concession €8/7; ⊙10am-5pm Tue-Sun Apr-Oct), one of the best places to view exquisite examples of Oberammergau's famously intricate woodcarving art. Local craftspeople can produce anything from an entire nativity scene in a single walnut shell to a life-size Virgin Mary.

The Drive ≫ The next stop at Schloss Linderhof is a short, snappy transfer along a picturesque valley. The monastery at Ettal is just a few kilometres off this route and worth a stop to sample the monks' Ettaler Klosterlikör, a sugary herbal *digestif*.

- - - - - - - - - - - - - -

TRIP HIGHLIGHT

❹ Schloss Linderhof

A trove of weird treasures, **Schloss Linderhof** (www.schlosslinderhof.de; adult/concession €8.50/7.50; ⊙9am-6pm Apr–mid-Oct, 10am-4pm mid-Oct–Mar) was Ludwig II's smallest but most sumptuous palace, and the only one he lived to see fully completed. Finished in 1878, the palace hugs a steep hillside

LUDWIG II – THE FAIRY-TALE KING

A cross in Berg on the shores of Starnberger See marks the spot where Ludwig II, the most beloved king ever to rule Bavaria, died under mysterious circumstances in 1886. His early death capped the life of a man at odds with the harsh realities of a modern world no longer in need of a romantic and idealistic monarch.

Prinz Otto Ludwig Friedrich Wilhelm was a sensitive soul, fascinated by romantic epics, architecture and music, but his parents, Maximilian II and Marie, took little interest in his musings and he suffered a lonely and joyless childhood. In 1864, he became king at 18 years old. Briefly engaged to the sister of Elisabeth (Sisi), the Austrian empress, he preferred the company of men. He also worshipped composer Richard Wagner.

Ludwig was an enthusiastic leader initially, but Bavaria's days as a sovereign state were numbered, and he became a puppet king after the creation of the German Reich in 1871. Ludwig withdrew completely to drink, draw up castle plans and view concerts and operas in private. His obsession with French culture and the 'Sun King', Louis XIV, inspired the fantastical palaces of Neuschwanstein, Linderhof and Herrenchiemsee.

Contrary to popular belief, it was only Ludwig – and not the state treasury – that was being bankrupted. However, by 1886 his ever-growing mountain of debt had put him at odds with his cabinet. In January 1886, several ministers and relatives arranged a hasty psychiatric test that diagnosed Ludwig as mentally unfit to rule. That June, he was removed to Schloss Berg on Starnberger See. A few days later he and his doctor took a Sunday evening lakeside walk and were found several hours later, drowned in just a few feet of water. King Ludwig II was dead, but the myth, and a tourist industry, had been born.

in a fantasy landscape of French gardens, fountains and follies. Linderhof was inspired by Versailles and dedicated to Louis XIV, the French 'Sun King'.

Linderhof's myth-laden, jewel-encrusted rooms are a monument to the king's excesses. The private bedroom is the largest, heavily ornamented and anchored by an enormous 108-candle crystal chandelier weighing 500kg. An artificial waterfall, built to cool the room in summer, cascades just outside the window.

Created by the famous court gardener Carl von Effner, the gardens and outbuildings, open April to October, are as fascinating as the castle itself. The highlight is the Moorish Kiosk, where Ludwig would preside over nightly entertainment from a peacock throne.

The Drive ⟫ From Schloss Linderhof you have no choice but to backtrack along the valley to the B23 which joins the B2 at Oberau. The journey to Garmisch-Partenkirchen is 26km and should take no more than 30 minutes.

TRIP HIGHLIGHT

❺ Garmisch-Partenkirchen

An incredibly popular hang-out for outdoorsy types, skiing fans and day trippers from Munich, the double-barrelled resort of Garmisch-Partenkirchen (G-P) is blessed with a fabled setting a snowball's throw from the Alps. The area offers some of the best skiing in the land, including runs on Germany's highest peak, the Zugspitze (2964m).

JAN GREUNE / GETTY IMAGES ©

HANS-PETER MERTEN / GETTY IMAGES ©

WHY THIS IS A CLASSIC TRIP
MARC DI DUCA, AUTHOR

It's no wonder this was chosen by Bavaria's nobility as the original touring route – a more varied and picturesque string of places you couldn't hope to find anywhere else in Germany. With 2000m-tall peaks, quaint Bavarian taverns, rivers flowing jade-green with snow melt and some of Germany's most intriguing castles – the magic of the German Alps meets you at every corner.

Top: Hausberg skiing region in Garmisch-Partenkirchen
Left: Lindau's historic town hall
Right: The emerald-green Königssee

ALEKSANDAR JAKSIC / GETTY IMAGES ©

No visit to G-P would be complete without a trip on the train to the top of the **Zugspitze** (www.zugspitze.de; return adult/child €51/29.50; 🚋 train 8.15am-2.15pm). The round trip starts in Garmisch aboard a cogwheel train (Zahnradbahn) that chugs along the mountain base to the Eibsee, an idyllic forest lake. From here, the Eibsee-Seilbahn, a super-steep cable car, swings to the top. When you're done admiring the views, the Gletscherbahn cable car brings you to the Zugspitze glacier at 2600m, from where the cogwheel train heads back to Garmisch.

Easily accessible from town, the narrow and dramatically beautiful 700m-long **Partnachklamm** (www.partnachklamm.eu; adult/concession €4/2.50; 🕗8am-6pm) is a hikeable gorge with walls rising up to 80m.

✕ 🛏 p245

The Drive >> Just 18km separate Garmisch-Partenkirchen from Mittenwald (along the B2 all the way), which most tackle as a day trip. It's a simple drive, and trains run hourly between the two.

------

⑥ Mittenwald

Nestled in a cul-de-sac under snowcapped peaks, sleepily alluring Mittenwald, 20km southeast of Garmisch-Partenkirchen, is the most natural spot

✓ **TOP TIP:**
GUEST CARD

Wherever you stay in the Alps, make sure your hotel reception supplies you with a guest card. This grants free or discounted admission to local attractions and free use of public transport within a given area.

imaginable for a resort. This drowsy village is known far and wide for its master violin makers, and its citizens seem almost bemused by its popularity. The air is ridiculously clean, and on the main street the loudest noise is a babbling brook.

Skiing on the Karwendel ski field is the main attraction here, but there is one fascinating off-piste sight – the **Geigenbaumuseum** (www. geigenbaumuseum-mittenwald. de; Ballenhausgasse 3; adult/ concession €4.50/3.50; ⊙11am-4pm Tue-Sun), a collection of over 200 locally crafted violins and the tools used to fashion them. It's also the venue for occasional concerts.

The Drive » The 57km scenic route between Mittenwald and Bad Tölz follows the B11 north as far as the stunningly beautiful Walchensee. From there take the 2072 along the lakeshore then through some marvellous Alpine terrain to the B13, Lengries and onto Bad Tölz.

- - - - - - - - - - - - - - -

7 Bad Tölz

A pretty spa town straddling the Isar River, Bad Tölz is a delightful spot known for its attractive, frescoed houses and ultramodern swimming complex, **Alpamare**

(☎08041-509 999; www. alpamare.de; Ludwigstrasse 14; day pass adult/child €35/25; ⊙9.30am-10pm). Europe's first covered aquapark, this huge centre has heated indoor and outdoor mineral pools, saunas, solariums, a wave and surfing pool, and a series of wicked water slides (including Germany's longest, the 330m-long Alpabob-Wildwasser). It even has its own hotel.

Bad Tölz is also the gateway to the Tölzer Land region and its emerald-green lakes, the Walchensee and the Kochelsee.

The Drive » Some 72km divide Bad Tölz from the shores of the Chiemsee. The quickest route is along the B72 and the A8 highway, but there are several other more picturesque options.

- - - - - - - - - - - - - - -

8 Chiemsee

Most foreign visitors arrive at the shores of the Bavarian Sea – as Chiemsee is affectionately known – in search of King Ludwig II's Schloss Herrenchiemsee. This is Bavaria's biggest lake (if you don't count

Lake Constance, which is only partially in the state), and its natural beauty and water sports make the area popular with Munich folk – many of the city's affluent residents own weekend retreats by the shimmering waters.

The towns of Prien am Chiemsee and, about 5km south, Bernau am Chiemsee are good bases for exploring the lake. Of the two towns, Prien is by far the larger and livelier.

The Drive » There's no car ferry to the Herreninsel. Take the hourly or half-hourly passenger ferry from Prien-Stock (€7.60 return, 15 to 20 minutes) or from Bernau-Felden (€7.90, 25 minutes, May to October). From the boat landing on Herreninsel, it's about a 20-minute walk through pretty gardens to the palace.

- - - - - - - - - - - - - - -

9 Schloss Herrenchiemsee

An island just 1.5km across the Chiemsee from Prien, Herreninsel, is home to Ludwig II's Versailles-inspired castle, **Schloss Herrenchiemsee** (☎08051-688 70; www.herren-chiemsee.de; adult/concession

€10/9; ⏲ tours 9am-6pm Apr-Oct, 9.40am-4.15pm Nov-Mar). Begun in 1878, it was never intended as a residence, but as a homage to absolutist monarchy, as epitomised by Ludwig's hero, Louis XIV. Ludwig splurged more money on this palace than on Neuschwanstein and Linderhof combined, but when cash ran out in 1885, one year before his death, 50 rooms remained unfinished. Ludwig spent only 10 days here.

The vast **Gesandten-treppe** (Ambassador Staircase), a double staircase leading to a frescoed gallery and topped by a glass roof, is the first visual knock-out on the guided tour, but that fades in comparison to the stunning **Grosse Spiegelgalerie** (Great Hall of Mirrors). This tunnel of light runs the length of the garden (98m, or 10m longer than that in Versailles).

Other highlights include the **Paradeschlaf-zimmer** (State Bedroom), featuring a canopied bed perching altar-like on a pedestal behind a golden balustrade, and the king's bedroom, the **Kleines Blaues Schlaf-zimmer** (Little Blue Bedroom), encrusted with gilded stucco and wildly extravagant carvings.

The Drive » The easy going way to cover the 90km from Prien to Berchtesgaden is to head south to Reit im Winkl, then east almost to Bad Reichenhall on the B305 nearly all the way. Stay on the B305 to Berchtesgaden. The journey takes a little under 1¾ hours and passes through the dramatic Chiemgauer Alpen range.

- - - - - - - - - - - -

⑩ Berchtesgaden

Wedged into Austria and framed by six formidable mountain ranges, the Berchtesgadener Land is a drop-dead-gorgeous corner of Bavaria. The area includes the Watzmann (2713m), Germany's second-highest mountain, and

DETOUR: MUNICH

Start: ⑦ **Bad Tölz**

Just over 50km north of Bad Tölz, Munich is one of Germany's top cities and a magnet for tourists from all over the globe. You could explore this affluent, stylish city for weeks and not see everything, but a few days can give you a taste of what Bavaria's capital is all about.

Most people start their exploration at the **Marienplatz**, a popular gathering spot that packs a lot of personality into a compact frame. It's anchored by the Mariensäule (Mary's Column). From Marienplatz it's a short walk to the city's top attraction, the **Residenz**. All the trappings of the lifestyles of Bavaria's Wittelsbach rulers are on display at the Residenzmuseum, which takes up around half of the palace.

Not far from the Residenz is the **Hofbräuhaus**, Munich's most famous beer hall, although there are many others that are just as characterful. Of the city centre's churches, two stand out: the landmark **Frauenkirche** and the late-baroque **Asamkirche**.

Munich has often been dubbed the 'city of art and beer' and when you've tried the beer, next comes the **Kunstareal**, a whole district of world-class art museums including the Alte Pinakothek, the Museum Brandhorst, the Neue Pinakothek and the Pinakothek der Moderne.

See also a Stretch Your Legs walking tour for Munich on p270.

Classic Trip

HITLER'S MOUNTAIN RETREAT

Of all the German towns tainted by the Third Reich, Berchtesgaden has a burden heavier than most. Hitler fell in love with nearby Obersalzberg in the 1920s and bought a small country home, later enlarged into the imposing Berghof.

After seizing power in 1933, Hitler established a part-time headquarters here and brought much of the party brass with him. They bought, or often confiscated, large tracts of land and tore down farmhouses to erect a 2m-high barbed-wire fence. Obersalzberg was sealed off as the fortified southern headquarters of the NSDAP (National Socialist German Workers' Party). In 1938, British prime minister Neville Chamberlain visited for negotiations (later continued in Munich), which led to the infamous promise of 'peace in our time' at the expense of Czechoslovakia's Sudetenland.

Little is left of Hitler's Alpine fortress today. In the final days of WWII, the Royal Air Force levelled much of Obersalzberg, though the Eagle's Nest, Hitler's mountaintop eyrie, was left strangely unscathed. The historical twist and turns are dissected at the impressive **Dokumentation Obersalzberg**.

the pristine Königssee, perhaps the country's most photogenic body of water.

Away from the stunning Alpine views, Berchtesgaden has some dark tourism sights bequeathed by the Nazis who chose nearby Obersalzberg as their headquarters. The **Dokumentation Obersalzberg** (☎08652-947 960; www.obersalzberg.de; Salzbergstrasse 41, Obersalzberg; adult/concession €3/free, audioguide €2; ☺9am-5pm daily Apr-Oct, 10am-3pm Tue-Sun Nov-Mar, last entry 1hr before closing) tells the story.

The **Eagle's Nest** (Kehlsteinhaus; ☎08652-2969; www.kehlsteinhaus.de; Obersalzberg; adult/child €16.10/9.30; ☺buses 7.40am-4pm mid-May–Oct) was built as a mountaintop retreat for Hitler, and gifted to him on his 50th birthday. It took some 3000 workers only two years to carve the precipitous 6km-long mountain road, cut a 124m-long tunnel and install a brass-panelled lift through the rock, and build the lodge itself (now a restaurant). It can only be reached by special shuttle bus from the Kehlsteinhaus bus station.

🛏 p245

The Drive » It's a short 6km drive from Berchtesgaden to Schönau on the northern shore of the Königssee. From there electric boats depart for lake tours.

TRIP HIGHLIGHT

⑪ Königssee

Crossing the serenely picturesque, emerald-green Königssee makes for some once-in-a-lifetime photo opportunities. Cradled by steep mountain walls some 5km south of Berchtesgaden, Königssee is Germany's highest lake (603m), with drinkably pure waters shimmering into fjordlike depths.

Escape the hubbub of the bustling lakeside tourist village of Schönau by taking an electric-boat tour to St Bartholomä, a quaint onion-domed chapel on the western shore. At some point, the boat will stop while the captain plays a horn towards the Echo Wall – the sound will bounce seven times. From St Bartholomä, an easy trail leads to the wondrous **Eiskapelle** (ice chapel) in about one hour.

You can also skip the crowds by meandering along the lake shore. It's a nice and easy 3.5km return walk to the secluded **Malerwinkel** (Painter's Corner), a lookout famed for its picturesque vantage point.

Eating & Sleeping

Lindau ❶

🍴 Valentin   Mediterranean €€€

(📞08382-504 3740; In der Grub 28; mains
€20-31, day specials €11.50-13.50; 🕐noon-2pm
& 6-10pm Wed-Mon) The chef carefully sources
the local ingredients that go into his Med-style
dishes at this sleek vaulted restaurant. Dishes
like spinach and pecorino ravioli and locally
caught trout with creamy lentils are beautifully
cooked and presented.

🛏 Reutemann &
Seegarten   Luxury Hotel €€€

(📞08382-9150; www.reutemann-lindau.
de; Ludwigstrasse 23; s €99-183, d €142-262;
🛜🏊) Wow, what a view! Facing the harbour,
lighthouse and lion statue, this hotel has plush,
spacious rooms done out in sunny shades, as
well as a pool big enough to swim laps, a spa,
gym and refined restaurant.

Füssen ❷

🍴 Zum Hechten   Bavarian €€

(Ritterstrasse 6; mains €8-19; 🕐10am-10pm)
Füssen's best hotel restaurant keeps things
regional with a menu of Allgäu staples like
schnitzel and noodles, Bavarian pork-themed
favourites, and local specialities such as
venison goulash from the Ammertal. Post-
meal, relax in the wood-panelled dining room
caressing a König Ludwig Dunkel, one of
Germany's best dark beers brewed by the
current head of the Wittelsbach family.

🛏 Hotel Sonne   Design Hotel €€

(📞08362-9080; www.hotel-sonne.de;
Prinzregentenplatz 1; s/d from €89/109; 🅿🛜)
Although traditional looking from outside,
this Altstadt favourite offers an unexpected
design-hotel experience within. Themed rooms
feature everything from swooping bed canopies
to big-print wallpaper, huge pieces of wall art

to sumptuous fabrics. The public spaces are
littered with pieces of art, period costumes and
design features – the overall effect is impressive
and unusual for this part of Germany.

Garmisch-Partenkirchen ❺

🍴 Gasthof Fraundorfer   Bavarian €€

(www.gasthof-fraundorfer.de; Ludwigstrasse
24; mains €8-19; 🕐7am-midnight Thu-Mon,
from 5pm Wed) If you came to the Alps to
experience yodelling, knee slapping and red-
faced locals in lederhosen, you just arrived at
the right address. Steins of frothing ale fuel the
increasingly raucous atmosphere as the evening
progresses and monster portions of plattered
pig meat push belt buckles to the limit. Decor
ranges from baroque cherubs to hunting
trophies and the 'Sports Corner'. Unmissable.

🛏 Reindl's Partenkirchner
Hof   Hotel €€€

(📞08821-943 870; www.reindls.de;
Bahnhofstrasse 15; d incl breakfast €140-230;
🅿@🛜) Though Reindl's doesn't look worthy
of its five stars from the outside, this elegant,
tri-winged luxury hotel is stacked with perks, a
wine bar and a top-notch gourmet restaurant.
Rooms are studies in folk-themed elegance and
some enjoy gobsmacking mountain views.

Berchtesgaden ❿

🛏 Hotel Edelweiss   Hotel €€€

(📞08652-979 90; www.edelweiss-
berchtesgaden.com; Maximilianstrasse 2; d incl
breakfast €200-236; 🏊) Smack dab in the town
centre, the Edelweiss is Berchtesgaden's sleek
new contender. The style is modern Bavarian,
meaning a combination of traditional woodsy
flair and such hip factors as a luxe spa, a rooftop
terrace restaurant-bar with wonderful mountain
views and an outdoor infinity pool. Rooms are
XL-sized and most have a balcony.

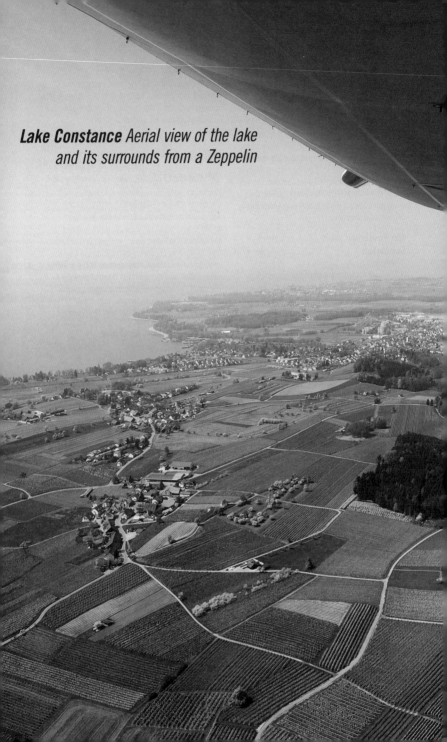

Lake Constance Aerial view of the lake
and its surrounds from a Zeppelin

Lake Constance

20

This circular route around Lake Constance (Bodensee) will take you from lakeside cafes to baroque churches, medieval cathedrals to sandy beaches, all of them sharing stupendous Alpine views.

TRIP HIGHLIGHTS

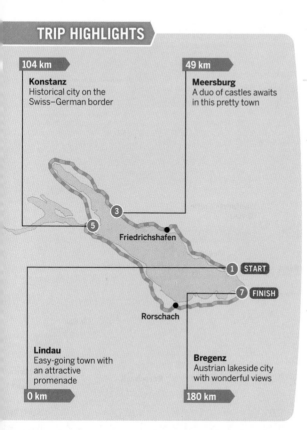

104 km

Konstanz
Historical city on the Swiss–German border

49 km

Meersburg
A duo of castles awaits in this pretty town

Friedrichshafen

START

FINISH

Rorschach

Lindau
Easy-going town with an attractive promenade

0 km

Bregenz
Austrian lakeside city with wonderful views

180 km

7 DAYS
180 KM / 112 MILES

GREAT FOR...

BEST TIME TO GO
Easter to October: winter fog doesn't obscure views and all sights are open.

ESSENTIAL PHOTO
Aerial shots from a Zeppelin over Lake Constance.

BEST FOR HISTORY
Meersburg's castle double act is unmissable for history fans.

20 Lake Constance

Shared by a trio of countries (Germany, Austria and Switzerland), Lake Constance is Central Europe's third-largest body of water. Taking in meadows and vineyards, orchards and wetlands, beaches and Alpine foothills, the lake's landscapes are like a 'greatest hits' of European scenery. Add to that heaps of culture, medieval architecture and relaxed lakeside promenades and you have yourself a highly enjoyable drive with many reasons to stop along the way.

TRIP HIGHLIGHT

❶ Lindau

Lindau is the starting point for Trip 19; see p237 for a full overview of the town's main attractions. Some of the town's lesser-known attractions are also worth an hour or two of exploration. The **Peterskirche** (Schrannenplatz; ☉daily) is a 1000-year-old church now transformed into a war memorial, but still hiding exquisite time-faded frescos of the Passion of Christ by Hans Holbein the Elder. The

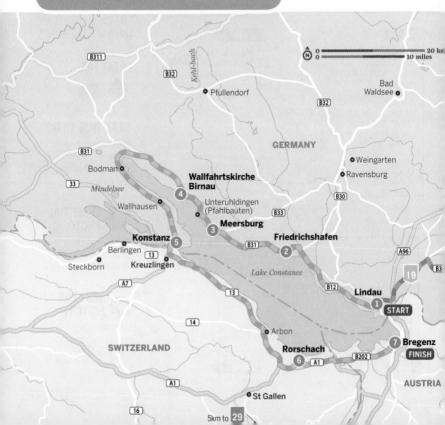

cool, dimly lit interior is a quiet spot for contemplation. Lions and voluptuous dames dance across the *trompe l'oeil* facade of the flamboyantly baroque Haus zum Cavazzen, which contains the **Stadtmuseum** (Marktplatz 6; adult/concession €7.50/3.50; ◷10am-6pm). Showcasing a fine collection of furniture, weapons and paintings, it also puts on stellar temporary exhibitions; recent ones featured works by Picasso, Chagall, Matisse and Emil Nolde.

✕ ⌒ p253

The Drive » This anticlockwise route is a fairly simple affair that follows a simple rule. If the lake is on your right, you're going the wrong way! From Lindau take the L116 as far as Kressbronn. From there take the L334 to Eriskirch where you have to join the B31 as far as Friedrichshafen. The journey is around 30km.

LINK YOUR TRIP

German Alpine Road

Both this route and the German Alpine Road kick off in Lindau.

Northern Switzerland

This route in Switzerland starts in St Gallen, only about 13km southwest of Rorschach.

COME FLY WITH ME

Real airship fans will justify the splurge on a trip in a high-tech, 12-passenger **Zeppelin NT** (📞07541-590 00; www.zeppelinflug.de). Flights lasting 30/45/60/90/120 minutes cost €200/295/395/565/745. Shorter trips cover lake destinations such as Schloss Salem and Lindau, while longer ones drift across to Austria or Switzerland. Take-off and landing are in Friedrichshafen. The flights aren't cheap but little beats floating over Lake Constance with the Alps on the horizon, and their slow pace means that you can make the most of the legendary photo ops.

❷ Friedrichshafen

Zeppelins, the cigar-shaped airships that first took flight in 1900 under the stewardship of high-flying Count Ferdinand von Zeppelin, will forever be associated with Friedrichshafen. Near the eastern end of Friedrichshafen's lakefront promenade, Seestrasse, is the **Zeppelin Museum** (www.zeppelin-museum.de; Seestrasse 22; adult/concession €8/4; ◷9am-5pm daily May-Oct, 10am-5pm Tue-Sun Nov-Apr), housed in the Bauhaus-style former Hafenbahnhof, built in 1932. The centrepiece is a full-scale mock-up of a 33m section of the *Hindenburg* (LZ 129), the largest airship ever built, measuring an incredible 245m long and outfitted as luxuriously as an ocean liner. The hydrogen-filled craft tragically burst into flames, killing 36, while landing in New Jersey in 1937. Other exhibits

provide technical and historical insights, including an original motor gondola from the famous Graf Zeppelin, which made 590 trips and travelled around the world in 21 days in 1929.

A promenade runs through the lakefront, sculpture-dotted Stadtgarten park along Uferstrasse, a great spot for a picnic or stroll.

⌒ p253

The Drive » The 19km drive from Friedrichshafen to Meersburg hugs the shore of the lake most of the way as it follows the B31. En route, the town of Immenstaad is a pretty stop, its old town gathered around a small promontory and pier.

TRIP HIGHLIGHT

❸ Meersburg

Tumbling down vine-streaked slopes to Lake Constance and crowned by a perkily turreted medieval castle, Meersburg lives up to all those clichéd knights-in-armour, damsel-in-distress fantasies. And if its tangle of cobbled lanes and half-timbered houses filled with jovial banter doesn't sweep you off your feet, the local pinot noir served in its cosy *Weinstuben* (wine taverns) certainly will.

Meersburg's two castles are the town's premier attractions. Looking across Lake Constance from its high perch, the **Altes Schloss** (adult/concession €9.50/6.50; 9am-6.30pm Mar-Oct, 10am-6pm Nov-Feb) is an archetypal medieval stronghold, complete with keep, drawbridge, knights' hall and dungeons. The **Neues Schloss** (www.schloesser-und-gaerten. de; adult/concession €5/2.50; 9am-6.30pm May-Oct, 11am-4pm Sat & Sun Nov-Apr) was built in 1710 by Prince-Bishop Johann Franz Schenk von Stauffenberg, and is a dusky-pink, lavishly baroque affair. A visit to the now state-owned palace takes in the extravagant bishops' apartments, replete with stucco work and frescos, Balthasar Neumann's

elegant staircase, and gardens with inspirational lake views.

The Drive » The quickest way to go between Meersburg and the next stop, the Wallfahrtskirche Birnau, is to stick to the B31 all the way (9km). The lakefront road is not a suitable route.

- - - - - - - - - - - - - -

4 Wallfahrtskirche Birnau

The exuberant, powder-pink **Wallfahrtskirche Birnau** (Pilgrimage Church; Uhldingen-Mühlhofen; 7.30am-7pm, to 5.30pm in winter) is one of Lake Constance's architectural highlights. It was built by the rococo master Peter Thumb of Vorarlberg in 1746. When you walk in, the decor is so intricate and profuse that you don't know where to look first. At some point your gaze will be drawn to the ceiling, where Gottfried Bernhard Göz worked his usual fresco magic.

The Drive » There are two ways of reaching Konstanz. The short way is to backtrack to

Meersburg and take the ferry. The long way is to head to the north of the lake then southeast along the western shore, a journey of around 46km.

- - - - - - - - - - - - - -

TRIP HIGHLIGHT

5 Konstanz

Sidling up to the Swiss border, bisected by the Rhine and outlined by the Alps, Konstanz sits prettily on the north-western shore of Lake Constance. Roman emperors, medieval traders and the bishops of the 15th-century Council of Constance have all left their mark on this alley-woven town, which was

TOP TIP: BODENSEE ERLEBNISKARTE

The three-day **Bodensee Erlebniskarte** (adult/child €72/37, not including ferries €40/20) is available at area tourist and ferry offices – it allows travel on almost all boats and mountain cableways on and around Lake Constance (including its Austrian and Swiss shores) and gives you entry to more than 160 tourist attractions and museums.

Friedrichshafen Engine compartment display in the Zeppelin Museum

mercifully spared from the bombs of WWII.

Crowned by a filigreed spire and looking proudly back on 1000 years of history, the sandstone **Münster** (tower adult/child €2/1; ⏰10am-6pm Mon-Sat, 10am-6pm Sun, tower 10am-5pm Mon-Sat, 12.30-5.30pm Sun) was the church of the diocese of Konstanz until 1821. The cathedral's interior is an architectural potpourri of Romanesque, Gothic, Renaissance and baroque styles. It's worth ascending the tower for broad views over the city and lake. On the lake itself, the sculpture-dotted promenade lures inline skaters, cyclists, walkers and ice-cream lickers. Just 4km northeast of the centre, the **Strandbad Horn** (Eichhornstrasse 100; ⏰mid-May–Sep) has sunbathing lawns, a kiddie pool and sports facilities.

✖ 🏠 p253

The Drive » The border with Switzerland doesn't come straight after the bridge over the Rhine in Konstanz, but a couple of kilometres further on. Have your passport ready just in case. After that, road 13 hugs the lake's shore all the way to Rorschach, a journey of around 40km.

6 Rorschach

The quiet waterfront resort of Rorschach on the Swiss side of the lake is backed by a wooded hill. Although something of a faded beauty, the town has some fine 16th- to 18th-century houses with oriel windows. Out on the lake is the 1920s **Badhütte** (Bathing Hut), attached to land by a small, covered bridge, which is a pleasant place for a drink.

The Drive » From Rorschach take road 7 east until the A1 highway. Stay on this until the signs for the exit to the border crossing with Austria. From

Bregenz Pfänder Cable Car

there the B202 heads into Bregenz, crossing the Rhine Canal on the way. The journey is 27km long.

- - - - - - - - - - - - -

TRIP HIGHLIGHT

7 Bregenz

Bregenz enjoys the most stupendous of views, with the lake spreading out like a liquid mirror; behind you the Pfänder (1064m) climbs to the Alps; to the right you see Germany, to the left the faint outline of Switzerland.

Three attractions stand out in Vorarlberg's capital. Designed by

Swiss architect Peter Zumthor, the giant glass-and-steel cube of the **Kunsthaus** (www.kunsthaus-bregenz.at; Karl-Tizian-Platz; adult/child €9/free; ☺10am-6pm Tue, Wed & Fri-Sun, to 9pm Thu; [🚹]) is said to resemble a lamp, reflecting the changing light of the sky and lake. The stark, open-plan interior is perfect for rotating exhibitions of contemporary art. The striking new home of the **Vorarlberg Museum** (www.vorarlbergmuseum. at; Kornmarktplatz 1; adult/child €9/free; ☺10am-8pm

Fri-Wed, to 9pm Thu Jul & Aug, 10am-6pm Fri-Wed, to 9pm Thu Sep-Jun) is a white cuboid that homes in on Vorarlberg's history, art and architecture. For an outdoor experience, the **Pfänder Cable Car** (www. pfaenderbahn.at; Steinbruch-gasse 4; one-way adult/child €7.10/5.70, return €12.20/9.80; ☺8am-7pm Dec-Oct) whizzes to the peak of the Pfänder, the wooded mountain rearing above Bregenz with a breathtaking panorama.

✕ �🛏 p253

Eating & Sleeping

Lindau ❶

✗ Valentin — Mediterranean €€€

(☎08382-504 3740; In der Grub 28; mains €20-31, day specials €11.50-13.50; ☺noon-2pm & 6-10pm Wed-Mon) The chef carefully sources the local ingredients that go into his Med-style dishes at this sleek vaulted restaurant. Dishes like spinach and pecorino ravioli and locally caught trout with creamy lentils are beautifully cooked and presented.

⌂ Reutemann & Seegarten — Luxury Hotel €€€

(☎08382-9150; www.reutemann-lindau. de; Ludwigstrasse 23; s €99-183, d €142-262; ☺☺) Wow, what a view! Facing the harbour, lighthouse and lion statue, this hotel has plush, spacious rooms done out in sunny shades, as well as a pool big enough to swim laps, a spa, gym and refined restaurant.

Friedrichshafen ❷

⌂ Hotel Restaurant Maier — Hotel €€

(☎07541-4040; www.hotel-maier.de; Poststrasse 1-3, Friedrichshafen-Fischbach; s €59-95, d €89-160; ☺☺) The contemporary, light-drenched rooms are immaculately kept at this family-run hotel, 5km west of Friedrichshafen and an eight-minute hop on the train. The mini spa invites relaxing moments, with its lake-facing terrace, steam room and sauna. Championing slow food, the wood-panelled restaurant is hailed far and wide for its regional food.

Konstanz ❺

✗ Münsterhof — German €€

(☎07531-363 8427; Münsterplatz 3; mains €9-22; ☺11.30am-1am Sun-Thu, to 2am Fri, to 3am Sat;) Tables set up in front of the Münster, a slick bistro interior and a lunchtime buzz have earned Münsterhof a loyal local following. Dishes from cordon bleu with pan-

fried potatoes to asparagus-filled *Maultaschen* (pork and spinach ravioli) in creamy chive sauce are substantial and satisfying. The €7.90 lunch is great value.

⌂ Riva — Boutique Hotel €€€

(☎07531-363 090; www.hotel-riva.de; Seestrasse 25; s €110-230, d €200-320;) This ultra-chic contender has crisp white spaces, glass walls and a snail-like stairwell. Zenlike rooms with hardwood floors feature perks such as (like it!) free minibars. A rooftop pool, spa area and gym, and a gourmet restaurant and terrace overlooking the lake, seal the deal.

Bregenz ❼

✗ Kornmesser — Austrian €€

(☎05574-548 54; www.kornmesser.at; Kornmarktstrasse 5; mains €14-30; ☺9.30am-11pm daily Apr-Sep, 9.30am-11pm Tue-Sun Oct-Mar) Baroque meets Bavaria at this attractively converted 18th-century *Gasthaus*. Wash down *Weisswürste* (herby veal sausages), pork knuckles and other hearty fare with Augustiner Bräu beer in the vaulted interior or chestnut-shaded beer garden.

✗ Wirtshaus am See — Austrian €€

(☎05574-422 10; www.wirtshausamsee.at; Seepromenade 2; mains €10.50-29; ☺9am-midnight) Snag a table on the lakefront terrace at this mock half-timbered villa, dishing up local specialities like buttery Bodensee whitefish and venison ragout. It's also a relaxed spot for quaffing a cold one.

⌂ Deuring-Schlössle — Historic Hotel €€€

(☎05574-478 00; www.deuring-schloessle. at; Ehre-Guta-Platz 4; d €218-252, ste €330-440; ☺☺☺) Perched above Bregenz in the Oberstadt, this is your archetypal fairy-tale hotel with a turret and ivy-draped walls. Rooms have medieval charm with antiques and low beams, while marble bathrooms, designer furnishings and wi-fi wing you back to the 21st century.

Heidelberg Famed for its Alte Universität building

Fantastic Road

21

This loop lives up to its name, taking you through a fantasy land of enchanting forests, gingerbread villages, turreted castles and mirror-like Alpine lakes.

TRIP HIGHLIGHTS

598 km

Baden-Baden
Home to a palatial spa and lavish casino

Heidelberg
START/FINISH

Stuttgart

Tübingen

Breisach

Konstanz
Spectacularly set on the shores of Lake Constance

322 km

Meersburg
A medieval Schloss, and a baroque one too

305 km

4–6 DAYS
707 KM / 440 MILES

GREAT FOR...

BEST TIME TO GO

June to August offers the loveliest summer weather.

ESSENTIAL PHOTO

Schloss Hohentübingen's terrace overlooks the river, old town and vine-streaked hills beyond.

BEST FOR FOODIES

Black Forest cake on its home turf.

21 Fantastic Road

On this ring encircling Baden-Württemberg you'll be dazzled by this German state's jewels: the ancient university city of Heidelberg, a string of storybook castles, sparkling Alp-framed lakes, a lush island-set garden and a swath of the thickly wooded Black Forest, where treasures include half-timbered villages huddled around cobbled squares, and the yesteryear grandeur of Baden-Baden, with its temple-like spa and opulent casino.

----

1 Heidelberg

Spirited Heidelberg (p196) is famed for its centuries-old university. The three-room **Universitäts-museum** (www.uni-heidelberg.de; Grabengasse 1; adult/child incl Studentenkarzer €3/2.50; ⏱10am-6pm Tue-Sun Apr-Sep, 10am-4pm Tue-Sat Oct-Mar), inside the Alte Universität building, has paintings, portraits, photos and documents about the university's mostly illustrious history.

From 1823 to 1914, students convicted of misdeeds such as public inebriation, duelling, loud nocturnal singing or freeing the local pigs were sent to its student jail, **Studentenkarzer** (Student

Jail; ☎06221-543 554; www.uni-heidelberg.de; Augustinergasse 2; adult/child incl Universitätsmuseum €3/2.50; ⏱10am-6pm Tue-Sun Apr-Sep, 10am-4pm Tue-Sat Oct-Mar), for at least 24 hours. Judging by the inventive wall graffiti, some found their stay highly amusing. Delinquents were let out to attend lectures or take exams. In certain circles, a stint in the Karzer was considered a rite of passage.

Heidelberg's student atmosphere peaks in its pubs, including its most historic, **Zum Roten Ochsen** (Red Ox Inn; www.roterochsen.de; Hauptstrasse 217; mains €11.90-24.50; ⏱5pm-12.30am Tue-Sat), with black-and-white frat photos on its dark wooden walls and names carved into the tables.

The Drive » Zooming along 120km of autobahns is the easiest way to reach Stuttgart. Southwest of Heidelberg take the A5 south for 9km. Join the eastbound A6 for 52km, and turn off onto the southbound A81 for another 52km.

- - - - - - - - - - - - - - -

❷ Stuttgart

The city where Bosch invented the spark plug and Daimler pioneered the gas engine has plenty to interest road-trippers, not least its two high-powered motoring museums.

The **Mercedes-Benz Museum** (☎0711-1730 000; www.mercedes-benz-classic. com; Mercedesstrasse 100; adult/concession/under 15yr €8/4/free; ☺9am-6pm Tue-Sun, last admission 5pm; 🚊S1 to Neckarpark) takes a chronological spin

§ LINK YOUR TRIP

15 **Bergstrasse**
Pick up the castle-lined, mountain-backed Bergstrasse in Heidelberg.

22 **Schwarzwald-hochstrasse**
Baden-Baden is the starting point for a glorious in-depth drive through the Black Forest along the Schwarzwaldhochstrasse.

257

through the Mercedes empire. Look out for legends like the 1885 Daimler Riding Car, the world's first gasoline-powered vehicle, and the record-breaking Lightning Benz that hit 228km/h at Daytona Beach in 1909.

At the **Porsche Museum** (📞0711-9112 0911; www.porsche.com/museum; Porscheplatz 1; adult/concession €8/4; ⏱9am-6pm Tue-Sun; 🚇Neuwirtshaus), groovy audioguides race you through the history of Porsche from its 1948 beginnings. Stop to glimpse the 911 GT1 that won Le Mans in 1998.

The Drive ›› From Stuttgart, it's 43km south via the B27 to Tübingen.

❸ Tübingen

In this bewitchingly pretty city, cobbled lanes lined with half-timbered townhouses twist up to a turreted 16th-century castle, **Schloss Hohentübingen** (Burgsteige 11; ⏱7am-8pm). An ornate Renaissance gate leads to the courtyard and the laboratory where Friedrich Miescher discovered DNA in 1869. Inside the castle, view the world's oldest figurative artworks, the locally unearthed 35,000-year-old Vogelherd figurines, at the **Museum Schloss Hohentübingen** (adult/concession €5/3; ⏱10am-5pm Wed-Sun, to 7pm Thu).

🍴 🛏 p261

The Drive ›› Back on the B27, drive south for 25km. At the Hechingen-Süd exit, take the K7111 (which becomes the K7110) for 2.3km to reach the lower and upper car parks for Burg Hohenzollern, from where it's a 800m or 600m walk, respectively, to the castle.

❹ Burg Hohenzollern

Rising dramatically from an exposed crag, its medieval battlements and silver turrets often veiled in mist, neo-Gothic **Burg Hohenzollern** (www.burg-hohenzollern.com; tour adult/concession €12/8, grounds admission without tour adult/concession €7/5; ⏱tour 10am-5.30pm mid-Mar–Oct, to 4.30pm Nov–mid-Mar) dates from 1867. It's the ancestral seat of the Hohenzollern family, the first and last monarchical rulers of the short-lived second German Empire (1871–1918).

The Drive ›› From Burg Hohenzollern, it's 110km southeast to Meersburg. When you cross the Danube at Sigmaringen, look out for the stunning Schloss Sigmaringen (rarely open to the public). The B31, bringing you into Meersburg, skirts Lake Constance's eastern shore.

TRIP HIGHLIGHT

❺ Meersburg

Tumbling down vine-laced slopes to Lake Constance, Meersburg's tangle of cobbled lanes

and half-timbered houses are the stuff of medieval fantasies. Looking across the lake from its lofty perch, the **Altes Schloss** (adult/concession €9.50/6.50; ⏱9am-6.30pm Mar-Oct, 10am-6pm Nov-Feb) is an archetypal medieval stronghold, complete with keep, drawbridge, knights' hall and dungeons. Founded by Merovingian king Dagobert I in the 7th century, the fortress is among Germany's oldest. The bishops of Konstanz used it as a summer residence between 1268 and 1803.

In 1710 Prince-Bishop Johann Franz Schenk von

Meersburg Looking across Lake Constance to the medieval town

Stauffenberg, perhaps tired of the dinginess and rising damp, swapped the Altes Schloss for the dusky-pink, lavishly baroque **Neues Schloss** (www.schloesser-und-gaerten. de; adult/concession €5/2.50; ⊙9am-6.30pm May-Oct, 11am-4pm Sat & Sun Nov-Apr). A visit to the now state-owned palace takes in the extravagant bishops' apartments, replete with stucco work and frescos, Balthasar Neumann's elegant staircase, and gardens with inspirational lake views.

The Drive ≫ From Meersburg's harbour, take the car ferry across Lake Constance to the B33 and follow it into Konstanz (10km including the ferry ride).

TRIP HIGHLIGHT

6 Konstanz

Konstanz is a highlight on a road filled with highlights, with its stunning location on the northwestern shore of Lake Constance, magnificent architecture and a fascinating history spanning Roman emperors, medieval traders and the bishops of the 15th-century Council of Constance. It also has a spirited student scene.

See p250 for details of the city's attractions.

✕ 🛏 p261

The Drive ≫ Take the B33 northwest for 50km and turn left (southwest) onto the B31. Pass beautiful Freiburg (well worth a stop if you have time); 6km later turn left onto the A5 towards Basel for 12km, before taking the B31 for 11km to reach Breisach.

7 Breisach

Breisach is where the Black Forest meets the French border. Lording over the town, the Romanesque and Gothic **St Stephansmünster** (⊙9am-5pm Mon-Sat) shelters a faded fresco

DETOUR:
MAINAU ISLAND

Start: ❻ Konstanz

From Konstanz, it's a quick 6km drive north via the B33 and L219 to the car park for Mainau Island, which is reached by a pedestrian-only causeway. (If you want to leave the car behind for a while, you can also take a ferry here from Konstanz.)

Jutting out over the lake and bursting with flowers, the lusciously green islet of Mainau is a 45-hectare Mediterranean **garden** (www.mainau.de; adult/concession €19/11 summer, €9.50/5.50 winter; ☉10am-7pm late Mar-late Oct, 10am-5pm rest of year) dreamed up by the Bernadotte family, relatives of the royal house of Sweden.

Crowds especially flock on weekends to admire sparkly lake and mountain views from the baroque castle, and to wander sequoia-shaded avenues and hothouses bristling with palms and orchids. Crowd-pullers include a Butterfly House, an Italian Cascade integrating patterned flowers with waterfalls, and a petting zoo. Tulips and rhododendrons bloom in spring, hibiscus and roses in summer.

cycle, Martin Schongauer's *The Last Judgment* (1491), and a magnificent altar triptych (1526) carved from linden wood.

Breisach's cobbled streets are lined with pastel-painted houses, and you'd never guess that 85% of the town was flattened in WWII, so successful has been the reconstruction. Vauban's star-shaped French fortress-town of Neuf-Brisach (New Breisach), which made the Unesco World Heritage list in 2008, sits 4km west of Breisach.

The Drive ≫ Vineyards fan out around you on this stretch of the trip. Head north via the L104 to reach the A5. Take it north towards Offenburg for 39km and link up with the B33. Following

the B33 east brings you to Gengenbach (a 77km drive in total), within the Black Forest.

❽ Gengenbach

Chocolate-box Gengenbach's chief 'sight' is its scrumptious **Altstadt** (old town) of half-timbered houses framed by vineyards and orchards. It's especially atmospheric during its Christmas festivities.

🛏 p261

The Drive ≫ It's a 96km journey to Baden-Baden. Take the B33 south; at Biberach, wind northeast for 35km to reach the high-altitude B500 (aka the Schwarzwaldhochstrasse or Black Forest High Road, which you can also explore on its own road trip; see p263). For

the next 46km, views stretch over the mist-wreathed Vosges Mountains, heather-flecked forests and glacial lakes.

TRIP HIGHLIGHT

❾ Baden-Baden

The Black Forest town of Baden-Baden recalls the grandeur of yesteryear with its colonnaded buildings and turreted art-nouveau villas beneath a backdrop of forest-covered mountains.

Gleaming with marble and glistening with mosaics, the palatial 19th-century **Friedrichs-bad** (☎07221-275 920; www.carasana.de; Römerplatz 1; 3hr ticket €25, incl soap-&-brush massage €37; ☉9am-10pm, last admission 7pm) thermal baths put the *baden* (bathe) in Baden.

Marlene Dietrich called Baden-Baden's sublime **casino** (www.casino-baden-baden.de; admission €5, guided tour €7; ☉2pm-2am Sun-Thu, 2pm-3am Fri & Sat, guided tours 9.30-11.45am) 'the most beautiful casino in the world'. Gents must wear a jacket and tie. To simply marvel at the opulence, take a 40-minute guided tour.

🍴 🛏 p261

The Drive ≫ From Baden-Baden, it's a quick 90km back to Heidelberg. Take the B500 (Schwarzwaldhochstrasse) northwest for 6.3km and turn northeast onto the A5. Along the way, you'll pass the town of Karlsruhe, which was the model for Washington, DC.

Eating & Sleeping

Tübingen ❸

✗ Wurstküche   German €€

(☎07071-927 50; Am Lustnauer Tor 8; mains €12.50-18.50; ☯11.30am-11pm Mon-Sat) The rustic, wood-panelled Wurstküche brims with locals quaffing wine and contentedly munching *Schupfnudeln* (potato noodles) and *Spanpferkel* (roast suckling pig).

⌘ Hotel am Schloss   Historic Hotel €€

(☎07071-929 40; www.hotelamschloss.de; Burgsteige 18; s €78, d €125-148, tr/q €225/290; P 🛜) So close to the castle you can almost touch it, this flower-bedecked hotel has dapper rooms ensconced in a 16th-century building. Rumour has it that Kepler was partial to the wine here; try a drop yourself before attempting the tongue twister above the bench outside: *dohoggeddiadiaemmerdohogged* (the same people sit in the same spot). And a very nice spot it is, too.

Konstanz ❻

✗ Zeitlos   German €

(☎07531-189 384; St Stephansplatz 25; snacks €4-10; ☯10am-1am Mon-Fri, 10am-6pm Sat & Sun) Behind Stephanskirche, this beamed, stone-walled bistro overflows with regulars. It's a cosy spot for brunch or filling snacks like *Wurstsalat* (sausage salad) and *Maultaschen*, the local take on ravioli. Sit in the ivy-draped courtyard in summer. Gluten-free dishes are available.

⌘ Glückseeligkeit Herberge   Guesthouse €

(☎07531-902 2075; www.herberge-konstanz. de; Neugasse 20; s €30-50, d €50-70; 🛜) What a sweet deal this little guesthouse is. Housed in a period building in the Altstadt, it shelters petite but attractively decorated rooms. The attic room has direct access to the roof terrace, which peers over a jumble of rooftops to the cathedral spire. There's also a shared lounge, kitchen and patio. E-bikes are available for rental.

Gengenbach ❽

⌘ Die Reichstadt   Boutique Hotel €€€

(☎07803-966 30; www.die-reichstadt.de; Engelgasse 33; s €140-160, ste €190-210, 4-course half-board per person €35; P 🛜) This boutique stunner on Engelgasse wings you to storybook heaven. Its 16th-century exterior conceals a pure, contemporary aesthetic, where clean lines, natural materials and subtle cream-caramel shades are enlivened with eye-catching details. A spa, sparkling wine on arrival, free fruit in the room and one of the top restaurants in town complete this pretty picture.

Baden-Baden ❾

✗ Café König   Cafe €

(Lichtentaler Strasse 12; cake €3.50-5; ☯8.30am-6.30pm) Liszt and Tolstoy once sipped coffee at this venerable cafe, which has been doing a brisk trade in Baden-Baden's finest cakes, tortes, pralines and truffles for 250 years. Black Forest gateau topped with clouds of cream, fresh berry tarts, moist nut cakes – oh, decisions!

✗ Weinstube im Baldreit   German €€

(☎07221-231 36; Küferstrasse 3; mains €12.50-19; ☯5-10pm Tue-Sat) Tucked down cobbled lanes, this wine-cellar restaurant is tricky to find, but worth looking for. Baden-Alsatian fare such as *Flammkuchen* (regional pizza) topped with Black Forest ham, Roquefort and pears is expertly matched with local wines. Eat in the ivy-swathed courtyard in summer, and the vaulted interior in winter.

⌘ Hotel Belle Epoque   Luxury Hotel €€€

(☎07221-300 660; www.hotel-belle-epoque.de; Maria-Viktoria-Strasse 2c; s €165-240, d €199-275, ste €325-695; 🛜) Nestling in manicured parkland, this neo-Renaissance villa is one of Baden-Baden's most characterful five-star pads. Antiques lend a dash of old-world opulence to the individually designed rooms. Rates include afternoon tea, with scones, cakes and fine brews served on the terrace or by the fireplace.

Ottenhöfen A storybook
Black Forest village nestled
among wooded hills

Schwarzwald-hochstrasse

22

What it says on the tin: the Black Forest High Road meanders scenically past glacial lakes, toytown villages and the gentle folds of valleys and forests that seem to roll on to infinity.

TRIP HIGHLIGHTS

0 km

Baden-Baden
Style, grace, a posh casino and famous thermal waters

24 km

Mehliskopf
Outdoor wonderland with a bob run and ski slopes

1 START

3

Wildgehege Breitenbrunnen

6

35 km

Mummelsee
Mystical forest lake for boating and hiking up to Hornisgrinde

7

Allerheiligen Wasserfälle

Freudenstadt
FINISH

Ottenhöfen
Real-deal Black Forest village with oodles of family activities

42 km

2–4 DAYS
81 KM / 50 MILES

GREAT FOR...

BEST TIME TO GO

Spring to autumn for seasonal colour (flowers and foliage).

📷 **ESSENTIAL PHOTO**

Snap the Black Forest peaks wreathed in morning mist.

☑ **BEST FOR FAMILIES**

Mehliskopf for its zippy bob run and high-rope course.

22 Schwarzwald-hochstrasse

Road trips in the deep, dark Black Forest don't get any lovelier than the Schwarzwaldhochstrasse. Why? This is a road with altitude, where the views over hill and dale are constant. Wind down the window for pine-fresh air as you wiggle south from the spa town of Baden-Baden to Freudenstadt, passing heather-flecked woodlands, luscious meadows, waterfalls, lakes and stout farmhouses. Autumn brings a dash of gold to the picture.

TRIP HIGHLIGHT

❶ Baden-Baden

Baden-Baden's air of old-world luxury and curative waters have attracted royals, the rich and celebrities over the years – Barack Obama and Bismarck, Queen Victoria and Victoria Beckham included. This chic Black Forest town boasts grand colonnaded buildings and whimsically turreted art-nouveau villas spread across the forested hillsides. Top billing goes to the grand

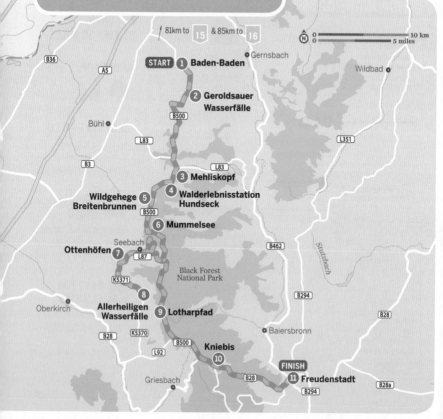

81km to 15 & 85km to 16

0 ——— 10 km
0 ——— 5 miles

START ❶ Baden-Baden
● Gernsbach
Wildbad ●

❷ Geroldsauer Wasserfälle

Bühl ●

❸ Mehliskopf

❹ Walderlebnisstation Hundseck

Wildgehege ❺ Breitenbrunnen

❻ Mummelsee

Seebach
Ottenhöfen ❼

Black Forest National Park

❽ Allerheiligen Wasserfälle
❾ Lotharpfad

Oberkirch ●

● Baiersbronn

Kniebis
❿

FINISH ⓫ Freudenstadt

Griesbach

neoclassical **Trinkhalle**
(Pump Room; Kaiserallee 3; ⊙10am-5pm Mon-Sat, 2-5pm Sun), a pump room embellished with 19th-century frescos of local legends, the sublime gilded **casino** (www.casino-baden-baden.de; admission €5, guided tour €7; ⊙2pm-2am Sun-Thu, 2pm-3am Fri & Sat, guided tours 9.30-11.45am) and the architecturally innovative **Museum Frieder Burda** (www.museum-frieder-burda. de; Lichtentaler Allee 8b; adult/concession €12/10; ⊙10am-6pm Tue-Sun), whose stellar collection features Picasso, Gerhard Richter and Jackson Pollock. If the sun's out, join the locals for a lazy mooch along the **Lichtentaler Allee**, a 2.3km ribbon of greenery shadowing the sprightly

LINK YOUR TRIP

15 **Bergstrasse**
From Baden-Baden, drive 86km north to Wiesloch and the Bergstrasse, a road trip taking in castles and vineyards aplenty.

16 **German Castle Road**
Like nothing better than a good castle? You'll be in your element on this history-packed road trip. Hook onto it in Heidelberg, 90km north of Baden-Baden.

SPA TIME

The bath-loving Romans were the first to discover the healing properties of Baden-Baden's springs in the city they called Aquae Aureliae. Rheumatism, arthritis, respiratory complaints, skin problems – all this and a host of other ailments can be healed, apparently, by this mineral-rich spring water.

To take the waters yourself, you could abandon modesty (and clothing) to wallow in thermal waters at **Friedrichsbad** (☎07221-275 920; www.carasana. de; Römerplatz 1; 3hr ticket €25, incl soap-&-brush massage €37; ⊙9am-10pm, last admission 7pm), a palatial 19th-century marble-and-mosaic-festooned spa, with a strict regime of hot-and-cold bathing, dunking and scrubbing. If you'd rather keep your bathing togs on, slip over to **Caracalla Spa** (☎07221-275 940; www. carasana.de; Römerplatz 11; 2/3/4hr €15/18/21; ⊙8am-10pm, last admission 8pm), a modern glass-fronted spa with a cluster of indoor and outdoor pools, grottoes and surge channels.

Oosbach, studded with fountains and carpeted with flowers.

✗ ⊨ p269

The Drive » The B500 south of Baden-Baden soon begins its steady climb through high meadows and spruce, pine and larch forest. After 7.5km, just after Gasthaus Auerhahn, bear left onto Geroldsauerstrasse, which soon becomes Wasserfallstrasse. It's a further 2km drive to Geroldsauer Wasserfälle.

- - - - - - - - - - - - -

2 Geroldsauer Wasserfälle
Word has it that German composer Brahms and French painter Courbet had a soft spot for the wispy **Geroldsauer Wasserfälle** (waterfalls), which plunge over mossy

boulders into a green pool. The 1.5km walk through forest and along the Grobbach stream is deliciously cool on a hot day and looks freshly minted for a picturebook about water sprites. The falls are at their loveliest when the rhododendrons are in bloom from early May to June.

The Drive » Backtrack to the B500 and follow it as it meanders south, affording bucolic views over forested hills, to Mehliskopf, 14km away.

- - - - - - - - - - - - -

TRIP HIGHLIGHT

3 Mehliskopf
Mehliskopf (www.mehliskopf. de; bob adult/concession €4.10/3.50, cart €4, day ski pass adult/concession €24/21, tower free; ⊙bob 10am-6pm

Wed-Sun year-round, carts 10am-6pm Sat & Sun Apr-Nov, high-rope course 10am-6pm Apr-Nov, ski lift 9am-8pm late Nov-Mar) rises 1007m, and its slopes are a magnet to families seeking low-key outdoor adventure. You can whiz downhill year-round on the bob run, picking up speeds of up to 40km/h on its hairpin bends and 360-degree loop, or on the downhill carts (over 14-year-olds). There's also a high-rope course in the forest and a lookout tower, with far-reaching views across the Northern Black Forest and the Rhine Plain. In winter, the focus switches to the snowpark's rails and obstacles, and downhill skiing.

The Drive >> Sidling up to Mehliskopf is the peak of Hundseck – your next stop.

④ Walderlebnis-station Hundseck

A sure-fire hit with the kids, this **forest discovery area** has child-geared trails including a circular 500m hunting path and a 2km quiz path, as well as a shorter barefoot path for feeling different textures underfoot.

The Drive >> Press on south along the ever-panoramic B500, veering right onto the L86 after around 5km. After a couple of kilometres you'll reach the Wildgehege Breitenbrunnen.

⑤ Wildgehege Breitenbrunnen

If wildlife encounters rank highly on your wish list, factor in a stop at this **game reserve** (Breitenbrunnen, Sasbachwalden) to come

eye to eye with stags, roe deer and wild boar.

The Drive >> Head back to the B500 for the dreamy drive overlooking a ripple of wooded hills to Mummelsee, around 3.5km south.

TRIP HIGHLIGHT

⑥ Mummelsee

This glacial **cirque lake** (lookout tower 10.30am-5pm Sat & Sun) makes a beautiful splash on a vast tract of forest. Lore has it that an underwater king and nymphs dwell in its inky depths – and indeed the lake is pure Brothers Grimm fairy-tale stuff. You can pedal across it by boat or stroll its shores. Should you want to ramble further, you can hike 1.5km up to 1164m Hornisgrinde, the highest peak in these parts, commanding far-reaching

LOCAL KNOWLEDGE: GOURMET PIT STOP

Swinging along country lanes 6km north of Freudenstadt brings you to Baiersbronn. It looks like any other Black Forest town, snuggled among meadows and wooded hills, but on its fringes sit two of Germany's finest restaurants, both holders of the coveted three Michelin stars.

Schwarzwaldstube (07442-4920; www.traube-tonbach.de; Tonbachstrasse 237, Baiersbronn-Tonbach; 5-/7-course menu €80/210, cookery courses around €170; 7pm-midnight Wed, noon-4.30pm & 7pm-midnight Thu-Sun) commands big forest views from its rustically elegant dining room. Here Harald Wohlfahrt performs culinary magic, while carefully sourcing and staying true to French cooking traditions.

Claus-Peter Lumpp has consistently won plaudits for his brilliantly composed, French-inflected menus at **Restaurant Bareiss** (07442-470; www.bareiss.com; Gärtenbühlweg 14, Baiersbronn-Mitteltal; lunch menu €95, dinner menus €168-210; noon-2pm & 7-9.30pm Wed-Sun). Dishes that appear deceptively simple on paper become things of beauty – rich in textures and aromas and presented with an artist's eye for detail.

HEINZ WOHNER / GETTY IMAGES ©

Mummelsee This cirque lake is surrounded by the Black Forest

views over the Black Forest from its lookout tower.

📖 p269

The Drive » From Mummelsee, bear south past slopes that fill with skiers in winter, then turn right onto the L87 (Ruhesteinstrasse) for the drive to Ottenhöfen, 14km away.

TRIP HIGHLIGHT

7 Ottenhöfen

As storybook Black Forest villages go, **Ottenhöfen** (www.ottenhoefen-tourismus. de) fits the bill nicely with its plethora of lovingly restored watermills (best explored on the 12km Mühlenweg), slender-spired church and farmhouses snuggled among low-rise, wooded hills. Climbers and hikers can head up to the knobbly peak of Karlsruher Grat. The surrounding area is criss-crossed with family-friendly walking trails and mountain-bike routes.

The Drive » The K5371 is a minor country road leading southeast of Ottenhöfen to Allerheiligen, 7.5km away.

8 Allerheiligen Wasserfälle

Allerheiligen's 90m-high **waterfalls** spill in silky threads over several cascades. From here, a short, round trail leads over bridges and up steps through the wooded gorge to a ruined Gothic abbey – an evocative sight with its nave open to the sky.

📖 p269

The Drive » From Allerheiligen, take the winding K5371 north back to the B500, then turn right heading south, where you'll pass Schliffkopf Wellness & Nature Hotel (p269) en route to the Lotharpfad. It's a 16km drive in total.

9 Lotharpfad

Hurricane Lothar swept across Europe in 1999, flattening some parts

NATIONALPARK SCHWARZWALD

An outdoor wonderland of heather-speckled moors, glacial cirque lakes, deep valleys, mountains and near-untouched coniferous forest, the **Nationalpark Schwarzwald** (Black Forest National Park; ☏07449-9299 8444; www.schwarzwald-nationalpark. de; Schwarzwaldhochstrasse 2, Seebach; ☺10am-6pm Tue-Sun May-Sep, 10am-5pm Tue-Sun Oct-Apr), which finally got the seal of approval (national park status) on 1 January 2014, is the Black Forest at its wildest and untamed best. Nature is left to its own devices in this 100-sq-km pocket in the northern Black Forest, tucked between Baden-Baden and Freudenstadt and centred on the Schwarzwaldhochstrasse (Black Forest High Road), the Murgtal valley and Mummelsee lake.

Hiking and cycling trails abound, as do discovery paths geared towards children. Stop by the information centre in Seebach for the low-down and to pick up maps. Details of guided tours and online maps are also available on the website.

of the Northern Black Forest, where trees fell like dominoes in wind speeds of up to 200km/h. The Lotharpfad is an 800m adventure trail that gives an insight into how the area is now being reforested.

The Drive » Back behind the wheel, drive gently south to reach the little village of Kniebis, 7km distant.

⑩ Kniebis

Serene and family-friendly, **Kniebis** (www.kniebis.de) backs onto a terrific landscape for all manner of outdoor activities – from hiking and biking to cross-country skiing and sledding. To cool off in summer, head over to the forest-rimmed **Waldschwimmbad** (www. waldschwimmbad-kniebis.de; adult/concession €2.50/1.50; ☺noon-8pm Mon-Fri, 11am-7pm Sat & Sun late May–mid-Sep), with its outdoor pool, kids' splash area and volleyball court.

The Drive » It's an easy 11km drive east on the B28, past forested hills, pastures and farmhouses, to Freudenstadt, marking the southern terminus of the Schwarzwaldhochstrasse.

⑪ Freudenstadt

Duke Friedrich I of Württemberg built a new capital in Freudenstadt in 1599, which was bombed to bits in WWII. Though its centre is underwhelming, statistics lovers will delight in ticking off Germany's biggest square (216m by 219m, for the record), **Marktplatz**, whose arcades harbour rows of shops and cafes with alfresco seating, and the 17th-century red-sandstone **Stadtkirche** (☺10am-5pm), with an ornate 12th-century Cluniac-style baptismal font, Gothic windows, Renaissance portals and baroque towers. The glass-fronted **Panorama-Bad** (www.panorama-bad. de; Ludwig-Jahn-Strasse 60; adult/concession 3hr pass €6.70/5.80; ☺9am-10pm Mon-Sat, 9am-8pm Sun) is a relaxation magnet with pools, steam baths and saunas. To rent out your own set of bike wheels, pop into **Intersport Glaser** (Katharinenstrasse 8; bike rental per day €14-24; ☺9.30am-6.30pm Mon-Fri, 9.30am-4pm Sat).

✕ 🛏 p269

Eating & Sleeping

Baden-Baden ❶

✗ Weinstube im Baldreit — German €€

(✆07221-231 36; Küferstrasse 3; mains €12.50-19; ⊙5-10pm Tue-Sat) Tucked down cobbled lanes, this wine-cellar restaurant is tricky to find, but worth looking for. Baden-Alsatian fare such as *Flammkuchen* (regional pizza) topped with Black Forest ham, Roquefort and pears is expertly matched with local wines. Eat in the ivy-swathed courtyard in summer, and the vaulted interior in winter.

▦ Hotel am Markt — Historic Hotel €€

(✆07221-270 40; www.hotel-am-markt-baden.de; Marktplatz 18; s €35-65, d €90-120; ᴾ🖥) Sitting pretty in front of the Stiftskirche, this 250-year-old hotel has 23 homely, well-kept rooms. It's quiet up here apart from your wake-up call of church bells, but then you wouldn't want to miss out on the great breakfast.

▦ Hotel Belle Epoque — Luxury Hotel €€€

(✆07221-300 660; www.hotel-belle-epoque.de; Maria-Viktoria-Strasse 2c; s €165-240, d €199-275, ste €325-695; 🖥) Nestling in manicured parkland, this neo-Renaissance villa is one of Baden-Baden's most characterful five-star pads. Antiques lend a dash of old-world opulence to the individually designed rooms. Rates include afternoon tea, with scones, cakes and fine brews served on the terrace or by the fireplace.

Mummelsee ❻

▦ Berghotel Mummelsee — Guesthouse €€

(✆07842-992 86; http://mummelsee.de/berghotel; Schwarzwaldhochstrasse 11; s €82-95, d €134-160, ste €180; ᴾ🖥) Sitting prettily on the shores of Mummelsee, this chalet-style lodge has rooms decked out in modern country style, with warm hues, local pine furnishings and balconies – the pick of which overlook the lake and forest. Warmed by a tiled oven, the wood-panelled restaurant dishes up regional fare (including a decent Black Forest gateau). Unwind in the little spa area and sauna.

Allerheiligen Wasserfälle ❽

▦ Schliffkopf Wellness & Nature Hotel — Hotel €€€

(✆07449-9200; www.schliffkopf.de; Schliffkopf; incl half-board s €163-173, d €256-356, ste €346-420; ᴾ🖥🏊) Right in the wooded heart of the Black Forest National Park, this hilltop hotel is an appealing pick, with spacious, warm-toned rooms, a spa, sauna and an outdoor pool. Splashing out on a wellness suite gets you a whirlpool bathtub. Rates include a five-course dinner that plays up seasonal, farm-fresh food.

Freudenstadt ⓫

✗ Turmbräu — German €€

(Marktplatz 64; mains €8-28; ⊙11am-midnight, to 3am Fri & Sat) This lively microbrewery doubles as a beer garden. Pull up a chair in ye-olde barn to munch *Maultaschen* (pork and spinach ravioli) and guzzle Turmbräu brews – a 5L barrel costs €39.

▦ Warteck — Hotel €€

(✆07441-919 20; www.warteck-freudenstadt.de; Stuttgarterstrasse 14; s €60-78, d €98-105; ᴾ🖥) In the capable hands of the Glässel family since 1894, this hotel sports modern, gleamingly clean rooms. The real draw, however, is the wood-panelled restaurant (mains €14.50 to €39), serving market-fresh fare like beetroot tortellini and rack of venison with wild mushrooms.

STRETCH YOUR LEGS
MUNICH

Start: Marienplatz

Finish: Englischer Garten

Distance: 4km / 2.5 miles

Duration: Three hours

This walk follows a route around the main sights in Munich's historical city centre. It takes in some of the Bavarian capital's finest churches, its top palace and its busiest piazzas, passing some of Central Europe's best shopping opportunities along the way.

Take this walk on Trip

Marienplatz

Leave your car at one of the many park and ride sites in Munich (see www. parkundride.de) and take the S-Bahn into the **Altstadt** (old town). This city centre walk kicks off at the epicentral heart and soul of Munich's Altstadt, the Marienplatz. This piazza is anchored by the **Marien-säule** (Mary's Column), built in 1638 to celebrate the victory over Swedish forces during the Thirty Years' War.

The Walk >> From Marienplatz head along Rindermarkt, past the Peterskirche with its climbable tower and out onto the expanse of the Viktualienmarkt.

Viktualienmarkt

The Viktualienmarkt is a feast of fla-vours and one of Central Europe's finest gourmet markets, with fresh fruits and vegetables, piles of artisan cheeses, hams and jams, chanterelles and truf-fles on display. The **Viktualienmarkt** (Viktualienmarkt 6; ☉9am-10pm; [U]Marienplatz, [S]Marienplatz) beer garden has been a Munich institution since 1807.

The Walk >> From the Viktualienmarkt, head northwest along Rosental until you reach Sendlinger Strasse. Take a left here and walk on – the Asamkirche is on your right.

Asamkirche

The late-baroque (1746) **Asamkirche** (Sendlinger Strasse 32; ☉9am-6pm Sat-Thu, 1-6pm Fri; [🚇]Sendlinger Tor, [U]Sendlinger Tor) is as rich and epic as a giant's treasure chest. Its creators dug deep into their talent box to swath every inch of wall space with gilt garlands and docile cherubs, false marble and oversize barley-twist columns.

The Walk >> Retrace your steps along Sendlinger Strasse for around 100m until you reach Hackenstrasse on the left. From here wind your way north until you hit pedestrianised Kaufingerstrasse. The Frauenkirche is just beyond.

Frauenkirche

The landmark **Frauenkirche** (Church of Our Lady; www.muenchner-dom.de; Frauenplatz 1; ☉7am-7pm Sat-Wed, to 8.30pm Thu, to 6pm Fri; [S]Marienplatz), built between 1468 and 1488, is Munich's spiritual heart. No other building in the central city stands taller than its onion-domed twin towers (99m).

The Walk » From the Frauenkirche's eastern end, head along Albertgasse then take a left into Weinstrasse until you reach the tramlines of Perusastrasse and Maximilianstrasse. Residenzstrasse and the entrance to the Residenz are on your left.

Residenz

Home to Bavaria's Wittelsbach rulers from 1508 until WWI, the Residenz is Munich's number-one attraction. The amazing treasures, as well as all the trappings of their lifestyles over the centuries, are on display at the **Residenzmuseum** (☎089-290 671; www.residenz-muenchen.de; Residenzstrasse 1; adult/concession/under 18yr €7/6/free; ☺9am-6pm Apr–mid-Oct, 10am-5pm mid-Oct–Mar, last entry 1hr before closing; ⓊOdeonsplatz), which takes up around half of the palace. If you have the time, it takes at least two hours to see everything.

The Walk » From the Residenz follow Residenzstrasse until you reach Odeonsplatz. Cross the exquisite Hofgarten diagonally until you reach Prinzregentenstrasse.

Eisbach Surfers

The last sport you might expect to see being practised in central Munich is surfing, but go to the southern tip of the English Garden at Prinzregentenstrasse and you'll see a crowd leaning over a bridge to cheer on daredevils as they hang on an artificially created wave in the Eisbach Stream.

The Walk » The Eisbach wave is at one of the entrances to the Englischer Garten, which extends north from here.

Englischer Garten

The sprawling English Garden is among Europe's biggest city parks, and is a popular playground for locals and visitors alike. Of its attractions, the one that may be of most interest post-walk is the **Chinesischer Turm** (☎089-383 8730; www.chinaturm.de; Englischer Garten 3; ☺10am-11pm; ▣Chinesischer Turm, ▣Tivolistrasse), Munich's oldest beer garden (1791).

The Walk » The nearest S-Bahn station to the Englischer Garten is at Marienplatz. The nearest U-Bahn (metro) station is at the southern end at Odeonsplatz.

Austria Trips

AUSTRIA IS A ROAD-TRIPPER'S FANTASY LAND. Not only are there spectacular backdrops of spellbinding landscapes and storybook architecture, but opportunities abound to get out and experience them.

Along these routes, you can scale soaring peaks, ski year-round, scuba-dive crystal-clear glacial lakes, raft white-water rapids, pelt down toboggan runs and delve into glittering ice caves and salt mines.

When you've had enough thrills and spills, Austria's multitude of cultural pursuits span medieval castles to monumental palaces, art-filled museums and magnificent churches, as well as the remains of Roman settlements and sobering WWII sites. You can taste cheese at Alpine dairies, schnapps at distilleries, and beer and wine in monasteries where they're still made by monks. Or just hop aboard a horse-drawn carriage to clip-clop through cobbled, lamp-lit city streets.

Salzburg Region Valley near the Krimmler Wasserfälle (Trip 24)
A JELLEMA / SHUTTERSTOCK ©

Austria Trips

23 **Along the Danube 2–4 Days**
Follow the Danube River as it flows through forests and vineyards. (p277)

Classic Trip

24 **Grossglockner Road 5–7 Days**
Twist and turn along three of Austria's most spectacular mountain passes. (p285)

25 **Tyrol & Vorarlberg 5–7 Days**
Walk through wildflower-filled pastures and savour local produce on this Alpine route. (p295)

26 **Castles of Burgenland 2–4 Days**
Visit castles and palaces along with celebrated wineries between Vienna and Graz. (p305)

27 **Salzkammergut 5–7 Days**
Spin around the Salzkammergut's jewel-like lakes beneath towering snow-capped mountains. (p313)

28 **Carinthian Lakes 2–4 Days**
Swim, boat, water ski or just unwind along 'Austria's Riviera', the Carinthian Lakes. (p323)

Salzburg View of the historic city and the Salzach River

DON'T MISS

Vienna

With its resplendent palaces, magnificent museums and opera house, Austria's capital is the belle of the country's ball. Waltz by on Trips 23 26

Lake Swimming

Many of Austria's Alp-framed lakes reach temperatures of up to 28°C in summer. Dive into them on Trips 24 25 26 28

Salzburg

Famed for its starring role in *The Sound of Music*, Salzburg's Unesco-listed Altstadt (old town) is a treasure. Visit on Trips 24 25 27

Skiing

Austria is synonymous with pure-white powder pistes. You can also ski the Stubai Glacier, near Innsbruck, in summer on Trip 24

Hiking

Through forests, up waterfall trails, down gorges, along wildflower-strewn meadows... You'll find some of Austria's best hiking on Trips 24 25

Passau *Cruising the Danube River*

Along the Danube

23

Follow the beautiful Danube River as it flows from the German city of Passau by the Austrian border through farmland, forest and vineyard-streaked hillsides to Austria's majestic capital, Vienna.

TRIP HIGHLIGHTS

205 km

Dürnstein
Richard the Lionheart was imprisoned here in a now-ruined castle

293 km

Vienna
View Vienna by foot, horse-drawn carriage or Ferris wheel

START
Passau

Linz

④

Krems an der Donau

⑦
⑨
Melk

⑩ FINISH

St Florian
Visit the abbey's exuberant basilica

92 km

Stift Göttweig
This Unesco-listed abbey serves its own monk-made wines

219 km

2–4 DAYS
293 KM / 182 MILES

GREAT FOR...

BEST TIME TO GO
Aim for summer: many places close between November and March.

ESSENTIAL PHOTO
St Florian's dazzling interior.

BEST FOR ART
Linz's contemporary Lentos gallery.

23 | Along the Danube

Immortalised in the stirring *Blue Danube* waltz by Austrian composer Johann Strauss II, this magnificent river ripples with the reflections of green forests, hilltop castles, and ribbons of vineyards, particularly on its prettiest stretch, the Wachau, between Melk and Krems an der Donau. Along the river's course are plenty of surprises too, including the cutting-edge city of Linz, and two monasteries producing, respectively, sublime beer and wine.

① Passau

Just inside the German border, Passau's pastel-shaded **Altstadt** (old town) sits atop a narrow peninsula jutting into the confluence of three rivers: the Danube, the Inn and the Ilz. Christianity generated prestige as Passau evolved into the largest bishopric in the Holy Roman Empire, as testified by the mighty cathedral **Dom St Stephan** (www.bistum-passau.de; Domplatz; ⊙6.30am-7pm).

Stroll the old town, which remains much as

it was when the powerful prince-bishops built its tight lanes, tunnels and archways with an Italianate flourish.

 p283

The Drive » Cross the Inn River where it joins the Danube and head east on ST2125 which, 3.3km later, becomes the B130 on entering Austria, and follows the Danube's southern bank. On your right, you'll pass Burg Krempelstein, built on the site of a Roman watch house. It's 26km all up to Engelhartszell an der Donau.

❷ Engelhartszell an der Donau

The little riverside village of Engelhartszell an der Donau is home to one of only eight licensed Trappist breweries outside Belgium, and the only one in Austria. At the 1293-founded abbey **Engelszell** (www.stift-engelszell.at; Stiftstrasse 6; ⏰ church 8am-7pm Apr-Oct, to 5pm Nov-Mar, shop 9am-5pm Apr-Oct, 10-11.30am & 2.30-4pm Sat & Sun Nov-Mar), you can purchase monk-made

LINK YOUR TRIP

26 Castles of Burgenland
Vienna is the starting point of this castle-strewn route.

27 Salzkammergut
From Passau, it's 115km southwest to Salzburg, from where you can explore the Salzkammergut's mountain-ringed lakes.

brews (dark Gregorius, amber Benno, and blond Nivard); the shop also sells liqueurs and cheeses produced here. Adjoining the shop is the abbey's gorgeous rococo church, completed in 1764.

The Drive >> Take the B130; at Aschach an der Donau, cross the river on the B131, and continue east to Ottensheim to join the B127 to Linz (52km in total).

- - - - - - - - - - - - - - -

3 Linz

The Austrian saying *In Linz beginnt's* (It begins in Linz) sums up this technology trailblazer. Its leading-edge **Ars Electronica Center** (www. aec.at; Ars Electronica Strasse 1; adult/child €8/6; ⊙9am-5pm Tue-Fri, to 9pm Thu, 10am-6pm Sat & Sun) has labs for interacting with robots, animating digital objects, converting your name to DNA and (virtually) travelling to outer space. After dark, the LED glass skin kaleidoscopically changes colour. Directly across the Danube is Linz's world-class contemporary-art gallery, the glass-and-steel **Lentos** (www.lentos. at; Ernst-Koref-Promenade 1; adult/child €8/4.50, guided tours €3; ⊙10am-6pm Tue-Sun, to 9pm Thu), with works by Warhol, Schiele and Klimt, among others.

But it's not all new in Austria's third-largest city: the **Mariendom** (Herrenstrasse 26; ⊙7.30am-7pm Mon-Sat, 8am-7.15pm Sun) is a neo-Gothic giant of a cathedral with a riot of pinnacles, flying buttresses and filigree traceried windows.

✗ ⮞ p283

The Drive >> Take the A1 southeast to Ebelsberg, then continue on the L564 to St Florian (21km all up).

- - - - - - - - - - - - - - -

TRIP HIGHLIGHT

4 St Florian

Rising like a vision above St Florian is its magnificent abbey, **Augustiner Chorherrenstift** (www. stift-st-florian.at; Stiftstrasse 1; tours €8.50; ⊙11am, 1pm & 3pm May-early Oct). Dating to at least 819, it has been occupied by the Canons Regular, living under Augustinian rule, since 1071. Today its imposing yellow-and-white facade is overwhelmingly baroque.

Compulsory guided tours of the abbey's interior take in the resplendent apartments adorned with rich stuccowork and frescos, including 16 emperors' rooms (once occupied by visiting popes and royalty) and a galleried library housing 150,000 volumes.

The **Stiftsbasilika** (⊙7am-dusk) is an exuberant affair with an altar carved from 700 tonnes of pink Salzburg marble, and a gold 18th-century organ.

The Drive >> Head northeast on the L566 to join the B1. Follow it for 7.5km then turn east on the B123 to cross the Danube, before turning west on the B3. After 2.4km take the L1411 for 2.5 signposted

STIFT ST FLORIAN/BEYER

kilometres to the Mauthausen Memorial (22km in total).

- - - - - - - - - - - - - - -

5 Mauthausen Memorial

Nowadays Mauthausen is a peaceful small town on the north bank of the Danube, but during WWII the Nazis turned the quarrying centre into the **KZ Mauthausen** concentration camp. Prisoners were forced into slave labour in the granite quarry and many died on the so-called *Todesstiege* (stairway of death) leading from the quarry to the camp. Some 100,000 prisoners perished or were executed in the

St Florian The beautiful pipe organ on display in the Stiftsbasilika

camp between 1938 and 1945. The complex is now a **memorial** (www.mauthausen-memorial.at; Erinnerungsstrasse 1; admission incl guided tour €5, audioguide €3; ⊘9am-5.30pm Mar-early Jul, 9am-5.30pm Tue-Sun early Jul-Oct, 9am-3pm Tue-Sun Nov-Feb); English-language audioguides relate its sobering history. It's not recommended for under 14s.

The Drive ⟫ Travelling east for 76km brings you to Melk. Along the river at Grein, look out for the dramatic castle Greinburg rising to your left.

⑥ Melk

Historically, Melk was of great importance to the Romans and later to the Babenbergs, who built a castle here. In 1089 the Babenberg margrave Leopold II donated the castle to Benedictine monks, who converted it into the fortified **Stift Melk** (Benedictine Abbey of Melk; www.stiftmelk.at; Abt Berthold Dietmayr Strasse 1; adult/child €10/5.50, with guided tour €12/7.50; ⊘9am-5.30pm May-Sep, tours 11am & 2pm Oct-Apr). Fire destroyed the original edifice; today its monastery church dominates the complex with its twin spires and high octagonal dome. The baroque-gone-barmy interior has regiments of cherubs, gilt twirls and polished faux marble.

The theatrical high-altar scene depicts St Peter and St Paul (the church's two patron saints).

The Drive ⟫ The Wachau is the loveliest along the mighty river's length: both banks here are dotted with ruined castles and terraced with vineyards. From Melk, follow the river northeast along the nothern bank for 28km, passing medieval villages Spitz, Wösendorf in der Wachau and Weissenkirchen, to reach Dürnstein.

TRIP HIGHLIGHT

⑦ Dürnstein

Picturesque Dürnstein is best known for the **Kuenringerburg** – the now-ruined castle above the town where Richard

281

TOP TIP: DANUBE CRUISES

Floating past vine-covered banks crowned by castles gives you a different perspective of the river. From Passau, **Wurm + Köck** (⌨0851-929 292; www.donauschiffahrt.de; Höllgasse 26) operates cruises between Regensburg, Germany, and Vienna from March to early November. One-way/return tickets for one stop start from €10.50/11.50; 10-stop tickets start from €26/29.

the Lionheart (Richard I of England) was imprisoned from 1192 to 1193, before being moved to **Burg Trifels** (p178) in Germany.

Of the 16th-century buildings lining Dürnstein's hilly, cobbled streets, the **Chorherrenstift** (www.stiftduernstein.at; Stiftshof; adult/child €3/1.50; ⌚9am-6pm Mon-Sat, 10am-6pm Sun Apr-Oct) is the most impressive. It's all that remains of the former Augustinian monastery originally founded in 1410, and received its baroque facelift in the 18th century.

The Drive » Head east along the river on the B3 for 7.5km to reach Krems an der Donau.

⑧ Krems an der Donau

Against a backdrop of terraced vineyards, Krems has an attractive cobbled centre and gallery-dotted **Kunstmeile** (Art Mile; www.kunstmeile-krems.at). Its flagship is the **Kunsthalle** (www.kunsthalle.at; Franz-Zeller-Platz 3; admission €10; ⌚10am-5pm Tue-Sun), a collection of galleries and museums, with changing exhibitions.

🛏 p283

The Drive » Leave Krems an der Donau on the B37 and cross the southbound L100. Stift Göttweig is well signposted (9km altogether from Krems).

TRIP HIGHLIGHT

⑨ Stift Göttweig

Surrounded by grape-laden vines, Unesco World Heritage–listed **Stift Göttweig** (Göttweig Abbey; ⌨02732-855 81-0; www.stift-goettweig.at; Furth bei Göttweig; adult/child €7.50/4; ⌚9am-6pm Jun-Sep, 10am-6pm Oct-May) was founded in 1083, but the abbey you see today is mostly baroque. Highlights include the Imperial Staircase with a heavenly ceiling fresco painted by Paul Troger in 1739, and the over-the-top baroque interior of the Stiftskirche (which has a Kremser Schmidt work in the crypt). Best of all is the opportunity to sip wine made here by the monks – including an exquisite Messwein rosé – on the panoramic garden terrace above the valley (you can also buy it at the abbey's shop).

The Drive » From Stift Göttweig, it's 79km to Vienna. The most scenic route, through farmland and forest, is south on the L100 to St Pölten, then east on the L120 to join the eastbound B44 at Ebersberg. Continue through the Wienerwald to the Austrian capital.

TRIP HIGHLIGHT

⑩ Vienna

Renowned for its imperial palaces, baroque interiors, opera houses and magnificent squares, Vienna is also one of Europe's most dynamic urban spaces. The best way to experience its blend of old and new is on a walking tour (p332).

A wonderfully atmospheric (if touristy) alternative is aboard a **Fiaker** (up to 4 passengers 20min/40min/1hr tour €55/80/110), which is a traditional-style open carriage drawn by a pair of horses. Drivers point out places of interest en route. Lines of horses, carriages and bowler-hatted drivers can be found at Stephansplatz, Albertinaplatz and Heldenplatz at the Hofburg.

Or survey the city from Vienna's 65m-high, 1897-built Ferris wheel, the **Riesenrad**. It's located at the **Prater** (www.wiener-prater.at; Ⓜ Praterstern), a sprawling park encompassing meadows, woodlands and an amusement park (the **Würstelprater**), between the Danube and Danube Canal (Donaukanal).

🍴🛏 p283

Eating & Sleeping

Passau ●

✗ Heilig-Geist-Stifts-
Schenke
Bavarian €€

(☎0851-2607; www.stiftskeller-passau.de;
Heilig-Geist-Gasse 4; mains €10-20; ⊙11am-
11pm, closed Wed; 🛜) Not only does this
historical inn have a succession of walnut-
panelled ceramic-stove-heated rooms, a
candlelit cellar (from 6pm) and a vine-draped
garden, but the food is equally inspired. Amid
the river fish, steaks and seasonal dishes there
are quite gourmet affairs such as beef fillet in
flambéed cognac sauce. Help it all along with
one of the many Austrian and German wines
in stock.

🛏 Hotel Schloss Ort
Boutique Hotel €€

(☎0851-340 72; www.hotel-schloss-ort.de;
Im Ort 11; s €68-121, d €97-184; P🛜) This
800-year-old medieval palace by the Inn River
conceals a tranquil boutique hotel, stylishly
done out with polished timber floors, crisp white
cotton sheets and wrought-iron bedsteads.
Many of the 18 rooms enjoy river views and
breakfast is served in the vaulted restaurant.
Parking is an extra €4.

Linz ●

✗ k.u.k. Hofbäckerei
Cafe €

(Pfarrgasse 17; coffee & cake €3-6; ⊙6.30am-
6.30pm Mon-Fri, 7am-12.30pm Sat) The Empire
lives on at this gloriously stuck-in-time cafe.
Here Fritz Rath bakes the best *Linzer Torte* in
town – rich, spicy and with lattice pastry that
crumbles just so.

🛏 Hotel am Domplatz
Design Hotel €€

(☎0732-77 30 00; www.hotelamdomplatz.at;
Stifterstrasse 3; d €125-145, ste €300; ❄@🛜)
Sidling up to the neo-Gothic Neuer Dom, this

glass-and-concrete cube reveals streamlined
interiors in pristine whites and blond wood that
reveal a Nordic-style aesthetic. Wind down with
a view at the rooftop spa.

Krems an der Donau ●

🛏 Arte Hotel Krems
Design Hotel €€

(☎02732-711 23; www.arte-hotel.at; Dr-Karl-
Dorrek-Strasse 23; s/d €109/159; P🛜)
This cutting-edge art hotel has 91 large,
well-designed rooms scattered with big retro
prints and patterns complementing the funky
'60s-style furniture.

Vienna ●

✗ Bierhof
Austrian €

(☎01-533 44 28; http://bierhof.at; 01, Haarhof
3; mains €10-19; ⊙11.30am-11.30pm; 🛜;
Ⓜ Herrengasse) A narrow passageway opens
to a courtyard where umbrella-shaded tables
beneath the trees make a charming spot to dine
on homemade classics like *Eiernockerl* (flour-
and-egg dumplings), *Tiroler Groest'l* (pork,
potatoes and bacon, topped with a fried egg),
Tiroler Leber (liver dumplings with apple sauce
and green beans) and *Weiner Schnitzel* with
parsley potatoes. The bar stays open until late.

🛏 Hotel Capricorno
Hotel €€

(☎01-533 31 04-0; www.schick-hotels.com/
hotel-capricorno; 01, Schwedenplatz 3-4; s/d
from €120/150; P🛜; Ⓜ Schwedenplatz)
Behind an unpromising mid-20th-century
facade, Hotel Capricorno was stunningly made
over in 2015 in lustrous velveteens in zesty lime,
orange, lemon and aubergine shades. Most
of its 42 rooms have balconies (front rooms
overlook the Danube Canal but rear rooms are
quieter). Rare-for-Vienna parking is available for
just €23 per day. It's a 10-minute walk from the
Stephansdom.

Grossglockner High Alpine Road
*A spectacular view of the Alps from this
legendary Austrian road*

Grossglockner Road

24

Austria's most exhilarating trip takes you on a wild roller-coaster drive over three legendary Alpine passes and packs in outdoor activities from year-round skiing to windsurfing and white-water rafting.

TRIP HIGHLIGHTS

335 km

Gerlos Alpine Road
Sing along the yodel hiking trail

START
● Salzburg

FINISH
● Bregenz

● Innsbruck

 ⑦

④

● Lienz

⑩

Silvretta High Alpine Road
Mountains reflect in the aquamarine reservoir

526 km

Grossglockner High Alpine Road
Traverse Austria's highest mountain

225 km

5–7 DAYS
644 KM / 401 MILES

GREAT FOR...

BEST TIME TO GO

The peak time to tackle this trip is midsummer.

📷 ESSENTIAL PHOTO

Europe's highest waterfalls, the three-tiered Krimmler Wasserfälle.

✓ BEST FOR DRIVERS

The Grossglockner's 36 heart-in-your-mouth hairpin bends.

Classic Trip

24 Grossglockner Road

Fair warning: if you're a faint-hearted driver (or passenger), this probably isn't the trip for you. (Take the gentler Tyrol & Vorarlberg route instead; see p295.) But if you're up for a serious adventure, this Austrian classic provides an opportunity to experience epic scenery, invigorating Alpine sports, and dizzying mountain passes with so many switchbacks they're used by high-performance car manufacturers and championship race drivers as test tracks.

① Salzburg

Salzburg's **trophy sights** (p302) huddle in the pedestrianised, Unesco World Heritage–listed **Altstadt** (old town). The tangled lanes are made for a serendipitous wander, leading to hidden courtyards and medieval squares framed by burgher houses and baroque fountains. You'll also see plenty of **icons** (p314) from the evergreen musical *The Sound of Music*.

Beyond **city strolling** (p330), there are plenty of opportunities to get active, from swimming at **Freibad Leopoldskron** (Leopoldskronstrasse 50; adult/concession €4.60/2.60; ☻9am-7pm May–mid-Sep), Salzburg's biggest lido, with diving boards, water slides and volleyball, to hiking up Salzburg's rival mountains, the 540m **Mönchsberg** and 640m **Kapuzinerberg**. Both mountains are thickly wooded and criss-crossed by walking trails, with photogenic views of the Altstadt's right bank and left bank, respectively.

The Drive » It's 47km south from Salzburg on the B159 to Werfen, mostly along the

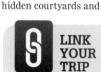

LINK YOUR TRIP

25 Tyrol & Vorarlberg

To make a mega-circuit of the Austrian Alps, pick up the Tyrol & Vorarlberg route in Bregenz.

28 Carinthian Lakes

Wind around the Carinthian Lakes from Lienz.

Classic Trip

Salzach River. After passing through a wide valley, you'll enter a tight, steep gorge; follow it until Werfen.

② Werfen

More than 1000m above Werfen in the Tennengebirge mountains is **Eisriesenwelt** (www.eisriesenwelt.at; adult/child €11/6, incl cable car €22/12; ☺8am-3.45pm May-Oct, to 4.45pm Jul & Aug). Billed as the world's largest accessible ice caves, this glittering ice spectacle spans 30,000 sq metres and 42km of narrow passages burrowing deep into the heart of the mountains. A highlight is the cavernous **Eispalast** (ice palace), where the frost crystals twinkle when a magnesium flare is held up to them. Wrap up warmly for subzero temperatures. Photography is not permitted inside the caves.

On a wooded clifftop beneath the majestic peaks of the Tennengebirge range, formidable fortress **Burg Hohenwerfen** (adult/child/family €11/6/26.50, incl lift €14.50/8/34.50; ☺9am-5pm Apr-Oct; 🚻) dates from 1077. Time your visit to be at the castle by 3.15pm for the falconry show.

🛏 p293

The Drive » Take the A10 south to the Millstätter See (which you can visit on a trip

through the Carinthian Lakes) and turn west onto the B100/E66 through the Drau Valley to Lienz (166km in total).

③ Lienz

Ringed by Dolomite peaks blushing reddish-pink at sunset, Lienz straddles the Isel and Drau Rivers, and lies just 40km north of Italy. An ancient **Roman settlement** (p328), today it's a famed ski town (for its Zettersfeld and Hochstein peaks, and especially its 100km of cross-country trails), but it has an energetic vibe year-round.

If you want to get up into the mountains, **Bergstatt** (📞0516-5835; www.bergstatt.at; Kranewitweg 5; rock climbing trips per adult/child from €75/55) has guides who can lead you on half-day, full-day and multiday rock-climbing, *via ferrata* or summit trips.

The Drive » Take the B107 north, passing picturesque villages including Winkler (with a wonderful Alpine hotel; p293) and Heiligenblut (look for the needle-thin spire of its pilgrimage church) to the Grossglockner High Alpine Road toll gates (43km in total).

TRIP HIGHLIGHT

④ Grossglockner High Alpine Road

A stupendous feat of 1930s engineering, the 48km **Grossglockner Road** (www.grossglockner.at; Hwy 107; car/motorcycle €34.50/24.50; ☺May-early Nov) swings giddily around 36 switchbacks, passing jewel-coloured lakes, forested slopes and above-the-clouds glaciers as it traverses the heart of the Hohe Tauern National Park, peaking at the bell-shaped **Grossglockner** (3798m), Austria's highest mountain.

En route, flag-dotted **Kaiser-Franz-Josefs-Höhe** (2369m) has memorable views of Grossglockner and the rapidly retreating Pasterze Glacier (best appreciated on the short and easy Gamsgrubenweg and Gletscherweg trails). Allow time to see the glacier-themed exhibition at the visitor centre and the crystalline Wilhelm-Swarovski observatory.

Get your camera handy for **Fuscher Törl** (2428m), with super views on both sides of the ridge, and **Fuscher Lacke** (2262m), a gemstone of a lake nearby. A small exhibition documents the construction of the road, built by 3000 men over five years during the Great Depression.

A 2km side road corkscrews up to **Edelweiss Spitze** (2571m), the road's highest viewpoint. Climb the tower for 360-degree views of more than 30 peaks topping 3000m.

Between toll gates, all attractions are free. Check the forecast before you hit the road, as the drive is not much fun in heavy fog, snow or a storm. It's often bumper-to-bumper by noon, especially in July and August; beat the crowds by setting out early.

The Drive » Descend the Grossglockner on the B107 to Bruck and take the B311 northeast to Zell am See.

❺ Zell am See

Resort town Zell am See's brightly painted chalets line the shore of the deep-blue Zeller See, framed by the Hohe Tauern's snowcapped peaks.

Mountain breezes create ideal conditions for windsurfing on the lake; **Windsurfcenter Zell Am See** (☎0664-644 36 95; http://windsurfcenter.members. cablelink.at; Seespitzstrasse 13; windsurfing/SUP/wetsuit rental per hr €10/8/3; ☺dawn-dusk May-Sep) rents equipment and runs courses.

The Drive » From the lake, it's 54km to the Krimmler Wasserfälle. Head west on the B168 and B165 to Krimml; when you arrive in the town the waterfalls come into view.

❻ Krimmler Wasserfälle

Europe's highest falls, at 380m, are the thunder-ous, three-tier **Krimmler Wasserfälle** (Krimml Falls; www.wasserfaelle-krimml.at; adult/child €3/1; ☺ticket office 8am-6pm mid-Apr–Oct). The **Wasserfallweg** (Waterfall Trail), which starts at the ticket office and weaves up-hill through mixed forest, has up-close viewpoints. It's 4km one way (about a 2½-hour round-trip walk).

The Drive » From the falls, it's 7.7km (and eight hairpin bends) to the Gerlos Alpine Road toll gates.

TOP TIP:
ALPINE ROAD TOLLS

Be aware that this trip's three top-draw drives – Grossglockner High Alpine Road, Gerlos Alpine Road and Silvretta High Alpine Road (p292) – incur tolls. There's also a smaller toll on the detour to the Stubaital (see boxed text, p292). Toll booths accept cash and credit cards.

TRIP HIGHLIGHT

❼ Gerlos Alpine Road

Open year-round, the **Gerlos Alpine Road** (www. gerlosstrasse.at; toll per car/ motorcycle €8.50/5.50) winds 12km through high moor and spruce forest, reach-ing an elevation of 1630m. The lookout above the turquoise Stausee (reser-voir) is a great picnic stop, with a tremendous vista of the Alps.

If you have the urge to burst out into song as you skip through wildflower-strewn meadows, take the 4.8km-long **Jodel Wanderweg** (Yodel Hiking Trail; ☎06565-82 43; www. jodelweg.at) in Königsleiten. You can go it alone and practise your high notes at eight stops with giant cowbells, alpine horns and listen-repeat audio clippings. Alternatively, join a free guided sing 'n' stroll hike with trail founder Christian Eder. The three-hour ambles begin at 10.30am every Wednesday from late June to mid-September at the **Dorfbahn** (adult/child €9/4.50) cable-car station;

reserve by 5pm the previ-ous day by phone.

The Drive » Continue west on the B165, passing the reservoir Durlassboden, before descending to Zell am Ziller along six hairpin bends (63km in total).

❽ Zell am Ziller

At the foot of knife-edge Reichenspitze (3303m), Zell am Ziller is a former gold-mining centre and popular ski base.

Year-round, you can take a wild toboggan ride on the 1.45km-long **Arena Coaster** (www.zillertalarena. com; Zillertal Arena; adult/ child coaster only €4.80/2.90, incl cable car €20.90/10.40; ☺9.30am-6pm late Jun-early Sep, shorter hours rest of year; ♿), which incorporates both a 360-degree loop and a 540-degree loop. It's accessible by cable car, or a steep 1.5km walk.

Aktivzentrum Zillertal (☎0664-505 95 94; www. aktivzentrum-zillertal.at; Freizeitpark Zell; ♿) offers paragliding (€55 to €130), white-water rafting on the Ziller (€35), canyoning (€35 to €65), *via ferrata*

Classic Trip

WHY THIS IS A CLASSIC TRIP
CATHERINE LE NEVEZ, AUTHOR

Awe-inspiring mountainscapes and adrenaline-pumping activities abound on this alpine itinerary, but the ultimate draw is the drive itself, peaking with its trio of dizzying high-altitude switchback passes – the Grossglockner High Alpine Road, Gerlos Alpine Road and Silvretta High Alpine Road. This is a route that reminds you that the highlight of road-tripping isn't the destination but the journey.

Top: Racing along Grossglockner High Alpine Road
Left: Bergisel ski jump in Innsbruck
Right: Krimmler Wasserfälle (Krimml Falls)

climbing (€45 to €85) and llama trekking (€20).

🛏 p293

The Drive ≫ Zell am Ziller sits 60km from Innsbruck. Take the B169 north then the A12 west.

- - - - - - - - - - - - - -

❾ Innsbruck

Hit Innsbruck's **cultural attractions** (p301), then head up to its ski jump, the **Bergisel** (www.bergisel.info; adult/child €9.50/4.50; ⊘9am-6pm), for a spectacular city and mountain panorama. Rising above Innsbruck like a celestial staircase, the glass-and-steel structure was designed by Iraqi architect Zaha Hadid.

Hadid also designed the space-age funicular **Nordkettenbahnen** (www.nordkette.com; one-way/return to Hungerburg €4.60/7.60, Seegrube €16.50/27.50, Hafelekar €18.30/30.50; ⊘Hungerburg 7am-7.15pm Mon-Fri, 8am-7.15pm Sat & Sun, Seegrube 8.30am-5.30pm daily, Hafelekar 9am-5pm daily), which whizzes from the Congress Centre to the slopes every 15 minutes. Walking trails head off in all directions from Hungerburg and Seegrube.

✕ 🛏 p293

The Drive ≫ Leave Innsbruck on the westbound A12 and veer southwest on the B188, passing a string of ski towns, to the Silvretta High Alpine Road toll gates (118km all up).

Classic Trip

TRIP HIGHLIGHT

❿ Silvretta High Alpine Road

Silhouetted by the Silvretta range and crowned by the 3312m arrow of Piz Buin, the Montafon Valley remains one of the most serene and unspoilt in the Austrian Alps.

The 23km-long **Silvretta High Alpine Road** (www.silvretta-bielerhoehe. at; car/motorcycle €15/12; ☺early Jun-late Oct) twists and turns beneath peaks rising to well over 2500m before climbing over the 2036m Bielerhöhe Pass via 34 tight switchbacks. At the top of the pass, the **Silvretta Stausee** (2030m), an aquamarine reservoir, mirrors the surrounding peaks on bright mornings.

The Drive » It's 100km to Rappenlochschlucht. Continue on the B188 and join the A14 at aromatic Bludenz. Continue northwest to Dornbirn, from where Rappenlochschlucht is 4km southeast on Gütlestrasse.

⓫ Rappenlochschlucht

The **Rappenlochschlucht** (Rappenloch Gorge; www. rappenlochschlucht.at) was gouged out by the thundering Dornbirner Ache. From the car park, there's a 375m trail to the **Staufensee**, a turquoise lake ringed by forest.

At the bottom of the Rappenlochschlucht, a 19th-century cotton mill is the unlikely home of the world's largest collection of Rolls-Royces at the **Rolls-Royce Museum** (www. rolls-royce-museum.at; Gütle 11a; adult/child €9/4.50; ☺10am-6pm daily Jul & Aug, 10am-6pm Tue-Sun Feb-Jun & Sep-Nov).

The Drive » Return to Dornbirn and head north on the B190 for 16km to Bregenz.

⓬ Bregenz

Bregenz (see also p296) sits on the shores of Lake Constance (in German, Bodensee), Europe's third-largest lake. The views here are extraordinary: before you the mirror-like lake; behind you, 1064m-high mountain the Pfänder, to the right, Germany, to the left, Switzerland.

A **cable car** (www. pfaenderbahn.at; Steinbruchgasse 4; one-way adult/child €7.10/5.70, return €12.20/9.80; ☺8am-7pm Dec-Oct) glides up the Pfänder. At the top, a 30-minute circular trail brings you close to deer, wild boar, ibex and whistling marmots at the year-round **Alpine Game Park Pfänder** (www.pfaender. at; Pfänder; ☺sunrise-sunset).

Some 5km south of central Bregenz is the nature reserve **Rheindelta** (www. rheindelta.org). Its mossy marshes, reeds and woodlands attract more than 300 bird species, including curlews, grey herons and rare black-tailed godwits.

✕ ⌂ p293

➡ DETOUR: STUBAITAL

Start: ➒ Innsbruck

Slip out of sandals and into skis at year-round skiing magnet, Stubai Glacier. A one-day summer **ski pass** (www.stubaier-gletscher.com) costs €43/21.50 per adult/ child and covers 26 lifts accessing 62km of slopes. Ski or snowboard and boot rental costs around €30/15 per adult/child. Summer skiing is between 2900m and 3300m and is dependent on weather conditions.

Lower down in the Stubai Valley, the **Wildewasserweg** waterfall trail wends for 9.2km (one way) to Sulzenau Glacier. En route, it passes the spectacular Grawa falls; there's a cafe with a panoramic viewing deck at its base.

The Stubai Glacier is just 38km south of Innsbruck. Take the A13 south to the toll gates (per car including passengers €3); keep right to take the B183 southwest along the valley.

Eating & Sleeping

Werfen ❷

🛏 Weisses Rössl   Pension €

(📞06468-5268; Markt 39; s/d €30/52) In the village centre, this good-value pension has great views of the fortress and the Tennengebirge from its rooftop terrace. Rooms are a blast from the 1970s, but all are large and cosy with sofas and cable TV.

Winklern

🛏 Hotel Tauernstern   Chalet €€

(📞04822-7205; www.tauernstern.at; Winklern 24, Winklern; s/d from €49/98; 🅿🛜) Sweeping valley views extend from the timber balconies of this mountain-set gem. Four-poster pine-and-stone beds, in-room fridges, a sauna and spa built from local wood and slate, and an exceptional gourmet restaurant using ingredients from local farms all make Tauernstern a fabulous pit stop before tackling the Grossglockner High Alpine Road.

Zell am Ziller ❽

🛏 Hotel Englhof   Boutique Hotel €€

(📞05282-3134; www.englhof.at; Zellbergeben 28; s/d/tr/ste from €55/103/153/110; 🛜) Beautiful blond-wood-panelled, white-linen-dressed rooms (many with balconies) and amenities like free DVD rental make Englhof a superb place to stay. But what really seals the deal is its in-house gourmet restaurant and world-class cocktail bar with Austria's second-largest collection of spirits (over 1400 varieties), mixing incredible cocktails like a Bloody Mary with frozen cherry tomatoes and barbecued black-pepper seasoning.

Innsbruck ❾

✖ Die Wilderin   Austrian €€

(📞0512-56 27 28; www.diewilderin.at; Seilergasse 5; mains €11-18; ⏱5pm-2am Tue-Sat, 4pm-midnight Sun) Take a gastronomic walk on the wild side at this modern-day hunter-gatherer of a restaurant, where chefs take pride in local sourcing and using top-notch farm-fresh and foraged ingredients. The menu sings of the seasons, be it asparagus, game, strawberries or winter veg. The vibe is urbane and relaxed.

🛏 Weisses Rössl   Guesthouse €€

(📞0512-58 30 57; www.roessl.at; Kiebachgasse 8; s €70-110, d €100-160; @🛜) An antique rocking horse greets you at this 16th-century guesthouse. The vaulted entrance leads up to spacious rooms recently revamped with blond wood, fresh hues and crisp white linen. The owner is a keen hunter and the restaurant (mains €10 to €18) has a meaty menu.

Bregenz ⓬

✖ Gebhardsberg   Austrian €€

(📞05574-908 61 60; www.greber.cc; Gebhardsbergstrasse 1; mains €14-26.50; ⏱11.30am-10pm daily May-Sep, 11.30am-10pm Tue-Sun Oct-Apr) Sweeping lake views taking in Switzerland and Germany extend from the dining room and terrace of this hilltop castle 1km south of the centre. Local specialities include *Käsespätzle* (hand-rolled noodles with cheese) with traditional apple sauce and fried onions, Lake Constance trout with almond butter and parsley potatoes, and white cheese strudel for dessert.

🛏 Schwärzler   Hotel €€

(📞05574-4990; http://schwaerzler.s-hotels. com; Landstrasse 9; s/d from €122/153; 🅿🛜♿) This turreted, ivy-clad place is a far cry from your average business hotel. Contemporary rooms are done out in earthy hues and blond wood, with comforts including bathrobes, flat-screen TVs and minibars. Regional produce from organic farms features on the breakfast buffet, and there's a 400-sq-metre pool and a sauna area. Parking costs €7.

Tyrol Backcountry skiers ascending to Brechhorn in the Kitzbühel Alps

Tyrol & Vorarlberg

25

Opportunities for outdoor pursuits abound here in the Alps, but there are also plenty of gentler pleasures, from rambles through wildflower-filled meadows to foodie tastings and artistic treasures.

TRIP HIGHLIGHTS

37 km

Feldkirch
Home to a medieval old town and fairy-tale castle

383 km

Salzburg
Resplendent Salzburg is the storybook vision of Austria

FINISH
11

START
● Bregenz
Schoppernau
7 8
2
● Landeck
St Anton am Arlberg

179 km

Stift Stams
Monumental abbey topped by twin silver cupolas

203 km

Innsbruck
Mountain-ringed city filled with art and architectural treasures

5–7 DAYS
383 KM / 238 MILES

GREAT FOR...

BEST TIME TO GO
Year-round is possible; you'll need snow tyres and chains in winter.

 ESSENTIAL PHOTO
Innsbruck's Gothic Hofkirche.

 BEST FOR FOODIES
The Bregenzerwald Käsestrasse (Bregenz Forest Cheese Road).

25 Tyrol & Vorarlberg

As you drive east from opera-festival-famed Bregenz on the shores of Lake Constance, you'll discover a different side of the Alps to the dizzying drives on and around the Grossglockner Road. On this food- and culture-filled trip through mountain valleys you'll visit Alpine dairies, schnapps distilleries and a medieval-castle-housed brewery, as well as dazzling, art-adorned palaces and churches.

❶ Bregenz

In a postcard-perfect setting on the shores of Lake Constance, framed by towering Alps, Bregenz offers plenty of swimming, boating and walking opportunities (see p292).

The white cuboid **Vorarlberg Museum** (www.vorarlbergmuseum.at; Kornmarktplatz 1; adult/child €9/free; ⏰10am-8pm Fri-Wed, to 9pm Thu Jul & Aug, 10am-6pm Fri-Wed, to 9pm Thu Sep-Jun) is emblazoned with what appears to be 16,656 flowers (actually PET bottle bases imprinted in concrete).

Permanent exhibitions home in on Vorarlberg state's history, art and architecture, with archaeological finds from Roman Brigantium, and paintings by Angelika Kauffmann.

Bregenz is most famous for the **Bregenzer Festspiele** (Bregenz Festival; ☎05574-4076; www.bregenzerfestspiele.com; ☉late Jul-late Aug), when opera is performed on a floating stage on the lake.

Palm-shaded **Beach Bar Bregenz** (www.beachbar-bregenz.com; Seepromenade 2; ☉4pm-midnight Mon-Fri, from 2pm Sat, from 11am Sun late Apr-early Sep) is perfect for enjoying cool

cocktails and chilled DJ beats in a *Strandkörbe* (wicker basket chair). Open-air cinema nights regularly take place.

🍴 p303

The Drive » It's a quick 33km zip from Bregenz via the southbound A14 to Feldkirch.

TRIP HIGHLIGHT

② Feldkirch

On the banks of the turquoise Ill River, Feldkirch sits at the foot of wooded mountains, vineyards and a castle-crowned hill. Its cobbled, arcaded lanes and pastel-coloured townhouses wing you

LINK YOUR TRIP

24 Grossglockner Road

Salzburg is the starting point for an action-packed trip through the Alps.

27 Salzkammergut

Set off from Salzburg to the Salzkammergut's sparkling mountain-ringed lakes.

back to late-medieval times. Towers surviving from the old fortifications include the 40m-high **Katzenturm** (Hirschgraben), where a bell weighing 7500kg still tolls.

Red-turreted **Schloss Schattenburg** (www. schattenburg.at; Burggasse 1; adult/child €6/4.50; ⊙9am-noon & 1.30-5pm Mon-Fri, 10am-5pm Sat & Sun Apr-Oct, shorter hours rest of year) is straight out of a fairy tale. Once the seat of the counts of Montfort, the castle now houses a small museum displaying religious art, costumes and weaponry.

Distinguished by its slender spire, Feldkirch's cathedral, **Domkirche St Nikolaus** (Domplatz; ⊙8am-6pm), has a large, forbidding interior complemented by late-Gothic features and dazzling stained glass.

✗ p303

The Drive » You'll know you're in the Alps on this 50km drive. From Feldkirch, take the B190 southeast, then the precipitous B193 northwest up to Schoppernau. Wind down your car windows to hear the melodic clinging of cow bells.

- - - - - - - - - - - -

❸ Schoppernau

Discover cheese-making secrets (including why Emmentaler is holey) at show dairy **Bergkäserei Schoppernau** (www. bergkaeserei.at; Unterdorf 248; ⊙8.30-11.30am & 3-6pm Mon-Fri, 8.30-11.30am & 3-5pm Sat). It's famed for its award-winning tangy *Bergkäse,* matured for up to 12 months. (And if it's not open, don't worry, a vending machine dispenses *Bergkäse* along with handmade butter, *Spätzle* noodles and fried onion round the clock.)

If the dairy whets your appetite for more melt-in-your-mouth cheese produced from the mountains' pristine pastures, set off from Schoppernau on a detour of the Bregenzerwald Käsestrasse (Bregenz For-est Cheese Road; see the boxed text, p300).

The Drive » From Schoppernau, it's an ultra-scenic 47km through deep valleys, steep ascents and switchback descents along the B200 and B198 to St Anton am Arlberg.

- - - - - - - - - - - -

❹ St Anton am Arlberg

In 1901 St Anton am Arlberg founded the first ski club in the Alps and downhill skiing was born. Strung out along the northern bank of the Rosanna River at the foot of 2811m-high Valluga, in winter St Anton is a cross

---

TIROLER SCHNAPSROUTE

For another flavour-packed detour, set out on the **Tiroler Schnapsroute** (www.schnapsroute.at). Like the Bregenzerwald Käsestrasse, this isn't a single road but instead refers to a region.

On a sunny plateau dotted with apple and plum orchards, the village of **Stanz** has just 204 residents but over 50 schnapps distilleries where you can taste and buy the local firewater.

From Landeck, it's a 2.5km drive northwest to Stanz. If you're still thirsty, other Schnapsroute villages include Grins, Elbigenalp, Prutz, Pfunds, Imsterberg and Arzl.

Innsbruck Inside the Gothic Hofkirche (Court Church)

between a ski bum's utopia and Ibiza in fast-forward mode – the terrain fierce, the nightlife hedonistic.

Walking in the mountains through meadows full of wildflowers and grazing cattle is the most popular summertime activity. A handful of cable cars and lifts (€5 to €23 one way, €6 to €25 return) rise to the major peaks. If you're planning to hike, pick up a detailed booklet and map from the **tourist office** (☎05446-226 90; www.stantonamarlberg.com; Dorfstrasse 8; ☻8am-6pm Mon-Fri, 9am-6pm Sat, 9am-noon & 2-5pm Sun). Also consider purchasing a **Wanderpass**

(3-/7-day pass €34/39), providing unlimited access to all lifts, or a **St Anton Card** (3-/7-day pass €55/77), which offers the same benefits plus entrance to the town's indoor and outdoor swimming pools.

The Drive ≫ A 25km deep valley drive via the B197 and B316 brings you to Landeck.

- - - - - - - - - - - - -

⑤ Landeck

Landeck is an ordinary town with an extraordinary backdrop: framed by an amphitheatre of forested peaks, it's bordered by the fast-flowing Inn and Sanna Rivers, and presided over by a hilltop

medieval castle that's visible from afar, 13th-century **Schloss Landeck** (www.schlosslandeck.at; Schlossweg 2; adult/child €7.50/4; ☻10am-5pm mid-Apr–late Oct, 1-5pm mid-Dec–early Jan; ⊞). Its museum showcases everything from Celtic figurines to hand-carved *Krampus* masks; there's also an art gallery here. Sweeping views over Landeck and the Lechtaler Alps extend from the tower.

In summer, the **Venet** (www.venet.at; adult/child one-way €14/8, return €16/9.50) cable car zooms up to Krahberg (2208m),

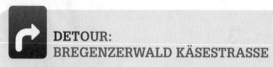

DETOUR:
BREGENZERWALD KÄSESTRASSE

Start: ❸ Schoppernau

Explore the Bregenzerwald's dairy country and local *Sennereien* (dairy farms) on the **Bregenzerwald Käsestrasse** (Bregenz Forest Cheese Road; www.kaesestrasse.at), which refers to the cheese-producing region rather than a specific route.

From Schoppernau, it's a 49km-long round trip. Country lanes lead to the pretty village of Egg en route to Lingenau. Peek inside the huge cellars of the ultramodern **Käsekeller Lingenau** (www.kaesekeller.at; Zeihenbühel 423, Lingenau; ⊙10am-6pm Mon-Fri, 9am-5pm Sat Apr-Sep, 10am-5pm Tue-Fri, 10am-4pm Sat Nov-Mar) to see robots brushing wagon-wheel-sized cheeses with salt water, watch a free 12-minute film (in English) and savour a tasting (three cheeses €5, with local wine €8).

Book ahead to take a factory tour of **Käse-Molke Metzler** (☎05512-3044; www. naturhautnah.at; Bruggan 1025, Egg; ⊙8am-noon & 1.30-6pm Mon-Fri, 8am-noon Sat). Tours costing €13.50/6.75 per adult/child include a lavish buffet of cheeses like creamy *Wälderkäsle*, made from cow's and goat's milk. If you'd like to try milking the goats and cows as well, the price is €25/12.50.

Old farmhouses tiled with wood shingles and studded with scarlet geraniums crowd the narrow streets of Schwarzenberg. Contemplate neoclassical art in the **Angelika Kauffmann Museum** (www.angelika-kauffmann.com; Brand 34, Schwarzenberg; adult/child €7/5; ⊙10am-5pm Tue-Sun May-late Oct). Admission covers entry to the neighbouring **Heimat Museum** (Heritage Museum), a pristine Alpine chalet. Displays focus on rural 19th-century life with traditional painted furniture, extraordinary headwear, hunting paraphernalia and filigree iron crosses. Dine on cheesy *Kässpätzle* (hand-rolled noodles with cheese, topped with crispy fried onion) in the wood-panelled parlour or garden at **Gasthof Hirschen** (☎05512-2944; www. hirschenschwarzenberg.at; Hof 14, Schwarzenberg; s/d/tr from €40/74/90; 🅿🛜) – mains €14 to €31.50 – or consider staying the night.

From Schwarzenberg, head southeast via peaceful Au back to Schoppernau.

---

where there's a web of marked walking trails.

A roller coaster of water thrashes the limestone cliffs at **Zammer Lochputz** (www.zammer-lochputz.at; adult/child €4/3; ⊙9.30am-5.30pm May-Sep, 10am-5pm Sat-Mon Oct), a gorge 4km northeast of Landeck, across the River Inn from Zams. Leading up through pine forest, a 2.9km round-trip trail passes viewpoints and interesting rock formations – look out for the head of a bull and a nymph.

The Drive ⟫ Travel via the B171 for 20km to Imst. Starkenberger Biermythos is 2.3km north of Imst just off the B189.

- - - - - - - - - - -

❻ Starkenberger Biermythos

At 200-year-old brewery **Starkenberger Biermythos** (☎05412-662 01; www. starkenberger.at; Griesegg 1, Tarrenz; tour €7; ⊙10am-5pm daily May-Oct, 10am-noon & 1-4pm Mon-Fri Nov-Apr), housed in a medieval castle, tours take you

through the brewing process and include a beer tasting. If you can't get enough of the stuff, you can even bathe in it by prior reservation – it does wonders for the complexion, apparently. A two-person beer bath costs €250 per couple.

The Drive ⟫ Take the northeast-bound B189 for 22km to the village of Krebsbach, then head south, crossing the Inn River, to reach Stams (29km all up).

7 Stift Stams

Monumental ochre-and-white abbey **Stift Stams** (www.stiftstams.at; Stiftshof 3; tours adult/child €4.70/2.50; ☺guided tours hourly 9-11am & 1-4pm Jun-Sep, 2pm Wed Oct-May) was founded in 1273 by Elisabeth of Bavaria, the mother of Konradin, the last of the Hohenstaufens. It's set in pristine grounds, with a facade topped by twin silver cupolas, a final flourish added when the abbey was revamped in baroque style in the 17th century. The exuberant church interior is dominated by the high altar: the intertwining branches of this version of the 'tree of life' support 84 saintly figures surrounding an image of the Virgin. Near the entrance is the Rose Grille, an exquisite iron screen made in 1716. Crane your neck to admire the ceiling's elaborate stuccowork, gilding and frescos.

Marmalade, juice, honey, liqueurs and schnapps made on the premises can be bought from the **Kloster shop** (☺9am-noon & 1-5pm Mon-Sat, 1-5pm Sun Jun-Sep, 9am-noon & 2-5pm Mon-Sat Oct-May), plus bread that's freshly baked here on Monday, Wednesday and Friday.

The Drive » Travel along the eastbound B171 for 37km to Innsbruck. Approaching the city you'll pass its airport – the views of planes descending into the valley are amazing.

8 Innsbruck

The mountains surrounding Innsbruck beg to be explored (see p291) but the city itself is also filled with treasures.

Innsbruck's pride and joy is the Gothic **Hofkirche** (www.tiroler-landesmuseum.at; Universitätstrasse 2; adult/child €5/free; ☺9am-5pm Mon-Sat, 12.30-5pm Sun), one of Europe's finest royal court churches. It was commissioned in 1553 by Ferdinand I, who enlisted top artists of the age such as Albrecht Dürer, Alexander Colin and Peter Vischer the Elder. Top billing goes to the empty black-marble sarcophagus of Emperor Maximilian I (1459–1519), a masterpiece of German Renaissance sculpture.

Built for Emperor Maximilian I, golden oriel ('awning') **Goldenes Dachl & Museum** (Golden Roof; Herzog-Friedrich-Strasse 15; adult/child €4/2; ☺10am-5pm, closed Mon Oct-Apr) glitters with 2657 fire-gilt copper tiles. Inside, look for the grotesque tournament helmets designed to resemble the Turks of the rival Ottoman Empire.

The cupola-crowned **Hofburg** (Imperial Palace; www.hofburg-innsbruck.at; Rennweg 1; adult/child €8/free; ☺9am-5pm) was built as a castle for Archduke Sigmund the Rich in the 15th century, expanded by Emperor Maximilian I in the 16th century and given a baroque makeover by Empress Maria Theresia in the 18th century.

Amid beautiful gardens, Renaissance **Schloss Ambras** (www.schlossambras-innsbruck.at; Schlosstrasse 20; adult/child/family €10/free/18; ☺10am-5pm; 🚗) was acquired in 1564 by Archduke Ferdinand II, then ruler of Tyrol, who transformed it from a fortress into a palace. Don't miss the **Spanische Saal** (Spanish Hall), the dazzling armour collection and the gallery's Velázquez and van Dyck originals.

✕ 🛏 p303

The Drive » From Innsbruck it's just a 10km trip east to Hall in Tirol along the B171 on the Inn River's northern bank.

9 Hall in Tirol

Tucked beneath the Alps, medieval Hall prospered from salt in the 13th century. You can visit a reconstructed salt mine, complete with galleries, tools and shafts, on a 45-minute guided tour at the **Bergbau Museum** (www.hall-wattens.at; Fürstengasse; adult/child €5/3; ☺tours 11.30am Mon, Thu & Sat).

Hall's winding lanes, lined with pastel-coloured townhouses that are lantern-lit after dark, are made for ambling. Bordering the main square is Hall's 15th-century **Rathaus** (Town Hall; Oberer Stadtplatz). Its distinctive courtyard is complete with crenellated edges and mosaic crests.

At **Burg Hasegg** (www.muenz-hall.at; Burg Hasegg 6; tower adult/child €5.50/4.50, mint €8/5.50, combined ticket €11.50/8; ⏱10am-5pm Tue-Sun Apr-Oct, 10am-5pm Tue-Sat Nov-Mar; [🚻]), a staircase spirals up 186 steps to the 5th floor for panoramic views. The castle had a 300-year career as a mint for silver *Thalers* (coins; the root of the modern word 'dollar'). Its history is unravelled in the Münze Hall, displaying water-driven and hammer-striking techniques; kids can mint their own coins here.

The Drive » It's a 92km drive from Hall in Tirol to Kitzbühel. East on the B171 along the widening valley, you'll pass Wattens, home to Austria's Swarovski crystal. From the village of Wörgl the incline ramps up. Turn east on the B178, passing beneath the awe-inspiring Kaisergebirge mountains, before heading south at St Johann on the B161 to Kitzbühel.

⑩ Kitzbühel

Kitzbühel began life in the 16th century as a silver and copper mining town, and preserves a charming medieval centre despite its winter persona. Ever since Franz Reisch slipped on skis and whizzed down the slopes of Kitzbüheler Horn in 1893, so

christening Austria's first Alpine ski run, Kitzbühel has carved out its reputation as one of Europe's foremost ski resorts.

In summer, it's a four-hour (14km) hike one way, or a speedy cable-car ride to the **Alpine Flower Garden** (Hornbahn cable-car return adult/child €22/12; ⏱8.30am-5pm May-Sep). Arnica, edelweiss and purple bellflowers are among the 400 Alpine blooms flourishing atop Kitzbüheler Horn. A road also twists up to the mountain (toll per car €6, plus €3 per person).

The **Museum Kitzbühel** (www.museum-kitzbuehel.at; Hinterstadt 32; adult/child €6.50/free; ⏱10am-5pm Fri-Wed, to 8pm Thu Apr-late Sep, reduced hours late Sep-Mar) traces Kitzbühel's heritage from its Bronze Age mining beginnings onwards. The big emphasis is on winter sports, and pays tribute to homegrown legends like ski racing champ Toni Sailer and winter landscape painter Alfons Walde.

🍴 🛏 p303

The Drive » Kitzbühel sits 85 fabulously scenic kilometres from Salzburg. Head northeast on the B161 then B178, passing the white-water rafting village of Lofer, and cross the German border (the road becomes the B21). On your left you'll see an opaque turquoise lake, the Saalachsee, before reaching Bad Reichenhall. The road crosses back into Austria and brings you into Salzburg.

- - - - - - - - - - - -

TRIP HIGHLIGHT

⑪ Salzburg

Salzburg is storybook Austria. Beside the fast-flowing Salzach River are the **Altstadt's** (old town) mosaic of domes and spires, and the formidable 900-year-old clifftop fortress, the **Festung Hohensalzburg** (p330), reached by the glass **Festungsbahn funicular** (Festungsgasse 4; one-way/return adult €6.70/8.30, child €3.70/4.50; ⏱9am-8pm), with the mountains beyond. This dazzling backdrop inspired the lordly prince-archbishops and homegrown genius Mozart.

You can visit the great composer's 1756 birthplace, the **Mozarts Geburtshaus** (p330), as well as his one-time residence, the **Mozart-Wohnhaus** (Mozart's Residence; www.mozarteum.at; Makartplatz 8; adult/child €10/3.50, incl Mozarts Geburtshaus €17/5; ⏱9am-5.30pm); both house museums.

Other unmissable stops include Salzburg's baroque cathedral, the **Dom** (p331), and the **Salzburg Museum** (www.salzburgmuseum.at; Mozartplatz 1; adult/child €7/3; ⏱9am-5pm Tue-Sun, to 8pm Thu; [🚻]), inside the baroque Neue Residenz palace, along with famed *The Sound of Music* sights (p314).

Salzburg is easily explored on a walking tour (p330).

🍴 🛏 p303

Eating & Sleeping

Bregenz ❶

✕ Kornmesser — Austrian €€

([☎]05574-548 54; www.kornmesser.at; Kornmarktstrasse 5; mains €14-30; ⊗9.30am-11pm daily Apr-Sep, 9.30am-11pm Tue-Sun Oct-Mar) Dine on local favourites in the vaulted interior or chestnut-shaded beer garden of this 18th-century baroque *Gasthaus*. These include pork knuckle with bread dumplings and potato salad, roast local trout with parsley potatoes, boiled beef with horseradish, pasta with picked-the-same-day chanterelles, and an 'emperor's pancake' (with stewed plums).

Feldkirch ❷

✕ Gutwinski — Austrian €€

([☎]05522-7217-5; www.gutwinski.cc; Rosengasse 4-6; mains €18-32; ⊗noon-2pm & 6-10pm Tue-Sat) In fine weather, head to Gutwinski's delightful tree-shaded terrace to dine on *Weiner Schnitzel* with parsley potatoes and cranberry compote, and *Tafelspitz* (boiled beef) with apple sauce, mashed potato and creamed spinach. When it's chilly, the candlelit interior, with champagne-coloured banquettes, makes an ideal refuge, as do the contemporary-meets-historic guest rooms upstairs (doubles from €168).

Innsbruck ❽

✕ Markthalle — Market €

(www.markthalle-innsbruck.at; Innrain; ⊗7am-6.30pm Mon-Fri, to 1pm Sat) Fresh-baked bread, Tyrolean cheese, organic fruit, smoked ham and salami – it's all under one roof at this riverside covered market.

⛏ Hotel Weisses Kreuz — Historic Hotel €€

([☎]0512-594 79; www.weisseskreuz.at; Herzog-Friedrich-Strasse 31; s €39-80, d €73-149; [P][@][☎]) Beneath the arcades, this atmospheric Altstadt hotel has played host to guests for 500 years, including a 13-year-old Mozart. With its wood-panelled parlours,

antiques and twisting staircase, the hotel oozes history with every creaking beam. Rooms are supremely comfortable, staff charming and breakfast is a lavish spread.

Kitzbühel ❿

✕ Huberbräu Stüberl — Austrian €€

([☎]05356-656 77; Vorderstadt 18; mains €8.50-18; ⊗8am-midnight Mon-Sat, from 9am Sun) An old-world Tyrolean haunt with vaults and pine benches, this tavern favours substantial portions of Austrian classics, such as schnitzel, goulash and dumplings, cooked to perfection.

⛏ Hotel Edelweiss — Hotel €€

([☎]05356-752 52; www.edelweiss-kitzbuehel.at; Marchfeldgasse 2; d incl half board €210-230; [P][☎]) Near the Hahnenkammbahn, Edelweiss oozes Tyrolean charm with its green surrounds, Alpine views, sauna and cosy interiors. Your kindly hosts Klaus and Veronika let you pack up a lunch from the breakfast buffet, and they serve delicious five-course dinners.

Salzburg ⓫

✕ Magazin — Modern European €€€

([☎]0662-84 15 84; www.magazin.co.at; Augustinergasse 13a; 2-course lunch €16, mains €33-39, tasting menus €68-71, cookery classes €150; ⊗10am-midnight Tue-Sat) Magazin shelters a deli, wine store, cookery school and restaurant. Seasonal flavours – smoked Alpine char with pickled root vegetables, saddle of venison with parsley potato purée and boletus mushrooms – are matched with wines from the 850-bottle cellar.

⛏ Hotel Amadeus — Historic Hotel €€

([☎]0662-87 14 01; www.hotelamadeus.at; Linzer Gasse 43-45; s €78-137, d €128-231, q €192-391; [☎]) Centrally situated on the right bank, this 500-year-old hotel has a boutique feel, with bespoke touches such as chandeliers and four-poster beds in the vibrantly coloured rooms. Guests are treated to free tea or coffee in the afternoon.

Vienna *The former Habsburg monarchy's summer palace, Schloss Schönbrunn*

Castles of Burgenland

26

Studded with fortified castles and lavish palaces, the countryside you'll traverse on this route is also threaded by vineyards that produce some of Austria's finest wines.

TRIP HIGHLIGHTS

46 km

Petronell-Carnuntum
Explore the remains of the Roman town of Carnuntum

START
Vienna

2

95 km

Rust
Home to reed-filled lakeshores and outstanding wines

3

Burg Forchtenstein

Burg Lockenhaus

Burg Güssing

FINISH 9

228 km

Graz
This vibrant city has a spectacular riverside setting

2–4 DAYS
228 KM / 142 MILES

GREAT FOR...

BEST TIME TO GO

May to September offers the most idyllic weather.

ESSENTIAL PHOTO

Buttercup-yellow Schloss Esterházy.

BEST FOR FOODIES

Vienna's Naschmarkt.

26 Castles of Burgenland

Austria's showpiece capital, Vienna, sets the stage for a dramatic voyage through this region's turbulent history. You'll visit the remains of the major political and military centre in the Roman Empire's northeastern territory, and a string of hilltop-perched castles (some reached by funicular or cable car), built as strongholds against marauding invaders, before finishing in the country's second-largest city, spirited Graz.

- - - - - - - - - - - - - -

❶ Vienna

Take in the Austrian capital's majestic sights on a walking tour (p332), or aboard a traditional **Fiaker** (horse-drawn carriage; see p282).

Vienna's splendour peaks at the Habsburgs' opulent summer palace, Unesco World Heritage–listed **Schloss Schönbrunn** (www.schoenbrunn.at; 13, Schönbrunner Schlossstrasse 47; Imperial Tour with audioguide adult/child €11.50/8.50, Grand Tour €14.50/9.50; ⊙8.30am-5.30pm; MHietzing). Of its 1441 rooms, 40 are open to the public. The fountain-filled, French-style formal gardens shelter the world's oldest zoo, the 1752-founded

Tiergarten, as well as a 630m-long hedge maze, and the **Gloriette**, whose roof offers panoramas over the palace grounds and beyond.

Grand *Kaffeehäuser* (coffee houses) aside, the best place to *nasch* (snack) is the historic **Naschmarkt** (06, Linke & Rechte Wienzeile; ⊙6am-7.30pm Mon-Fri, to 6pm Sat; MKarlsplatz, Kettenbrücken-gasse), with food-laden stalls, delis, sit-down cafes and takeaway stands.

✕ ⏤ p311

The Drive 》 The 37km drive from Vienna is unavoidably industrial until you clear the city's outskirts. Take the A4 southeast for 19km. After passing the airport, take the exit to the B9 and follow it eastwards for a further 18km.

TRIP HIGHLIGHT

② Petronell-Carnuntum

The Roman town of Carnuntum was the most important political and military centre in the empire's northeast; with a population of 50,000 people at its peak, it made Vienna look like a village in comparison. The town developed around AD 40 and was abandoned some 400 years later.

The three main Roman attractions are covered by one ticket (adult/child €11/6). Modern-day Petronell-Carnuntum is home to the fascinating open-air museum **Freilichtmuseum Petronell** (www.carnuntum.co.at; Hauptstrasse 1a, Petronell-Carnuntum; ⊙9am-5pm mid-Mar–mid-Nov), with buildings painstakingly reconstructed using ancient techniques, including a cloth merchant's

LINK YOUR TRIP

23 Along the Danube
From Vienna, you can follow the Danube River to Passau, just over the German border, to do this route in reverse.

28 Carinthian Lakes
Graz is the starting point for a drive around the crystal-clear Carinthian Lakes.

house, an upper-class city mansion and Roman public baths. Situated 2.7km east, the grass-covered **Amphitheater Bad Deutsch-Altenburg** (Wienerstrasse 52, Petronell-Carnuntum; ⊙9am-5pm mid-Mar–mid-Nov) seated 15,000. The town of Bad Deutsch-Altenburg, a further 1km northeast, harbours archaeological finds at the **Museum Carnuntinum** (Badgasse 40-46; ⊙10am-5pm mid-Mar–mid-Nov).

The Drive » The 49km drive southwest to Rust becomes increasingly picturesque. Travel through farmland via the B211 and E60 to the vast lake Neusiedler See. Here, you enter wine country, with vineyards covering the hillsides. Wine villages along this stretch of the B50 that offer tastings and cellar-door sales include Purbach am See, Donnerskirchen and Oggau am Neusiedler See.

③ Rust

The reed-filled lake and hidden boatsheds of the charming village of Rust give it a sleepy, swampy feel on a steamy day. From the end of March, dozens of storks make their homes on chimneys in town to rear their young. The clacking of expectant parents can be heard until late August.

The tower of the central **Katholische Kirche** (Haydengasse; ⊙10.30am-noon & 2.30-5pm Mon-Sat, 3-5pm Sun) is a good vantage point for observ-

ing storks. For a close-up view, check out the **web-cam** (or 'nestcam') outside the tourist office, located at the **Rathaus** (town hall) on Conradplatz.

In 1524 the emperor granted local vintners the right to display the letter 'R' on their wine barrels and today the corks still bear this distinctive insignia. Wineries where you can sample the local drop are scattered through the village's streets.

📷 p311

The Drive » Driving northwest along the B52 for 15km through rolling countryside ribboned with vineyards brings you to Eisenstadt's Schloss Esterházy.

④ Schloss Esterházy

Dating from the 14th century, giant, sunny yellow **Schloss Esterházy** (www.esterhazy.at; Esterházyplatz 1; adult/child palace tour €9/7, Haydn Explosive €7/5, wine museum €7/5; ⊙tours hourly 10am-6pm May-Sep, 10am-5pm Apr & Oct, 10am-5pm Fri-Sun Nov-Mar), in Burgenland's small capital, Eisenstadt, received one makeover in baroque and a later one in the neoclassical style. Many of the 256 rooms are occupied by the provincial government, but several can be seen on tours. The highlight is the frescoed **Haydnsaal** (Haydn Hall), where during Joseph Haydn's employment by the Esterházys from 1761 to 1790 the great composer

conducted an orchestra on a near-nightly basis. Haydn's music accompanies you as you walk past exhibitions on his life and work. Austria's largest **wine museum** is also here, along with a *Vinothek* serving local vintages.

The Drive » It's 26km through mostly open countryside to Burg Forchtenstein via the B50.

⑤ Burg Forchtenstein

Straddling a dolomite spur, **Burg Forchtenstein** (www.esterhazy.at; Melinda-Esterházy-Platz 1; guided tour of castle & arsenal adult/child €9/7;

Rust Storks make their homes on chimneys in town

🕙10am-6pm late Mar-Oct) was built in the 14th century and enlarged in 1635 by the Esterházys (who still own it today). Apart from a grand view from its ramparts, the castle's highlights include an impressive collection of armour and weapons, portraits of regal Esterházys in the **Ahnengalerie** (Ancestral Gallery; adult/child €9/7), and spoils from the Turkish wars (it was the only castle in the area not to fall to the Turks). Its **Schatzkammer** (Treasury; adult/child €9/7) contains a rich collection of jewellery and porcelain. Combination tickets (adult/child €13/6.50) for

two of the attractions are also available.

The Drive » From Burg Forchtenstein, head up into heavily forested hills on the L223. Join the southbound L149 to Kirchschlag in der Buckligen Welt, then head southeast on the B55 (54km in total).

6 Burg Lockenhaus

Burg Lockenhaus
(📞02616-239 40; www.ritterburg.at; Günserstrasse 5; adult/child €8/4; 🕙10am-3pm late Mar–mid-Apr, 9am-4pm mid-late Apr, 9am-5pm May-Oct) is infamous for its former resident Elizabeth Báthory, aka the 'Blood Countess'. During her

reign of terror early in the 17th century, she reputedly tortured and murdered over 600 mainly peasant women for her own sadistic pleasure. The castle has long been cleansed of gruesome horrors but still contains an impressive torture chamber, complete with an iron maiden.

🛏 p311

The Drive » Head south on the B56 for 66km, skirting the Hungarian border, before following the road west to Güssing.

7 Burg Güssing

Arresting **Burg Güssing** (📞03322-434 00; www.burgguessing.info;

Batthyanystrasse 10; adult/child €6/4; ⊙10am-5pm Tue-Sun Easter-Oct; **P**) rises dramatically over the Strembach River and peaceful town, reached by a modern 100m **funicular railway** (Schrägaufzug; tickets €1; ⊙10am-5pm Tue-Sun Easter-Oct). A mix of ruins and renovations, the castle contains plenty of weapons from the Turks and Hungarians, striking portraits from the 16th century and a tower with 360-degree views of the surrounding countryside.

The Drive ›› You'll traverse hilly forest and farmland on this scenic stretch. Take the B57 southwest to Heiligenkreuz im Lafnitztal. Continue south on the L116, grazing the Hungarian border (literally across the road), and rejoin the B57. The L207 then L224 travel northwest, passing the delightful swimming and pedal-boating lake Seebad Riegersburg, before heading uphill to Schloss Riegersburg (50km altogether).

- - - - - - - - - - - -

8 Schloss Riegersburg

Perched on a 200m-high rocky outcrop, **Schloss Riegersburg** (http://veste-riegersburg.at; Riegersburg 1; adult/child €12/7; ⊙9am-6pm May-Sep, 10am-6pm Apr & Oct) is a hugely impressive 13th-century castle built due to invading Hungarians and Turks; today it houses a Hexenmuseum on witchcraft, a Burgmuseum featuring the history of the Liechtenstein family,

---

WINES OF BURGENLAND

Burgenland's wine is some of Austria's finest, due to the 300 days of sunshine per year, rich soil and excellent drainage. Although classic white varieties have a higher profile, the pick of the local wines is arguably the red Blaufränkisch, whose 18th-century pedigree here predates its arrival in the Danube region and Germany.

Eiswein (wine made from grapes picked late and shrivelled by frost) and selected late-picking sweet or dessert wines are being complemented by *Schilfwein*, made by placing the grapes on reed *(Schilf)* matting so they shrivel in the heat.

Southern Burgenland is best known for Uhudler, a typically rosé-coloured wine with a fruity taste.

---

who acquired it in 1822, and an impressive collection of weapons. A war memorial is a reminder of fierce fighting in 1945, when Germans occupying the castle were attacked by Russian troops.

A cable car on the north side whisks you up in 90 seconds (uphill/downhill €4/2); it costs €2 to walk up the footpath.

The Drive ›› From Riegersburg, it's just 57km north via the B66 and west via the B65 to the lively city of Graz.

- - - - - - - - - - - -

TRIP HIGHLIGHT

9 Graz

Austria's second-largest city bursts with energy thanks to its spirited student population. Surrounding the fast-flowing river gushing through its centre is a vision of green parkland, red rooftops, Renaissance courtyards and baroque palaces, plus modern designs.

Rising 473m, **Schlossberg** (1hr ticket for lift or funicular €2.10; ⊒4, 5 Schlossbergplatz) is the site of the original fortress where Graz was founded. It's topped by the city's most visible icon – the **Uhrturm** (clock tower). Its wooded slopes can be reached by bucolic (and strenuous) paths, but also by lift or Schlossbergbahn funicular.

Graz's elegant palace, **Schloss Eggenberg** (Eggenberger Allee 90; adult/child €11.50/5.50; ⊙tours 10am-4pm Tue-Sun Palm Sun-Oct; ⊒1 Schloss Eggenberg), was created for the Eggenberg dynasty in 1625. Admission is via a highly worthwhile guided tour during which you'll learn about each room's idiosyncrasies, the stories portrayed by the frescos and the Eggenberg family itself.

 p311

Eating & Sleeping

Vienna ❶

✖ Figlmüller   Bistro, Pub Food €€

(📞01-512 61 77; www.figlmueller.at; 01, Wollzeile 5; mains €9.50-20.50; ⏰11am-9.30pm; 🛜; Ⓜ Stephansplatz) The Viennese would simply be at a loss without Figlmüller. This famous *Beisl* (bistro pub) has some of the biggest and best schnitzels in the business.

✖ Meierei im Stadtpark   Austrian €€

(📞01-713 31 68; http://steirereck.at; 03, Am Heumarkt 2a; set breakfasts €20-24, mains €10.50-20, 6-cheese selection €11-14; ⏰8am-11pm Mon-Fri, 9am-7pm Sat & Sun; 🖋; Ⓜ Stadtpark) Embedded in the greenery of the Stadtpark, the Meierei serves a bountiful breakfast until noon. It's most famous, though, for its goulash served with leek roulade (€18), and its selection of 120 types of cheese.

🛏 Hotel Rathaus Wein & Design   Boutique Hotel €€

(📞01-400 11 22; www.hotel-rathaus-wien.at; 08, Lange Gasse 13; s/d/f/ste €150/210/240/400; ✳ @ 🛜; Ⓜ Rathaus) Each of the open-plan, minimalist-chic rooms at this boutique hotel is dedicated to an Austrian winemaker and the minibar is stocked with premium wines from the growers themselves.

Rust ❸

🛏 Mooslechners Bürgerhaus   Hotel €€€

(📞02685-6162; www.hotelbuergerhaus-rust. at; Hauptstrasse 1; d from €240; P 🛜) This exquisite hotel has spiral staircases inside a 1537 former bakery. Some of its Biedermeier-style rooms have vaulted ceilings and drapes around the beds. It caters superbly for children, with cots on hand, and the option of an extra bed at a discount. Its restaurant (closed Monday) serves rustic regional specialities and local wines in a magical garden setting.

Burg Lockenhaus ❻

🛏 Burghotel Lockenhaus   Historic Hotel €€

(📞02616-2394; www.ritterburg.at; s/d €98/136; P) For an atmospheric castle stay, the Burghotel Lockenhaus has antique furnished rooms, and a sauna. Breakfast costs €8; there's an extra €20 supplement for heating from October to March. Apartments with kitchenettes attached to the castle wall are also available (s/d €52/80).

Graz ❾

✖ Der Steirer   Austrian, Tapas €€

(📞0316-70 36 54; www.dersteirer.at; Belgiergasse 1; tapas €2, lunch menu €7.90, mains €10-22.50; ⏰11am-midnight; 🖋; 🚋1, 3, 6, 7 Südtiroler Platz) This Styrian neo-*Beisl* and wine bar has a small but fantastic selection of local dishes, including a great goulash, and Austrotapas if you just feel like nibbling.

🛏 Schlossberg Hotel   Hotel €€

(📞0316-8070-0; www.schlossberg-hotel. at; Kaiser-Franz-Josef-Kai 30; s €115-135, d €150-185, ste €210-250; P @ 🛜 🏊; 🚋4, 5 Schlossbergbahn) Central but secluded, four-star Schlossberg is blessed with a prime location at the foot of its namesake. Rooms are well sized and decorated in the style of a country inn. The rooftop terrace with views is perfect for an evening glass of wine.

Hallstatt *Salzkammergut's loveliest village sits between the mountains and lakeshore*

Salzkammergut

27

The Salzkammergut's gemstone-coloured lakes glittering beneath the soaring, snowcapped Alps set the scene for a magical drive between enchanting villages along the waters' edge.

TRIP HIGHLIGHTS

137 km

St Wolfgang
Take a steam train high above town

Kammer

Traunkirchen

START/FINISH

Salzburg

9

Bad Ischl

11 10

Hallstatt
Salzkammergut's prettiest village, home to an intriguing salt mine

195 km

Obertraun
Explore the dazzling Dachstein ice caves

190 km

5–7 DAYS
270 KM / 168 MILES

GREAT FOR...

BEST TIME TO GO
The lakes are at their sparkling best from June to September.

ESSENTIAL PHOTO
D-o-w-n through the glass floor of the 5 Fingers viewing platform.

BEST FOR HISTORY
Salt mine Salzwelten, detailing the area's 'white gold'.

27 Salzkammergut

Captivating scenery is reason enough to set out on this trip, but the Salzkammergut's beauty goes well below the surface. You'll explore iridescent ice caves and fascinating salt mines, and visit magnificent churches, including the wedding-scene church from *The Sound of Music.* Fans of the iconic musical can visit a multitude of other filming locations on this trip, particularly in romance-steeped Salzburg.

① Salzburg

A walking tour (p330) is an ideal way to discover this exquisite city.

Along with architectural standouts (p302) and outdoor activities (p287), some of Salzburg's most magnificent buildings featured in *The Sound of Music,* and can be visited on a DIY tour (see the boxed text, p319). They include the stately baroque square, the **Residenzplatz** (p331), with its horse-drawn carriages and palatial **Residenz** (www.domquartier.at; Residenzplatz 1;

DomQuartier ticket adult/child €12/5; ⊙10am-5pm Wed-Mon). Another splendid palace, the **Schloss Mirabell** (Mirabellplatz 4; ⊙Marble Hall 8am-4pm Mon, Wed & Thu, 1-4pm Tue & Fri, gardens 6am-dusk), was built by Prince-Archbishop Wolf Dietrich for his mistress Salome Alt in 1606 and given an early-18th-century baroque makeover that included its lavish, stucco **Marmorsaal** (Marble Hall). Benedictine convent, 1300-year-old **Stift Nonnberg** (Nonnberg Convent; Nonnberggasse 2; ⊙7am-dusk), has beautiful Romanesque frescos.

A highlight is Hellbrunn Park at early-17th-century Italianate villa **Schloss Hellbrunn** (www. hellbrunn.at; Fürstenweg 37; adult/child/family €10.50/5/25; ⊙9am-5.30pm, to 9pm Jul & Aug; ⊞); the summer palace was built by Prince-Archbishop Markus Sittikus as an escape from his Residenz duties.

✗ ⊨ p321

The Drive » It's 28km from Salzburg along the eastbound B158, past resort lake the Fuschlsee, to St Gilgen.

----

❷ St Gilgen

St Gilgen's historic centre, 400m west of the Wolfgangsee's shore, huddles around Mozartplatz and the photogenic **Rathaus** (town hall).

Mozart's mother was born in St Gilgen and the family is the focus at St Gilgen's **Mozarthaus** (www.mozarthaus.info; Ischler Strasse 15; adult/child €4/2.50; ⊙10am-noon Sat & Sun May-Oct), especially Mozart's sister 'Nannerl', also an accomplished composer and musician.

Cosy little museum **Muzikinstumente-**

Museum der Völker (Folk Music Instrument Museum; www.hoerant.at; Aberseestrasse 11; adult/child €4/2.50; ⊙9-11am & 3-7pm Tue-Sun Jun–mid-Sep, reduced hours rest of year) is home to 1500 musical instruments from all over the world, collected by a family of music teachers; there are opportunities to hear and play the instruments.

The eclectic collection at the **Heimatkundliches Museum** (www. heimatkundliches-museum. at; Pichlerplatz 6; adult/child €4/2.50; ⊙10am-noon & 3-6pm Tue-Sun Jun-Sep) spans embroidery (originally manufactured in the building) to animal specimens (about 4700) and religious objects.

The Drive » Leaving St Gilgen, take the B154 northeast past the small Krottensee. At its northern end, you'll enter a tight, forested mountain pass, then descend to the Mondsee. Continue northwest along the lakeshore to the town of Mondsee at the lake's northwestern end (14km in total).

LINK YOUR TRIP

24 **Grossglockner Road**
This adventure-filled trip also starts in Salzburg.

25 **Tyrol & Vorarlberg**
Salzburg is the end point for this bucolic Alpine drive.

3 Mondsee

The lively – if touristy – town of Mondsee extends along the northern tip of the crescent-shaped, warm-water lake of the same name.

A must-see for *The Sound of Music* lovers is the 15th-century Gothic former monastery **Basilica Minor St Michael** (www.pfarre-mondsee.com; Kirchengasse 1; admission by donation; ☻9am-7pm). Its lemon-yellow baroque facade (added in 1740) and interior, centred on a soaring high altar, featured in the Captain and Maria's wedding scene in the film. Pope John Paul II upgraded it from a parish church to a *basilica minor* in 2005.

Next door to the basilica, the **Museum Mondseeland und Pfahlbaumuseum** (www.mondseeland.org/mondseeland; Marschal-Wrede-Platz; adult/child €3/1.50; ☻10am-6pm Tue-Sun early Jul-early Sep, 10am-5pm Tue-Sun May-early Jul & early Sep-early Oct, 10am-

5pm Sat & Sun early-late Oct) has displays on Stone Age finds and the monastic culture of the region.

Segelschule Mondsee (☎06232-354 82 00; www.segelschule-mondsee.at; Robert Baum Promenade 3; windsurfer & kayak rental per hr/day €10/55, sailing-boat rental per hr/day from €16/70; ☻9am-6pm May-Sep) offers windsurfing, kayaking and sailing-boat rental as well as courses.

The Drive >> From Mondsee it's a 13km drive, taking the B151 along the Mondsee's northern shoreline, flanked by farmland with picturesque swimming spots en route, to Unterach am Attersee.

4 Unterach am Attersee

The Attersee is the largest of the Salzkammergut's lakes. The village of Unterach am Attersee has little in the way of sights but is a relaxing spot to swim or rent a SUP (stand-up paddleboard) from **SUP Attersee** (www.sup-attersee.at; Strandbad Badgasse, Unterach am Attersee; SUP rental per hr/day €12/50; ☻11am-7pm Jul-Aug, noon-6pm Sat & Sun Apr-Jun & Sep).

From Unterach am Attersee, you can cruise on the lake with **Attersee-Schifffahrt** (www.atterseeschifffahrt.at; ☻May–mid-Sep), which runs a five-stop southern lake tour (adult/child €11/5.50, one hour 10 minutes), an 11-stop southern lake tour (€17/8.50, 2½ hours), and an 18-stop full lake tour (€20/10, 3½ hours).

The Drive >> Take the B152 along the Attersee's southern then eastern shores for 24km to

CANADASTOCK / SHUTTERSTOCK ©

**TOP TIP:
SALZKAMMERGUT
SAVINGS**

Save money by picking up a **Salzkammergut Erlebnis-Card** (Salzkammergut Adventure Card; €4.90), available from tourist offices and hotels. The nontransferable card offers discounts of up to 30% at popular attractions, sights and activities for 21 days. Details of seasonal savings and conditions are available on the comprehensive website www.salzkammergut.at.

Salzburg The splendid gardens of Schloss Mirabell

Kammer (signposted Kammer-Schörfling am Attersee, with its neighbouring town of Schörfling).

- - - - - - - - - - - -

⑤ Kammer

A treat for art lovers, Kammer, on the shores of the Attersee, is home to the **Gustav Klimt-Themenweg** (Gustav Klimt Artist Trail; Kammer), a 2km-long lakeside trail including information boards with prints of works by symbolist painter Gustav Klimt (1862–1918), a seminal Vienna Secession movement member. Klimt spent regular spells on the Attersee, painting many of his renowned landscapes here; the trail passes his summer residences. There are also some boards in other lake settlements.

The **Gustav Klimt Zentrum** (www.klimt-am-attersee.at; Hauptstrasse 30, Kammer; adult/child €6/3; ⏰10am-6pm late Jun-Aug, 10am-5pm Wed-Sun Apr-late Jun & Sep-Oct) rents audioguides for the trail (€3). High-tech multimedia exhibits here provide an overview of Klimt's life and works on the Attersee; the museum also has a cinema screening informative films (mainly in German with English subtitles). There's often an original on-loan work displayed here.

The centre neighbours privately owned **Schloss Kammer**, dating from the mid-13th century.

From Kammer, Attersee-Schifffahrt runs a seven-stop northern lake tour (adult/child €11/5.50, one hour 10 minutes).

The Drive » A 24km drive brings you to Seeschloss Ort. From Kammer, follow the A1 east and exit onto the B145. Just south of Gmunden, as the road descends to the Traunsee, you'll spot Seeschloss Ort out in the lake.

6 Seeschloss Ort

On the Traunsee's eastern side, pretty nature reserve Toscana Park forms a backdrop to **Seeschloss Ort** (www.gmunden.ooe.gv.at; Orth 1; adult/child €3/free; ☺10am-5pm May-late Oct). Reached by a pedestrian bridge, this lake-set castle on a small island is believed to have been built on the ruins of a Roman fortress. Dating from 909 or earlier, it was rebuilt in the 17th century after a fire. There's a picturesque courtyard, a late-Gothic external staircase and sgraffito from 1578. You can walk around the outside for free.

The Drive » Traunkirchen lies 10km south of Seeschloss Ort on the Traunsee just off the B145.

7 Traunkirchen

Traunkirchen sits on a picturesque spit of land on the western shore of the Traunsee, guarded by immense mountain peaks. A beautiful 450m path wends around the headland. There's a great **paddling pool** in the lake for kids.

In the **Pfarrkirche** (Parish Church) is the wooden **Fischerkanzel** (Fisherman's Pulpit; Klosterplatz 1; ☺8am-5pm), carved in 1753 and depicting the miracle of the fishes, with the Apostles standing in

a tub-shaped boat and hauling in fish-laden nets.

There are plenty of lake cruises; to explore under your own steam you can rent pedal boats and electric boats from **Schifffahrt Loidl** (☎0664-371 56 40; www.schifffahrt-traunsee.at; Ortsplatz; pedal/electric boat rental per hr €7/12; ☺8am-5pm May-early Oct).

✗ 🛏 p321

The Drive » It's 22km from Traunkirchen southwest on the B145 to Bad Ischl. As you come into Ebensee, you'll cross the Traun River; 3km south of Ebensee, you'll cross the river again and follow its northern bank.

8 Bad Ischl

This spa town's reputation was enhanced after the Habsburg Princess Sophie took an infertility cure here in 1828. Within two years she had given birth to Emperor Franz Josef I, who made Bad Ischl his summer home for the next 60 years. The fateful letter he signed declaring war on Serbia, sparking WWI, bore a Bad Ischl postmark.

The **Stadtmuseum** (www.stadtmuseum.at; Esplanade 10; adult/child €5.40/2.70; ☺10am-5pm Thu-Sun, 2-7pm Wed Apr-Oct & Dec, 10am-5pm Fri-Sun Jan-Mar) showcases Bad Ischl's history inside the building where Franz Josef and Princess Elisabeth of Bavaria were engaged

(the day after they met at a ball).

Franz Josef's Italianate **Kaiservilla** (www.kaiservilla.at; Jainzen 38; adult/child €13.50/7.50, grounds only €4.50/3.50; ☺9.30am-5pm Apr-Sep, 10am-4pm Oct, 10am-4pm Sat & Sun Dec, 10am-4pm Wed Jan-Mar) was bought by Sophie as an engagement present for her son and Elisabeth. Tours give illuminating insights into the family's life.

The Drive » St Wolfgang sits 16km west from Bad Ischl via the B158 and the L116 and L546.

TRIP HIGHLIGHT

9 St Wolfgang

Charming St Wolfgang slinks down the steep banks of the Wolfgangsee. Its narrow streets can get clogged with day trippers but early evenings offer tranquil strolling along the forested lakeshore past creaking wooden boathouses.

St Wolfgang became famous as a place of pilgrimage, and the faithful still come to the **Wallfahrtskirche** (Pilgrimage Church; www.pfarre-sankt-wolfgang.at; Markt; donation €1; ☺8am-6pm May-Sep, 8am-4pm Oct-Apr), a 14th-century pilgrim church. It's a spectacular gallery of religious art, with glittering altars (from Gothic to baroque), an extravagant pulpit, a fine organ and countless statues and paintings.

DIY SALZBURG SOUND OF MUSIC TOUR

Did you know that there were 10, not seven Trapp children, the eldest of whom was Rupert (so long Liesl)? Or that in 1938 the Trapp family left quietly for the United States instead of climbing every mountain to Switzerland?

No matter. Sing as you stroll on a self-guided tour of *The Sound of Music* filming locations. Let's start at the very beginning:

» **The Hills Are Alive** The opening scenes were actually filmed around the Salzkammergut lakes. Maria makes her twirling entrance on Alpine pastures just across the German border in Bavaria.

» **A Problem Like Maria** Nuns waltzing on their way to mass at Benedictine **Stift Nonnberg** (Nonnberg Convent; Nonnberggasse 2; ⊘7am-dusk) is fiction, but it's a fact that the real Maria von Trapp intended to become a nun here.

» **I Have Confidence** Residenzplatz is where Maria playfully splashes the spouting horses of the Residenzbrunnen fountain.

» **So Long, Farewell** The grand rococo palace Schloss Leopoldskron, a 15-minute walk from Festung Hohensalzburg, is where the lake scene was filmed. Its Venetian Room was the blueprint for the Trapps' lavish ballroom, where the children bid their farewells.

» **Do-Re-Mi** The Pegasus fountain, the steps with fortress views, the gnomes...the Mirabellgarten at **Schloss Mirabell** (Mirabellplatz 4; ⊘Marble Hall 8am-4pm Mon, Wed & Thu, 1-4pm Tue & Fri, gardens 6am-dusk) might inspire a rendition of 'Do-Re-Mi', especially if there's a drop of golden sun.

» **Sixteen Going on Seventeen** Liesl and Rolf's glass-paned pavilion hides out in Hellbrunn Park at **Schloss Hellbrunn** (www.hellbrunn.at; Fürstenweg 37; adult/child/family €10.50/5/25; ⊘9am-5.30pm, to 9pm Jul & Aug; ⏴).

» **Edelweiss and Adieu** The Felsenreitschule (Summer Riding School) is the backdrop for the Salzburg Festival in the movie, where the Trapp Family Singers win the audience over with 'Edelweiss' and give the Nazis the slip with 'So Long, Farewell'.

» **Climb Every Mountain** To, erm, Switzerland. Or content yourself with Alpine views from Untersberg, which appears briefly at the end of the movie when the family flees the country.

The lovable crimson-coloured steam train that appeared with Maria and the children in *The Sound of Music,* the **Schafbergbahn** (www.wolfgangsee schifffahrt.at; Schafbergbahn-strasse; adult/child one-way €22.70/11.40, return €33/16.50; ⊘late Apr-late Oct), chugs from St Wolfgang to the summit of the 783m-high Schafberg. During the season there are seven departures daily, starting from 9.15am, then hourly from 10am to 3pm. Journey time is 40 minutes one way.

The Drive » The prettiest drive from St Wolfgang back to Bad Ischl is along the narrow L546 through undulating open countryside. From Bad Ischl, head south on the B145 to Bad Aussee, and take the L701 west on a tight, heavily forested descent before crossing the Traun River into Obertraun (53.5km all up).

TRIP HIGHLIGHT

⑩ Obertraun

Obertraun offers easy access via cable car to the extraordinary

Dachstein Eishöhle (www.dachstein-salzkammergut.com; tour incl cable car adult/child €29.70/16.20; ☺core tour 9.20am-4pm May-late Oct). Millions of years old, these glittering ice caves extend into the mountain for almost 80km in places. Dress warmly! Also here is the non-ice **Mammuthöhle** (Mammoth Cave; www.dachstein-salzkammergut.com; tour incl cable car adult/child €29.70/16.20; ☺core tour 10.30am-2.30pm early May-late Oct), among the deepest and longest caves in the world.

Another cable car runs up to the 2109m-high **Krippenstein** (www.dachstein-salzkammergut.com; cable car return adult/child €28.60/15.80; ☺mid-Jun–late Oct) and its vertigo-inducing **5 Fingers viewing platform**, protruding from a sheer cliff face. Each 'finger' has a different form, with one reminiscent of a diving board. A glass floor allows you to peer below your feet into a gaping void.

Allow a whole day to see one or both caves and the viewpoint. A combination ticket for all three, including cable cars, is €41.90/23.10 per adult/child.

The Drive » From Obertraun it's just 4.5km to Hallstatt via the L547 along the southern edge of the beautiful Hallstätter See.

TRIP HIGHLIGHT

⑪ Hallstatt

Hallstatt's pastel-coloured houses cast shimmering reflections onto the glassy waters of the Hallstätter See.

The village is strung along a narrow stretch of land between the towering mountains and lakeshore. The **Beinhaus** (Bone House; Kirchenweg 40; admission €1.50; ☺10am-6pm May-Oct), a small charnel house, contains rows of neatly stacked skulls, painted with decorative designs and the names of their former owners. It stands in the grounds of the 15th-century Catholic **Pfarrkirche** (Parish Church), which has some attractive Gothic frescos and three winged altars inside.

Salt in the surrounding hills has made it a centre of salt mining. The Hallstatt Period (800 to 400 BC) refers to the early Iron Age in Europe, named after the village and the Iron Age settlers and Celts who worked the salt mines here.

The fascinating **Salzwelten** (www.salzwelten.at; funicular return plus tour adult/child/family €26/13/54, tour only €19/9.50/40; ☺9.30am-4.30pm late Apr-late Oct) is situated high above Hallstatt on Salzberg (Salt Mountain). Tours (in English and German) detail how salt is formed and the history of mining, and take visitors into the depths on miners' slides – the longest is 60m. The **Hallstätter Hochtal** (Hallstatt High Valley) near the mine was also an Iron Age burial ground. Audioguides from the base station of the **funicular** (one-way adult/child €7/3.50) to the mine take you through the numbered stations and explain the site and rituals of burial.

✗ 📇 p321

The Drive » Take the L547 north along the cliff-framed Hallstätter See until you reach the Gosaubach River. Then head west on the B166 through the Gschütt mountain pass and the hot-air ballooning town of Gosau to Lindenthal. Take the B162 northwest to Golling an der Salzach, then the B159 north to return to Salzburg (77km in total).

Eating & Sleeping

Salzburg ❶

✖ Bärenwirt — Austrian €€

(📞0662-42 24 04; www.baerenwirt-salzburg.
at; Müllner Hauptstrasse 8; mains €9.50-20;
🕙11am-11pm) Sizzling and stirring since 1663,
Bärenwirt is Austrian through and through.
Go for hearty *Bierbraten* (beer roast) with
dumplings, locally caught trout or organic wild
boar bratwurst. A tiled oven warms the woody,
hunting-lodge-style interior in winter, while the
river-facing terrace is a summer crowd-puller.
The restaurant is 500m north of Museumplatz.

✖ Carpe Diem Finest Finger Food — Fusion €€€

(📞0662-84 88 00; www.carpediem
finestfingerfood.com; Getreidegasse 50;
3-course lunch €21.50, mains €37.50-39.50;
🕙8.30am-midnight) This avant-garde,
Michelin-starred lounge-restaurant sits in pride
of place on Getreidegasse. A food-literate crowd
flock here for cocktails and finger-food cones,
mini taste sensations with fillings like tomato
panna cotta with Jerusalem artichoke and
scallop-rhubarb.

✖ Villa Trapp — Hotel €€€

(📞0662-63 08 60; www.villa-trapp.com;
Traunstrasse 34; s €65-130, d €114-280,
ste €290-580) Did you know that there were 10,
not seven Trapp children, the eldest of whom
was Rupert (so long Liesl)? Or, perhaps, that in
1938 the Trapp family left quietly for the United
States instead of climbing every mountain to
Switzerland? For the truth behind the Hollywood
legend, stay the night at Villa Trapp, tucked
away in Salzburg's biggest private park in the
Aigen district, 3km east of the Altstadt.

Traunkirchen ❼

✖ Restaurant Bootshaus — Austrian €€€

(📞07617-2216; www.dastraunsee.at;
Klosterplatz 4; mains €31-37, 4-/5-/6-course
menu €65/75/85; 🕙6-9pm Thu, Fri & Mon,
noon-2pm & 6-9pm Sat & Sun) A stunningly
converted *Bootshaus* (boat house) at the lake's
edge with panoramic views is the setting for
locally sourced ingredients given the gourmet
treatment by chef Lukas Nagl: Traunsee crab
soup; sautéed porcini mushrooms picked in the
surrounding forest and served with avocado
cream; venison with cherry sauce; and lake-
caught carp with asparagus and horseradish.
Sublime wine pairings are available.

🛏 Hotel Post — Hotel €€

(📞07617-230 70; www.hotel-post-traunkirchen.
at; Ortsplatz 5; s/d from €98/158; P 🛜) All 55
of the spacious, contemporary and supremely
comfortable rooms at this chalet-style hotel
have balconies (with window boxes blazing
with geraniums in summer); rooms at the
front have dress-circle views of the mountain-
framed lake. In-room amenities include mini
bars; downstairs, the restaurant serves hearty
traditional Austrian fare (mains €11.80 to €23).

Hallstatt ⓫

✖ Restaurant zum Salzbaron — European €€

(📞06134-8263; Marktplatz 104; mains €16-23;
🕙11.30am-10pm; 🛜🅿) One of the best
gourmet acts in town, the Salzbaron is perched
alongside the lake inside the Seehotel Grüner
Baum and serves a seasonal pan-European
menu; local trout features strongly in summer.

🛏 Pension Sarstein — Guesthouse €

(📞06134-8217; Gosaumühlstrasse 83 ; d
€64-80, apt €70-120; 🛜) The affable Fischer
family take pride in their little guesthouse, a few
minutes' walk along the lakefront from central
Hallstatt. The old-fashioned rooms are nothing
flash, but they are neat, cosy and have balconies
with dreamy lake and mountain views. Family-
sized apartments come with kitchenettes.

Weissensee Houses sit on the shore of
Austria's highest swimmable glacial lake

Carinthian Lakes

This spin through the Carinthian Lakes region not only offers stunning Alpine scenery but the opportunity to get out on – and into – the sparkling clear waters.

TRIP HIGHLIGHTS

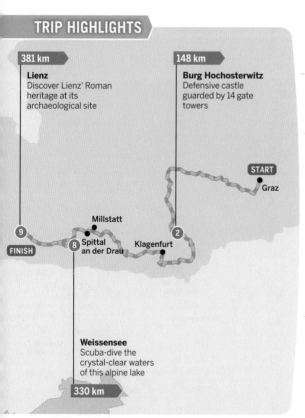

381 km

Lienz
Discover Lienz' Roman heritage at its archaeological site

148 km

Burg Hochosterwitz
Defensive castle guarded by 14 gate towers

Millstatt

Spittal an der Drau

Klagenfurt

START
Graz

9
FINISH
8
2

Weissensee
Scuba-dive the crystal-clear waters of this alpine lake

330 km

2–4 DAYS
381 KM / 237 MILES

GREAT FOR...

BEST TIME TO GO

May to September offers the best weather for boating and swimming.

ESSENTIAL PHOTO

Lake views from the top of the Aussichtsturm Pyramidenkogel.

BEST FOR FAMILIES

'Miniature world' Minimundus.

Carinthian Lakes

On this multilake trip in the country's summer playground, dubbed 'Austria's Riviera', water babies of all ages can swim, boat, water ski and wakeboard, as well as scuba-dive high up in the Alps at Weissensee, the country's highest swimmable glacial lake. Along the way, you'll discover a wealth of cultural attractions too, from Roman archaeological finds to medieval castles, a splendid Benedictine abbey and cutting-edge contemporary art galleries.

❶ Graz

Austria's second-largest city might be famed for its historic treasures, including palatial **Schloss Eggenberg** (p310), but you'll find edgy new art and architecture here, too.

Inside the Joanneumsviertel museum complex, the **Neue Galerie** (www.museum-joanneum.at; Joanneumsviertel; adult/child €8/3; ◷10am-5pm Tue-Sun; 🚊1, 3, 4, 5, 6, 7 Hauptplatz) has a stunning collection showcasing richly textured and colourful works

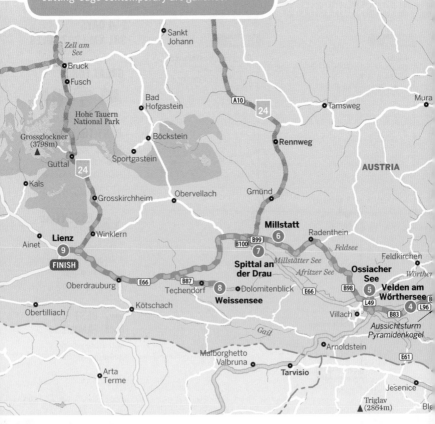

by painters such as Ernst Christian Moser.

World-class art space **Kunsthaus Graz** (www. kunsthausgraz.at; Lendkai 1; adult/child €8/3; ⊙10am-5pm Tue-Sun; 🚊1, 3, 6, 7 Südtiroler Platz) looks something like a space-age sea slug. Exhibitions here change every three to four months.

In the middle of the Mur River, floating landmark **Murinsel** (🚌4, 5 Schlossplatz/Murinsel, 🚊1, 3, 6, 7 Südtiroler Platz) is a curvilinear metal and plastic island/bridge containing a cafe, kids' playground and a small stage.

 p329

The Drive » Avoid the faster but tunnel-dominated highways and drive the scenic 170km to Burg Hochosterwitz through farmland and mountains. Take the B70 then B77 northwest to Judenburg and join the B317. Take the L84 past the Längsee and head east on the B82; the castle's car park is a 3km drive uphill.

TRIP HIGHLIGHT

❷ Burg Hochosterwitz

Storybook fortress **Burg Hochosterwitz** (www. burg-hochosterwitz.com; Hochosterwitz 1; adult/child incl tour €12/8; ⊙9am-6pm May-Sep, 10am-5pm Apr & Oct)

LINK YOUR TRIP

24 **Grossglockner Road**

Pick up this dizzying Alpine drive in Lienz.

26 **Castles of Burgenland**

This castle- and winery-lined route ends in Graz.

Oberzeiring
Fohnsdorf · Knittelfeld
Jnzmarkt-auenburg
Judenburg
[B77]
Peggau
Stübing ·
Gleisdorf
Graz · 26
❶ START
Koflach
Voitsberg
[B70]
· Kalsdorf
[B317]
· Knappenburg
Stainz ·
Friesach
· Wolfsberg
Deutschlandsberg
Leibnitz ·
Treibach-Althofen
· St Andrä
Ehrenhausen ·
Eibiswald ·
· Arnfels
[L84]
[B82]
Burg ❷
Hochosterwitz
[S37] · Völkermarkt
Völkermarkter Stausee
❸ **Klagenfurt** [B82]
Keutschacher See
p328
[B91] [B85]
acher usee
Dravograd
Maribor
Ravne na Koroškem · Slovenj Gradec
Slovenska Bistrica
SLOVENIA
[B91]
Ščavnica
· Velenje
[A1]
⊙N 0 ————— 40 km
0 ————— 20 miles

rises from the slopes of a Dolomite mountain, with 14 gate towers on the path up to the final bastion. The towers were built between 1570 and 1586 by its former owner, Georg Khevenhüller, to ward off invading Turks. Each gate presented different challenges to attackers – some have embedded spikes, which could be dropped straight through unwary invaders passing underneath.

From the car park a lift (€6), sometimes out of service, ascends to the castle; otherwise it's a steep but smooth-going 620m walk.

The Drive » From the base of the hill, head east to Brückl then southeast on the B82, past the Völkermarkter Stausee, to join the westbound B85 to the Ferlacher Stausee. The B91 leads north to Klagenfurt (84km in total).

❸ Klagenfurt

Busy Klagenfurt isn't comparable with Graz or Vienna but it's still an enjoyable, sunny city that offers easy access to the beautiful Wörthersee, which, due to its thermal springs, is one of the region's warmer lakes, averaging 21°C in summer.

At the town's western limit is the wide green space of **Europapark**. Its family-friendly *Strandbad* (beach) on the shores of the Wörthersee offers splashy fun. The park's biggest draw is **Minimundus** (www.minimundus.at; Villacher Strasse 241; adult/child €13/8; ⏰9am-7pm Mar-Sep; 👶), a 'miniature world' with 140 replicas of the world's architectural icons, downsized to a scale of 1:25.

✕ 🛏 p329

The Drive » Take the B83 west along the Wörthersee's northern shore for 16.5km, through the resort town of Pörtschach am Wörthersee to Velden am Wörthersee.

❹ Velden am Wörthersee

The Wörthersee stretches from east to west between Klagenfurt and Velden.

The Wörthersee's top nightlife resort, Velden is also the venue of various high-adrenaline sports events on summer weekends. It's a vibrant place packed with people of all ages enjoying everything from ice creams to cocktails.

Paragliding, water skiing, wakeboarding and electric boat rental are all offered by lakeside beach club **Strand Club** (☎04274-511 01; www.strandclub.com; Seepromenade 15; paragliding single/tandem per 15min €70/100, water skiing/wakeboarding per 30min €60, electric boat rental per hr €30; ⏰activities dawn-dusk Apr-Oct, bar 7am-midnight Apr-Oct, cafe 7am-10pm Apr-Oct); **prices include wetsuit hire.**

The Drive » Continue west on the B83 and take the L49 north, passing Burg Landskron, which has summer falconry shows, to Annenheim, on the western shores of Ossiacher See (18km all up).

CARINTHIAN / SHUTTERSTOCK ©

❺ Ossiacher See

The pretty Ossiacher See has plenty of lake swimming and boating opportunities.

Boats run by **Ossiachersee Schifffahrt** (www.ossiachersee-schifffahrt.at; day ticket adult/child €13.50/6.80, half-day lake boat tour €9/4.50; ⏰up to 8 services daily Apr-Oct) complete a criss-cross 2½-hour circuit between St Andrä and Steindorf as part of a regular service. The company also runs half-day lake tours.

The Drive » It's a 39km drive from Annenheim to Millstatt. Head northwest on the B98. En route you'll pass the Afritzer See

Carinthia Hilltop fortress Burg Hochosterwitz

and the Feldsee, as well as the northern shore of the Millstätter See, to reach Millstatt.

---

⑥ Millstatt

Stretching 12km long but just 1.5km wide, the Millstätter See, Carinthia's second-largest lake, was gouged out during the Ice Age about 30,000 years ago and has temperatures of about 22°C to 26°C in summer. Millstatt, on the north shore, is the most appealing of its small towns.

Millstatt's main attraction is its Romanesque Benedictine abbey, **Stift Millstatt** (www.stifts museum.at; Stiftsgasse 1; adult/child €3/2.50; ⊙10am-4pm

May-Oct). Founded in 1070, it contains the Stiftsmuseum, an attractive 11th-century abbey church and a graveyard. The abbey grounds and magnificent arcades and cloisters are free to enter.

The Drive » The 9km drive from Millstatt follows the Millstätter See shore on the B98 before veering south through a steep forested valley on the B99 to Spittal an der Drau.

---

⑦ Spittal an der Drau

Spittal is a key economic and administrative centre in upper Carinthia. Its name comes from a

12th-century hospital and refuge that once succoured travellers here.

Adjoining a small but attractive park with splashing fountains and bright flowerbeds is the impressive Italianate palace **Schloss Porcia & Museum für Volkskultur** (Local Heritage Museum; www. museum-spittal.com; Burgplatz 1; adult/child €8/4; ⊙9am-6pm mid-Apr–mid-Oct, 1-4pm Mon-Thu mid-Oct–mid-Apr; ♿). Inside, arcades line a central courtyard used for summer theatre performances. The top floors contain the Local Heritage Museum, which has extensive displays about the region.

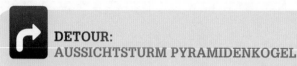

DETOUR:
AUSSICHTSTURM PYRAMIDENKOGEL

Start: ❸ Klagenfurt

Phenomenal views over the sparkling lakes and surrounding countryside extend from the Pyramidenkogel. The 851m-high mountain is topped by a stunning contemporary 70.6m tower (the world's highest of its kind), the **Aussichtsturm Pyramidenkogel** (☎04273-2443; www.pyramidenkogel.info; Linden 62, Keutschach am See; adult/child €11/5.50, slide per ride €4; ☺9am-9pm Jun-Aug, 9am-8pm May & Sep, 10am-7pm Apr & Oct, 10am-6pm Mar), made of steel with wooden beams spiralling up its exterior. Two of its three viewing platforms are open; one, the lower-level Sky Box, is glass encased.

After climbing 441 steps or riding the glass lift/elevator and taking in the panoramas, you can return to ground level on Europe's highest covered **slide**, down 120 tube-enclosed metres, dropping 52m in about 20 seconds at speeds of up to 25km/h. Recover with a drink in the cafe at the tower's base.

From Klagenfurt, it's an 18km side trip: head west to the Wörthersee's southern shore and follow the L96 along the lakefront to Reifnitz. Turn left on L97B and follow it to the lake, Keutschach See. Take L97C northwest until you reach the tower.

The Drive » Traversing 44km along a farmed valley framed by towering Alps via the B100 and B87 brings you to the least developed of Carinthia's lakes, the Weissensee.

❽ Weissensee

Wedged within a glacial cleft in the Gailtal Alps, the pristine nature reserve Weissensee holds Austria's highest swimmable glacial lake, with an altitude of 930m and summer temperatures of above 20°C. Just 1km or so wide in most parts, it stretches for almost 12km.

Boat services on Weissensee operated by **Weissensee Schifffahrt** (www.schifffahrt-mueller.at; 1-8 stops €2.50-7.50, day ticket €11; ☺up to 10 services daily mid-May–mid-Oct) are as much an excursion through the picturesque landscape as

a way of getting around the lake. The crystal-clear waters offer incredible visibility for dazzling views of the lake's 22 fish species. **Yachtdiver** (☎0664-460 4080; www.yachtdiver.at; Techendorf 55; dives from €12, equipment rental from €29, courses from €35; ☺9am-6pm) runs scuba-diving trips for experienced divers and courses for beginners, as well as ice-diving expeditions in winter.

The Drive » Take the B87 back to the B100 and head west to lively Lienz (a 48km journey).

❾ Lienz

Towering **Dolomite peaks** rise like an amphitheatre around Lienz.

The Romans settled here some 2000 years ago. Their legacy is explored at the regional history museum inside the medi-

eval castle **Schloss Bruck** (www.museum-schlossbruck. at; Schlossberg 1; adult/child €7.50/2.50, combined admission with Aguntum €10.50/8.50; ☺10am-6pm, closed Mon Sep-May), and at the archaeological site **Aguntum** (www.aguntum. info; Stribach 97; adult/child €7/4, combined admission with Schloss Bruck €10.50/8.50; ☺9.30am-4pm May-Oct), where excavations are unearthing details of this two-millenia-old *municipium,* which was a centre of trade and commerce under Emperor Claudius. Visit the glass-walled museum to learn more before exploring the ruins. An exhibition features fun elements such as traditional Roman recipes.

The town's medieval cobbled centre is an atmospheric place to stroll.

✕ 🛏 p329

Eating & Sleeping

Graz ❶

✖ El Gaucho — Steak €€

(☎0316-830 083; www.elgaucho.at/graz; Landhausgasse 1; mains €15-36; ☻kitchen 5-11pm Mon-Fri, 11.30am-11pm Sat & Sun; 🚋1, 3 ,4, 5, 6, 7 Hauptplatz) Set inside the evocative Renaissance Landhaus building, El Gaucho would seem an unlikely place to feast on succulent Argentine and local steaks (with sides like truffle gnocchi that can be ordered as mains). The scene is lit in relaxing crimson and decorated with hanging glass bubbles, but in summer the best seats are in the buzzing courtyard. Service is outstanding.

✖ Landhauskeller — Austrian €€

(☎0316-83 02 76; Schmiedgasse 9; mains €11.50-28.50; ☻11.30am-midnight Mon-Sat; 🚋1, 3 ,4, 5, 6, 7 Hauptplatz) What started as a spit-and-sawdust pub in the 16th century has evolved into an atmospheric, medieval-style restaurant serving specialities such as its four different sorts of *Tafelspitz* (prime broiled beef).

⎉ Hotel zum Dom — Hotel €€

(☎0316-82 48 00; www.domhotel.co.at; Bürgergasse 14; s €74, d €89-169, ste €189-294; P ✲ 🛜; 🚋30 Palais Trauttmansdorff/Urania, 🚋1, 3, 4, 5, 6, 7 Hauptplatz) Ceramic art crafted by a local artist lends character to graceful Hotel zum Dom, whose individually furnished rooms come either with steam/power showers or whirlpools. One suite even has a terrace whirlpool.

Klagenfurt ❸

✖ Restaurant Maria Loretto — Austrian €€

(☎0463-244 65; Lorettoweg 54; mains €16-26; ☻10am-midnight Wed-Mon) Situated on a headland above Wörthersee, this characterful restaurant is easily reached by foot from the *Strandbad*. It does a very good trout and some flavoursome meat dishes. Reserve for an outside table.

⎉ Hotel Geyer — Hotel €€

(☎0463-578 86; www.hotelgeyer.com; Priesterhausgasse 5; s €70-88, d €102-135, q €155-170; P 🛜) Expect modern and comfortable rooms in this three-star hotel. Bonuses are the sauna and steam bath, and free use of the fitness centre around the corner.

Lienz ❾

✖ Kirchenwirt — Austrian €€

(☎04852-625 00; www.kirchenwirt-lienz.at; Pfarrgasse 7; mains €9.50-29; ☻9am-11.30pm Sun-Thu, to 1.30am Fri & Sat) Up on a hill opposite Stadtpfarrkirche St Andrä, this is Lienz's most atmospheric restaurant. Dine on a selection of local dishes under the vaults or on the streamside terrace. The lunch special costs under €10.

⎉ Goldener Fisch — Hotel €€

(☎04852-621 32; www.goldener-fisch.at; Kärntnerstrasse 9; s/d €65/110; P 🛜) The chestnut-tree-shaded beer garden is a big draw at this family-friendly hotel. The rooms are light and modern – if not fancy – and you can wind down in the sauna and herbal steam baths.

STRETCH YOUR LEGS
SALZBURG

Start/Finish: Stift Nonnberg

Distance: 6.4km

Duration: Three to four hours

This walk is Salzburg in a nutshell, taking you high above its rooftops and spires, up to its whopper of a fortress, down to the Salzach River and over to Mozart's birthplace and the palaces and churches of its resplendent, Unesco-listed Altstadt.

Take this walk on Trips

Stift Nonnberg

With views to make you yodel out loud, the high-on-a-hill Benedictine convent **Stift Nonnberg** (Nonnberg Convent; Nonnberg-gasse 2; ⊘7am-dusk) found fame as the nunnery in *The Sound of Music*.

The Walk ≫ There is an underground car park at Unipark Nonntal, a five-minute walk southeast of Stift Nonnberg. Walking on from Stift Nonnberg, take the high, panoramic Festungsgasse then make the stiff final climb to the fortress.

Festung Hohensalzburg

Every inch the storybook fortress, clifftop **Festung Hohensalzburg** (www.salzburg-burgen.at; Mönchsberg 34; adult/child/family €8/4.50/18.20, incl Festungsbahn funicular €11.30/6.50/26.20; ⊘9am-7pm) proudly guards 900 years of history. Roam the ramparts for views over the city's spires, the Salzach River and the mountains.

The Walk ≫ Skirt the top of Mönchsberg along shady wooded trails, following the signs for Museum der Moderne.

Museum der Moderne

Straddling Mönchsberg's cliffs, the contemporary glass-and-marble **Museum der Moderne** (www.museumdermoderne.at; Mönchsberg 32; adult/child €8/6; ⊘10am-6pm Tue-Sun, to 8pm Wed) shows first-rate temporary exhibitions of 20th- and 21st-century art. While you're up here, linger over coffee or lunch at **M32** (☏0662-84 10 00; www.m32.at; Mönchsberg 32; 2-course lunch €16, mains €26-36; ⊘9am-1am Tue-Sun; ✈♦).

The Walk ≫ Your scenic walk continues along Mönchsberg, with cracking views of the city. As you descend, you reach Augustiner Bräustübl.

Augustiner Bräustübl

Since 1621, monastery-run brewery **Augustiner Bräustübl** (www.augustinerbier.at; Augustinergasse 4-6; ⊘3-11pm Mon-Fri, from 2.30pm Sat & Sun) has been serving potent homebrews in Stein tankards in the vaulted hall and beneath the chestnut trees in the 1000-seat beer garden.

The Walk ≫ Cross Müllner Hauptstrasse and amble down to the Kaipromenade shadowing the Salzach River, then turn right to cross Museumsplatz and Gstättengasse. You'll emerge on shop-lined, sign-crammed Getreidegasse.

Mozarts Geburtshaus

Wolfgang Amadeus Mozart, Salzburg's most famous son, was born in bright-yellow **Mozarts Geburtshaus** (Mozart's Birthplace; www.mozarteum.at; Getreidegasse 9; adult/child €10/3.50, incl Mozart-Wohnhaus €17/5; ☺9am-5.30pm) in 1756 and spent the first 17 years of his life here. Today's museum harbours a collection of instruments, documents and portraits.

The Walk » Continue straight then veer right onto Alter Markt to reach Residenzplatz.

Residenzplatz

With its horse-drawn carriages, palace and street entertainers, this stately baroque square is the Salzburg of a thousand postcards. Its centrepiece is the Residenz-brunnen, a fountain ringed by horses and topped by a conch-shell-bearing Triton. Allow ample time for a romp of the **Residenz** (www.domquartier.at; Residenzplatz 1; DomQuartier ticket adult/child €12/5; ☺10am-5pm Wed-Mon), the crowning glory of Salzburg's new DomQuartier.

The Walk » No need to walk far – Residenzplatz sidles up to Domplatz.

Dom

Gracefully crowned by a bulbous copper dome and twin spires, the **Dom** (Cathedral; Domplatz; ☺8am-7pm Mon-Sat, 1-7pm Sun) stands out as a masterpiece of baroque art. In the nave, Arsenio Mascagni's ceiling frescos recount the Passion of Christ.

The Walk » Stroll west along Franziskanergasse, then turn left and left again to reach Erzabtei St Peter.

Erzabtei St Peter

A missionary named Rupert founded abbey church and monastery **Erzabtei St Peter** (St Peter's Abbey; St Peter Bezirk 1-2; catacombs adult/child €2/1.50; ☺church 8am-noon & 2.30-6.30pm, cemetery 6.30am-7pm, catacombs 10am-6pm) in around 700, making it the oldest in the German-speaking world. The cemetery is home to the catacombs – cave-like crypts hewn out of the Mönchsberg cliff face.

The Walk » It's a 12-minute walk east back to the starting point, Stift Nonnberg.

STRETCH YOUR LEGS
VIENNA

Start/Finish: Café Central

Distance: 3.4km

Duration: Four hours

Vienna's grandeur unfolds in all its glory on this city stroll, from the timeless elegance of its *Kaffeehäuser* (coffee houses) to its monumental Hofburg palace, museums, parks and opulent opera house, as well as magnificent churches.

Take this walk on Trips

Café Central

Park just around the corner on Freyung and fortify yourself with coffee and a slice of *Altenbergtorte* cake at grand **Café Central** (www.palaisevents.at/cafecentral.html; 01, Herrengasse 14; ⊘7.30am-10pm Mon-Sat, 10am-10pm Sun; ⊛; Ⓜ Herrengasse).

The Walk ≫ Walk southeast on Herrengasse for 350m, then through the Michaelertor palace gate to the imposing Hofburg.

Hofburg

Nothing symbolises Austria's culture and heritage more than the **Hofburg** (Imperial Palace; www.hofburg-wien.at; 01, Michaelerkuppel; ⊟1A, 2A Michaelerplatz; Ⓜ Herrengasse, ⊟D, 1, 2, 71, 46, 49 Burgring), seat of the Habsburgs from 1273 to 1918. Its oldest section is the 13th-century **Schweizerhof** (Swiss Courtyard). The palace owes its size and architectural diversity to one-upmanship; sections were added by new rulers, including the Gothic Burgkapelle (Royal Chapel), early baroque Leopold Wing, 16th-century Amalia Wing and 18th-century Imperial Chancery Wing.

The Walk ≫ It's a 750m stroll southwest through Heldenplatz, passing the twin museums Naturhistorisches and Kunsthistorisches on Maria-Theresien-Platz, to the MuseumsQuartier.

MuseumsQuartier

The **MuseumsQuartier** (Museum Quarter; www.mqw.at; 07, Museumsplatz; ⊘information & ticket centre 10am-7pm; Ⓜ Museumsquartier, Volkstheater) is a remarkable ensemble of museums, cafes, restaurants and bars inside former imperial stables. With over 60,000 sq metres of exhibition space, the complex is one of the world's most ambitious cultural spaces.

The Walk ≫ Head southeast through the MuseumsQuartier's arched laneways to Mariahilfer Strasse. Turn left and continue 350m northeast to the Burggarten.

Burggarten

The **Burggarten** (Castle Garden; www.bundesgaerten.at; 01, Burgring; ⊘6am-10pm Apr-Oct, 7.30am-5.30pm Nov-Mar; Ⓜ Museumsquartier, ⊟D, 1, 2, 71) is a leafy oasis amid the city's hustle and bustle. The marble statue of Mozart is the park's most famous tenant, but there's also a statue of Emperor Franz Josef. Don't miss the **Schmetterlinghaus** (butterfly house), and the **Palmenhaus** bar, housed in a beautifully restored *Jugendstil* (art-nouveau) palm house.

The Walk » From the garden's northeastern edge, walk southeast on Hanuschgasse for 200m to the city's opera house, the Staatsoper.

Staatsoper

The neo-Renaissance **Staatsoper** (www.wiener-staatsoper.at; 01, Opernring 2; Ⓜ Karlsplatz, 🚊 D, 1, 2, 71) is Vienna's foremost opera and ballet venue. Built between 1861 and 1869, it initially appalled the Viennese public, earning the nickname 'stone turtle'. Performances here are unforgettable; you also can visit its museum and/or take a guided tour.

The Walk » Head north on Kärntner Strasse for 600m to the Stephansdom, and pause to check out the glorious tiled roof.

Stephansdom

Vienna's soaring, filagreed Gothic masterpiece, the **Stephansdom** (St Stephan's Cathedral; www.stephanskirche.at; 01, Stephansplatz; ⏰ 6am-10pm Mon-Sat, from 7am Sun, main nave

& Domschatz audio tours 9-11.30am & 1-4.30pm Mon-Sat, 1-3.30pm Sun; Ⓜ Stephansplatz), is locally – and ironically – nicknamed Steffl (Little Stephan). A church has stood here since the 12th century; reminders include the Romanesque Riesentor (Giant Gate) and Heidentürme. Inside, a magnificent stone pulpit, sculpted in 1515, presides over the main nave.

The Walk » Take Goldschmiedgasse northwest for 230m to Petersplatz and the domed Peterskirche.

Peterskirche

The **Peterskirche** (Church of St Peter; www.peterskirche.at; 01, Petersplatz; ⏰ 7am-8pm Mon-Fri, 9am-9pm Sat & Sun; Ⓜ Stephansplatz) was built in 1733 according to plans by the celebrated baroque architect Johann Lukas von Hildebrandt. Interior highlights include a fresco on the dome painted by JM Rottmayr and a golden altar depicting the martyrdom of St John of Nepomuk.

The Walk » Head northwest on Graben and Naglergasse for 200m. Turn left onto Haarhof for 90m, then right onto Wallnerstrasse for 80m; Café Central is in front of you.

Switzerland Trips

A place of heart-stopping natural beauty and head-spinning efficiency, Switzerland lies in the centre of Europe yet exhibits a unique blend of cultures. Dazzling outdoor scenery such as the ever-admired Alps, pristine lakes, lush meadows and chocolate-box chalets combines with local traditions, cosmopolitan cities and smooth infrastructure. In short, Switzerland makes it easy for you to dive deep into its heart: distances are manageable and variety is within easy reach: you can be perusing a farmers market for picnic provisions in the morning, then feasting on them on a mountaintop come lunchtime. At nightfall, try gazing at stars in the night sky from cosy digs or revelling in the cultural offerings of one of Switzerland's urbane cities.

Zermatt View of Lake Riffelsee and the magnificent Matterhorn (Trip 32)
KARL THOMAS / GETTY IMAGES ©

Switzerland Trips

29 Northern Switzerland 3 Days
Architectural marvels and epic water features colour this oft-overlooked northern delight. (p339)

30 Lake Geneva & Western Switzerland 4 Days
A glorious lake, stunning vineyards, enchanting villages and fairy-tale castles. (p347)

31 Geneva to Zürich 7 Days
Mountains, pastures, lakes and small-town charm, book-ended by Switzerland's biggest cities. (p355)

Classic Trip

32 The Swiss Alps 7 Days
The greatest of the great outdoors: perfect peaks, gorgeous glaciers, verdant valleys. (p365)

33 Graubünden & Ticino 5 Days
Big-sky wilderness, off-the-beaten-track beauty, pretty towns and unique local flavours. (p377)

DON'T MISS

The Matterhorn

Symbol of Switzerland, this magical mountain demands to be photographed. See it for yourself on Trip 32

Lavaux

Swiss wine is a well-kept secret, but this dreamy Unesco-listed spot will have you wanting to share its charms with the world. Imbibe on Trips 30 31

Rheinfall

Its thunderous roar is the perfect soundtrack to the panoramic lift to the Kanzelli viewing platform as part of Trip 29

Züri-West

Switzerland dispenses with its staid reputation in this hip neighbourhood full of great bars, clubs, cafes and restaurants. Explore it on Trip 31

Tremola Road

All hairpin bends and cobblestones, this section of the historic St Gotthard Pass is a true joyride. Experience it along Trip 33

The Swiss Alps A skier enjoying the slopes near Davos (Trip 33)

Basel *The city's Marktplatz is dominated by the vivid Rathaus*

Northern Switzerland

29

Combine Switzerland's natural and man-made wonders with this art- and architecture-rich trip through the powerhouse north, all with a distinct Swiss-German accent.

TRIP HIGHLIGHTS

244 km

Basel
Design-driven museum capital with an arty edge

102 km

Stein am Rhein
Sublime Old Town with charm in spades

Schaffhausen

7

6 4

St Gallen
START

Ligerz
FINISH

Rheinfall
Europe's biggest waterfall knows how to grab your attention

124 km

**3 DAYS
339 KM / 211 MILES**

GREAT FOR...

BEST TIME TO GO

Any time of year, although the warmer months are best.

 ESSENTIAL PHOTO

The half-timbered heart of Stein am Rhein.

☑ **BEST FOR CULTURE**

From St Gallen's rococo ebullience to Basel's myriad museums and architectural gems.

29 | Northern Switzerland

The best of Switzerland is blended to perfection with a little northern exposure. This route allows travellers to tiptoe off the tourist trail and experience lesser-known places such as Appenzell before returning for the heavy-hitting urban pleasures of museum-rich Basel. Impressive natural wonders like the Rheinfall compete with architectural jaw-droppers such as St Gallen's Stiftsbibliothek, while tucked-away vineyards delight the senses.

❶ St Gallen

Located in Switzerland's northeast, St Gallen's riotously beautiful rococo library, **Stiftsbibliothek** (www.stibli.ch; Klosterhof 6d; adult/child Sfr12/9; ⊙10am–5pm), in its Catholic abbey, is a must-see. The 16th-century library (one of the world's oldest), along with the rest of the monastery complex, forms a Unesco World Heritage site. Filled with 170,000 priceless books and manuscripts painstakingly handwritten by monks in the Middle Ages, it's a dimly lit confection of ceiling frescos, stucco, cherubs and parquetry.

The Drive » Driving through the verdant countryside from St Gallen, take gently winding Rte 447 for part of the way to reach Appenzell's centre.

- - - - - - - - - - - -

❷ Appenzell

Appenzell is a feast for the eyes and the stomach. Behind the gaily decorative pastel-coloured facades of its traditional buildings lie cafes, *confiseries* (sweets and cake shops), cheese shops, delicatessens, butchers and restaurants

offering local specialities. It's also perfect for a lazy wander along the **Sitter River** or the photogenic **Altstadt** (old town) with its **Landsgemeindeplatz**, featuring elaborately painted hotels and restaurants. Vis-

iting the **Brauerei Locher** (www.appenzellerbier.ch; Brauereiplatz 1; visitor centre admission free, beer tasting Sfr8.50; ☺1-5pm Mon, 10am-12.15pm & 1-5pm Tue-Fri, 10am-5pm Sat & Sun Apr-Oct, 10am-12.15pm & 1-5pm Tue-Fri, 10am-4pm Sat

LINK YOUR TRIP

30 Lake Geneva & Western Switzerland

Head south from Ligerz for 77km to Gruyères, the end point of Trip 30, which can easily be done in the opposite direction.

31 Geneva to Zürich

Geneva lies 145km southwest of Ligerz, allowing a loop through the country, back to the north.

Nov-Dec & Feb-Mar) is great for brew lovers, and you can come to grips with local history at the **Appenzell Museum** (Hauptgasse 4; adult/child Sfr7/3; ☺10am-noon & 2-5pm) nearby.

✖ p345

The Drive » From Appenzell, retrace your drive to St Gallen (Rte 447), then head to Arbon (the A1 and A1.1) on the shore of Lake Constance. From Arbon drive to Romanshorn, then take Rte 13 to Schloss Arenenberg, on the Untersee, a total of 70km.

③ Schloss Arenenberg

Lake Constance (Bodensee) is the German Mediterranean, with a mild climate, gardens and palm trees. Nicknamed the 'Swabian Sea', it's Central Europe's third-largest lake, straddling Switzerland, Germany and Austria. It's a cool place to wind down, even when driving. The lakeside road (Rte 13) between Kreuzlingen and Stein am Rhein is dotted with quaint half-timbered Thurgau villages such as **Gottlieben**, **Steckborn** and **Berlingen**. Near the latter is **Schloss Arenenberg** (www.napoleonmuseum. tg.ch; Salenstein; adult/child Sfr12/5; ☺10am-5pm summer, closed Mon winter), a handsome lakefront mansion in beautiful grounds where France's Napoleon III grew up.

The Drive » Departing the castle, continue on lakeside Rte

13 for 18km, until you arrive in Stein am Rhein.

TRIP HIGHLIGHT

④ Stein am Rhein

Stein am Rhein appears to have leaped from the pages of a fable, with its leafy river promenade and gingerbread houses. The effect is overwhelming in cobblestone **Rathausplatz** (town hall square), hailed as Switzerland's most beautiful town square, where houses, some half-timbered, others covered in frescos, line up for a permanent photo op, the fresco-festooned **Rathaus** (town hall) soaring above it all. Situated between the Rathaus and the Rhine is the **Klostermuseum St Georgen** (www.klostersankt georgen.ch; adult/child Sfr5/3; ☺10am-5pm Tue-Sun Apr-Oct), on the site of a Benedictine monastery built in 1007. What you see today, including the cloister and magnificent *Festsaal* (grand dining room), is largely a late-Gothic creation.

✖ 🛏 p345

The Drive » It's a straightforward 20km, 20-minute drive along Rte 13 from Stein am Rhein to Schaffhausen, passing small towns and agricultural holdings.

⑤ Schaffhausen

Quaint medieval Schaffhausen is known for ornate frescos and oriel bay windows (called *Erker*), which grace the houses of

its Old Town. The colourful frescos of 17th-century **Zum Goldenen Ochsen** (Vorstadt 17) and 16th-century **Zum Grossen Käfig** depict, respectively, a golden ox and the parading of Turkish sultan Bajazet in a cage by the triumphant Mongol conqueror Tamerlane. A block east, eye-catching 1492 **Haus zum Ritter** (Vordergasse 65) boasts a detailed Renaissance-style fresco of a knight. Good city **walking tours** (adult/child Sfr14/7; ☺10am Tue & 2pm Sat May–mid-Oct) kick off from the tourist office in summer. The 16th-century circular **Munot** (☺8am-8pm

Schaffhausen Massive surge of thunderous Rheinfall (Rhine Falls)

May-Sep, 9am-5pm Oct-Apr) fortress lords it over a vineyard-streaked hill.

Completed in 1103, **Allerheiligen Münster** (All Saints' Cathedral; Münster-platz; ⊙10am-noon & 2-5pm Tue-Sun, cloister 7.30am-8pm Mon-Fri, 9am-8pm Sat & Sun), with its beautifully simple cloister, is a rare specimen of the Romanesque style in Switzerland. The art collection of **Museum zu Allerheiligen** (www.allerheiligen.ch; Klosterstrasse 16; adult/child Sfr12/free; ⊙11am-5pm Tue-Sun) has works by Otto Dix and Lucas Cranach the Elder.

✗ p345

The Drive » Taking Rte 4 out of Schaffhausen, it's a very quick trip (5.5km) to Rheinfall, with parking at Schloss Laufen.

- - - - - - - - - - -

TRIP HIGHLIGHT

6 Rheinfall

Ensnared in wispy spray, thunderous **Rheinfall** (Rhine Falls; www.rheinfall.ch) might not compete with Niagara in height (23m), width (150m) or water flow (700 cu metres per second in summer), but Europe's largest waterfall is stunning nonetheless. Trails thread up and along its shore, and viewpoints provide abundant photo ops.

The 1000-year-old medieval castle **Schloss Laufen** (www.schlosslaufen. ch; adult/child Sfr5/3.50; ⊙8am-7pm Jun-Aug, shorter hours Sep-May) overlooks the falls at closer quarters. Buy a ticket at its souvenir shop to walk or take the panoramic lift down to the **Känzeli viewing platform** to fully appreciate the crash-bang spectacle.

During summer, **ferries** (www.maendli.ch; Schloss Laufen to Schlössli Worth adult/child Sfr2/1, round trip Sfr8/4) flit in and out of the water at the bottom of the falls. The best is the round trip that stops at the tall rock in the middle of the falls, from where you can climb to the top and watch the water rush all around.

The Drive » From Rheinfall, get on the A4, then change to the A1 and eventually the A3 to get to Basel in the quickest way possible (128km).

- - - - - - - - - - - - - -

TRIP HIGHLIGHT

❼ Basel

Business-minded Basel's delightful medieval Old Town is centred on **Markt-platz**, in turn dominated by the astonishingly vivid red facade of the 16th-century **Rathaus**. Blending Gothic exteriors with Romanesque interiors, the 13th-century **Münster** (Cathedral; www.baslermuenster.ch; Münsterplatz; ⊙10am-5pm Mon-Fri, to 4pm Sat, 11.30am-5pm Sun) was largely rebuilt after an earthquake in 1356. Renaissance humanist Erasmus of Rotterdam (1466–1536) lies buried in the northern aisle. For views, climb the soaring Gothic **towers**, or visit leafy **Münster Pfalz** for sublime Rhine watching.

The astounding private-turned-public collection, **Fondation Beyeler** (☎061 645 97 00; www.fondation beyeler.ch; Baselstrasse 101, Riehen; adult/child Sfr25/6; ⊙10am-6pm, to 8pm Wed), assembled by former art dealers Hildy and Ernst Beyeler, is housed in a light-filled, open-plan building designed by Renzo Piano. The collection has works by Picasso,

> ### ACID BASE
>
> In 1943 a chemist for Sandoz, Albert Hofmann (1906–2008), accidentally absorbed an experimental compound through his fingertips while searching for a migraine cure and took the world's first 'acid trip'.
>
> Hofmann's discovery was soon taken up by artists and writers such as Aldous Huxley, and by the 1960s flower-power generation.
>
> Basel remains the epicentre of Switzerland's multibillion-franc pharmaceutical industry, with industry giants such as Roche and Novartis based here.

Rothko, Miró and Max Ernst.

Built by Ticino architect Mario Botta, **Museum Jean Tinguely** (☎061 681 93 20; www.tinguely.ch; Paul Sacher-Anlage 2; adult/child Sfr18/free; ⊙11am-6pm Tue-Sun) showcases the playful, mischievous and wacky concoctions of sculptor-turned-mad scientist Jean Tinguely. Pop across the German border to the dazzling **Vitra Design Museum** (www.design-museum.de; Charles-Eames-Strasse 1, Weil am Rhein; adult/child €10/free; ⊙10am-6pm). The main building, designed by Frank Gehry, is surrounded by an ever-expanding bevy of installations by other cutting-edge architects.

✕ ⨎ p345

The Drive » For this last drive, enjoy the longer and slower (95km, 1¾ hours) route through the lush Jura countryside: Rte 18 down to Delémont, then Rte 16 to Biel-Bienne and finally scenic Rte 5 along the beautiful vineyard- and village-lined Bielersee to Ligerz.

- - - - - - - - - - - - - -

❽ Ligerz

This hidden delight sees lush green vines stagger down the steep hillside towards Lake Biel's northern shore. The quaint lakeside hamlet of Ligerz is, simply put, a heavenly place to savour local wines in relaxed surrounds. There's a small **wine museum** (Rebbaumuseum am Bielersee 'Hof'; ☎032 315 21 32; www.rebbaumuseum.ch; adult/child Sfr6/free; ⊙1.30-5pm Sat & Sun May-Oct) and the old-fashioned **Vinifuni funicular** (www.vinifuni.ch; adult one-way Sfr6), which climbs through the vines to hilltop Prêles. On clear days the views across the vines to the snowcapped Bernese Alps are a revelation. A 30-minute lakeside walk to Twann takes you to **Vinothek Viniterra Bielersee** (☎032 315 77 47; www.vinothek-viniterra-bielersee.ch; Im Moos 4; ⊙5-9pm Tue-Fri, 2-8pm Sat, 2-7pm Sun).

✕ ⨎ p345

Eating & Sleeping

Appenzell ➋

✖ Gasthaus Linde Swiss €€

(☎071 787 13 76; Hauptgasse 40; mains Sfr19-32; ⊙noon-2pm & 7-10pm Fri-Wed) This warm, wood-panelled tavern oozes local character and does excellent Appenzell beer fondue. More adventurous diners can tuck into offal specialities.

Stein am Rhein ➍

✖ Burg Hohenklingen Swiss €€

(☎052 741 21 37; www.burghohenklingen. com; Hohenklingenstrasse 1; mains Sfr29.50-52.50; ⊙10am-10pm Tue-Sun) For medieval atmosphere, you can't beat this 12th-century hilltop fortress, with superb views over Stein am Rhein. Tuck into Swiss classics in the Rittersaal (Hall of Knights). It's a 30-minute uphill walk from the Old Town.

⎚ B&B Stein am Rhein B&B €

(☎052 741 45 44; Bollstieg 22; s/d/f Sfr70/130/170; ⚟) Huddled away in a green, quiet corner of town is this charming B&B. The kindly Keller family make you feel instantly at home in their chalet with bright, well-kept rooms kitted out with pine furnishings. Families are *wilkommen*, and biking and kayaking tours can be arranged.

Schaffhausen ➎

✖ Oberhof Swiss €€

(☎052 632 07 70; www.oberhof-schaffhausen. ch; Stadthausgasse 15; mains Sfr31-49; ⊙11.30am-11pm Mon-Fri, 4-11pm Sat) There's always a buzz at Oberhof, which hides a slick, contemporary interior behind its historic facade. The menu skips from creative salads and Thai curries to surf and turf and vegan dishes – everything is super-fresh, nicely presented and served with a smile.

Basel ➐

✖ Volkshaus Basel Brasserie, Bar €€

(☎061 690 93 11; www.volkshaus-basel.ch; Rebgasse 12-14; mains Sfr28-56; ⊙11.30am-2pm & 6-10.30pm Mon-Fri, 11.30am-10.30pm Sat) This stylish Herzog & de Meuron–designed venue is part resto-bar, part gallery and part performance space. For relaxed dining, head for the atmospheric beer garden, in a shady, cobblestoned courtyard. The menu ranges from brasserie classics to more innovative offerings. The hip bar is open 10am to 1am Monday to Saturday.

⎚ Hotel Krafft Hotel €€

(☎061 690 91 30; www.krafftbasel.ch; Rheingasse 12; s Sfr110-150, d Sfr175-265; ⚟) Design-savvy urbanites will love this renovated historic hotel. Sculptural modern chandeliers dangle in the creaky-floored dining room overlooking the Rhine, and minimalist Japanese-style tea bars adorn each landing of the spiral stairs.

Ligerz ➑

✖ Restaurant Aux Trois Amis Swiss €€

(☎032 315 11 44; www.aux3amis.ch; Untergasse 17; mains Sfr28-52; ⊙11am-11pm Thu-Sat, Mon & Tue, to 8pm Sun) A quintessential village bistro with a centuries-old vined facade. In summer, its tree-shaded terrace heaves with punters eating, drinking and gazing at the tumbling vines and the slate-blue water rippling towards St Peter's Island.

⎚ Hotel Kreuz Hotel €€

(☎032 315 11 15; www.kreuz-ligerz.ch; Hauptstrasse 17; s Sfr120-150, d Sfr185-220; P⚟) This lakefront hotel in an old patrician's house with painted shutters has been run by the same welcoming family for generations. It has a Renaissance soul and a garden by the water (swimming allowed). Its bistro serves wine produced from its own vines and great local dishes.

Lavaux Lake Geneva and the wine-
growing area of St-Saphorin

Lake Geneva & Western Switzerland

30

By turns hugging the shore of Lake Geneva and venturing into the lush dairy lands of French-speaking Switzerland, this trip offers dazzling views, rare wines and bucolic bliss.

TRIP HIGHLIGHTS

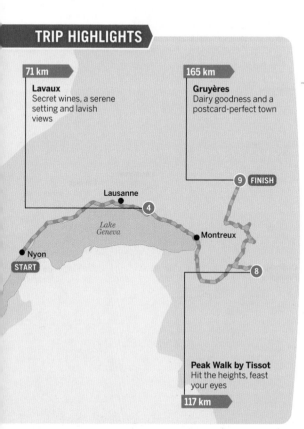

71 km

Lavaux
Secret wines, a serene setting and lavish views

165 km

Gruyères
Dairy goodness and a postcard-perfect town

9 FINISH

Lausanne

4

Lake Geneva

● Montreux

● Nyon
START

8

Peak Walk by Tissot
Hit the heights, feast your eyes

117 km

**4 DAYS
165 KM / 103 MILES**

GREAT FOR...

BEST TIME TO GO

From May to September, when the vineyards put on a show.

 ESSENTIAL PHOTO

Lavaux's terraced vineyards overlooking Lake Geneva.

 BEST FOR FOODIES

Lausanne's dining scene has come into its own and fondue is a regional staple.

347

Lake Geneva & Western Switzerland

Touring Lake Geneva (Western Europe's biggest lake, known as Lac Léman to locals) is a treat; the 570-sq-km lake is the region's summer playground, embellished by the Alps, historic vineyards, chic urban centres, petite *plages* (beaches), beautiful villages, classic castles and the constant play of light and wind upon its surface. Plus, this is the perfect spot to enjoy rare wines, fondue and heavenly meringues under double cream.

❶ Nyon

The wine-producing region between Lausanne and Geneva is known as La Côte (The Coast). From Geneva to Nyon is a 40-minute trip (24km) via Rte 1, which skirts the lake. Of Roman origin, Nyon is a pretty fishing village pierced at its hilltop heart by the white turrets of a textbook castle. **Château de Nyon** (www.chateaudenyon.ch; Place du Château) was started in the 12th century, modified 400 years later and now houses the **Caveau des Vignerons** (Place du

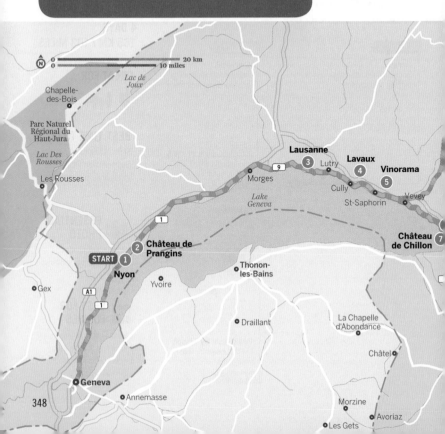

Château; ✪2-9pm Fri & Sat, 11am-8pm Sun), where you can taste five Nyon wines (and charcuterie) for Sfr25. Don't miss the view of Lake Geneva from the terrace. Nyon's ancient history is on display at the **Musée Romain** (Roman Museum; ☎022 361 75 91; www.mrn.ch; Rue Maupertuis 9; adult/child Sfr8/free, 1st Sun of month free; ✪10am-5pm Tue-Sun Apr-Oct, 2-5pm Tue-Sun Nov-Mar), which lies in the foundations of a 1st-century basilica.

✕ p353

The Drive » From Rte 1 in Nyon, it's a short hop (3km) through the leafy landscape to Château de Prangins. Drive along Rte 1, continuing until the château's car

park (make a right turn just after the bus stop named 'Prangins, Les Abériaux'. You'll need to walk from there (signed).

– – – – – – – – – – – – –

② Château de Prangins

A stone's throw from Nyon, charming 18th-century **Cheteâu de Prangins** (www.chateau deprangins.ch; adult/child Sfr10/free; ✪10am-5pm Tue-Sun) houses one of the branches of the **Musée National Suisse**. Swiss history from 1730 to 1920 is covered in satisfying detail, and the lovely *potager* (vegetable garden) and nature trail warrant exploration.

The Drive » Avoid the motorway and stick with Rte 1 for just under an hour (36km). You'll be rewarded with views of the lake, verdant countryside, small towns, orchards and some impressive hedges that stand between you and the discreetly super-rich.

– – – – – – – – – – – – –

③ Lausanne

One of Switzerland's lovelier cities, Lausanne has overcome a reputation for culinary stagnation and

now has a buzzing food scene, with solid drinking choices. Dominated by the grand Gothic **Cathédrale de Notre Dame** (Place de la Cathédrale; ✪9am-7pm Apr-Sep, to 5.30pm Oct-Mar), the city has a full cultural calendar, pretty lakefront, delightful **Old Town** and fab food **market** (Old Town; ✪8am-2pm Wed & Sat). Must-see sights include the aforementioned, and also the wonderful **Musée Olympique** (Olympic Museum; ☎021 621 65 11; www. olympic.org/museum; Quai d'Ouchy 1; adult/child Sfr18/10; ✪9am-6pm May–mid-Oct, 10am-6pm Tue-Sun mid-Oct–Apr) and **Fondation de l'Hermitage** (☎021 320 50 01; www.fondation-hermitage. ch; Rte du Signal 2; adult/child Sfr18/free; ✪10am-6pm Tue, Wed & Fri-Sun, to 9pm Thu).

✕ 🍴 p353

The Drive » From Lausanne, take Rte 9 for a few kilometres until just after Lutry. Turn left on Rte Petite Corniche, passing through petite medieval towns such as Aran and Epesses. The road becomes Rte de la Corniche, taking you up to

LINK YOUR TRIP

31 Geneva to Zürich
Head north for 32km via the A12 from Gruyères to beautiful bilingual Fribourg, in the same canton (county).

32 The Swiss Alps
The fastest route to Arosa, starting point of the A to Z of Swiss Alps, is 330km away, heading west along the A1 and then the A3.

Chexbres. From there, drive east back down to the lakeside, then head west along Rte 9 to St-Saphorin.

TRIP HIGHLIGHT

4 Lavaux

East of Lausanne, the 830-hectare serried ranks of 800-plus-year-old **vineyards** stagger up the steep terraced slopes of Lake Geneva from the Lavaux wine region. They're sufficiently magnificent to be a Unesco World Heritage site. Walking between vines and tasting wines are key reasons to explore the string of villages beaded along this 40km stretch of fertile and wealthy shore. This drive starts as a loop of sorts once you reach **Lutry**, heading up into the vines and villages, before heading down and back along the shore. The prettiest town here and the focus of untold 'I could live here' fantasies is **St-Saphorin**, a little gem with closely packed centuries-old

houses, narrow streets, wine cellars, a church dating from 1530 and a great lunch-spot auberge.

✗ 🛏 p353

The Drive ›› It's a 1.4km, two-minute drive from St-Saphorin to Vinorama. You may even want to walk it, so that you can take advantage of the wine tasting and then walk off its effects.

5 Vinorama

Lavaux Vinorama
(☎021 946 31 31; www.lavaux-vinorama.ch; Rte du Lac 2; ☺10.30am-8.30pm Mon-Sat, to 7pm Sun, closed Mon & Tue Nov-Jun) marries edgy modern architecture with the region's best tipples (some 260 of them). It sits in a designer bunker (fronted by a 15m-long bay window decorated with 6000 metallic pixels inspired by the veins of a vine leaf), at the foot of a terraced vineyard by the lake. Wine-tasting packages cost from Sfr13 to Sfr22, and platters of local cheese or dry sausage cost Sfr12 or Sfr14, respectively.

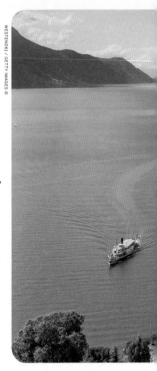

The Drive ›› From Vinorama, it's an easy 14km drive along Rte Cantonal (Rte 9) to Montreux. For the hotel, turn left onto Av des Alpes (100m after Hôtel Villa Toscane). Continue until the roundabout and take the fourth exit for Rue de la Gare (heading up), then continue until you take a slight left onto Rue du Pont, eventually turning left onto Rue du Temple.

6 Montreux

No place does palm trees and yellow awnings better than Montreux on a sunny day. The town's golden microclimate and prized position belie the fact that the place is fairly quiet outside of the

TEN O'CLOCK AND ALL IS WELL!

From the height of Lausanne's cathedral bell tower, a *guet* (night watchman) still calls out the hours into the night, from 10pm to 2am. Four times after the striking of the hour he calls out: 'C'est le guet! Il a sonné dix, il a sonné dix!' (Here's the night watchman! It's 10 o'clock, it's 10 o'clock!'). In earlier times the *guet* kept a lookout for fires around town and other dangers. He was also charged with making sure the townsfolk were well behaved during solemn moments of church services.

Montreux The resort town sits on the northeastern edge of Lake Geneva

Montreux Jazz Festival
(www.montreuxjazz.com;
⊙Jul). The main draw is
the **Queen Studio Experience** (www.mercuryphoenix
trust.com; Rue du Théâtre 9,
Casino Barrière de Montreux;
⊙10.30am-10pm), where
fans of Queen and the
beloved Freddie Mercury
get a kick out of seeing
the studio where Queen
recorded numerous
albums (they owned the
joint from 1979 to 1993).
Evocative memorabilia includes Freddie's
handwritten lyrics and
flamboyant Zandra
Rhodes' stage wear, plus
the original mixing desk.
At lakefront Place du

Marché, in front of the
town's covered market,
there's a 3m-tall **statue**
of Freddie, 'lover of life,
singer of songs'.

🛏 p353

The Drive » Drive along
Rte 9 for 3km until you reach
the castle, located in Veytaux
(parking available).

- - - - - - - - - - - -

**❼ Château de
Chillon**

The magnificent 13th-
century fortress **Château
de Chillon** (☎021 966
89 10; www.chillon.ch; Av
de Chillon 21; adult/child
Sfr12.50/6; ⊙9am-7pm Apr-
Sep, 9.30am-6pm Mar & Oct,

10am-5pm Nov-Feb, last entry
1hr before close) is a maze of
courtyards, towers and
halls filled with arms,
period furniture and
artwork. The landward
side is heavily fortified,
but lakeside presents a
gentler face. Don't miss
the medieval frescos in
the Chappelle St Georges
and the spooky Gothic
dungeons. The fortress
gained fame in 1816 when
Byron wrote *The Prisoner of Chillon*, a poem
about François Bonivard,
thrown into the dungeon
for his seditious ideas
and freed by Bernese
forces in 1536. Byron
carved his name into the

pillar to which Bonivard was supposedly chained.

The Drive » From Château de Chillon, Rte 9 heads east to exit 17. From here take Rte 11 through Aigle (making sure to catch sight of its castle surrounded by vineyards), before ascending via the same winding road through forested countryside topped with rocky peaks to Col du Pillon (parking), just past Les Diablerets. All told, it's 38km (about 45 minutes).

TRIP HIGHLIGHT

⑧ Peak Walk by Tissot

Opened in 2014, the feat of engineering known as **Peak Walk** (Col du Pillon, Les Diablerets; ☺9am-4.30pm, closed 2 weeks mid-Oct) allows you to stroll between sky-scraping peaks and feast on views of iconic mountains such as Eiger, Mönch, Jungfrau, the Matterhorn and Mont Blanc. The 107m-long span has viewfinders (with names

of the peaks) that overlook the famous Glacier3000 ski station. From the car park at Col du Pillon, take the **cable car** (return adult/child under 9 Sfr79/free) to Cabane and then to the Mario Botta–designed station at Scex Rouge (15 minutes; 2971m).

The Drive » Rte 11 and Rte 190 connect Col du Pillon with Gruyères (55km, 70 minutes) through countryside and quaint chalet-filled villages (Les Mosses has a sweet wood-shingled church). From Col du Pillon, retrace your drive on Rte 11 and follow signs to Bulle. From Montbovon, the road skirts the train tracks, but just past Estavannens, take a left (Rte de Gruyères).

TRIP HIGHLIGHT

⑨ Gruyères

This dreamy village of 15th to 17th-century houses tumbling down a hillock has a cobblestone heart and the

postcard-perfect **Château de Gruyères** (☎026 921 21 02; www.chateau-gruyeres.ch; Rue du Château 8; adult/child Sfr10/3; ☺9am-6pm Apr-Oct, 10am-4.30pm Nov-Mar) as its crowning glory. The hard AOC Gruyère cheese (the village name is Gruyères but the 's' is dropped for the cheese) has been made for centuries in the surrounding Alpine pastures; learn all about it at **La Maison du Gruyère** (☎026 921 84 00; www.lamaisondugruyere.ch; Place de la Gare 3; adult/child Sfr7/3; ☺9am-7pm Jun-Sep, to 6pm Oct-May), with daily cheesemaking demonstrations, a shop and information about area walks. It's 1.5km from Gruyères, in Pringy. An adult combined ticket with the château costs Sfr14.50.

✕ ⊨ p353

Eating & Sleeping

Nyon ❶

✕ Hôtel-Restaurant de la Plage
Swiss €€

(☎022 364 10 35; www.hoteldelaplage.info; Chemin de la Falaise, Gland; mains Sfr37-86; ⏲noon-2pm & 7-9.30pm Tue-Sun Feb–mid-Dec; P 🐾) This low-key lakeside hotel, 7km north of Nyon, gets packed, thanks to some of Lake Geneva's best *filets de perche* (perch fillets), pan-fried in a divinely buttery, herbed secret recipe sauce; fries and green salad included. Unless you specify otherwise, you automatically get two (very large) servings.

Lausanne ❸

✕ Eligo
Modern European €€

(☎021 320 00 03; www.eligo-restaurant.ch; Rue du Flon 8; mains Sfr32-58, 4-/6-course dinner Sfr90/150; ⏲noon-2pm & 7-10pm Tue-Sat) With a name from the Latin 'to choose', Lausanne's glam newcomer, replete with chic concrete-and-wood interior and Chef Guillaume Reineix at the helm, keeps it simple with a judicious menu grounded in local, market-fresh ingredients and technical prowess. Reservations are advised.

🛏 Hotel Carlton
Hotel €€

(www.carltonlausanne.com; Av de Cour 4; s/d/ste from Sfr125/155/215; P ❄ 🛜) The Carlton is known for discreet elegance, having hosted luminaries such as Serge Gainsbourg. With a shaded terrace and 47 elegant, soundproofed rooms (all with marble bathroom), the hotel is located in a residential area close to sights such as the Olympic Museum.

Lavaux ❹

✕ Auberge de l'Onde
Swiss €€€

(☎021 925 49 00; www.aubergedelonde.ch; St-Saphorin; bar mains Sfr28-40, rotisserie mains Sfr38-62; ⏲noon-2pm & 7-9.30pm Wed-Sun) A wonderful spot for rotisserie meats and imaginative Med-influenced dishes. It's also great for a cheeky glass of wine or coffee in the *pinte* (bar) at ground level.

🛏 Hotel Lavaux
Hotel €€

(☎021 799 93 93; www.hotellavaux.ch; Rte Cantonal; s/d with lake view from Sfr164/210; P 🛜) Perfectly placed to take in views across the lake or of the famous Lavaux vineyards, Lavaux's nattiest hotel has sleekly simple and contemporary rooms, and a summer terrace perfect for sundowners.

Montreux ❻

🛏 Tralala Hôtel
Boutique Hotel €€

(☎021 963 49 73; www.tralalahotel.ch; Rue du Temple 2; r/ste from Sfr110/200; ❄ @ 🛜) This Old Town boutique hotel references Montreux's extraordinary musical heritage. The 33 rooms come in three sizes – S ('Small & Sexy'), L or XL – and each pays homage to a different artist.

Gruyères ❾

✕ Le Chalet de Gruyères
Swiss €€

(☎026 921 21 54; www.chalet-gruyeres.ch; Rue du Bourg 53; fondue & raclette from Sfr30; ⏲noon-10pm) A quintessential Gruyères address, this cosy wooden chalet strung with cow bells and flowers has all-day fodder (fondue, raclette, grilled meats).

🛏 La Ferme du Bourgoz
B&B €

(☎026 921 26 23; www.lafermedubourgoz. ch; Chemin du Bourgo 14; s/d from Sfr80/100; P) Authentic cheese dreams are guaranteed at the cheesemaking Murith family's home. Simple, cosy rooms and unbeatable farm-fresh breakfasts, plus chunks of their Gruyère for sale.

Jungfrau Region Hikers taking
in the view of Eiger's north face

Geneva to Zürich

31

Connect the dots between Switzerland's two biggest cities on a trip that takes you through its enigmatic heartland, historic cities, spine-tingling ascents and a world-famous mountain trio.

TRIP HIGHLIGHTS

0 km

Geneva
Cosmopolitan city and Old Town grace galore

481 km

Zürich
Culturally vibrant city with a post-industrial edge

FINISH
9

Bern

Lucerne

8

Fribourg

Stanserhorn
An open-air cable car; the perfect Lake Lucerne panorama

402 km

1
START

7 DAYS
481 KM / 300 MILES

GREAT FOR...

BEST TIME TO GO

Late spring, summer and autumn, when the light and weather are best.

ESSENTIAL PHOTO

The verdant Emmental region exemplifies pastoral perfection.

BEST FOR CULTURE

Zürich's mighty museums and relentless nightlife are intoxicating.

31 Geneva to Zürich

Rather than take a straight line from Geneva to Zürich, this trip gives you room to roam some of Switzerland's finest sights: small cities with charming Old Towns, heaven-sent lakes with dreamy views, winding roads through countryside that is by turns bucolic and wild, an adventure capital with the perfect setting, a train ride to the top of Europe and scenic ascents that will have you gasping, all book-ended by Switzerland's cultural capitals.

TRIP HIGHLIGHT

❶ Geneva

Cosmopolitan Geneva is a rare blend: a multicultural population chattering in every language under the sun, a distinctly French feel, one of the world's most expensive cities, a stronghold of the Protestant Reformation, a synonymity with numbered bank accounts and a humanitarian haven.

With a whole day and night, schedule time for Geneva's magnificent **Old Town**. Waterside attractions exert a strong pull, so make a beeline for the emblematic **Jet d'Eau** (Quai Gustave-Ador) and the egalitarian public swimming baths at **Bains des Pâquis** (☎022 732 29 74; www.bains-des-paquis.ch; Quai du Mont-Blanc 30; ☺9am-8pm mid-Apr–mid-Sep).

Plenty of museums will tempt you: among the best are the **Musée d'Art Moderne et Contemporain** (MAMCO; ☎022 320 61 22; www.mamco.ch; Rue des Vieux-Grenadiers 10; adult/child Sfr8/free; ☺noon-6pm Tue-Fri, 11am-6pm Sat & Sun) the **Musée International de la Croix-Rouge et du Croissant-Rouge** (International Red Cross & Red Crescent Museum; www. redcrossmuseum.ch; Av de la Paix 17; adult/child Sfr15/7; ☺10am-6pm Tue-Sun Apr-Oct, to 5pm Nov-Mar), the new **ICT Discovery** (☎022 730 61 55; www.ictdiscovery.org; Rue de Varembé 2; ☺10am-1pm & 2-5pm Mon-Fri) and the lavish timepieces of **Patek Philipe Museum** (☎022 807 09 10; www.patekmuseum. com; Rue des Vieux-Grenadiers 7; adult/child Sfr10/free; ☺2-6pm Tue-Fri, 10am-6pm Sat).

If you're after a behind-the-scenes glimpse of the UN or the Large Hadron Collider, prebook a tour of the **Palais des Nations**

(☏022 907 48 96; www.unog.
ch; Av de la Paix 14; adult/child
Sfr12/7; ☺10am-4pm Mon-Sat
Jul & Aug, 10am-noon & 2-4pm
Mon-Sat Sep-Jun) or **CERN**
(☏022 767 84 84; www.cern.
ch; Meyrin; ☺ guided tour 11am
Mon-Sat, 1pm Mon, Tue, Thu &
Fri), respectively.

See also the Stretch
Your Legs walking tour
for Geneva on p388.

LINK YOUR TRIP

29 Northern Switzerland
From end-point Zürich
it's an easy one-hour,
85km drive heading east
to St Gallen, the starting
point of this trip.

32 The Swiss Alps
It's a two-hour
(147km) drive eastward
from Zürich to Arosa,
the starting point of the
Swiss Alps whirl.

p363

The Drive » From Geneva, head west via the A1 until the A9 (follow signs to Vevey/Montreux). Take exit 11 and follow signs for Lutry. From Lutry, take Rte 9 (direction Vevey) until Cully, then head up Rte de la Corniche to Chexbres. Next follow Rte du Genevrex and get on the A9, followed by the A12 to Fribourg (143km total).

- - - - - - - - - - - - - -

② Fribourg

Nowhere is Switzerland's language divide felt more keenly than in Fribourg (Freiburg or 'Free Town'), a medieval city where the inhabitants on the west bank of the River Sarine speak French, and those on the east bank of the Sanne speak German. Sights that merit a look-see include the bohemian **Espace Jean Tinguely – Niki de Saint Phalle** (☑026 305 51 40; www.mahf.ch; Rue de Morat 2; adult/child Sfr6/free; ⊙11am-6pm Wed & Fri-Sun, to 8pm

Thu), the evocative **Old Town** filled with Gothic facades, the **Musée d'Art et d'Histoire** (☑026 305 51 40; www.mahf.ch; Rue de Morat 12; adult/child Sfr8/free; ⊙11am-6pm Tue, Wed & Fri-Sun, to 8pm Thu) and the outsize **Cathédrale de St Nicolas de Myre** (www.cathedrale-fribourg.ch; Rue des Chanoines 3; tower adult/child Sfr3.50/1; ⊙9.30am-6pm Mon-Fri, 9am-4pm Sat, 2-5pm Sun, tower 10am-noon & 2-5pm Mon-Fri, 10am-4pm Sat, 2-5pm Sun Apr-Oct) with its 74m-tall **tower**. Be sure to make time for a couple of the city's bohemian cafe-bars, such as Le Port (p363) or **Café Culturel de l'Ancienne Gare** (☑026 322 57 72; Esplanade de l'Ancienne-Gare 3; ⊙9am-11.30pm Mon-Thu, 9am-3am Fri, 1pm-3am Sat, 11am-midnight Sun).

p363

The Drive » We've chosen a longish (103km, one hour and 50 minutes) scenic route along

winding roads through lovely small towns in Fribourg and Bern cantons, with unspoiled countryside aplenty. Head first to the village of Charmey via Rte 189, then to Boltingen. Next take Rte 11 to Speiz on Lake Thun, from where you'll follow Rte 8 to Interlaken.

- - - - - - - - - - - - - -

③ Interlaken

Once Interlaken made the Victorians swoon with mountain vistas from the chandelier-lit confines of grand hotels; today it makes daredevils scream with adrenaline-loaded adventures. Straddling the glittering Lakes Thun and Brienz and dazzled

LOCAL KNOWLEDGE:
FRIBOURG'S FILTHY
FUNICULAR

Nowhere else in Europe does a funicular lurch up the mountainside with the aid of stinky sewage water (on certain days it smells as you'd expect). Constructed in 1899 and managed by the Cardinal Brewery until 1965 (when the municipality took over), the **Funiculaire de Fribourg** links the lower town with the upper. It runs every six minutes, and the ride in one of two counterbalancing water-powered carriages from the lower Pertuis station (121m; Place du Pertuis) to the upper station (618m; Rte des Alpes) takes two minutes.

Bern The city's Zytglogge (Clock Tower) is an important landmark

by the pearly whites of Eiger, Mönch and Jungfrau, the scenery is mind-blowing. Check out the views from **Harder Kulm** (www.harderkulm.ch), or do a daredevil activity with **Outdoor Interlaken** (☎033 826 77 19; www.outdoor-interlaken.ch; Hauptstrasse 15; ⏰8am-7pm), organised in advance. Leave the car in Interlaken after spending the night here and head to the Top of Europe (Jungfraujoch) very early the next morning.

🛏 p363

The Drive » From Interlaken to Bern is a one-hour (54km)

drive via Lake Thun's Seestrasse, past turreted Schloss Oberhoffen and art-nouveau-meets-neorenaissance Schloss Hünegg. After Thun, you'll get to the country's capital quickly via the A6.

- - - - - - - - - - - -

❹ Bern

Wandering through the picture-postcard **Old Town**, with its laid-back, riverside air, it's hard to believe that Bern (Berne in French) is the Swiss capital, but it is, and a Unesco World Heritage site to boot. The flag-festooned, cobbled centre, rebuilt in distinctive grey-green sandstone after a devastating 1405

fire, is a delight, with 6km of covered arcades, cellar shops and bars, and fantastical folk figures frolicking on 16th-century fountains, such as the **Kindlifresserbrunnen** (Kornhausplatz). Be sure to visit Bern's **Münster** (www.bernermuenster.ch; Münsterplatz 1; tower adult/child Sfr5/2; ⏰10am-5pm Mon-Sat, 11.30am-5pm Sun May–mid-Oct, noon-4pm Mon-Fri, 10am-5pm Sat, 11.30am-4pm Sun rest of year), the beautiful **Zytglogge** (Marktgasse), the famous **Bären Park** (Bear Park; www.baerenpark-bern.ch; ⏰9.30am-5pm), the architecturally daring

ISLAND DINING

Genevan living is easy in summer when a constant crowd throngs the lakefront quays to hang out in pop-up terrace bars such as **La Terrasse** (www.laterrasse.ch; Quai du Mont-Blanc 31; ☺8am-midnight Apr-Sep), the fashionista spot by the water to see and be seen. Meander away from Quai du Mont-Blanc to uncover a brilliant trio of beloved summertime shacks on the water's edge – alfresco and effortlessly cool.

The right-bank address is refreshingly casual: Rhône-side **Terrasse Le Paradis** (☎079 665 35 73; www.terrasse-paradis.ch; Quai Turrettini; sandwiches & salads Sfr10-14; ☺10am-9pm Jun-Sep) is the type of cafe that practically begs you to pull out a book and stay all day in its deckchairs arranged down steps to the water while sipping beakers of homemade *citronnade* (lemonade). 'Paradise' does not serve alcohol, but the pots of green-mint tea flow and the wholly affordable sandwiches, salads and legendary *taboulé* hit the spot.

Le Bateau Lavoir (Passerelle des Lavandières; ☺11am-midnight Mon-Thu, 11am-2am Fri, 5pm-2am Sat May-Sep) is an eye-catching boat with rooftop terrace moored between the old market hall and Pont de la Coulouvrenière. Its cabin-size dining area cooks fondue and other basic local dishes, the crowd is hip and there is a 360-degree lake view. Its very design and name evokes the wash-house boats – yes, where undies et al were washed – that floated here in the 17th century.

Then there's **La Barje** (Terrasse des Lavandières; www.labarje.ch; Promenade des Lavandières; ☺11am-midnight Mon-Fri, 3pm-midnight Sat & Sun Apr-Sep), not a barge at all but a vintage caravan with tin roof and candy-striped facade, parked on the grassy banks of the Rhône near the Bâtiment des Forces Motrices. The beer and music are plentiful, outside concerts and art performances pull huge crowds, and proceeds go towards helping young people in difficulty.

Zentrum Paul Klee (☎031 359 01 01; www.zpk.org; Monument im Fruchtland 3; adult/child Sfr20/7, audioguide Sfr6; ☺10am-5pm Tue-Sun) and the well-endowed **Kunstmuseum** (Museum of Fine Arts; ☎031 328 09 44; www.kunstmuseumbern.ch; Hodlerstrasse 8-12; adult/child Sfr7/free; ☺10am-9pm Tue, to 5pm Wed-Sun).

✕ 🛏 p363

The Drive » Leave Bern via the A6 and take Krauchthalstrasse (35 minutes, about 24km) through verdant countryside to Burgdorf. From Burgdorf to Affoltern im Emmental, 6km to the east, is a scenic drive past old farmsteads proudly bedecked with flower boxes, neat woodpiles and kitchen gardens. Rte 23 between Affoltern and Langnau im Emmental is 21km (25 minutes).

- - - - - - - - - - - -

❺ Emmental Region

After so much city time, the postcard-perfect landscapes of rural Switzerland beckon, with the bucolic idyll that is the Emmental region, where iconic and holey Emmental (Swiss) cheese is produced. To see how the cheese is made, head to **Emmentaler Schaukäserei** (☎034 435 16 11; www.showdairy. ch; Schaukäsereistrasse 6, Affoltern; ☺9am-6.30pm Apr-Oct, to 5pm Nov-Mar) in Affoltern.

The region's gateway towns of Burgdorf and Langnau im Emmental preside over a mellow patchwork of quiet villages, grazing cows and fabulous farm chalets with vast barns and overhanging roofs, strung out along the banks of the Emme river. Burgdorf (literally 'castle village') is split into an Upper and Lower Town. The natural highlight of the Oberstadt (Upper Town) is the 12th-century **Schloss** (castle), with its drawbridge, thick stone walls and trio of museums.

The Drive » From Langnau im Emmental, take Rte 10 for 30 minutes (23km), crossing over from Bern canton to Lucerne canton, until you reach Schüpfheim, the heart of the Entlebuch biosphere.

- - - - - - - - - - -

6 Unesco Biosphere Entlebuch

The 39,000-plus-sq-km **Entlebuch area** (www.biosphaere.ch; a mixed mountain and highland ecosystem) was declared a Unesco Biosphere Reserve in 2001. Far from being a lonely wilderness outpost, the reserve is home to some 17,000 people keen to preserve their traditional dairy-farming lifestyle. The landscape of karst formations, sprawling moors (some 25% of the area), Alpine pastures and mountain streams, which rise from 600m to some 2350m above sea level, makes for some stirring scenery. The park office is in Schüpfheim.

The Drive » Driving through Entlebuch from Schüpfheim, you'll take the Panoramastrasse (which deserves to be more famous) to the town of Giswil (Obwalden canton; 50 minutes, 37km). Next, follow the signs to Lucerne (Luzern in German) along the A8 (30 minutes, 30km).

- - - - - - - - - - -

7 Lucerne

Recipe for a gorgeous Swiss city: take a cobalt lake ringed by mountains of myth (Pilatus, Rigi), add a well-preserved medieval **Altstadt** (Old Town), then sprinkle with covered bridges **Kapellbrücke** (Chapel Bridge) and **Spreuerbrücke** (Spreuer Bridge; btwn Kasernenplatz & Mühlenplatz), sunny plazas, candy-coloured houses and waterfront promenades. Legend has it that an angel with a light showed the first settlers where to build a chapel in Lucerne, and today it still has amazing grace.

One minute it's nostalgic (its emotive **lion monument**; Löwendenkmal; Denkmalstrasse), the next highbrow, with concerts at acoustic marvel **Kultur und Kongresszentrum** (KKL; ☏tour reservations 041 226 79 50; www.kkl-luzern.ch; Europaplatz; guided tour adult/child Sfr15/9) and the peerless Picasso collection of **Museum Sammlung Rosengart** (☏041 220 16 60; www.rosengart.ch; Pilatusstrasse 10; adult/student Sfr18/16; ⏱10am-6pm Apr-Oct, 11am-5pm Nov-Mar). Crowd-pleasers such as **Verkehrshaus** (Swiss Museum of Transport; ☏041 370 44 44; www.verkehrshaus.ch; Lidostrasse 5; adult/child Sfr30/15; ⏱10am-6pm Apr-Oct, to 5pm Nov-Mar; 👶) and the city's surrounding natural wonders never fail to impress, while balmy summers and golden autumns ensure this 'city of lights' shines constantly.

🍴 🛏 p363

The Drive » A fast 15-minute, 15km journey along the A2 will get you from Lucerne to Stans' Stansstaderstrasse 19, from where the journey up to Stanserhorn begins.

- - - - - - - - - - -

TRIP HIGHLIGHT

8 Stanserhorn

Looming above the lake, 1898m **Stanserhorn** (www.stanserhorn.ch) boasts 360-degree vistas of **Lake Lucerne**, **Mt Titlis**, **Mt Pilatus** and the **Bernese Alps**, among others. Getting to the summit is half the fun. The journey starts with a ride on a vintage 19th-century funicular from Stans to Kälti; from here, the nearly transparent **CabriO** (☏041 618 80 40; www.cabrio.ch; Stansstaderstrasse 19, Stans, ticket office; all-inclusive funicular & cable-car fare adult/child one-way Sfr37/9.25, return Sfr74/18.50, online boarding pass Sfr5; ⏱mid-Apr–early Nov), launched in 2012 as the world's first cable car with an open upper deck, takes you the rest of the way, offering amazing on-the-go views.

On sunny days and when large numbers of travellers are expected, you'll need to book an online 'boarding pass' to confirm your time of departure and subsequent return.

At the summit there's the star-shaped **Rondorama**, the region's only revolving restaurant, which rotates 360 degrees every 43 minutes. Kids love the nearby **marmot park**, where the

DETOUR:
JUNGFRAUJOCH: THE TOP OF EUROPE

Presided over by monolithic **Eiger**, **Mönch** and **Jungfrau** (Ogre, Monk and Maiden), the crown jewels of Bernese Oberland's Alpine scenery, will make your heart skip a beat.

The 'big three' peaks have an enduring place in mountaineering legend, particularly the 3970m Eiger, whose fearsome north wall remained unconquered until 1938. Today, it takes only 2½ hours from Interlaken Ost (return fare Sfr204.40) by train to **Jungfraujoch** (3454m), Europe's highest station. From May through to October, the Good Morning Ticket costs Sfr145 if you take the first train (6.35am from Interlaken Ost) and leave the summit by 1pm.

From Kleine Scheidegg (the last stage of the journey), the train burrows through the Eiger before arriving at the Sphinx meteorological station. Opened in 1912, the tunnel took 3000 men 16 years to drill. Along the way, the Eigerwand and Eismeer stops have panoramic windows offering glimpses across rivers of crevassed ice. Good weather is *essential* for this journey; check beforehand on www.jungfrau. ch and always take warm clothing, sunglasses and sunscreen. Within the Sphinx weather station there's a nice sculpture gallery, restaurants, indoor viewpoints and a souvenir shop. Outside there are views of the 23km-long **Aletsch Glacier**. On cloudless days, the views stretch as far as the Black Forest in Germany.

When you tire (as if!) of the view, you can zip across the frozen plateau on a flying fox, dash downhill on a sled or snow disc, or enjoy a bit of tame skiing or boarding at the **Snow Park**. A day pass covering all activities costs adult/child Sfr45/25.

If you cross the glacier along the prepared path, in around an hour you reach the **Mönchsjochhütte** (☎033 971 34 72; www.moenchsjoch.ch; dm/d with half-board Sfr28/64; ☺late Mar–mid-Oct) at 3650m, where hardcore rock climbers psyche themselves up to tackle the Eiger or Mönch.

critters can be observed in a near-natural habitat.

The Drive » Retrace your route along the A2 and head in the direction of Lucerne before changing to the A4 and following the signs to Zürich (50 minutes, 65km).

TRIP HIGHLIGHT

9 Zürich

Culturally vibrant, efficiently run and attractively set at the meeting of river and lake, Zürich is constantly recognised as one of the world's most liveable cities. It's a savvy, hard-working financial centre,

yet Switzerland's largest and wealthiest metropolis has an artsy, postindustrial edge. Much of the Old Town, with its winding lanes and quaint squares, is lovingly intact. Must-see sights include the glorious **Fraumünster** (www.frau muenster.ch; Münsterhof; ☺9am-6pm Apr-Oct, 10am-4pm Nov-Mar), with its Marc Chagall stained-glass windows, the **Grossmünster** (www.grossmuenster.ch; Grossmünsterplatz; ☺10am-6pm Mar-Oct, to 5pm Nov-Feb) with its salt-and-pepper-shaker steeples, and the excellent **Kunsthaus** (☎044

253 84 84; www.kunsthaus.ch; Heimplatz 1; adult/child Sfr15/ free, Wed free; ☺10am-8pm Wed-Fri, to 6pm Tue, Sat & Sun), which holds an impressive permanent collection. For contemporary cool, walk around Züri-West (p386). In summer, the fun revolves around the pools of the lake and river, such as **Seebad Utoquai** (☎044 251 61 51; Utoquai 49; adult/ child Sfr7/3.50; ☺7am-8pm mid-May–mid-Sep), **Frauenbad** (Stadthausquai) and **Männerbad** (Badweg 10).

✘ p363

Eating & Sleeping

Geneva ❶

✖ Brasserie des Halles
de l'Île
European €€

(☎022 311 08 88; www.brasseriedeshallesdelile.ch; Place de l'Île 1; mains Sfr20-50; ⓣ10.30am-midnight Sun & Mon, to 1am Tue-Thu, to 2am Fri & Sat) An old market hall on an island, this industrial-style venue produces a cocktail of aperitifs, after-dark DJs and fresh fare. Best seat in the house is a terrace hanging over the water.

Fribourg ❷

✖ Le Port
Cafe, Bar €€

(☎026 321 22 26; www.leport.ch; Planche-Inférieure 5; ⓣ10am-11pm Tue-Sun) In a former gas warehouse on the banks of the Sarine, the Port bursts with energy. Hang out on its shady riverside terrace enjoying lunchtime platters, or live bands and dancing at night.

🛏 Auberge aux 4
Vents
Boutique Hotel €€

(☎026 347 36 00; www.aux4vents.ch; Res Balzli Grandfrey 124; s Sfr130-170, d Sfr180-260, s/d/tr/q with shared bathroom Sfr65/130/170/200; P 🛏) 'Stylish' scarcely does justice to this eight-room inn, with its dreamy Blue Room sporting a bathtub that rolls out on rails through the window for a soak beneath the stars.

Interlaken ❸

🛏 Victoria-Jungfrau Grand
Hotel & Spa
Luxury Hotel €€€

(☎033 828 26 10; www.victoria-jungfrau.ch; Höheweg 41; d Sfr400-800, ste Sfr600-1000; P @ 🛜 🛏) The impeccable service here evokes a bygone era, with the perfect melding of well-preserved art-nouveau features, modern luxury, stellar dining and plum Jungfrau views.

Bern ❹

✖ Altes Tramdepot
Swiss €€

(☎031 368 14 15; www.altestramdepot.ch; Am Bärengraben; mains Sfr18-37; ⓣ11am-12.30am) At this cavernous microbrewery, Swiss staples compete against microbrews for your appetite.

🛏 Hotel Goldener Schlüssel
Hotel €€

(☎031 311 02 16; www.goldener-schluessel.ch; Rathausgasse 72; s Sfr148-185, d Sfr190-260; 🛜) This comfortable 500-year-old hotel has updated rooms in the Old Town.

Lucerne ❼

✖ Grottino 1313
Italian €€

(☎041 610 13 13; www.grottino1313.ch; Industriestrasse 7; 2-course lunch menu Sfr20; ⓣ11am-2pm & 6-11.30pm Mon-Fri, 6-11.30pm Sat, 9am-2pm Sun) A welcome escape, this relaxed yet stylish eatery with a candlelit interior serves seasonal menus featuring creative pasta dishes, meats cooked over an open fire and scrumptious desserts.

🛏 Château Gütsch
Hotel €€€

(☎041 289 14 14; www.chateau-guetsch.ch; Kanonenstrasse; d Sfr330-570, ste Sfr445-1260; 🛜) The setting is incomparable at this fairy-tale hilltop palace dating from 1888. Many rooms and suites enjoy sweeping views over Lake Lucerne, as do the bar and breakfast terrace. The decor features lavish details such as silver claw-footed bathtubs.

Zürich ❾

✖ Alpenrose
Swiss €€

(☎044 271 39 19; Fabrikstrasse 12; mains Sfr26-42; ⓣ11am-midnight Wed-Fri, 6.15-11pm Sat & Sun) With its timber-clad walls, 'No Polka Dancing' warning and multiregional Swiss cuisine, the Alpenrose exudes charm. Specialities include *Pizokel*, a savoury kind of *Spätzli* (egg noodles) from Graubünden.

Zermatt *The Matterhorn's majestic peak rises in the distance*

Classic Trip

The Swiss Alps

32

From Arosa to Zermatt, this zigzagging trip is the A to Z of Switzerland's astounding Alpine scenery, with majestic peaks, formidable panoramas, cable-car rides and local charm.

TRIP HIGHLIGHTS

612 km

Zermatt
Switzerland's Alpine heart beats strongest here

77 km

Vals
A modern architectural jewel embellishes this remote spa town

Grindelwald

Schilthorn (2970m)

Andermatt

● Arosa
START

2

11

12
FINISH

Aletsch Glacier
A mesmerising marvel, viewed from on-high

538 km

---

7 DAYS
612 KM / 382 MILES

GREAT FOR...

BEST TIME TO GO

This trip can be done year-round, although certain mountain passes may be closed to vehicular traffic.

ESSENTIAL PHOTO

The magical Matterhorn is the ultimate mountain photo op.

BEST FOR OUTDOORS

Whatever the season, the Alps offer activities galore.

Classic Trip

32 The Swiss Alps

A natural barrier, the Alps are both a blessing and a burden when it comes to tripping around Switzerland. The soul-stirring views are stupendous, but you have to get over, around them or go through them to reach the next one. Starting in Graubünden's Arosa and finishing in Valais' Zermatt, this trip visits five cantons via hairpin bends, valley highways, tunnels, passes and cable cars to bring you the best.

① Arosa

Framed by the peaks of **Weisshorn**, **Hörnli** and moraine-streaked **Schiesshorn**, Arosa is a great Alpine all-rounder: perfect for downhill and cross-country skiing in winter, hiking and downhill biking in summer, and heaps of activities for families year-round. Although only 30km southeast of Chur (Switzerland's oldest city), getting here involves a series of 365 hairpin bends so challenging that Arosa cannot be reached by postal buses. Once here, you may want to revel in the beauty of the Mario Botta–designed **Tschuggen Bergoase Spa** (http://en.tschuggen.ch/spa; Tschuggen Grand Hotel; nonguest morning/evening pass Sfr65, massage from Sfr80; ⊗7am-9pm), an architectural statement built at the foot of the mountains. The recurring leaf-shaped motifs throughout the structures look particularly striking when illuminated at night.

✕ p375

The Drive » The trip from Arosa to Vals takes 79km and 1¾ hours. First, head back towards Chur, then take Rte 19 to Ilanz, from where you drive a delightful road that passes through Uors and St Martin before arriving at Vals (1252m). About 2km short of the village, you emerge into Alpine pastures, liberally scattered with chalets and shepherds' huts.

② Vals

Shadowing the course of the babbling **Glogn** (Glenner) stream south, the luxuriantly green **Valsertal** (Vals Valley) is full of sleepy hamlets and thundering waterfalls. Vals stretches 2km along its glittering stream. The secret of this chocolate-box village and its soothing waters is out since Basel-born architect Peter Zumthor worked architectural magic to transform **Therme Vals** (☎081 926 89 61; www.therme-vals.ch; adult/child Sfr80/52, with Vals guest card Sfr45/30; ⊗11am-8pm) into a temple of cutting-edge cool.

Using 60,000 slabs of local quartzite, Zumthor created one of the country's most enchanting thermal spas. Aside from heated indoor and outdoor pools, this greystone labyrinth hides all sorts of watery nooks and crannies, cleverly lit and full of cavernous atmosphere. You can drift away in the bath-warm Feuerbad (42°C) and perfumed Blütenbad, sweat it out in the steam room and cool down in the teeth-chattering Eisbad.

🛏 p375

The Drive » Take the road back to Ilanz, then continue on

Landquart
E43

Chur
28

ns-
ax
Ilanz

Arosa ①

3 START

A13

Zillis

Silvaplana

Maloggia

hiavenna

ITALY San Martino

SS36

SS38

ravedona Morbegno

Ice
mo

Vezio

Parco
Regionale
Bergamasche

Pasturo Lenna

LINK YOUR TRIP

30 **Lake Geneva & Western Switzerland**
Zermatt is three hours (245km) east of Geneva, which is the starting point of Trip 30.

31 **Geneva to Zürich**
Arosa is a two-hour drive east (147km) on the A3 from Zürich, the end point of Trip 31.

Rte 19 until you reach Disentis/Mustér (50km, 55 minutes).

③ Disentis Abbey

Disentis/Mustér's Benedictine monastery, **Kloster Disentis** (www.kloster-disentis.ch; Via Claustra 1, Disentis/Mustér; museum adult/child Sfr7/3; ⏱ museum 2-5pm Tue, Thu & Sat Jun-Oct), which rises like a vision above the town, has a lavishly stuccoed baroque church attached. A monastery has stood here since the 8th century, but the present immense complex dates from the 18th century. Left of the church entrance is a door to the **Klostermuseum**, crammed with memorabilia. Head left upstairs to the **Marienkirche**, a chapel with Romanesque origins filled with ex-voto images from people in need of (or giving thanks for) a miraculous intervention from the Virgin Mary. If you're peckish, a handy (and very good-value) on-site cafe/takeaway has soups, salads and specialities.

The Drive » Disentis is an exhilarating (40 minutes, 32km) drive along Rte 19 and the twisting Oberalp Pass (2044m), which connects Graubünden and Uri cantons. In winter, the Oberalp Pass is closed to cars, but a car train

> **LOCAL KNOWLEDGE: ZUMDORF**
>
> If the grand scale of this trip seems overwhelming, the antidote surely lies in a quick detour to Switzerland's smallest village, **Zumdorf** (Uri canton), little more than a cluster of small buildings on the Furkastrasse and a population that can be counted on one hand. Despite its diminutive size, it has a place to eat, **Restaurant Zum Dörfli** (📞 041 887 01 32; www.zumdoerfli.ch; Furkastrasse; mains Sfr26-40), specialising in Swiss dishes (especially rösti) and venison (when in season). Find it 6km southwest of Andermatt's centre.

connects Sedrun on Rte 19 and Andermatt (three services daily in winter, two in spring). Reservations are essential. Call 📞 027 927 77 40 or visit www.matterhorngotthardbahn.ch.

TRIP HIGHLIGHT

④ Andermatt

Blessed with austere mountain appeal, Andermatt (Uri canton) contrasts low-key village charm (despite a recent five-star development) with big wilderness. Once an important staging-post on the north–south St Gotthard route, it's now bypassed by the tunnel, but remains a major crossroads near four major Alpine passes (Susten, Oberalp, St Gotthard and Furka), making it a terrific base for **hiking** and **cycling**. The tourist office distributes free booklets outlining these opportunities.

One popular hike leads from the Oberalp Pass to sparkly **Lai da Tuma**, the

source of the Rhine; the 11km round trip takes three to four hours, with 500m elevation gain.

A walk around and along **Gotthardstrasse** reveals textbook dark-wood central Swiss architecture, often weighed down with either geraniums or snow.

Skiers in the know flock to 2963m **Gemsstock** (www.skiarena.ch; cable car one-way/return Sfr36/50) mountain, reached by the Gemsstock-bahn cable car (undergoing a major overhaul at the time of research), for the snow-sure winter slopes.

🛏 p375

The Drive » From Andermatt to Engelberg, take Rte 2 to Göschenen, then get on the A2/E35 and follow the signs for Lucerne. The road will skirt the bottom of Lake Uri for some lovely water views. Continue on this road until you take exit 33 (Stans-Süd), then follow Rte 374 all the way to Engelberg (one hour, 77km in total).

5 Engelberg

Wonderful Engelberg (literally 'Angel Mountain'), backed by the glacial bulk of **Mt Titlis** (www.titlis.ch) – central Switzerland's tallest mountain – and frosted peaks, which feature in many a Bollywood production, is divine. After visiting the 12th-century Benedictine **Engelberg Monastery** (Kloster Engelberg; ☎041 639 61 19; www.kloster-engelberg.ch; church admission free, tours adult/child Sfr8/free; ⏱1hr tour 10am & 4pm Wed-Sat), get closer to the heavens via the world's first revolving **cable car** (www.titlis.ch/en/tickets/cable-car-ride; adult/child return Sfr89/44.50; ⏱8.30am-5pm). The cable car pirouettes over the dazzling **Titlis Glacier**, peaks rising like shark fins ahead, before you step out onto Titlis station's **terrace** (3020m), with a panorama that stretches to Eiger, Mönch and Jungfrau in the Bernese Oberland. For even more thrilling views, step onto the adjacent **Cliff Walk** (www.titlis.ch/en/glacier/cliff-walk; ⏱9.15am-4.45pm) – opened in 2012, this 100m-long, 1m-wide, cable-supported swinging walkway is Europe's highest suspension bridge.

There are some 360km of marked hiking trails in and around Engelberg. For gentle ambles and gorgeous scenery, head for **Brunni** on the opposite side of the valley. The **Brunni cable car** (www.brunni.ch; cable car one-way/return Sfr18/30, incl chairlift one-way/return Sfr26/42) goes up to Ristis at 1600m, where a chairlift takes you to the Swiss Alpine Club's refurbished **Brunni Hütte**. From here you can watch a magnificent sunset before spending the night, should you wish.

🛏 p375

The Drive » As Engelberg is a 'dead end' retrace your route back to the A2, heading west, before turning onto the A8 (direction Interlaken), and

---

AROUND GRINDELWALD: FIRST

From Grindelwald, a cable car zooms up to **First**, the trailhead for 100km of paths, half of which stay open in winter. From here, you can trudge up to **Faulhorn** (2681m; 2½ hours), even in winter, via the cobalt **Bachalpsee** (Lake Bachalp). As you march along the ridge, the unfolding views of the Jungfrau massif are entrancing. Stop for lunch and 360-degree views at Faulhorn. From here, you might like to continue on to Schynige Platte (another three hours) and return by train.

Other great walks head to **Schwarzhorn** (three hours), **Grosse Scheidegg** (1½ hours), **Unterer Gletscher** (1½ hours) and **Grindelwald** itself (2½ hours).

First has 60km of well-groomed pistes, which are mostly wide, meandering reds suited to intermediates. The south-facing slopes make for interesting skiing through meadows and forests. Freestylers should check out the kickers and rails at Bärgelegg or have a go on the superpipe at Schreckfeld station.

Faulhorn happens to be the starting point for **Europe's longest toboggan run**, accessible only on foot. Bring a sled to bump and glide 15km over icy pastures and through glittering woodlands all the way back down to Grindelwald via Bussalp. Nicknamed 'Big Pintenfritz', the track lasts around 1½ hours, depending on how fast you slide.

Year-round, you can get your pulse racing on the **First Flyer**, a staggeringly fast zip-line from First to Schreckfeld. The mountains are but a blur as, secure in your harness, you pick up speeds of around 84km/h.

Opened in 2015, the **First Cliff Walk** is a summit trail with a 40m-long suspension bridge, climbing stairs and an observation deck, with suitably impressive views of the local landscape and the jaw-dropping mountains.

WHY THIS IS A CLASSIC TRIP
SALLY O'BRIEN,
AUTHOR

Even though I now call Switzerland home, the Alpine scenery still has an other-worldly effect on me. The abundance of snow-capped peaks, mountains with fairy-tale names that 'pop up' at numerous vantage points, time-defying glaciers, gravity-defying railways. And then there's the moment you catch sight of the Matterhorn...

Top: Mountain biking around Andermatt
Left: Climbers on the Matterhorn
Right: Aletsch Glacier

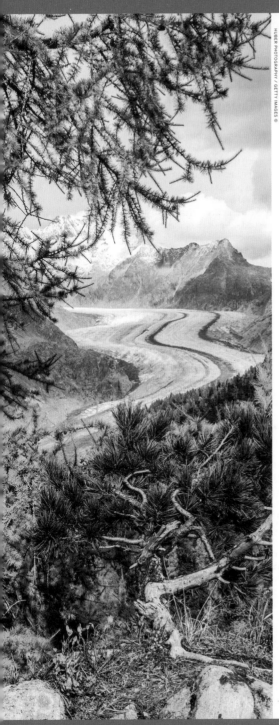

continuing alongside bright-blue Brienzersee to Giessbachfälle (one hour and 10 minutes, 71km).

6 Giessbachfälle

Illuminating the fir forests like a spotlight in the dark, the misty **Giessbachfälle** (Giessbach Falls) plummet 500m over 14 rocky ridges. Europe's oldest **funicular**, dating to 1879, creaks up from the boat station (one-way/return Sfr5/10), but it's only a 15-minute walk up to the most striking section of the falls.

The Drive » Get back onto the A8 and follow the road along the Brienzersee until exit 25 (Wilderswil/Grindelwald), then continue as the road winds its way through rural countryside up to Grindelwald (39km, 45 minutes).

7 Grindelwald

Grindelwald's sublime natural assets are film-set stuff: the chiselled features of the north face of **Eiger**, the glinting tongues of **Oberer** and **Unterer Glaciers** and the crown-like peak of **Wetterhorn**. Skiers and hikers cottoned onto its charms in the late 19th century, which makes it one of Switzerland's oldest resorts. And it has lost none of its appeal, with geranium-studded Alpine chalets and verdant pastures aplenty.

Turbulent waters carve a path through the craggy glacier gorge known

Classic Trip

as **Gletscherschlucht** (Glacier Gorge; adult/child Sfr7/3.50; ⏰10am-5pm May-Oct, to 6pm Jul & Aug), a 30-minute walk south of the centre. A footpath weaves through tunnels hacked into cliffs veined with pink and green marble. It's justifiably a popular spot for canyon and bungee-jumping expeditions.

Grindelwald is outstanding **hiking** territory, veined with trails that command arresting views to massive north faces, crevasse-filled glaciers and snow-capped peaks. High-altitude walks can be reached by taking cable cars from the village.

🍴 🛏 p375

The Drive › From Grindelwald, follow the signs to Lauterbrunnen, which is 20km (15 minutes) away by car.

- - - - - - - - - - - -

⑧ Lauterbrunnen

Laid-back Lauterbrunnen's wispy **Staubbachfall** (Staubbach Falls; ⏰8am-8pm Jun-Oct) inspired both Goethe and Lord Byron to pen poems to their ethereal beauty. Today the postcard-perfect village, nestled deep in the valley of 72 waterfalls, including the **Trümmelbachfälle** (Trümmelbach Falls; www. truemmelbachfaelle.ch; adult/ child Sfr11/4; ⏰9am-5pm), attracts a less highfalutin crowd.

Hikes heading up into the mountains from the waterfall-laced valley include a 2½-hour uphill trudge to car-free **Mürren** and a more gentle 1¾-hour walk to **Stechelberg**. In winter, you can glide past frozen waterfalls

on a well-prepared 12km cross-country trail.

The Drive › From Lauterbrunnen, head to Stechelberg (10 minutes, 6km), where you'll leave the car (paid parking available) and take the cable car to Schilthorn (adult/ child Stechelberg–Schilthorn return Sfr102/51).

- - - - - - - - - - - -

⑨ Schilthorn

There's a tremendous 360-degree, 200-peak panorama from the 2970m **Schilthorn** (www. schilthorn.ch), best appreciated from the **Skyline viewing platform** or **Piz Gloria revolving restaurant**. On a clear day, you can see from **Titlis** around to **Mont Blanc**, and across to the German Black Forest.

Some visitors seem more preoccupied with practising their delivery of the line, 'The name's Bond, James Bond', because a few scenes from

---

💬 **LOCAL KNOWLEDGE:**
WINE TIME

The canton of Valais, which features so much of Switzerland's stunning Alpine scenery, is also the largest and best producer of wine in the country, so sampling it in situ at the end of a day's driving is a great idea.

Drenched in extra sunshine and light from above the southern Alps, much of the land north of the Rhône River in western Valais is planted with vines. Unique to the Valais are the bisses (narrow irrigation channels) that traverse the vineyards.

Dryish white Fendant, the perfect accompaniment to fondue and raclette, and best served crisp cold, is the region's best-known wine, accounting for two-thirds of Valais wine production. Dôle, made from Pinot noir and Gamay grapes, is the principal red blend and is full bodied, with a firm fruit flavour.

When ordering wine in a wine bar or restaurant, use the uniquely Swiss approach of deci (decilitre – ie a 10th of a litre) multiples. Or just order a bottle...

THE HIGH LIFE

Charming as Zermatt is, heading out of town and up to the mountains is a rush like no other.

Europe's highest cogwheel railway, the **Gornergratbahn** (www.gornergrat.ch; Bahnhofplatz 7; one-way adult/child Sfr42/21; ⏰7am-9.50pm), has climbed through picture-postcard scenery to Gornergrat (3089m) – a 30-minute journey – since 1898. Sit on the right-hand side to gawp at the Matterhorn. Tickets allow you to get on and off en route; there are restaurants at Riffelalp (2211m) and Riffelberg (2582m). In summer an extra train runs once a week at sunrise and sunset – the most spectacular trips of all.

Views from Zermatt's cable cars are all remarkable, but the **Matterhorn Glacier Paradise** (www.matterhornparadise.ch; adult/child Sfr99/49.50; ⏰8.30am-4.20pm) is the icing on the cake. Ride Europe's highest-altitude cable car to 3883m and marvel at 14 glaciers and 38 mountain peaks over 4000m from the Panoramic Platform (only open in good weather). Don't miss the Glacier Palace, an ice palace complete with glittering ice sculptures and an ice slide to swoosh down bum first. End with some exhilarating snow tubing outside in the snowy surrounds.

On Her Majesty's Secret Service were shot here in 1968–69. The **Bond World 007** interactive exhibition gives you the chance to pose for photos secret-agent style and relive movie moments in a helicopter and bobsled.

The Drive » When you descend back to Stechelberg, head to Kandersteg via the road down to Interlaken. Get on the A8/Rte 11, then take exit 19 (direction Spiez/Kandersteg/Adelboden). The 60km trip takes one hour.

- - - - - - - - - -

⑩ Kandersteg

Turn up in Kandersteg wearing anything but muddy boots and you'll attract a few odd looks. Hiking is this town's raison d'être, with 550km of surrounding trails. An amphitheatre of spiky peaks studded with glaciers and jewel-coloured lakes such as **Blausee** (www.blausee.ch; adult/child Sfr7/3; ⏰9am-5pm) and **Oeschinensee** (www.oeschinensee.ch; cable-car one-way/return Sfr18/26; ⏰cable car 8am-6pm) creates a sublime natural backdrop to the rustic village of dark-timber chalets.

In winter, there are more than 50km of cross-country ski trails, including the iced-over Oeschinensee. The limited 15km of downhill skiing is suited to beginners. Kandersteg's frozen waterfalls attract ice climbers and the village hosts the spectacular annual **Ice Climbing Festival** (⏰Jan).

The Drive » From Kandersteg, take the **BLS Lötschberg Tunnel** (www.bls.ch/e/autoverlad/tickets-goppenstein.php), which connects with Goppenstein (in Valais) at regular intervals daily. The trip takes 15 minutes and costs from Sfr25 per car if booked online. From Goppenstein, head east from Rte 9. Once past Brig, the deep valley narrows and the landscape switches to rugged wilderness, with a string of bucolic villages of timber chalets and onion-domed churches (47km).

- - - - - - - - - -

TRIP HIGHLIGHT

⑪ Aletsch Glacier

The Aletsch Glacier is a seemingly never-ending, 23km-long swirl of ice with deep crevasses that slices past thundering falls, jagged spires of rock and pine forest. It stretches from Jungfrau in the Bernese Oberland to a plateau above the Rhône and is, justly so, a Unesco World Heritage site.

Picture-postcard riverside Fiesch on the valley floor is the best place to access it. From the village, ride the

Classic Trip

cable car (www.eggishorn. ch; adult/child 6-16yr return from Fiesch Sfr57/28.50) up to Fiescheralp and continue up to Eggishorn (2927m). Streaming down in a broad curve around the Aletschhorn (4195m), the glacier is just like a frozen six-lane superhighway. In the distance to the north rise the glistening summits of Jungfrau (4158m), Mönch (4107m), Eiger (3970m) and Finsteraarhorn (4274m). To the southwest of the cable-car exit, you can spy Mont Blanc and the Matterhorn.

p375

The Drive » It takes one hour (56km) to get from Fiesch to Täsch via Rte 19 to Visp, then the winding rural road to Täsch itself. You'll park the car here before boarding the train to car-free Zermatt.

- - - - - - - - - -

TRIP HIGHLIGHT

⑫ Zermatt

You can almost sense the anticipation on the train from Täsch.

Then, as you arrive in car-free Zermatt, the pop-up-book effect of the one-of-a-kind **Matterhorn** (4478m) works its magic. Like a shark's fin it rises above the town, with moods that swing from pretty and pink to dark and mysterious. Since the mid-19th century, Zermatt has starred among Switzerland's glitziest resorts. Today skiers cruise along well-kept pistes, spellbound by the scenery, while style-conscious darlings flash designer threads in the town's swish lounge bars.

Meander main-strip **Bahnhofstrasse** with its boutiques and stream of horse-drawn sleds or carriages and electric taxis, then head towards the noisy Vispa river along **Hinterdorfstrasse**. This old-world street is crammed with archetypal Valaisian timber granaries propped up on stone discs and stilts to keep out pesky rats; look for the fountain commemorating Ulrich Inderbinen (1900–2004), a Zermatt-born mountaineer who climbed the Matterhorn 370 times, the last time at age 90.

A walk in Zermatt's **Mountaineers' Cemetery** (Kirchstrasse) in the garden of St Mauritius Church is sobering. Numerous gravestones tell of untimely deaths on Monte Rosa, the Matterhorn and Breithorn. In July 2015 a **memorial** to 'the unknown climber' was unveiled to mark the 150th anniversary of the Matterhorn's first ascent.

The **Matterhorn Museum** (027 967 41 00; www.matterhornmuseum.ch; Kirchplatz; adult/child Sfr10/5; 11am-6pm Jul-Sep & mid-Dec–Apr, 3-6pm Oct–mid-Dec) provides a fascinating insight into Valaisian village life, the dawn of tourism in Zermatt and the lives the Matterhorn has claimed. Short films portray the first successful ascent of the Matterhorn on 14 July 1865, led by Edward Whymper, a feat marred by tragedy on the descent when four team members crashed to their deaths in a 1200m fall down the North Wall. The infamous rope that broke is on display.

p375

Eating & Sleeping

Arosa ❶

✕ Burestübli   Swiss €€

(☎081 377 18 38; Hotel Arlenwald, Prätschli; mains Sfr25-42; ⊙8am-midnight) This woodsy chalet has magical above-the-treetop views. Come winter, pots of gooey fondue and mugs of glühwein fuel floodlit dashes through the snow.

Vals ❷

🛏 Hotel Therme   Design Hotel €€€

(☎081 926 80 80; www.therme-vals.ch; Vals; s Sfr290-390, d Sfr390-590; P 🛜) Peter Zumthor revamped many rooms at this famous spa hotel, with others given a Japanese touch (thanks to Tadao Ando and Kengo Kuma). The restaurants emphasise local and organic ingredients.

Andermatt ❹

🛏 River House Boutique Hotel   Design Hotel €€

(☎041 887 00 25; www.theriverhouse.ch; Gotthardstrasse 58; s Sfr150-210, d Sfr200-280; P 🛜) At this stylish eco-hotel in a 250-year-old building, the owners have created unique and beautiful rooms, some with river views. The excellent on-site restaurant features local produce and Swiss wines.

Engelberg ❺

🛏 Ski Lodge Engelberg   Hotel €€

(☎041 637 35 00; www.skilodgeengelberg.com; Erlenweg 36; s/d/tr/q Sfr150/270/360/450; P 🛜) Run by sociable Swedish pro skiers, this delightful lodge fuses art-nouveau flair with 21st-century comfort. Après-ski activities include gazing at snowy peaks from an outdoor spa and chef Jonas' stellar New Nordic cuisine.

Grindelwald ❼

✕ C & M   Swiss €€

(☎033 853 07 10; Almisgässli 1; snacks Sfr5-9, mains Sfr29-49; ⊙8.30am-11pm Wed-Mon) Just as appetising as the seasonally inspired dishes are the stupendous views to Unterer Gletscher from this gallery-style cafe's sunny terrace.

🛏 Gletschergarten   Historic Hotel €€

(☎033 853 17 21; www.hotel-gletschergarten.ch; Obere Gletscherstrasse 1; s Sfr130-170, d Sfr230-300; P 🛜) The sweet Breitenstein family make you feel at home in their timber heirloom-filled chalet. Rooms have balconies facing Unterer Gletscher and Wetterhorn.

Aletsch Glacier ⓫

🛏 Fiesch Youth Hostel   Hostel €

(www.youthhostel.ch/en/hostels/fiesch; Sport Ferien Resort; dm with shared bathroom per person from Sfr35, d with private bathroom per person Sfr50) This 1970s bunker-like complex plays host to 1001 activities and has spotless rooms (many recently updated).

Zermatt ⓬

✕ Snowboat   International €

(☎027 967 43 33; www.snowboat.ch; Vispastrasse 20; mains Sfr19-26; ⊙noon-midnight) This is a hybrid eating-drinking, riverside address with yellow deckchairs on its rooftop terrace. Head here for barbecue-sizzled burgers, creative salads and great cocktails.

🛏 Suitenhotel Zurbriggen   Boutique Hotel €€

(☎027 966 38 38; www.zurbriggen.ch; Schluhmattstrasse 68; high season d/ste/apt from Sfr290/420/490) Owned by Swiss Alpine skiing legend Pirmin Zurbriggen, this modern hotel has a handy position near the cable-car station for Matterhorn Glacier Paradise. Suites have south-facing balconies and Matterhorn views, plus there's a wellness area.

Locarno *Santuario della Madonna del Sasso overlooks the pretty town*

Graubünden & Ticino

33

Graubünden is raw natural beauty; broad-shouldered Alpine grandeur married with unique local culture. Meanwhile, Ticino's la dolce vita blends Alpine scenery tempered with Italian flair.

TRIP HIGHLIGHTS

490 km

St Gotthard Pass
Thrilling touring, twinned with sweeping views

101 km

Swiss National Park
Wilderness wonderland at the edge of Switzerland

START
Chur

Davos

4

13
FINISH

St Moritz

Bellinzona
11

410 km

Locarno
Lake Maggiore's sweet sanctuary

5 DAYS
490 KM / 305 MILES

GREAT FOR...

BEST TIME TO GO

Spring or summer for enjoying the natural beauty.

ESSENTIAL PHOTO

Sublimely pretty Val Fex when sprinkled with wildflowers.

BEST FOR CULTURE

Graubünden is home to Romansch, an official language of Switzerland spoken regularly by only 60,000 people.

33 Graubünden & Ticino

The wild beauty of Switzerland dominates, tracing valley floors sheltered by hulking mountains, pristine forests and brilliantly blue lakes. Cities on this route are reassuringly relaxed and even a bit retro, the villages embrace their quiet appeal, and at the end of it all climbs one of Europe's most exciting drives. Start in Graubünden, with its unique language and identity, then finish with a hearty 'Ciao Bella' in riviera-rich Ticino.

1 Chur

The Alps rise like an amphitheatre around Chur, Switzerland's oldest city, inhabited since 3000 BC.

The **Bündner Kunstmuseum** (www.buendner-kunstmuseum.ch; Postplatz; adult/child Sfr12/free) in the neoclassical Villa Planta gives an insight into the artistic legacy of Graubünden-born Alberto Giacometti (1877–1947) and his talented contemporaries, including Giovanni Segantini and Ernst Ludwig Kirchner.

The city's most iconic landmark is **Martinskirche** (St Martin's Church; Kirchgasse 12), with its distinctive spire and clock face. The 8th-century church was rebuilt in the late-Gothic style in 1491 and is dramatically lit by a trio of Augusto Giacometti **stained-glass windows**.

Chur is a 1¼-hour drive from Zürich along the A3, passing the fantastically fjord-like **Walensee**. The limestone Churfirsten mountains rise like an iron curtain along the lake's north flank, occasionally interrupted by a coastal hamlet or upland pasture and, about halfway along the lakefront, seemingly cracked open by **Seerenbachfälle**, Switzerland's highest waterfall.

The Drive » Chur to Tamina Therme is a simple 18-minute, 20km drive along the A13.

2 Bad Ragaz

The graceful little spa town of Bad Ragaz opened in 1840 and has attracted the bath-loving likes of Douglas Fairbanks and Mary Pickford. The fabled waters are said to boost the immune system and improve circulation. The sleek and stylish **Tamina Therme** (📞081 303 27 40; www.taminatherme.ch; Hans-Albrecht-Strasse; weekday ticket adult/child Sfr36/22; ⏰8am-10pm Sun-Thu, to 11pm Fri), a couple of kilometres south of Bad Ragaz, has several pools for wallowing in the 36.5°C thermal waters, as well as massage jets, whirl

LINK YOUR TRIP

29 Northern Switzerland

End point St Gotthard Pass is a 2½-hour drive northeast from St Gallen, starting point of Trip 29.

31 Geneva to Zürich

Starting point Chur is only a 75-minute (120km) drive southeast from Zürich, the end point of Trip 31.

pools, saunas and an assortment of treatments and massages, not to mention Alp views and a good cafe. Dine and sleep in nearby Maienfeld.

✖ 🛏 p385

The Drive » From Maienfeld, take Landstrasse for just over 5km until turning left onto the N28 road east from Landquart. Here you enter the broad Prättigau Valley, which stretches east to Davos for 39km. This high Alpine country is punctuated by villages and burned-wood Walser houses built by this rural folk since migrating here from eastern Valais from the 13th century onward.

----

❸ Davos

Unlike nearby Klosters, Davos is more cool than quaint. But what the resort lacks in Alpine prettiness, it makes up for with seductive skiing and a great après-ski scene. It is also the annual meeting point for the crème de la crème of world capitalism, the World Economic Forum. Global chat fests aside, Davos inspired Thomas Mann to pen *The Magic Mountain*.

Davos' giant cube of a museum, **Kirchner Museum** (www.kirchnermuseum. ch; Ernst-Ludwig-Kirchner-Platz; adult/child Sfr12/5; ☺10am-6pm Tue-Sun), showcases the world's largest Ernst Ludwig Kirchner (1880–1938) collection, with some 50 paintings. The German Expressionist painted

extraordinary scenes of the area around Davos, which he called home from 1918. When the Nazis classified Kirchner a 'degenerate artist' and emptied galleries of his works, he was overcome with despair and took his own life in 1938.

🛏 p385

The Drive » From Davos, turn onto Rte 28 (Flüelastrasse), continuing for 34km (40 minutes) until you reach Zernez, where the headquarters of the Swiss National Park are located. This route includes (weather permitting) the Flüela Pass (2383m). If the pass is closed, you'll need to travel through the Vereina Tunnel (car train) from Selfranga to Sagliains (www.rhb. ch/en/car-transporter).

TRIP HIGHLIGHT

❹ Swiss National Park

Spanning 172 sq km, Switzerland's first and only national park (established 1 August 1914) is a nature-gone-wild swathe of dolomitic peaks, shimmering glaciers, larch woodlands, pastures, waterfalls and high moors strung with topaz-blue lakes. It's a real glimpse of the Alps before the dawn of tourism.

Some 80km of well-marked hiking trails lead through the park, where, with a little luck and decent binoculars, ibex, chamois, marmots and golden eagles can be sighted. The **Swiss National Park Centre**

BORIS-B / SHUTTERSTOCK ©

(🕿081 851 41 41; www.national park.ch; Zernez; exhibition adult/ child Sfr7/3; ☺8.30am-6pm Jun-Oct, 9am-noon & 2-5pm Nov-May) in **Zernez** should be your first port of call for information on activities and accommodation. An audioguide gives you the low-down on conservation, wildlife and environmental change. The tourist office here can also provide details on park hikes.

Zernez itself is an attractive cluster of stone chalets, outlined by the profile of its baroque church and the stout medieval tower of its castle, **Schloss Wildenberg**.

Davos Resorts abound in this Alpine area

The Drive » The views between Zernez and Müstair along Rte 28 are stupendous, with wild Alpine scenery and the Ofen/Fuorn Pass (2149m). The drive takes 40 minutes (39km).

- - - - - - - - - - -

❺ Müstair

Nestled in a remote corner of Switzerland, just before the Italian border, Müstair is one of Europe's early Christian treasures and a Unesco World Heritage site. When Charlemagne supposedly founded a monastery and a church here in the 8th century, this was a strategically placed spot below the Ofen Pass,

separating northern Europe from Italy and the heart of Christendom.

Vibrant Carolingian (9th century) and Romanesque (12th century) frescos smother the interior of the church of Benedictine **Kloster St Johann** (St John's Convent; www. muestair.ch; guided tour adult/child Sfr10/5; ☺9am-noon & 1.30-5pm Mon-Sat, 1.30-5pm Sun). Beneath Carolingian representations of Christ in Glory in the apses are Romanesque stories depicting the grisly ends of St Peter (crucified), St Paul (decapitated) and St Stephen (stoned). The **museum** (adult/child Sfr12/6;

☺9am-noon & 1.30-5pm Mon-Sat, 1.30-5pm Sun) next door takes you through part of the monastery complex, with Carolingian art and other relics.

The Drive » From Müstair to Zuoz is 56km (one hour). This is mostly retracing your drive back to Zernez along Rte 28, before heading southwest along Rte 27, which sticks close to the River Inn as it snakes through the valley floor.

- - - - - - - - - - -

❻ Zuoz

Little Zuoz is a quintessential Engadine town, with colourful **sgraffito houses**, flower boxes bursting with geraniums

LOCAL KNOWLEDGE:
MUST-TRY BÜNDNER SPECIALITIES

Pizokel Stubby wheat-and-egg noodles, seasoned with parsley and often served with speck, cheese and onions.

Bündnerfleisch Seasoned and air-dried beef or game.

Capuns A hearty dish consisting of egg pasta and sausage or Bündnerfleisch, which is wrapped in chard, flavoured with herbs and cooked in milky water.

Maluns Potatoes soaked for 24 hours, then grated and slowly roasted in butter and flour. Apple mousse and Alpine cheese add flavour.

Nusstorte Caramelised nut tart usually made with walnuts.

Bündner Gerstensuppe Creamy barley soup with smoked pork, beef, speck, leeks, celery, cabbage, carrots and potatoes.

and Augusto Giacometti **stained-glass windows** illuminating the church chancel. Though skiing is fairly limited (albeit good), Zuoz is unquestionably one of the Oberengadin's prettiest towns, and a great place to unwind for a night.

🛏 p385

The Drive » Follow Rte 27 for 18km along the valley path, admiring the landscape of broad-shouldered mountains, and small towns.

- - - - - - - - - - - -

7 St Moritz

Switzerland's original winter wonderland and the cradle of Alpine tourism, St Moritz has been luring royals, celebrities and serious money since 1864. With its shimmering aquamarine lake, emerald forests and aloof mountains, the town looks a million dollars, which you could prob-

ably drop during a quick shopping spree on **Via Serlas**.

The real riches lie outdoors with superb carving on **Corviglia** (2486m), hairy black runs on **Diavolezza** (2978m) and kilometres of **hiking** and **biking** trails when the snow melts.

🍴 p385

The Drive » Part of the 10km-long drive (take Rte 27, then Rte 3) from St Moritz to Sils-Maria skirts the startlingly turquoise, wind-buffeted Silvaplanersee, a kitesurfing and windsurfing mecca. Sils-Maria is situated between Silvaplanersee and another equally beautiful lake, the Silsersee.

- - - - - - - - - - - -

8 Sils-Maria

Sils-Maria (Segl in Romansch) is a cluster of pastel-painted, slate-roofed chalets set against a backdrop of rugged, glacier-capped mountains. German philoso-

pher Friedrich Nietzsche spent his summers here from 1881 to 1888 writing texts, including *Thus Spake Zarathustra*. Housed in a geranium-bedecked chalet, the little memorabilia-filled **Nietzsche Haus** (www.nietzschehaus.ch; Via da Marias 67; adult/child Sfr8/free; ⏲3-6pm Tue-Sun) was his summer retreat.

Nearby car-free **Val Fex** features high pastures freckled with wildflowers in summer and streaked gold with larch forests in autumn, and a glacier crowning a host of rocky peaks. Nietzsche, Thomas Mann and Marc Chagall were among those who found the space here to think and dream.

Reaching the valley is an experience in itself, whether you hike (around 2½ hours from Sils-Maria) or arrive by horse-drawn carriage.

For the latter, head to Dorfplatz in Sils-Maria from where carriages depart. The scenic journey for up to four people costs from Sfr60/100 one-way/return to Fex-Platta, Sfr70/120 to Fex-Cresta and Sfr90/160 to Hotel Fex; exact times and prices depend on group numbers.

🛏 p385

The Drive » From Sils-Maria, head back past the Silvaplanersee, then turn left onto Rte 3. This takes you to the Julier Pass (open year-round; 2284m) and then up towards Thusis. Next head south on Rte 13, which you drive along for just under 5km to get to Via Mala (64km total, one hour and 10 minutes).

- - - - - - - - - - - - -

9 Via Mala

The narrow, breathtakingly sheer and narrow gorge Via Mala ('Bad Path') was once part of a pack-mule trail to Italy.

Today you can descend to its depths (some cliffs reach 300m) via 321 steps and try to imagine what an arduous and inhospitable schlep this must have been back in the day.

The Drive » Head to Lake Lugano via Rte 13 and watch as the landscape changes from stoic Graubünden mountains to the velvety hills of Ticino, via the San Bernardino Pass (2066m). It takes around two hours and is 130km.

- - - - - - - - - - - - -

10 Lugano

Ticino's lush, mountain-rimmed Lago di Lugano (Lake Lugano) isn't its only liquid asset. The largest city in the canton is also the country's third-most-important banking centre. Suits aside, Lugano is a vivacious city, with chic boutiques, bars and pavement cafes huddling in the spaghetti maze of

steep cobblestone streets that untangle at the edge of the lake and along the flowery promenade.

For a bird's-eye view of Lugano and the lake, head for the hills. A funicular from Cassarate hauls you up to the summit of 925m **Monte Brè** (www.montebre. ch; funicular one-way/return Sfr16/25) from March to December. The peak is the trailhead for hiking and mountain-biking trails that grant expansive views of the lake and reach deep into the Alps.

🛏 p385

The Drive » Hop on the A2 heading north. Take exit 48 (Monte Ceneri) and then Rte 2 and A13, following the signs to Locarno (45 minutes, 43km).

- - - - - - - - - - - - -

TRIP HIGHLIGHT

11 Locarno

With its palm trees and much-vaunted 2300 hours of sunshine a year,

---

SCHLOSS SCHAUENSTEIN

Lauded as one of Switzerland's greatest chefs, Michelin-starred Andreas Caminada is king of fairy-tale **Schloss Schauenstein** (📞081 632 10 80; www.schauenstein.ch; Schlossgasse 77, Fürstenau; 3-/4-/5-/6-course menu Sfr198/219/235/249; ⏰lunch Thu-Sun, dinner Wed-Sun), which, in turn, has featured in San Pellegrino's list of the world's 50 best restaurants. The rarefied experience belies the simplicity of many of the ingredients, often local, all handled with imagination and exquisite technique. The excellent wine list features many of Switzerland's best vintages, along with international offerings.

The castle's guesthouse (rooms/suites from Sfr370/580, breakfast Sfr42) features three rooms decorated with sleek contemporary furnishings and three suites that combine period fixtures and modern features. The manicured grounds come with an outdoor pool and terrace. Reserve well in advance for both (up to eight months), or try your luck with listings of last-minute table cancellations via the website or by phoning.

Find it in Fürstenau, just off Rte 13 from Chur, before Thusis and Via Mala.

Locarno, the lowest town in Switzerland, attracts sun lovers to its warm, Mediterranean-style setting, and has done so since the late 19th century.

The impossibly photogenic **Santuario della Madonna del Sasso** (◔6.30am-6.30pm) overlooks the town and is a must-see sight. It was built after the Virgin Mary supposedly appeared in a vision to a monk, Bartolomeo d'Ivrea, in 1480. There's a highly adorned church and several rather rough, near-life-size statue groups (including one of the Last Supper) in niches on the stairway. The best-known painting in the church is *La Fuga in Egitto* (Flight to Egypt), painted in 1522 by Bramantino. A **funicular** (adult one-way/return Sfr4.80/7.20, child Sfr2.20/3.60; ◔8am-10pm) runs every 15 minutes from the town centre past the sanctuary to Orselina, but a more scenic, pilgrim-style approach is the 20-minute walk up the chapel-lined Via Crucis (take Via al Sasso off Via Cappuccini).

The Drive ≫ Take the A13 and then Rte 13; follow the signs to Bellinzona (30 minutes, 24km).

---

12 Bellinzona

At the convergence of several Alpine valleys, Bellinzona is visually striking. Its three grey-stone medieval castles have attracted everyone from Swiss invaders to painter William Turner.

The main one, **Castelgrande** (www.bellinzonaune sco.ch; Via Salita Castelgrande; ◔grounds 10am-6pm Mon, 9am-10pm Tue-Sun, Murata 10am-7pm), rising from a rocky central hill, was a Roman frontier post and Lombard defensive tower. It's now one of Bellinzona's best places to eat, and wandering the vineyard-surrounded grounds is unforgettable.

The three castles didn't stop Swiss-German confederate troops from overwhelming the city in 1503, thus deciding Ticino's fate for the following three centuries. Castelgrande is the easiest castle to access, but both **Castello di Montebello** (www.bellinzonaunesco. ch; Salita al Castello di Montebello; castle admission free, museum adult/child Sfr5/2; ◔10am-6pm Sep, Oct, May & Jun, to 7pm Jul & Aug, closed Nov-Apr) and **Castello di Sasso Corbaro** (www.bellinzonaunesco.ch; Via Sasso Corbaro; castle admission free, museum & tower adult/child Sfr5/2; ◔10am-6pm Sep, Oct, May & Jun, to 7pm Jul & Aug, closed Nov-Apr) reward the effort.

---

 p385

The Drive ≫ Coming from Bellinzona on the A2, take exit 41 (direction Nufenen/Bedretto/Passo San Gottardo) before continuing on Rte 2 towards San Gottardo (one hour, 72km).

TRIP HIGHLIGHT

13 St Gotthard Pass

An exhilarating drive if ever there was one, this famous mountain pass (2108m) at the heart of Europe connects cantons Ticino and Uri (namely, Andermatt). It can be bypassed by the tunnel (road and train), but if you want spectacular scenery and a sense of really getting over the Alps, then taking the famous cobblestone **Tremola Road** (on the southern side of the pass, connecting the highest point with the Italian-speaking town of Airolo) via 37 tortuous twists, is a must. Once at the top, visit the **Museo Nazionale San Gottardo** (☏091 869 15 25; www.passosangottardo.ch/en/musei/museo-nazionale.html; ◔9am-6pm Jun-Oct). This museum covers the commercial, political and cultural significance of the pass and is housed in a former customs house and hotel. From here, you can connect easily with Andermatt.

Eating & Sleeping

Maienfeld

✖ Schloss Brandis
Swiss €€

(📞081 302 24 23; www.schlossbrandis.ch; mains Sfr26-62; ⊙11am-10pm) Schloss Brandis is a lofty 15th-century tower housing one of Graubünden's best restaurants. The beamed, lantern-lit dining room, the garden or the vaulted cellar are great spots for Maienfeld riesling soup and excellent autumn game.

🛏 Schlaf Fass
Guesthouse €€

(http://schlaf-fass.ch; Weingut zur Bündte; d/q Sfr150/300, fondue dinner per person Sfr20) Bed down here in one of two quirky and snug wine barrels. The table converts into a bed with red-and-white-check duvets to snuggle under, and you'll wake up to soothing vineyard views.

Davos ❸

🛏 Waldhotel Davos
Historic Hotel €€€

(📞081 415 15 15; www.waldhotel-bellevue.ch; Buolstrasse 3; s Sfr205-275, d Sfr390-460; 🅿🛜🏊) The Magic Mountain in Thomas Mann's eponymous 1924 novel, this sanatorium-turned-hotel has had an update, and even standard rooms have balconies. When you tire of mountain views, head to the spa's saltwater pools and saunas. The restaurant matches Grisons cuisine with wines from the award-winning cellar. It closes in summer.

Zuoz ❻

🛏 Castell
Design Hotel €€€

(📞081 851 52 53; www.hotelcastell.ch; Via Castell 300; d Sfr250-410, ste Sfr410-480; 🅿🛜) Some of Europe's leading architects have transformed this turn-of-the-century hotel, with art-slung spaces, chic rooms and a restaurant serving seasonally inspired cuisine, into a family-friendly design trailblazer. Unwind in the hammam, the movie room or the great outdoors.

St Moritz ❼

✖ Ecco On Snow
Gourmet €€€

(📞081 836 63 00; www.giardino-mountain.ch; Via Maistra 3, Giardino Mountain; menus Sfr142-208; ⊙7pm-midnight Wed-Sun) Two-Michelin-starred Ecco On Snow is where chef Rolf Fliegauf gives flight to culinary fantasy. Exquisitely presented dishes with strong, assured flavours revolve around primary ingredients – Wagyu beef and horseradish, lime, caramel, fig and the like.

Sils-Maria ❽

🛏 Hotel Privata
Hotel €€

(📞081 832 62 00; http://hotelprivata.ch; Via da Marias 83; s Sfr170-220, d Sfr280-440; 🛜) This family-run, dreamy, country-style hotel has huge pine-clad rooms, antique-style furniture and forest views from the herb and flower garden.

Lugano ❿

🛏 Guesthouse Castagnola
Guesthouse €€

(📞078 632 67 47; www.gh-castagnola.com; Salita degli Olivi 2; apt Sfr120-180; 🅿🛜) Kristina and Mauro aim to please at their B&B, in a beautifully restored 16th-century townhouse. Exposed stone and earthy colours dominate in apartments with Nespresso machines and flat-screen TVs. A generous breakfast (Sfr10 extra) is served in the courtyard.

Bellinzona ⓬

✖ Ristorante Castelgrande
Italian €€

(📞091 814 87 87; www.ristorantecastelgrande.ch; Castelgrande; mains Sfr29-39, menus Sfr68-80; ⊙7-10pm Tue-Sun Sep-Jun) It's not often you get the chance to eat inside a Unesco World Heritage site. The medieval castle setting alone is enough to bewitch. Seasonal specialities such as pike perch fillets with vanilla-cauliflower purée are married with top-notch wines.

STRETCH YOUR LEGS
ZÜRICH

Start: Im Viadukt

Finish: Frau Gerolds Garten

Distance: 2.6km

Duration: Three hours

This tour of Zürich West (a quarter made up of former working-class districts Kreis 4 and Kreis 5 and now a hedonistic night-time playground nicknamed Züri-West) takes you through a postindustrial landscape dedicated to culture, commerce and carousing.

Take this walk on Trip

Im Viadukt

This once down-at-heel storage facility under a stone railway viaduct (hand-built by 6000 workers in the late 19th century) was reborn in 2010 as **Im Viadukt** (www.im-viadukt.ch; Gewerbeschule; ⊘ market 10am-8pm Mon-Thu, 8am-8pm Fri & Sat), with local shops, hip eateries and a food market with great coffee.

The Walk » After perusing Im Viadukt, it's a quick 300m stroll from the market's Limmatstrasse entrance up to the Migros Museum.

Migros Museum

In the former **Löwenbräu-Areal brewery**, the well-funded **Migros Museum** (☎044 277 20 50; www.migrosmuseum.ch; Limmatstrasse 270; adult/child Sfr12/free, free Thu after 5pm, combined ticket with Kunsthalle Sfr20; ⊘11am-6pm Tue, Wed & Fri, to 8pm Thu, 10am-5pm Sat & Sun) focuses on innovative artwork, with exhibitions on interesting themes. The collection was started in the 1950s by Gottlieb Duttweiler, founder of the Migros chain of supermarkets, Switzerland's largest retailer. Upstairs, **Kunsthalle Zürich** (☎044 272 15 15; www.kunsthallezurich.ch; adult/child Sfr12/free, free Thu after 5pm, combined ticket with Migros Museum Sfr20; ⊘11am-6pm Tue, Wed & Fri, to 8pm Thu, 10am-5pm Sat & Sun) has contemporary art exhibitions.

The Walk » From the Migros Museum, continue up Limmatstrasse, then cross Hardstrasse into Hardturmstrasse. Veer left along Förrlibuckstrasse and follow it before turning left at Duttweilerstrasse. The 1.2km-long walk passes the city's industrial heritage (the MAN plant) and its industro-glam present (cafes and eateries).

Museum Für Gestaltung

Exhibitions at this impressive **design museum** (☎043 446 67 67; www.museum-gestaltung.ch; Pfingstweidstrasse 96; adult/child Sfr12/free; ⊘10am-5pm Thu-Sun & Tue, to 8pm Wed) feature anything from classic photographers to plastic garbage. The permanent collection of 500,000-odd objects covers four categories: graphics, design, applied art and posters. Find it in its new home, the Schaudepot.

The Walk » From the design museum, walk to the end of Duttweilerstrasse, turn left and follow Pfingstweidstrasse. Turn left at Technoparkstrasse and right at Schiffbaustrasse.

Schiffbau

Once a mighty shipyard fabricating lake steamers and turbine-engine parts, the enormous **Schiffbau** (Schiffbaustrasse) now plays host to the impressive three-staged **Schauspielhaus** (www.schauspielhaus.ch) theatre, a slick restaurant and a jazz club.

The Walk » From Schiffbaustrasse turn right onto Hardstrasse. Cross it, then turn left into Geroldstrasse, whose illegal clubs started the quarter's night-time rebirth. Follow U-shaped Geroldstrasse (the bottom of which almost connects with the tail-end of Im Viadukt) to the Freitag skyscraper.

Freitag Tower

Zürich's Freitag brothers recycle truck tarps into carry-all chic and every item,

from purses to laptop bags, is original. This flagship **Freitag store** (☎043 366 95 20; www.freitag.ch; Geroldstrasse 17; ⏰11am-7.30pm Mon-Fri, 10am-6pm Sat) is pure industrial whimsy – 19 shipping containers stacked 26m high. Its rooftop has spectacular city views.

The Walk » From the top of the Freitag tower, descend to street level and walk a few metres.

Frau Gerolds Garten

The wildly popular addition to Zürich's scene that is **Frau Gerolds Garten** (www.fraugerold.ch; Geroldstrasse 23/23a; ⏰bar-restaurant 11am-midnight Mon-Sat, noon-10pm Sun Apr-Oct, market & shops 11am-7pm Mon-Fri, to 6pm Sat year-round; ♿) is pure fun. Strewn with shipping containers, multicoloured lights and sandwiched between flower beds and a rail yard, it has numerous eating and drinking options, and even some hip shops. In winter, its restaurant moves indoors to a pavilion.

STRETCH YOUR LEGS
GENEVA

Start: Jardin Anglais

Finish: Place du Bourg-de-Four

Distance: 2km

Duration: Three hours

Geneva's beautiful Old Town (Vieille Ville) is the perfect spot for a charmingly edifying stroll, thanks to its mix of sights and a history lesson worthy of its status as one of the Protestant Reformation's key cities.

Take this walk on Trips

Jardin Anglais

Before strolling up the hill to the Old Town, visit the flower clock in Geneva's waterfront **garden** (Quai du Général-Guisan), landscaped in 1854 on the site of an old lumber-handling port and merchant yard. The **Horloge Fleurie** (Flower Clock), Geneva's most photographed clock, is crafted from 6500 plants and has ticked since 1955. Its second hand, 2.5m long, is claimed to be the world's longest.

The Walk ›› From the clock, cross Quai du Général-Guisan. Head south through the shopping district to Cour de St-Pierre, which faces the cathedral. It's about a seven-minute stroll.

Cathédrale St-Pierre

Begun in the 11th century, Geneva's **cathedral** (www.espace-saint-pierre.ch; Cour de St-Pierre; admission free, towers adult/child Sfr5/2; ⊙9.30am-6.30pm Mon-Sat, noon-6.30pm Sun Jun-Sep, 10am-5.30pm Oct-May) is predominantly Gothic with an 18th-century neoclassical facade. Between 1536–64 Protestant John Calvin preached here; see his uncomfortable-looking seat in the north aisle. Inside the cathedral, 77 steps spiral up to the attic – a fascinating glimpse at its architectural construction – from where another 40 lead to the top of the panoramic **northern and southern towers** (adult/child Sfr5/2). Views of the Old Town and the Jet d'Eau are marvellous. In summer, free carillon (5pm) and organ (6pm) concerts fill the cathedral and its surrounding square with music.

The Walk ›› Exit the cathedral and head for the Site Archéologique de la Cathédrale St-Pierre; a few dozen footsteps should cover it.

Site Archéologique de la Cathédrale St-Pierre

This small **archaeological site** (☎022 310 29 29; www.site-archeologique.ch; Cour St-Pierre; adult/child Sfr8/4; ⊙10am-5pm Tue-Sun) in the basement of Cathédrale St-Pierre has 4th-century mosaics in the Roman crypt and the tomb of an Allobrogian chieftain. Its entrance is at the right of the cathedral's main portico.

The Walk » Head to the other side of the cathedral (a one-minute walk) to spend an hour at the Reformation Museum.

Musée International de la Réforme

This modern **museum** (☎022 310 24 31; www.musee-reforme.ch; Rue du Cloître 4; adult/child Sfr13/6; ⏰10am-5pm Tue-Sun) in an 18th-century mansion has state-of-the-art exhibits on the Reformation: printed bibles, the emergence of 16th-century Geneva as 'Protestant Rome', John Calvin and present-day Protestantism. A combined ticket covering the museum, Cathédrale St-Pierre and Site Archéologique de la Cathédrale St-Pierre is Sfr18/10 per adult/child.

The Walk » From Cour de St-Pierre, walk down Rue Otto Barblan. Turn left onto Rue du Puits-St-Pierre and continue past Maison Tavel (the city's longest-standing private residence, now a museum) to the bottom of Rue Henri Fazy, which overlooks Parc des Bastions and has the world's

longest bench. Turn down Rampe de la Treille and follow it to the park's gates.

Parc des Bastions

It's all statues – plus free life-size chess boards hosting lively games – in green Parc des Bastions. A laid-back stroll with locals along its tree-lined promenade reveals the 4.5m-tall po-faced figures of Bèze, Calvin, Farel and Knox on **Reformation Wall**, which stretches for 100m. There are play facilities for kids and a skating rink in winter.

The Walk » From Promenade des Bastion's eastern end, walk along Rue St-Léger. Continue under the bridge and ahead until Place du Bourg-de-Four ends at the fountained terrace area.

Place du Bourg-de-Four

Eateries, bars and locals crowd Place du Bourg-de-Four, Geneva's oldest square. In summer, it's filled to bursting with gossiping local denizens. Stalwart **La Clémence** (☎022 312 24 98; www.laclemence.ch; Place du Bourg-de-Four 20; ⏰7am-1am Mon-Thu & Sun, to 2am Fri & Sat) is a popular place to linger over a coffee.

ROAD TRIP ESSENTIALS

Germany, Austria & Switzerland Driving Guide

With stunning landscapes, superb highways and spectacular, vertigo-inducing mountain passes and hairpin bends, this region is made for road tripping.

DRIVING LICENCE & DOCUMENTS

Drivers must carry the following at all times:

➡ passport or EU national-ID card

➡ valid EU driving licence or International Driving Permit

➡ car-ownership papers

➡ Green Card insured by your insurers as proof of third-party insurance

INSURANCE

Third-party liability insurance is compulsory for all vehicles, including cars brought from abroad. Normally, private cars registered and insured in another European country do not require additional insurance, but check with your insurer before leaving home. You could face huge costs by driving when uninsured or underinsured. Germans are fussy about their cars and even nudging someone's bumper may result in you having to pay for a new one.

Keep a record of who to contact at your insurance company in case of a breakdown or accident.

HIRING A CAR

To hire a car in Austria, you'll need to be at least 19. In Germany and Switzerland it's usually 25. Region-wide, you need a credit card and a driving licence issued at least one year ago.

If you plan to take your car across a country border, tell the rental company beforehand and double-check for add-on fees and age requirements.

All car-hire companies provide mandatory third-party liability insurance, but prices and conditions for collision-damage waiver insurance (CDW) vary greatly – CDW is optional, but driving without it is not recommended. Purchasing CDW reduces the deductible/excess you'll be liable for if your car is damaged or stolen. Your credit card may cover CDW if you use it to pay for the rental; verify conditions and details with your card issuer.

International car-hire companies have branches at airports, major train stations and larger towns. Rates vary considerably. Child or infant safety seats may be hired for about €5 per day; reserve when booking.

Reserve cars in advance online: prebooked and prepaid packages are cheaper than on-the-spot rentals. If you're flying into Geneva Airport in Switzerland, it's cheaper to rent on the French side.

Driving Fast Facts

➡ **Right or left?** Drive on the right

➡ **Manual or automatic?** Manual

➡ **Legal driving age** 18

➡ **Top speed limit** On motorways no limit in Germany, 130km/h in Austria, 120km/h in Switzerland

➡ **Signature cars** BMW Coupé, Trabant, Volkswagen Beetle

Road Trip Websites

AUTOMOBILE ASSOCIATIONS

ADAC (www.adac.de) Germany's main motoring organisation; roadside assistance available to members of its affiliates, including Britain's AA, the AAA in the US and Canada's CAA.

ÖAMTC (www.oeamtc.at) Free 24-hour breakdown service to members in Austria, with reciprocal agreements with motoring clubs abroad.

Swiss Touring Club (www.tcs.ch) Driving in Switzerland.

ROAD RULES

RAC (www.rac.co.uk)

AA (www.theaa.com)

MAPS & TRAFFIC INFO

ADAC (http://maps.adac.de) Online route planner for entire region.

Swiss Motorways (www.autobahnen.ch) Real-time traffic information for Switzerland.

Rental cars with automatic transmission are rare; book well in advance.

International car-hire companies:

Alamo (www.alamo.com)

Avis (www.avis.com)

Budget (www.budget.com)

Europcar (www.europcar.com)

Hertz (www.hertz.com)

National (www.nationalcar.com)

Sixt (www.sixt.com)

Internet-based discount brokers:

Auto Europe (www.autoeurope.com)

DriveAway Holidays (driveaway.com.au)

Easycar (www.easycar.com)

Holiday Autos (www.holidayautos.co.uk)

BRINGING YOUR OWN VEHICLE

➡ Any foreign vehicle entering Germany, Austria or Switzerland must display a sticker or licence plate identifying its country of registration.

➡ Right-hand-drive vehicles brought from the UK or Ireland must have deflectors affixed to headlights to avoid dazzling oncoming traffic.

MAPS

➡ Even if your car has a navigation system, a good map or road atlas is essential, especially when negotiating the labyrinth of country roads.

➡ Maps costing a few euros are sold at bookstores, train stations, airports and petrol stations. Publishers include **Freytag & Berndt** (www.freytagberndt.com), **ADAC** (www.adac. de) and **Falk** (www.falk.de).

ROADS & CONDITIONS

The region has an excellent network of well-built, well-signposted and well-maintained roads comprising autobahns (autoroutes in French-speaking Switzerland), national roads, narrow country lanes and corkscrew mountain passes.

➡ **Autobahns** (highways or motorways beginning with A, signalled by white-on-blue signs in Germany and Austria, white-on-green signs in Switzerland) Multilane divided highways, kitted out every 40km to 60km with elaborate service areas with petrol stations, toilets and restaurants.

Autobahns are free to use in Germany. In Austria and Switzerland motorists must buy a motorway-tax sticker (vignette in German and French, *contrassegno* in Italian) to display on the windscreen. Buy vignettes in advance from motoring organisations or in situ (in cash) at border crossings, petrol stations, Austrian post offices and Tabak shops.

In Austria, a vignette costs €8.70/25.30/84.40 for 10 days/two months/one calendar year. In Switzerland, motorists pay Sfr40, valid for one year, from 1 December to 31 January of the following year. A separate vignette is required for trailers and caravans.

For more information, see www.asfinag.at (Austria) and www.vignette.ch (Switzerland).

➡ **Bundesstrassen** (*routes nationales* in French-speaking Switzerland) Secondary 'B' roads.

➡ **Landstrassen** (L) Local roads designed for scenic rides rather than speed.

➡ **Alpine mountain passes** Many passes in Austria and Switzerland are blocked by snow from October or November to May. Conditions are posted at the foot of each pass and signs (a criss-crossed white tyre on a blue circular background) indicate if snow chains are compulsory; always carry snow chains when motoring in mountainous areas.

Major Swiss Alpine passes are negotiable year-round, albeit by tunnel for part of the year – this is the case at the Great St Bernard, St Gotthard and San Bernardino passes.

In Austria and Switzerland, some roads and tunnels demand an additional toll (not covered by the motorway vignette).

In Switzerland, putting your car on a train to traverse the **Furka Pass** (www.mgbhan.ch), **Lötschberg Tunnel** (www.bls.ch) or **Vereina Tunnel** (www.rhb.ch) costs Sfr20 to Sfr40.

ROAD RULES

Enforcement of traffic laws is strict. Across the region, speed- and red-light cameras, and radar traps are common and notices are sent to the car's registration address. For many infractions fines are doled out on the spot.

Road Distances (km)

	Bregenz	Berlin	Bremen	Hanover	Dresden	Düsseldorf	Frankfurt	Hamburg	Munich	Stuttgart	Geneva	Zürich	Chur	Bern	Basel	St Gallen	Salzburg	Vienna	Linz
Berlin	681																		
Bremen	687	376																	
Hanover	571	273	115																
Dresden	553	187	460	357															
Düsseldorf	550	568	290	278	550														
Frankfurt	370	507	376	327	451	205													
Hamburg	777	282	115	150	453	425	482												
Munich	170	576	696	629	457	564	392	777											
Stuttgart	205	613	591	495	492	387	183	650	228										
Geneva	356	1020	1049	1106	938	743	646	1151	529	454									
Zürich	101	758	787	844	674	560	384	889	267	192	292								
Chur	87	851	770	695	758	678	492	884	261	290	409	118							
Bern	210	892	807	864	809	597	407	1004	443	331	171	125	242						
Basel	180	795	710	767	712	503	310	907	346	234	267	113	228	97					
St Gallen	32	702	770	628	521	564	410	597	205	248	371	81	102	204	191				
Salzburg	374	679	845	929	508	729	535	933	133	359	678	401	360	506	463	339			
Vienna	670	808	964	844	673	855	655	984	374	592	923	670	650	784	746	600	301		
Linz	507	648	804	684	513	695	495	824	214	432	763	510	490	624	586	439	138	189	
Innsbruck	193	751	857	741	575	733	548	947	164	378	480	277	187	341	343	199	181	477	314

Green in the City

To decrease air pollution, some Austrian and German cites have low-emissions environmental zones that may only be entered by cars displaying an Umweltplakette or environmental badge. This includes foreign vehicles. Buy the sticker (€32) online from www.feinstaubvignette.de. Badgeless drivers caught in green zones are fined €80.

Speed Limits

➡ Unless signposted otherwise, a limit of 50km/h applies in towns and built-up areas; this often drops to 30km/h in residential areas.

➡ Maximum speed is 100km/h on single-lane freeways and national roads; this drops to 80km/h on main roads outside towns in Switzerland and to 70km/h on some country roads in Austria.

➡ The speed limit on autobahns is 130km/h in Austria (110km/h at night between 10pm and 5am, except on the A1 between Vienna and Salzburg and the A2 between Vienna and Villach) and 120km/h in Switzerland.

➡ In theory, there is no speed limit on German autobahns. In reality, there are numerous stretches where slower speeds of 100km/h apply.

Headlights

➡ **Switzerland** Headlights must be turned on at all times, day and night; the fine for not doing so is Sfr40.

➡ **Germany & Austria** Usual rules apply: use headlights after dusk, in the dark or when visibility is poor.

➡ **Region-wide** Use dipped headlights in tunnels.

Winter Tyres

➡ **Austria** Compulsory from 1 November to 15 April.

➡ **Switzerland & Germany** Not obligatory but highly recommended in winter.

Alcohol

➡ **Region-wide** The blood-alcohol limit is 0.05% (0.5g per litre of blood) – the equivalent of two standard glasses of wine for a 75kg adult.

➡ **Austria** The limit drops to 0.01% for drivers who have held their licence for less than two years.

➡ **Germany** No alcohol is tolerated for drivers aged under 21 or those who have held their licence for less than two years.

Child Seats

➡ Up to age 12 (age 14 in Austria), children shorter than 1.5m must use a size-appropriate car seat or booster.

➡ Children cannot ride in the front until aged 13 in Germany and 14 in Austria.

➡ Providing they are strapped in the appropriate seat or booster for their weight, children of any age can ride in the front seat in Switzerland.

Other Rules

➡ All passengers, front and back, must wear seat belts.

➡ Mobile phones may only be used with a hands-free kit or speakerphone.

➡ Give priority to traffic, including bicycles, approaching from the right (unless a priority road sign indicates otherwise).

➡ Stationary trams have priority; wait behind while tram passengers board and alight.

➡ On mountain roads the ascending vehicle has priority; Swiss postal buses always have right of way.

➡ All vehicles in Germany must carry a breakdown warning triangle and first-aid kit; in Austria you also need a reflective jacket. In Switzerland only the warning triangle is required by law, but the other items are recommended.

PARKING

➡ Street parking in city centres, often limited to up to two hours, is controlled by parking meters from 8am to 7pm Monday to Saturday. Buy a ticket at the coin-fed ticket machine and display it on your dashboard.

➡ For all-day city parking, pay to park in a parking lot or garage; some close at night.

Driving Problem-Buster

I can't speak German/French/Italian; will that be a problem? German is the dominant language – learn at least the basics before arriving. Road signs are mostly international and English is widely spoken in Germany and Austria (less so in Switzerland).

What should I do if my car breaks down? Safety first: turn on your warning lights, put on your reflective vest (required by law in Austria) and place a reflective triangle 30m to 100m behind your car to warn approaching motorists. Call the local automobile association (or phone number listed on your insurance) for breakdown assistance or walk to the nearest orange roadside call box, placed every 2km on most autobahns.

What if I have an accident? For minor accidents with no injuries, fill out a European Accident Statement, included in rental-car glove compartments. Report the accident afterwards to your insurance and/or rental-car company. If necessary, call the police (☎112).

What should I do if I am stopped by the police? Show your passport (or EU national-ID card), driving licence and proof of insurance.

Do I need to buy a vignette, even if I am only using the Swiss/Austrian autobahn for a few kilometres? Unfortunately, yes. And don't even think about not sticking it on your windshield (for a friend to reuse) or only partially affixing it. An unstuck vignette is considered invalid by road police and will incur you an on-the-spot fine of up to €240/Sfr100 in Austria/Switzerland.

Is it dangerous driving on German autobahns with no speed limit? It can be if you don't keep your wits about you. If you're unaccustomed to high speeds, be extra careful when passing another vehicle. It takes only seconds for a car appearing far away in the rear-view mirror to close in at 200km/h or more. Pass as quickly as possible, then quickly return to the right lane.

➡ Region-wide, public car parks allocate special parking spaces for women, extra well lit and close to exits.

FUEL

➡ Petrol stations, mainly self-service, are ubiquitous except in sparsely populated rural areas. Petrol is sold in litres.

➡ Unleaded (bleifrei, sans plomb, senza piombo) petrol is standard and diesel is widely available. Expect to pay around €1.50/1.20 per litre for unleaded and €1.25/1.15 for diesel in Germany/Austria; Sfr1.55 and Sfr1.53, respectively, in Switzerland.

➡ Filling up is most expensive at autobahn/autoroute rest stops, cheapest at hypermarkets and large supermarkets.

SAFETY

➡ Never leave anything valuable in your car, even in the boot (trunk). Thieves often identify and target rental cars.

RADIO

➡ In Germany, private Berlin radio station **Flux FM** (www.fluxfm.de) has a mix of indie rock, alternative rock and interesting newcomers. For mainstream rock and pop, try **Radio 1** (www.radioeins.de).

➡ News in English in Germany is aired by **BBC World Service** (90.2 FM); find US news bulletins on **Rock Star** (87.9 FM; www.rocksender.de).

➡ In Austria, cruise to traffic news and drivable tunes with **Hitradio Ö3** (http://oe3.radio.net).

➡ Pick up Switzerland's English-language radio station, **WRS** (www.worldradio.ch), around Lake Geneva.

Germany, Austria & Switzerland Travel Guide

GETTING THERE & AWAY

AIR

International Airports
Rental cars are available at all international airports listed below.

Germany
Frankfurt Airport, Düsseldorf and Munich are the main gateways for overseas air traffic. Until the opening of Berlin Branden- burg Airport in 2017, flights to Berlin will arrive at **Tegel** (TXL; ☑030-6091 1150; www. berlin-airport.de; ☐Tegel Flughafen) and **Schönefeld** (SXF; ☑030-6091 1150; www. berlin-airport.de; ☐Airport-Express; RE7 and RB14) airports.

Berlin Brandenburg Airport (BBI; www. berlin-airport.de)

Köln Bonn Airport (CGN; Cologne-Bonn Airport; ☑02203-404 001; www.koeln-bonn- airport.de; Kennedystrasse)

Düsseldorf International Airport (DUS; www.dus-int.de)

Hamburg Airport (HAM; www.airport.de; ☐Hamburg Airport)

Frankfurt Airport (FRA; www.frankfurt- airport.com; ☎; ☐Flughafen Regionalbahnhof)

Munich Airport (MUC; ☑089-975 00; www.munich-airport.de)

Stuttgart Airport (SGT; ☑0711-9480; www.stuttgart-airport.com)

Austria
Vienna is the main hub, but international flights to smaller airports or **Airport Bra- tislava** (Letisko; ☑+421 2 3303 3353; www. bts.aero), 60km east of Vienna, can be cheaper.

Vienna International Airport (VIE; www. viennaairport.com)

Salzburg Airport (☑0662-858 00; www. salzburg-airport.com; Innsbrucker Bundes- strasse 95)

Innsbruck Airport (INN; ☑0512-22 525; www.innsbruck-airport.com; Fürstenweg 180)

Graz Airport (GRZ; ☑0316-29 020; www. flughafen-graz.at)

Blue Danube Airport Linz (☑043-7221 600; www.linz-airport.at; Flughafenstrasse 1, Hörsching)

Switzerland

Geneva Airport (www.gva.ch)

Zürich Airport (ZRH; ☑043 816 22 11; www.zurich-airport.com)

CAR & MOTORCYCLE

Entering the region should be swift and pain- less thanks to the Schengen Agreement, which abolished passport and customs formalities between Germany, Austria, Swit- zerland and bordering EU countries.

TRAIN

➡ Rail services link the region with virtually every country in Europe. Main rail hubs include Munich, Vienna, Zürich and Basel. Rental cars are readily available at these and other major train stations.

➡ Book tickets and get information from **Rail Europe** (www.raileurope.com). In the UK contact **Railteam** (www.railteam.co.uk), an alliance of European high-speed train operators including German railways **Deutsche Bahn** (www.bahn.com), Austria's **ÖBB** (ww.oebb. at) and **Swiss Federal Railways** (www. sbb.ch).

From the UK, hourly **Eurostar** (www.euro-star.com) trains scoot from London (St Pancras International) to Paris (Gare du Nord) in 2¼ hours or Brussels (two hours), from where you can continue by regular or high-speed train to Germany. For Vienna, go to Frankfurt then pick up a connection to Vienna. For Geneva and other Swiss cities, take a French TGV from Paris (Gare de Lyon).

Useful train-travel resources:

RailPassenger Info (www.railpassenger.info)

The Man in Seat 61 (www.seat61.com)

DIRECTORY A–Z

ACCOMMODATION

From simple mountain huts to five-star hotels fit for kings – you will find a wide choice of accommodation. Standards are high, and even basic accommodation is likely to be clean and comfortable. Tourist offices keep lists and details.

Seasons

➡ Seasonal variations are common in holiday regions, less in the cities where rates are generally constant year-round. Exceptions are Christmas and New Year.

➡ In 'business' cities such as Munich, Geneva and Zürich, pricier weekday rates drop slightly at weekends.

➡ In mountain resorts prices are seasonal: low season (mid-September to mid-December and mid-April to mid-June) is the cheapest time to visit, mid-season (January to mid-February and mid-June to early July and September) begins to get pricey, and high season (July, August, Christmas, and mid-February to Easter) is the busy period.

Reservations

➡ Book in advance during high season in July, August, Christmas, Easter, and between December and April in ski areas.

➡ At other times, a day or two in advance can be sufficient; a week or more in advance is recommended for Friday and Saturday nights.

Practicalities

➡ **Time** The region uses the 24-hour clock and is on Central European Time, one hour ahead of GMT/UTC. During daylight-saving time (last Sunday in March to last Sunday in October) it's two hours ahead.

➡ **TV & DVD** TV is DVB-T (digital) and PAL (analogue); DVDs are zone 2.

➡ **Floors** 'Ground floor' is street level. The 1st floor (2nd floor in the US) is the floor above that.

➡ **Weights & Measures** Metric system.

➡ You'll need to confirm online after making a phone booking; many places can be booked online, often with a best-price guarantee.

➡ Many tourist offices make hotel reservations, some for a small fee, others for free.

Camping

➡ Campsites are often in a scenic out-of-the-way place by a river or lake. Facilities often include washing machines, electricity, on-site shops and, occasionally, cooking facilities. Camping gas canisters are often available.

➡ Most campsites open April to September; a handful open year-round. Prices start at €3/Sfr10 per person, plus €6/Sfr10 for a small tent and €3/Sfr5 for a car. Pay extra for hot showers, resort tax, electricity and sewage disposal. A **Camping Card International** (www.campingcardinternational.com) may yield savings.

➡ Wild camping (*wildes camping* in German, *camping sauvage* in French) is not allowed. In Austria, free camping in campervans is allowed in autobahn rest areas and alongside other roads, as long as you're not causing an obstruction; It's illegal to pitch a tent in these areas.

Useful organisations:

www.campingclub.at Austrian Camping Club.

www.germany.travel/camping Searchable database with detailed information on 750 German campgrounds.

www.sccv.ch Swiss Camping and Caravanning Federation.

B&Bs & Pensionen

➡ B&Bs make for some of Switzerland's most charming accommodation – a room in a private home (anything from castle to farm), which includes breakfast, often made from home-made produce.

➡ In Germany and Austria, *Pensionen* are the B&B equivalent. *Gasthöfe/Gasthäuser* (inns) are similar but usually have restaurants serving regional food to a local clientele. Amenities, room size and decor vary, often within a single establishment. What rooms lack in amenities, though, they often make up for in charm, authenticity and friendly hosts.

➡ Tourist offices have lists of B&Bs and *Pensionen* in their area – urban rarities but plentiful in the countryside.

➡ Online listings include www.bnb.ch, www.bed-and-breakfast.de and www.bedandbreakfast.de.

Farmstays

For motorists there is no greater way to end a day on the road than by pulling into a gorgeous old farmstead, strung with geraniums in bloom and with the milk urn sitting on the doostep waiting to be filled.

Farmstays offer a great opportunity to get close to nature in relative comfort. Kids can interact with animals and help with chores. Accommodation ranges from bare-bones rooms with shared facilities to fully furnished holiday apartments. Minimum stays are common. Farms may be organic, dairy, equestrian or wine estates.

Switzerland

Switzerland's **Aventure sur la paille/ Schlaf im Stroh** is the ultimate roll in the hay. When the cows are out to pasture in summer, Swiss farmers charge travellers Sfr20 to Sfr30 per adult and Sfr10 to Sfr20 per child under 15 to sleep on straw in their hay barns or lofts.

➡ Farmers provide cotton under-sheets and woolly blankets, but guests need their own sleeping bags (bring a pocket torch/flashlight).

➡ Rates include a hearty farmhouse breakfast.

➡ A morning shower (Sfr2) and evening meal (Sfr20 to Sfr30) are usually available for an extra charge.

Agritourism Switzerland (www.agro tourismus.ch) Lists 170-odd Swiss farms offering accommodation, including farmhouses that welcome B&B guests or self-caterers keen to rent a renovated barn or cottage.

Austria

➡ In rural Austria stay in a *Bauernhof* (farmhouse) with rooms or apartments to rent, often for a minimum of three nights but sometimes for one – check when booking. Nightly rates vary between €35 and €100 per person.

➡ In mountainous regions, isolated *Almhütten* (Alpine meadow huts) – usually part of a farmstead – provide a welcome break from the road and an opportunity to stretch your legs; some can only be accessed by cable car, on foot or by mountain bike on forest tracks. Most close October to April or May.

➡ Bio- or Öko- ('eco') hotels are less rural, but in picturesque settings, often with wellness facilities such as saunas and steam baths. See www.biohotels.info.

➡ **Urlaub in der Almhütte** (www.urlaubauf deralm.com; www.farmholidays.com) lists farmstays; contact tourist offices for local mountaintop *Almhütten*.

Germany

The German Agricultural Association inspects and quality-controls hundreds of farms and publishes details on www. landreise.de. Another source is www. landsichten.de.

Hostels

➡ Hostels (*Jugendherberge* in German, *auberge de jeunesse* in French, *alloggio per giovanni* in Italian) range from older, institutional affairs to modern establishments bordering on designer accommodation.

➡ Facilities are often excellent: four- to six-bed dorms with shower/toilet, plus double and family rooms are the norm; internet facilities, free wi-fi and a restaurant or cafe are commonplace.

→ Many hostels are affiliated with **Hostelling International** (HI; www.hihostels.com), bookable by email or online. If you don't have an HI membership card from your home country, buy one for €18/Sfr22 (valid for one year) or collect six individual Welcome Stamps (€3.50/Sfr6 per night). Average nightly rates in mixed or gender-segregated dorms are about €22/Sfr35 per night, including sheets.

→ Private, independent hostels – prevalent in big German cities like Berlin, Cologne and Hamburg – attract a convivial, international crowd.

→ Indies range from classic backpacker pads with large dorms and a communal spirit to modern 'flashpacker' properties similar to budget hotels. Indie hostels have no curfew and staff tend to be savvy, multilingual and keen to help with tips and advice.

National hostelling organisations:

Deutsches Jugendherbergswerk (DJH; www.jugendherberge.de) Manages Germany's 530 HI-affiliated hostels.

Independent Hostels of Germany (www.german-hostels.de) Alliance of some 60 independent hostels in 34 German cities.

ÖJHV (www.oejhv.at) and **ÖJHW** (www.jugendherberge.at) Austria's two hostelling organisations provide info on the country's 100-plus HI-affiliated hostels.

Swiss Youth Hostels (www.youthhostel.ch) Swiss HI-affiliated hostels.

Swiss Hostels (www.swisshostels.com) Formerly called 'Backpacker', these hostels tend to be more flexible in their regulations, reception times and opening hours; membership not required.

Hotels

→ You'll find everything from small family-run properties to international chains and luxurious designer abodes.

→ Increasingly popular are budget designer chains geared towards lifestyle-savvy travellers, such as **Motel One** (www.motelone.com) in Germany and Austria.

→ In older, family-run hotels, rooms vary dramatically in size, decor and amenities. The cheapest may have shared facilities, while others have a shower but no private toilet; only pricier ones have their own bathrooms.

→ Midrange hotels have comfortable clean rooms and a decent buffet breakfast with cold cuts of meat, cheeses, eggs and bread rolls (except in French-speaking Switzerland where croissants, bread and jam prevail). Rooms have private bathroom with shower, flat-screen TV, often a minibar, and a place to sit or a desk. Internet and wi-fi is available, usually free.

→ Luxurious, top-end places include Germany's fairy-tale castles, palaces and country manors. Mod cons blend with baronial ambience and old-world trappings such as four-poster beds, antique armoires and heavy drapes – the stuff of road-trip dreams. See www.thecastles.de or www.germany-castles-hotels.com.

→ A growing number of properties are entirely nonsmoking; others set aside rooms or entire floors for smokers.

ELECTRICITY

→ European two-pin plugs are standard in Austria and Germany.

230V/50Hz

→ Swiss three-pin plugs slot into recessed, three-holed, hexagonally shaped sockets. These plugs usually take the standard European two-pronged plug, but to be safe, bring an adapter for Switzerland.

230V/50Hz

FOOD

Whether you're digging into a creamy wedge of real McCoy black forest gateau in southeast Germany, savouring fish on the shores of Austria's Salzkammergut's looking-glass lakes or devouring an oven-crisp rösti or cheesy fondue in the Swiss Alps, food is integral to your road-trip experience.

The region has endless eateries; categories listed here are perfect for breaking a road trip or feasting in style. You'll find cafes, ranging from bakery-cafes for a quick coffee and sandwich to all-organic delis, and restaurants covering the whole spectrum from pizzeria bites to Michelin-starred finery.

Advance reservations are recommended for high-end eateries and popular, family-run rural inns.

Germany

Gaststätten & Gasthöfe Rural inns with a laid-back feel, local crowd and solid menu of *gutbürgerliche Küche* (home cooking).

Stehcafé Stand-up cafe for coffee and snacks at speed.

Cafe-Konditorei Traditional cake shop and cafe.

Ratskeller Atmospheric town-hall basement restaurant, frequented more by tourists than locals.

Imbiss Handy speed-feed stops for savoury fodder, such as wurst-in-a-bun, kebabs or pizza.

Apfelweinwirtschaft Frankfurt's historic *Ebbelwei* (apple-wine) taverns. Warm, woody and serving good, honest, regional fare.

Biergarten Beer garden, often with tree shade and a meaty menu.

Austria

Beisln/Gasthäuser Rural inns with homely interiors and menus packed with hearty dishes such as *Tafelspitz* (boiled beef in broth), schnitzel and goulash.

Neo-Beisln New-wave *Beisln* often with retro-cool decor and a creative, market-fresh take on classics.

Konditoreien Traditional cake-shop cafes.

Kaffeehäuser Vienna's 'living rooms' cook up delectable tortes, cakes and arm-long coffee menus; inexpensive breakfast, lunch and snacks, too.

Imbiss Snack or takeaway joint, the most famous being the *Würstelstand* (sausage stand).

Brauereien Many microbreweries and brewpubs serve grub, too.

Switzerland

Auberge Countryside inn serving traditional Swiss fare.

Kaffeebar Cafe in German-speaking Switzerland serving coffee and other typical drinks.

Stube Cosy bistro in rural or Alpine areas, serving traditional fare such as cheesy fondues and raclette.

Grotto Rustic, summer-cool restaurants in the Italian-speaking canton of Ticino.

Osteria Casual eatery in Ticino serving good-value, traditional fare.

Eating Price Ranges

The following price ranges refer to a two-course meal, excluding drinks.

€ less than €15/Sfr25

€€ €15-30/Sfr25-50

€€€ more than €30/Sfr50

GAY & LESBIAN TRAVELLERS

➡ Attitudes to homosexuality across the region are progressive; but more so in German cities such as Berlin, Cologne, Hamburg, Frankfurt and Munich.

➡ Many cities have gay and lesbian bars, and pride marches in spring.

➡ The age of consent for gay sex is 14 in Germany and Austria, 16 in Switzerland. Same-sex partnerships, but not marriage, are recognised.

Publications

Blu (www.blu.fm) Magazine with searchable, up-to-the-minute location and event listings.

L-Mag (www.l-mag.de) Bimonthly mag for lesbians.

Websites & Apps

German National Tourist Office (www.germany.travel) Dedicated LGBT pages.

My Switzerland (www.myswitzerland.com) Gay-friendly accommodation and events.

BGLAD (www.bglad.com) International online resource and directory.

Spartacus World (www.spartacusworld.com) Hip hotel, style and event guide.

Patroc Gay Travel Guide (www.patroc.com) Travel information.

INTERNET ACCESS

➡ Public wireless access points can be found at airports, train stations, some city parks, town squares and other public spaces.

➡ Some tourist offices, and many cafes and bars, sport free wi-fi and allow customers to linger with laptops.

➡ Most hotels offer free wi-fi; some have a computer guests can use to surf the internet for free or a small fee.

MONEY

ATMs

ATMs are widespread and accessible 24 hours. They accept most international bank or credit cards and have multilingual instructions. Your bank or credit-card company will usually charge a 1% to 2.5%

Tipping Guide

By law restaurant and bar prices include a service charge, so there is no need to tip. In reality, locals leave a bit extra if satisfied with the service.

Bars Round to nearest euro

Hotel cleaning staff €1 to €2 per day

Hotel porters €1 to €1.50 per bag

Restaurants 10%

Taxis 10%–15%

Toilet attendants €0.50

Tour guides €1 to €2 per person

---

fee, and there may also be a small charge at the ATM end.

Cash

You'll always find a better exchange rate in-country, but if arriving in the region by air late at night, bring enough euros or Swiss francs to take a taxi to your hotel.

Businesses throughout Switzerland, including most hotels and some restaurants and souvenir shops, accept euros. Change will be given in Swiss francs at that day's exchange rate.

Credit & Debit Cards

The use of credit cards is less widespread than in the UK or USA and not all shops, hotels or restaurants accept them. Euro-Card/MasterCard and Visa are the most popular.

Moneychangers

Change money at banks, airports and nearly every train station until late into the evening. Banks tend to charge about 5% commission; some money-exchange bureaus don't charge commission.

OPENING HOURS

These are standard hours; hours can fluctuate by an hour or so either way:

Banks 8am or 9am to 3pm Monday to Friday (to 4.30pm in Switzerland)

Bars 6pm or 7pm to anywhere between midnight and 4am

Cafes 7am or 8am to 11pm or midnight

Nightclubs 11pm to early morning

Post offices 8am to noon and 2pm to 6pm Monday to Friday, 8am to noon Saturday (in Germany 9am to 6pm Monday to Friday, to 1pm Saturday)

Restaurants 11am to 2.30pm and 6pm to 10pm or 11pm, five or six days a week (not before noon in Switzerland)

Shops 9am to 6.30pm or 7pm Monday to Friday, 9am to 5pm or 6pm Saturday, often late-night opening to 9pm Thursday

Supermarkets 9.30am to 8pm Monday to Saturday (shorter hours outside cities)

PUBLIC HOLIDAYS

The following public holidays (*Gesetzliche Feiertage* in German, *jours fériés* in French) are observed in the entire region:

New Year's Day 1 January

Good Friday March/April

Easter Sunday & Monday March/April

Ascension Day 40th day after Easter

Whit Sunday & Monday Seventh week after Easter

May Day 1 May

Christmas Day 25 December

St Stephen's Day 26 December

➡ In Austria and German states with predominantly Catholic populations (such as Bavaria and Baden-Württemberg), the following are also public holidays: Epiphany (6 January), Corpus Christi (10 days after Whit Sunday), Assumption Day (15 August), All Saints' Day (1 November) and Immaculate Conception (8 December).

➡ Some Swiss cantons observe their own special holidays and religious days, eg Berchtold Day (2 January), Labour Day (1 May), Corpus Christi (May or June), Assumption (15 August) and All Saints' Day (1 November).

➡ Austria and Switzerland celebrate their own national day with a public holiday: Swiss National Day (1 August) and Austrian National Day (26 October).

TELEPHONE

Mobile Phones

➡ Mobile phone numbers begin with the following digits:

Germany ☏0151, ☏0178, ☏0157 or ☏0170

Austria ☏0650 or any higher digit up to ☏0699

Switzerland ☏076, ☏078 or ☏079

➡ All three countries use GSM 900/1800, compatible with the rest of Europe and Australia but not with the North American GSM 1900; check with your provider about roaming charges.

➡ If you're spending the bulk of your time motoring in one country, it may be cheaper to buy a local SIM card (€15 to €30) and rev it up with prepaid credit. Buy recharge cards at newsagents and supermarkets.

➡ Mobile-phone operators:

Germany Blau (www.blau.de), T-Online (www.t-online.de), Vodafone (www.vodafone.de)

Austria T-Mobile (www.t-mobile.at), A1 (www.a1.net), 3 (www.drei.at)

Switzerland Orange (www.orange.ch), Sunrise (www.sunrise.ch), Swisscom Mobile (www.swisscom-mobile.ch)

Phone Codes

➡ **Calling the region from abroad** Dial your country's international dialling access code, then the respective country code and the phone number *without* the initial 0.

➡ **Calling internationally from Germany, Austria or Switzerland** Dial 00, the relevant country code, area code if necessary (dropping the initial 0) and telephone number.

➡ **Area codes** German and Austrian telephone numbers have an area code (starting with 0 and up to six digits long). If dialling from a landline within the same town or city, you don't need to dial the area code. You must use it when calling from a *Handy* (mobile). Area codes do not exist in Switzerland, although phone numbers in the same city or region share a common three-digit prefix (which must always be dialled).

➡ **Directory enquiries** From a German landline call ☏11828 for numbers within Germany or ☏11834 for numbers outside Germany; for an English-speaking operator call ☏11837. In Austria call ☏0900 11 88 77 for international directory assistance.

Important Numbers

Country code Germany ☑49, Austria ☑43, Switzerland ☑41

International access code ☑00

Emergency number ☑112

Roadside assistance Germany ☑01802 22 22 22, Austria ☑120, Switzerland ☑140

➡ **Search for Swiss phone numbers online at** http://tel.local.ch/en

Phonecards

Germany Buy Deutsche Telekom phonecards (€5, €10 or €20) for public pay phones at post offices and newsagents. For long-distance or international calling, prepaid cards issued by other companies are better value – find them at newsagents and telephone-call shops.

Austria Public pay phones still accept coins as well as a wide range of competitive phonecards, sold at post offices, Telekom Austria shops, call shops and *Tabak* (tobacconist) kiosks.

Switzerland Save money on the normal international tariff by buying a prepaid Swisscom card worth Sfr10, Sfr20, Sfr50 or Sfr100.

TOILETS

➡ Toilets in the region are sit-down affairs.

➡ Public toilets are generally clean and in reasonable supply. Free-standing 24-hour self-cleaning toilet pods are common; pay €0.50 and take no more than 15 minutes.

➡ Toilets in main train stations are often maintained by private companies such as McClean – pay €1.50/Sfr2 for the privilege.

TOURIST INFORMATION

Towns and cities have clearly signposted tourist offices (*Verkehrsbüro* in German, *office du tourisme* in French, *ufficio turistico* in Italian) where you can pick up free information and city maps, and sometimes book hotel rooms and tours. Somebody always speaks English.

National tourist boards:

German National Tourist Office (www.germany-travel)

Austria Info (www.austria.info)

Switzerland Tourism (www.myswitzerland.com)

TRAVELLERS WITH DISABILITIES

➡ The region is fairly progressive when it comes to barrier-free travel. Access ramps and/or lifts are available in many public buildings, including train stations, museums, concert halls and cinemas.

➡ Trains, trams, underground trains and buses are increasingly accessible; train stations have a mobile lift for boarding trains and city buses are ramp-equipped.

➡ Some car-rental agencies offer hand-controlled vehicles and vans with wheelchair lifts; reserve well in advance.

For information, contact the national tourist boards or these organisations:

Deutsche Bahn Mobility Service Centre (☑01806-996 633, ext 9 for English; www.bahn.com) Train access information and route-planning assistance; search 'barrier-free travel' on its website.

Mobility International Switzerland (www.mis-ch.ch)

VISAS

➡ Visas for stays of up to three months are not required for citizens of the EU, much of Eastern Europe, the USA, Canada, Australia and New Zealand. For stays exceeding 90 days in a 180-day period, contact your nearest German/Austrian/Swiss embassy or consulate and begin your visa application well in advance.

➡ Nationals from other countries need a Schengen Visa. It allows unlimited travel within the entire zone for a 90-day period. Apply to the consulate of the country you are entering first, or your main destination.

➡ For up-to-date details on visa requirements, go to the **German Federal Foreign Office** (www.auswaertiges-amt.de), **Austria's Ministry of Foreign Affairs** (www.bmaa.gv.at) or **Swiss Federal Office for Migration** (www.bfm.admin.ch).

Language

German is easy for English speakers to pronounce because almost all of its sounds are also found in English. If you read our coloured pronunciation guides as if they were English, you'll have no problems being understood. Note that kh is like the 'ch' in 'Bach' or the Scottish 'loch' (pronounced at the back of the throat), r is also pronounced at the back of the throat (almost like a g, but with some friction), zh is pronounced as the 's' in 'measure', and ü as the 'ee' in 'see' but with rounded lips. The stressed syllables are indicated with italics.

The sounds used in spoken French can almost all be found in English. There are a couple of exceptions: nasal vowels (represented in our pronunciation guides by o or u followed by an almost inaudible nasal consonant sound m, n or ng), the 'funny' u (ew in our guides) and the deep-in-the-throat r. Bearing these few points in mind and reading our pronunciation guides below as if they were English, you'll be understood just fine.

GERMAN BASICS

Hello.	*Guten Tag.*	*goo*·ten tahk
Goodbye.	*Auf Wiedersehen.*	owf *vee*·der·zay·en
Yes./No.	*Ja./Nein.*	yah/nain
Please.	*Bitte.*	*bi*·te
Thank you.	*Danke.*	*dang*·ke
You're welcome.	*Bitte.*	*bi*·te
Excuse me.	*Entschuldigung.*	ent·*shul*·di·gung
Sorry.	*Entschuldigung.*	ent·*shul*·di·gung

Do you speak English?
Sprechen Sie Englisch? (pol) — *shpre*·khen zee *eng*·lish
Sprichst du Englisch? (inf) — *shprikhst* doo *eng*·lish

I don't understand.
Ich verstehe nicht. — ikh fer·*shtay*·e nikht

DIRECTIONS

Where's ...?
Wo ist ...? — vaw ist ...

How far is it?
Wie weit ist es? — vee vait ist es

Can you show me (on the map)?
Können Sie es mir (auf der Karte) zeigen? — *ker*·nen zee es meer (owf dair *kar*·te) *tsai*·gen

How can I get there?
Wie kann ich da hinkommen? — vee kan ikh dah *hin*·ko·men

Turn ...	*Biegen Sie ... ab.*	*bee*·gen zee ... ab
at the corner	*an der Ecke*	an dair *e*·ke
at the traffic lights	*bei der Ampel*	bai dair *am*·pel
left	*links*	lingks
right	*rechts*	rekhts

ON THE ROAD

I'd like to hire a ...	*Ich möchte ein ... mieten.*	ikh *merkh*·te ain ... *mee*·ten
4WD	*Allrad- fahrzeug*	*al*·raht· fahr·tsoyk
car	*Auto*	*ow*·to
motorbike	*Motorrad*	*maw*·tor·raht
How much is it per ...?	*Wie viel kostet es pro ...?*	vee feel *kos*·tet es praw ...
day	*Tag*	tahk
week	*Woche*	*vo*·khe

Does this road go to ...?
Führt diese Straße nach ...? — fürt *dee*·ze *shtrah*·se nahkh ...

Want More?

For in-depth language information and handy phrases, check out Lonely Planet's *German* and *French Phrasebooks*. You'll find them at **shop.lonelyplanet.com**.

(How long) Can I park here?
(Wie lange) Kann ich hier parken? — (vee *lang*·e) kan ikh heer *par*·ken

Where's a petrol station?
Wo ist eine Tankstelle? — vaw ist *ai*·ne *tangk*·shte·le

I need a mechanic.
Ich brauche einen Mechaniker. — ikh *brow*·khe *ai*·nen me·*khah*·ni·ker

My car/motorbike has broken down (at ...).
Ich habe (in ...) eine Panne mit meinem Auto/Motorrad. — ikh *hah*·be (in ...) *ai*·ne *pa*·ne mit *mai*·nem *ow*·to/*maw*·tor·raht

I've run out of petrol.
Ich habe kein Benzin mehr. — ikh *hah*·be kain ben·*tseen* mair

I have a flat tyre.
Ich habe eine Reifenpanne. — ikh *hah*·be *ai*·ne *rai*·fen·pa·ne

- -

EMERGENCIES

Help!
Hilfe! — *hil*·fe

I'm lost.
Ich habe mich verirrt. — ikh *hah*·be mikh fer·*irt*

- -

FRENCH BASICS

Hello. | *Bonjour.* | bon·*zhoor*
Goodbye. | *Au revoir.* | o·rer·*vwa*
Yes./No. | *Oui./Non.* | wee/non
Excuse me. | *Excusez-moi.* | ek·skew·zay·*mwa*
Sorry. | *Pardon.* | par·*don*
Please. | *S'il vous plaît.* | seel voo play
Thank you. | *Merci.* | mair·*see*

You're welcome.
De rien. — der ree·en

Do you speak English?
Parlez-vous anglais? — par·lay·voo ong·*glay*

I don't understand.
Je ne comprends pas. — zher ner kom·pron pa

- -

DIRECTIONS

Can you show me (on the map)?
Pouvez-vous m'indiquer (sur la carte)? — poo·vay·voo mun·dee·kay (sewr la kart)

Where's ...?
Où est ...? — oo ay ...

- -

EMERGENCIES

Help!
Au secours! — o skoor

I'm lost.
Je suis perdu/perdue. — zhe swee·pair·dew (m/f)

- -

ON THE ROAD

I'd like to hire a/an ... | *Je voudrais louer ...* | zher voo·dray loo·way ...
4WD | *un quatre-quatre* | un kat·kat
automatic/ manual | *une auto-matique/ manuel* | ewn o·to·ma·teek/ ma·nwel
motorbike | *une moto* | ewn mo·to

How much is it daily/weekly?
Quel est le tarif par jour/semaine? — kel ay ler ta·reef par zhoor/ser·men

Does that include insurance?
Est-ce que l'assurance est comprise? — es·ker la·sew·rons ay kom·preez

Does that include mileage?
Est-ce que le kilométrage est compris? — es·ker ler kee·lo·may·trazh ay kom·pree

What's the speed limit?
Quelle est la vitesse maximale permise? — kel ay la vee·tes mak·see·mal per·meez

Is this the road to ...?
C'est la route pour ...? — say la root poor ...

Where's a service station?
Où est-ce qu'il y a une station-service? — oo es·keel ya ewn sta·syon·ser·vees

Please check the oil/water.
Contrôlez l'huile/l'eau, s'il vous plaît. — kon·tro·lay lweel/lo seel voo play

I need a mechanic.
J'ai besoin d'un mécanicien. — zhay ber·zwun dun may·ka·nee·syun

The car/motorbike has broken down.
La voiture/moto est tombée en panne. — la vwa·tewr/mo·to ay tom·bay on pan

I had an accident.
J'ai eu un accident. — zhay ew un ak·see·don

405

BEHIND THE SCENES

SEND US YOUR FEEDBACK

We love to hear from travellers – your comments help make our books better. We read every word, and we guarantee that your feedback goes straight to the authors. Visit **lonelyplanet. com/contact** to submit your updates and suggestions.

Note: We may edit, reproduce and incorporate your comments in Lonely Planet products such as guidebooks, websites and digital products, so let us know if you don't want your comments reproduced or your name acknowledged. For a copy of our privacy policy visit lonelyplanet.com/privacy.

AUTHOR THANKS

NICOLA WILLIAMS

Many thanks to my expert co-authors who responded to my pesky questions with appropriate speed, graciousness and authority. *Danke* to my own increasingly grown-up, trilingual road-tripping tribe – Niko, Mischa and Kaya – who've quit being car-sick and are now the ones deciding where our next road trip will be.

KERRY CHRISTIANI

A heartfelt *dankeschön* to friends and family in the Schwarzwald, especially Hans and Monika in Villingen and Anja at the Brickstone Hostel, Ulm. Big thanks to Claus Schäfer in Triberg for the interviews. I'd also like to thank all the tourist board pros

I met on the road and my Lonely Planet co-authors for being great to work with. Finally, thanks to my husband for his ongoing support and for introducing me to the Black Forest all those years ago.

MARC DI DUCA

Huge thanks go to parents-in-law Mykola and Vira for looking after the boys while I was away. Also much gratitude goes to Oleksandr in Erding for night 'researching' the output of Bavaria's breweries, Andrea in Nuremberg and the staff at tourist offices across the region, but in particular those in Coburg, Passau, Regensburg and Bayreuth.

CATHERINE LE NEVEZ

Vielen Dank first and foremost to Julian, and to all of the locals and fellow travellers en route

for insights, information and good times. Huge thanks too to Destination Editor Gemma Graham and everyone at LP. As ever, *merci encore* to my parents, brother, *belle-sœur* and *neveu*.

TOM MASTERS

Huge thanks to Thomas Beach, my main man in Leipzig. To Álvaro Rodríguez Martín for company in Saxon Switzerland and for not choking to death in that restaurant in Görlitz. Thanks also to Moritz Estermann, Marius Rauschenbach, Sadia Belhadi, KiKi Hahn and Mario Dzurila for their help with research.

SALLY O'BRIEN

Many thanks to the friends, acquaintances, locals and tourists who shared their opinions with me on the subject

THIS BOOK

This 1st edition of Lonely Planet's *Germany, Austria & Switzerland's Best Trips* was researched and written by Nicola Williams, Kerry Christiani, Marc Di Duca, Catherine Le Nevez, Tom Masters, Sally O'Brien, Andrea Schulte-Peevers, Ryan Ver Berkmoes and Benedict Walker.

This guidebook was produced by the following:

Destination Editor Gemma Graham

Product Editors Elin Berglund, Jenna Myers

Senior Cartographer Valentina Kremenchutskaya

Cartographer Julie Dodkins

Book Designer Virginia Moreno

Assisting Editors Nigel Chin, Kate Evans, Kellie Langdon, Anne Mulvaney

Cover Researcher Campbell McKenzie

Thanks to Sasha Baskett, Andi Jones, Kate Morgan, Claire Naylor, Karyn Noble, Lorna Parkes, Kirsten Rawlings, Alison Ridgway, Angela Tinson, Tasmin Waby, Lauren Wellicome, Tony Wheeler of Switzerland's best trips. As always, my family was an enormous help in matters practical, and terrific company on the road – *gros becs à vous*, as we say in these parts.

ANDREA SCHULTE-PEEVERS

Big heartfelt thanks to the many wonderful people who've plied me with tips, insights, information, ideas and encouragement in my research for this guide.

RYAN VER BERKMOES

Thanks to Claudia Stehle as always for taking me to the dark depths of Northern Germany. And the happy ending to my fairy tale: Alexis Averbuck.

BENEDICT WALKER

A massive thanks to my friends in Germany, to Gemma and Nicola from LP and to Mum for believing in me. I dedicate my writing to Aunty Bonnie, who started all this when I was a kid, who made books matter and who'll never be forgotten.

PUBLISHER THANKS

Climate map data adapted from Peel MC, Finlayson BL & McMahon TA (2007) 'Updated World Map of the Köppen-Geiger Climate Classification', *Hydrology and Earth System Sciences*, 11, 163344.

Front cover photographs: (clockwise from top) Tarasp village and castle, Graubünden, Switzerland, nagelestock.com/Alamy; Old mill, Austria, JK Photo/Shutterstock; Convertible at the shore of Wolfgangsee, Austria, Andrea Altemueller/Getty.

Back cover photograph: Gosausee, Salzkammergut, Austria, daitoZen/Getty.

INDEX

INDEX W–Z

Andrea Schulte-Peevers Born and raised in Germany and educated in London and at UCLA, Andrea has travelled the distance to the moon and back in her visits to some 75 countries. She has written about her native land for two decades and authored or contributed to some 80 Lonely Planet titles, including all editions of the Germany country guide and the Berlin city guide. Andrea discovered her love for road trips while living in California for nearly 20 years and now puts pedal to the metal crisscrossing Europe from her home base in Berlin.

Read more about Andrea at: https://auth. lonelyplanet.com/profiles/andreaschultepeevers

Ryan Ver Berkmoes Ryan once lived in Germany. He spent three years in Frankfurt, during which time he edited a magazine until he got a chance for a new career with... Lonely Planet. One of his first jobs was working on LP's Germany coverage. He loves smoked fish, which serves him well in the north, and he loves beer, which serves him well everywhere in Germany. Follow him at ryanverberkmoes.com and @ryanvb.

Read more about Ryan at: https://auth. lonelyplanet.com/profiles/ryanvb

Benedict Walker Benedict got his driving licence a little later than most and made up for lost time fast: he's at his happiest behind the wheel on a country road, music blaring. Having lost a few years buzzing around the backroads of Australia, NZ, Japan, Canada and the US, he found it was an honour to get back to Germany's jaw-dropping history, culture and verdant nature.

My Favourite Trip 8 **German Avenues Route** I love how much this trip packs in without being exhausting, just a hop-skip-and-a-jump from the headiness of Berlin.

Marc Di Duca A well-established travel guide author, Marc has explored many corners of Germany over the last 25 years but it's to the quirky variety and friendliness of Bavaria that he returns most willingly. When not hiking Alpine valleys, eating snowballs in Rothenburg ob der Tauber or brewery hopping in Bamberg, he can be found in Sandwich, Kent, where he lives with his wife, Tanya, and their two sons.

Read more about Marc at: https://auth.lonelyplanet.com/profiles/Madidu

Catherine Le Nevez Catherine's wanderlust kicked in when she first roadtripped across Europe – including Germany and Austria – aged four, and she's been roadtripping here ever since, completing her Doctorate of Creative Arts in Writing, Masters in Professional Writing, and post-grad qualifications in Editing and Publishing along the way. A freelance writer for decades, over the last dozen-or-so years she has written scores of Lonely Planet guides and articles covering destinations all over Europe and beyond.

My Favourite Trip 13 **Moselle Valley** This is Germany at its most magical: hilltop castles, half-timbered villages, vineyards in every direction, and truly exceptional wines.

Read more about Catherine at: https://auth.lonelyplanet.com/profiles/catherine_le_nevez

Tom Masters Tom hails from London, but has lived in Berlin since 2009 and has travelled widely all over Germany in that time. During research for this book, he particularly enjoyed his time discovering Leipzig's secret life beyond the Altstadt, walking in Saxon Switzerland, the gorgeousness that is Görlitz and getting to know Dresden. More of Tom's work can be found online at www.tommasters.net.

Read more about Tom at: https://auth.lonelyplanet.com/profiles/tommasters

Sally O'Brien Australian-born Sally, a Lonely Planet writer since 2001, has called Switzerland home since 2007. Swapping her surfboard for a snowboard, the beach for the lake and the BBQ for the caquelon, she loves exploring Switzerland's charming cities, the sublime Alps and lakes, and catching cable cars and trains to stunning vantage points. It's only fitting that she became a naturalised Swiss citizen while on the road for this guide. She lives with her husband, Denis, and their sons in the Lake Geneva region. Sally tweets @swissingaround.

Read more about Sally at: https://auth.lonelyplanet.com/profiles/swissingaround

OUR WRITERS

OUR STORY

A beat-up old car, a few dollars in the pocket and a sense of adventure. In 1972 that's all Tony and Maureen Wheeler needed for the trip of a lifetime – across Europe and Asia overland to Australia. It took several months, and at the end – broke but inspired – they sat at their kitchen table writing and stapling together their first travel guide, *Across Asia on the Cheap*. Within a week they'd sold 1500 copies. Lonely Planet was born.

Today, Lonely Planet has offices in Franklin, London, Melbourne, Oakland, Beijing and Delhi, with more than 600 staff and writers. We share Tony's belief that 'a great guidebook should do three things: inform, educate and amuse'.

Nicola Williams Border hopping is a way for life for British writer Nicola Williams, who lives on Lake Geneva's southern shore. Every journey from her lakeside home begins with a boat ride across Europe's largest lake or a drive around its vine-stitched shore. When not road-tripping for work, she can be found motoring with her trio of trilingual kids to Germany to visit family in Cologne (and celebrate Karneval), to Switzerland to ski beside the Aletsch Glacier, to Austria to hike childhood haunts ... Follow her travels at @Tripalong.

My Favourite Trip `32` **The Swiss Alps** For outdoor action and top of-the-world views.

Read more about Nicola at: https://auth. lonelyplanet.com/profiles/NicolaWilliams

Kerry Christiani Having lived for six years in the Black Forest, Kerry returned to this neck of the woods (her second home) to write her chapters. Summer hikes in the forest, bike rides on Lake Constance and going on the trail of Mozart and Maria in Salzburg kept her busy for this edition. She tweets @kerrychristiani and lists her latest work at www.kerrychristiani.com.

Read more about Kerri at: https://auth. lonelyplanet.com/profiles/KerryChristiani

MORE WRITERS

Published by Lonely Planet Publications Pty Ltd
ABN 36 005 607 983
1st edition – Feb 2016
ISBN 978 1 74360 695 7
© Lonely Planet 2016
Photographs © as indicated 2016
10 9 8 7 6 5 4 3 2
Printed in China

MIX
Paper from responsible sources
FSC™ C021741

Paper in this book is certified against the Forest Stewardship Council™ standards. FSC™ promotes environmentally responsible, socially beneficial and economically viable management of the world's forests.